The Shalom Seders

Three Haggadahs

Compiled by New Jewish Agenda

Introduction by Arthur Waskow ◆ Preface by Grace Paley

Excerpts by Moshe Leib Lilienblum and Aaron David Gordon from
The Zionist Idea edited by Arthur Hertzberg. Translation copyright
©1959 by Arthur Hertzberg. Reprinted by permission of Doubleday &
Company, Inc.

Excerpts from *My Home, My Prison* by Raymonda Hawa Tawil are
copyright ©1979 by Raymonda Hawa Tawil and Peretz Kidron and
Adam Publishers. Reprinted by permission of Holt, Rinehart and
Winston, Publishers.

Excerpts from *The Longest War* by Jacobo Timerman are copyright
©1982 by African International Productions, N.V., and reprinted by permission of Alfred A. Knopf, Inc.

''Zog Nit Keynmell'' by Hersh Glik is translated by Aaron Kramer
and used with his permission.

''Pastures of Plenty,'' words and music by Woody Guthrie, are
copyright ©1960 and 1963 by Ludlow Music, Inc., New York, N.Y.
Used by permission.

Excerpts from *The Disinherited: Journal of a Palestinian Exile* by
Fawaz Turki are copyright ©1972 by Fawaz Turki. Reprinted by permission of Monthly Review Press.

Excerpts from *Abba Eban: An Autobiography* are copyright ©1977 by
Abba Eban, and reprinted by permission of Random House, Inc.

Excerpt from *Israel and the World* by Martin Buber are copyright
©1948, 1963 by Schocken Books, Inc. Reprinted by permission of the
Publisher.

Excerpts from *My Home, My Land* by Abu Iyad are copyright ©1981
by Times Books. Reprinted by permission of Times Books, a division of
Quadrangle/The New York Times Book Co., Inc.

Library of Congress Cataloging in Publication Data

Haggadah (Reform, New Jewish Agenda)
    The shalom seders.

    1. Haggadot-Texts.   2. Seder—Liturgy—Texts.
3. Reform Judaism—Liturgy—Texts.   I. New Jewish Agenda
(Organization)   II. Title
BM675.P4Z6685 1984   296.4'37   83-25857
ISBN 0-915361-03-5 (pbk.)

Adama Books, 306 West 38 Street, New York, New York 10018

Printed in Israel

Contents

Given the collective nature of the effort that brought forth these Haggadahs, it is impossible to acknowledge everyone who contributed by name. We particularly want to thank the members of the Philadelphia Chapter of New Jewish Agenda and Kadima-Agenda in Seattle. Arthur Waskow deserves special thanks for making the *shidduchim* that produced this volume. Rhonda Zangwill, Pamela Nelson, Clare Kinberg, Ruth Bernards, and Richard Thorns provided technical assistance with the editing and publicity. We also want to thank Sandy Kadet, Dennis Sheheen, and Mark Solomon for their help. The art of Amnon Danziger, Beth Haber, Nina Raab, and Irwin Rosenhouse enhanced the beauty of the text. Reena Bernards and Jeffrey Dekro, Agenda's Co-Directors, coordinated the project. And finally, we want to thank our friend and ally, Esther Cohen of Adama Books, whose vision and perseverance made this all possible.

N.J.A.

I lived my childhood in a world so dense with Jews that I thought we were the great imposing majority and kindness had to be extended to the others because, as my mother said, everyone wants to live like a person. In school I met my friend Adele who together with her mother and father were not Jewish. Despite this they often seemed to be in a good mood. There was the janitor in charge of coal and my father, unusually smart, spoke Italian to him. They talked about Italian literature because the janitor was equally smart. Down the hill under the Southern Boulevard El, families lived, people in lovely shades of light and darkest brown. My mother and sister explained that they were treated unkindly; they had in fact been slaves in another part of the country in another time.

Like us? I said.

Like us, my father said year after year at seders when he told the story in a rush of Hebrew, stopping occasionally to respect my grandmother's pained face, or to raise his wine glass to please the grownups. In this way I began to understand in my own time and place, that we had been slaves in Egypt and brought out of bondage for some reason. One of the reasons, clearly, was to tell the story again and again—that we had been strangers and slaves in Egypt and therefore knew what we were talking about when we cried out against pain and oppression. In fact, we were obligated by knowledge to do so.

But this is only one page, one way to introduce these Haggadah makers, story tellers, who love history and tradition enough to live in it and therefore by definition be part of its change.

Grace Paley

Introduction

Birthpangs

Freedom is always a-borning . . . and so is the Haggadah, the telling of freedom. Its old questions lead always to new questions; so these Haggadahs are retellings, with new questions.

But the Seder is not only a retelling of the past. It is itself a new birth of freedoms: the Haggadah teaches us that *we*, not our forebears only, are liberated from Mitzra-yim—not only from old Egypt, but from every "tight spot," every narrow place.

Every year and every generation, Passover comes as a moment of birth. Indeed, it was midwives who first resisted Pharaoh, because they revered God's command to choose life rather than to kill new-born infants as Pharaoh commanded. Even before that, shepherds may have celebrated the birthing of lambs with Pesach; farmers, the sprouting of barley with matzah. Pesach came to birth when Moses, Miriam, and Aaron led a whole people through the narrow birth canal and broke the Red Sea waters. And in every generation since . . .

The Haggadah teaches us to rewrite the Haggadah. "All who go beyond telling about the departure from Mitzra-yim—all these are worthy of praise." And so it teaches us about that night when five rabbis gathered to talk of resistance to Rome as well as redemption from Egypt. And we ourselves teach about the Passover night when the Jews of the Warsaw Ghetto rose up against the Nazis.

So tonight: let us tell our own story, bring about a new birth of freedom.

Tonight . . . the Pharaohs hold 50,000 pieces of the center of the sun in their hands, to fling upon our heads and burn the earth to ashes.

Tonight . . . the poor are homeless.
Tonight . . . we are lonely, depressed, disheartened.
Tonight . . . we will begin our liberation.

In the last 15 years, there has been a growing wave of energy among American Jews, moving toward the renewing and remaking of Jewish thought and practice. Since the Passover Seder is one of the deepest and richest moments of Jewish life, this movement for Jewish renewal has found one of its most joyful tasks in the remaking and renewing of the Seder.

The three Haggadahs that are here collected are not individual idiosyncracies; all of them grow out of this movement for Jewish renewal. They grow especially out of the interest of some wings of the movement that are reexamining political questions in the light of Jewish tradition and Jewish historical experience. Indeed, one of the most interesting and vital expressions of Jewish renewal has been the emergence of a new national organization of progressive Jews, some religious and some secular, who have begun to apply Jewish ideas, practices and liturgies to political questions. That group, New Jewish Agenda, has brought together the three Haggadahs collected here. These three Haggadahs are quite different from each other, but their very differences express the range of people who are learning to struggle with and learn from each other. For practically everyone who has been searching toward a "Jewish politics" Passover and the story of the liberation from Pharaoh seems like a good place to begin. In 1982, about two-thirds of Agenda's local chapters wrote their own Haggadahs and held their own Seders.

All of the "Shalom Seders" are rooted in the traditional Haggadah; all of them differ from it in profound and fruitful ways. For this new generation of Jews know that the very name of the people Israel means God-wrestler. And they are indeed wrestling with Jewish tradition. Wrestling: not bowing down to it, and not turning away. Their wrestling is a fusion of making love and doing battle. Through this wrestle, new paths of being Jewish are emerging.

One aspect of the new Jewish renewal is reaching out to other peoples, not by diluting or dissolving Jewishness, but by shaping intensely Jewish symbols and practices in new ways. So Jews began to shape the Seder in ways that other people might welcome, without dissolving into universalism. Each of these Haggadahs reaches out to welcome everyone.

Recently, there has been an unprecedented wave of interest among Christians in experiencing the Jewish Seder: sometimes for its own sake as a liberating experience, sometimes as an act of friendship with Jews, sometimes as a way of joining in The Last Supper.

So the confluence of these two new streams can be found in these Haggadahs which can be used by Jews and Christians together or separately.

The new paths of Jewish life affirm the constant process of rebirth. They recognize in principle, with joy instead of fear, that Judaism needs to grow and transform just as individual Jews and the Jewish people need to transform. Each of these three Haggadahs has gone through a process of self-transformation, and each is still intended to be changed, reworked, rewoven. Each includes space for the participants to speak their minds and wrestle anew — so that from year to year the Seder cannot possibly be the same. Only the frameworks are intended to remain. The very fact that New Jewish Agenda has brought together three very different Haggadahs points toward this sense of openness.

The first — "The Rainbow Seder" — is in one sense the oldest, for it is the fifth reincarnation of *The Freedom Seder* that I wrote in 1969. Yet it is deeply changed. *The Freedom Seder* emerged from the moment of agony at Passover 1968 when Martin Luther King had just been killed, dozens of American cities had exploded, and the United States Army was still standing armed upon the streets of Washington, D.C. It brought together the age-old story of the Exodus with tales of efforts of modern Jews and blacks and other people toward their liberation.

The Freedom Seder was first used on April 4, 1969, the first anniversary of King's death and the third night of Passover, by about 300 "Jews for Urban Justice" and 100 Christians. It was told and sung in the basement of a church deep in the black community of Washington, D.C. — a church whose pastor was the Reverend Channing Phillips. (In 1968, in the tumultuous Chicago Convention of the Democratic Party, Phillips had become the first black person ever nominated for President at a major party convention.) Fourteen years later, Phillips had joined the Reverend William Sloane Coffin as minister of Riverside Church in New York City. Their congregants had been studying the Bible as a guide to modern life, and they asked to do a Passover Seder. Phillips remembered the Freedom Seder—and asked me to help create a new Seder at Riverside Church.

In the meantime, I had been deeply changed through passionate involvement in the movement for Jewish renewal. The Freedom Seder had acted almost as a *bar mitzvah* for me—a gateway for my first conscious, choosing entry into Jewish life. But once inside the gate!—there everything seemed both different and the same. I began to experience the riches of Jewish experience and tradition. I began to learn that those riches spoke more deeply to the hopes and values that I held, than did the secular mindsets I was used to. I began to understand, and learn from, some of the bitter criticisms that had been directed at the Freedom Seder. Yet I also kept learning that my hopes and values were indeed deeply Jewish themselves—deeply rooted in Jewish tradition and experience. Everything was different—yet the same.

And then, in Washington and Philadelphia, I worked with a number of different groups—including New Jewish Agenda—to create Rainbow Sign, a project that applied Jewish perspectives to the prevention of a world nuclear holocaust. So when the moment came to share a Seder with Riverside Church, all these learnings had become a part of me. And so they came to be interwoven in what is now "The Rainbow Seder."

"The Rainbow Seder" is the product of an intensely collective experience and process, which was then distilled through one writer. The other two Haggadahs in this book are even more communal in their process, for they were written and rewritten by small groups of people who wrestled with each other.

The newest of the Haggadahs is "The Seder of the Children of Abraham." It springs from the Philadelphia chapter of New Jewish Agenda, whose members were struggling to deal with the agony of seeing Israel over and over again at war, over and over again losing the lives and limbs of its own people, over and over again inflicting on other peoples the loss of life and limb. Three members of the Agenda chapter who were rabbinical students—Devorah Bartnoff, Mordechai Liebling, and Brian Walt—joined with Catherine Essoyan, an Armenian-American who had spent years of her childhood in Beirut while her father worked there; had studied and worked closely with American Jews as well as with Palestinian-Americans; and had grown to know and understand the hurts, the angers, the desires, and the hopes of Jews and Palestinians. Together they wrote a Haggadah that celebrated both sides of the family split that divided the Children of Abraham —celebrated both Sarah and Hagar, both Isaac and Ishmael, both the Jewish State of Israel and the Palestinian people. What they accomplished was a remarkable transformation in the Haggadah. Pharaoh was transformed into the endless, oppressive war between the two peoples—liberation into the need for hope for both peoples to make a decent peace with one another.

Together with others from the New Jewish Agenda chapter in Philadelphia, these four created a Third Night Seder with about 120 participants. A few Palestinians took part in the Seder; many of those present felt how important—and how difficult—it would be for reasonably equal numbers of Jews and Palestinians to sit face to face in a Seder for the Children of Abraham.

"A Haggadah of Liberation" is the work of Kadima ("Forward"), the Seattle chapter of New Jewish Agenda. But the Seder began before Kadima or Agenda existed. It began as the work of a group of Jewish women in Portland, Oregon, in 1971. They wrote it together, creating one Haggadah— literally one copy—written on sheets of rice paper. They wrote it together because they felt that even the new Haggadahs of the late '60s ignored and excluded women, and they wanted to tell the stories of women's liberation— beginning with the freedom-minded midwives who were the first to resist the Pharaoh's murderous edicts.

Having written the rice-paper Haggadah as women, they shared it for several years in Seders that included men too. One of them, Bria Chakofsky, carried the rice-paper Haggadah with her when she moved across the continent to Brooklyn. One Seder that used the rice-paper telling became the heart of "This Year in Brooklyn: A Seder to Celebrate Ourselves," a story in *Off Our Backs*, a journal of women's liberation. When Chakofsky returned west, this time to Seattle, she became part of a progressive Jewish group called Kadima. The group grew. Her rice-paper Haggadah became clearly insufficient as Kadima's Seders grew to include hundreds of people. And the original content of the Haggadah also became insufficient, as the people grew and changed. So the Cultural Committee of Kadima (which then became the Seattle chapter of New Jewish Agenda) began every year to revise the Haggadah; and the most recent revision is what is published here. It expresses that side of the movement for Jewish renewal that sees energy for redemption and social transformation as coming from human struggle.

What do these stories teach us? That in our day the Seder can only be what it says it wants to be—a moment to experience liberation in the present, not just to remember it in the past—if we constantly reshape the Haggadah to express our growing, changing sense of freedom. Here are some ways to use it:

- Plan ahead. Leave yourself time. For the next decade, Passover begins on the nights of April 16, 1984; April 5, 1985; April 23, 1986; April 13, 1987; April 1, 1988; April 19, 1989; April 9, 1990; April 4, 1991; April 17, 1992; April 5, 1993; March 26, 1994.
- If you are preparing a communal or organizational Seder for more than about 20 people, begin at least two months in advance to plan for choosing a place and time (which night of Passover?), reaching out to participants, reworking the Haggadah, cooking the food, asking particular people to read and sing, etc.
- If you would like to join with New Jewish Agenda for a Seder, call the office in New York (212/227-5885) to ask about a nearby chapter.
- If you are planning a smaller Seder of friends and family, begin at least two weeks before Passover—perhaps on the night of the new moon of the month of Nisan. Reread these three Haggadahs, and the traditional one as well. (An excellent annotated version is the one edited by E.D. Goldschmidt and Nahum Glatzer, *The Passover Haggadah*, published by Schocken Books.) You might also want to read the Preface and the chapters on Passover in my book on the Jewish festivals, *Seasons of Our Joy* (Bantam). Mull over how they speak to you, *this year*. How many Seders do you want to have?
- You might collect your non-Passover food and on the day before Passover give it to a soup kitchen or a group of the unemployed or poverty-

bound who are organizing for social change. (Perhaps add some money to the gift.)

• Ask people who will be sharing the Seder with you to prepare some brief readings, dances, poetry, art, songs—that express their own sense of freedom. Plan to leave space in the Seder for people to share these expressions.

• Encourage people to look at four levels of freedom—physical, emotional, intellectual, and spiritual—and four spheres of freedom—the individual; the face-to-face family or community; the broader nation, culture, or people; and the whole human race as part of the web of all life.

• At the Seder itself, treat each of the symbolic ritual items as a focus for experiencing and expressing freedom at all four levels and spheres. For instance, experience and share the taste of the wine, the emotional loosening created by the wine, the intellectual meaning of the wine, and the spiritual wholeness that arises from integrating all these aspects of the wine. Try doing the washing of hands first alone, inward, focusing on the feel of the cool water, the loosening-up—and then wash each other's hands so as to focus on sharing with a community. When you eat the bitter herb, talk about what is *bitter* in your own life; the life of the friendship group as a group; the life of the Jewish people or the American nation as a whole; the life of Planet Earth.

• Conversely, take part of the intellectual aspect of the Haggadah and express it in a physical or emotional way: for instance, make a dance of guided meditation out of "Serfs we were to Pharaoh in Mitzrayim . . ." or a mime of the ten plagues. (What would ten such plagues be today? Are we already experiencing them—not just accidental troubles but upheavals that signal some profound dis-order?)

• Consider doing some kind of political act during the week of Passover, as an act of resistance to the Pharaohs of our day: saving some time together to write letters to members of Congress, doing a vigil, marching an "exodus," deciding to boycott a product, refusing taxes, or assisting at a rape crisis center, or a walk-in soup kitchen.

It is we ourselves, not our forebears only, who are slaves in the narrow places; it is we ourselves who must give birth to freedom. Tonight.

Arthur Waskow

The Table

When the Seder begins, the table should be arranged with the following:

1. A plate with three sheets of matzah, covered by a napkin.

2. A plate with a roasted whole egg; a burnt or roasted shank bone or chicken bone; a raw horse-radish root; sprigs of parsley or spring onion; charoset (a mixture of chopped nuts, chopped apples or raisins, cinnamon, and wine); and chopped horseradish.

3. A cup for each person, a few bottles of wine, and an empty cup in the center of the table, for Elijah.

4. Two unlit candles—or, for "The Rainbow Seder," eight unlit candles: one white, placed near the initial speaker; the others of seven different colors, in different places on the table.

5. A bowl of salt water or vinegar.

6. A bowl of plain water for washing the hands, and a towel.

7. Flowers on the table.

The Rainbow Seder

The Rainbow Seder

Turn out all lights.

A speaker:

In the beginning, darkness covered the face of the deep. Then the rushing breath of God hovered over the waters. Let us breathe together. Let us catch our breaths from slavery, from anxiety, and from the need to *do,* to *make.* Let us be conscious of the Breath of Life, the One Who breathes us.

Pause for seven breaths. Then say:

God breathed, "Be Light!" And Light came into being.

Light the white candle. All say together:

We are the generation
That stands between the fires.
Behind us is the flame and smoke
That rose from Auschwitz and from
   Hiroshima.
Before us is the nightmare of a Flood
   of Fire:
A thermonuclear holocaust
That could make every human city
A crematorium without a chimney.
It is our task to make from fire
Not an all-consuming blaze
But the light in which we see each other;
All of us different,
All of us made in the image of God.
We light this fire to see more clearly
That the earth, the human race,
   is not for burning.
We light this fire to see more clearly
The rainbow in our many-colored faces.

Blessed are you, YHWH* our God, Ruler of the Universe, who give us light that we may become a light for peace and freedom for all peoples.

Blessed are you, YHWH our God, Ruler of the Universe, who make us holy by your commandments and command us to light these lights for your holy day.

Barukh atah Adonai elohenu melekh ha-olam asher kid-shanu b'mitzvotav vitzivanu l'hadlik ner shel yomtov.

בָּרוּךְ אַתָּה יְיָ אֱלֹהֵינוּ מֶלֶךְ הָעוֹלָם. אֲשֶׁר קִדְּשָׁנוּ בְּמִצְוֹתָיו וְצִוָּנוּ לְהַדְלִיק נֵר שֶׁל יוֹם טוֹב:

---

*These four letters may be said out loud in several ways—"Lord," "Holy One of Being," "Y-h-w-h." See "A Note on the Names of God," p. 35

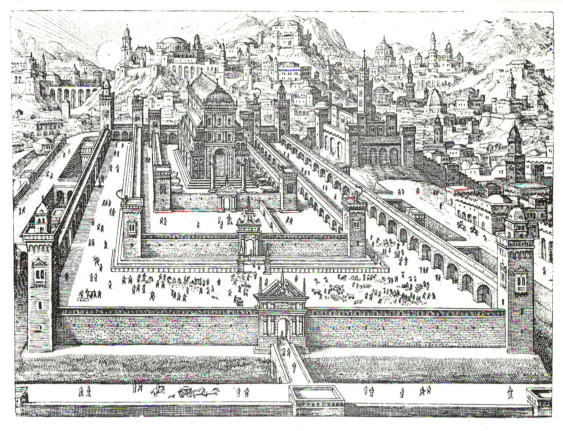

Pass the lit white candle down the table so that others use it to light the seven colored candles. Raise the cup of wine and say:

Blessed are you, YHWH our God, Ruler of the Universe, who create the fruit of the vine.

Barukh atah Adonai elohenu melekh ha-olam boray p'ri ha-gafen.

בָּרוּךְ אַתָּה יְיָ אֱלֹהֵינוּ מֶלֶךְ הָעוֹלָם. בּוֹרֵא פְּרִי הַגָּפֶן:

Blessed are you, YHWH our God, Ruler of the Universe, who made of one humus, one earth, all the humans of the earth; who breathed into our earthiness the spirit of freedom; who made us holy so that we might know and say what is holy.

Blessed are you, YHWH our God, who with love have given us and allowed us to give you solemn days for joy, festivals and seasons for gladness.

Blessed are you, YHWH our God, who imagined this day of the Feast of Unleavened Bread, the season of our freedom, a holy convocation, a memorial of the departure from Mitzra-yim, the tight spot. Blessed are you, YHWH, who make holy the people of Israel—all who are God-wrestlers*— who make holy humankind, freedom, and the seasons.

Blessed are you, YHWH our God, Ruler of the Universe, who have given us life and lifted us up and enabled us to reach this season.

Barukh atah YHWH elohenu melekh ha-olam sheh-hekhianu v'kimanu v'higianu lazman hazeh.

בָּרוּךְ אַתָּה יְיָ אֱלֹהֵינוּ מֶלֶךְ הָעוֹלָם. שֶׁהֶחֱיָנוּ. וְקִיְּמָנוּ. וְהִגִּיעָנוּ לַזְּמַן הַזֶּה:

Yisrael, "Israel," means the one who wrestles with God.

15

Drink the first cup of wine, and fill Elijah's cup. Pass around a basin to wash and dry the hands. Take pieces of parsley or spring onion, dip them in vinegar or salt water, pass them around the table, and say:

Blessed are you, YHWH our God, Ruler of the Universe, who create the fruit of the earth.

Barukh atah YHWH elohenu melekh ha-olam boray p'ri ha a-da-mah.

בָּרוּךְ אַתָּה יְיָ אֱלֹהֵינוּ מֶלֶךְ הָעוֹלָם. בּוֹרֵא פְּרִי הָאֲדָמָה:

Everyone then eats this piece of parsley. Then, break the middle matzah in two and hide the larger piece somewhere in the house, for an Afikoman. Uncover the matzah, lift up the dish and say:

This is the bread of the pressing-down that our forebears ate in the land of Mitzra-yim. Let all who are hungry eat, and all who are in need come and celebrate the Passover.

Ha Lakhma anya di-akhalu avahatana b'ara d'mitzrayeem. Kol dikhvin yetey v'yekhvol; Kol ditzrikh yetey v'yifsakh. Hashata hakha; l'shanah ha ba-ah b'ara d'yisrael. Hashata avdai; l'shanah ha ba-ah b-nai khorin.

הָא לַחְמָא עַנְיָא דִי־אֲכָלוּ אֲבָהֳתַנָא בְּאַרְעָא דְמִצְרָיִם. כָּל־דִּכְפִין יֵיתֵי וְיֵכוֹל. כָּל־דִּצְרִיךְ יֵיתֵי וְיִפְסַח. הָשַׁתָּא הָכָא. לְשָׁנָה הַבָּאָה בְּאַרְעָא דְיִשְׂרָאֵל. הָשַׁתָּא עַבְדֵי. לְשָׁנָה הַבָּאָה בְּנֵי חוֹרִין:

This pressed-down bread was the bread of oppression. But sometimes oppression was so deep that even this bread could not be eaten. In Bergen-Belsen Death Camp the prisoners said this prayer:

> Our Father in heaven, behold it is evident and known to thee that it is our desire to do thy will and to celebrate the festival of Passover by eating matzah and by observing the prohibition of leavened food. But our heart is pained that the enslavement prevents us and we are in danger of our lives. Behold, we are prepared and ready to fulfill thy commandment: "And ye shall live by them and not die by them." We pray to thee that thou mayest keep us alive and preserve us and redeem us speedily so that we may observe thy statutes and do thy will and serve thee with a perfect heart. Amen.

In the world today there are still some who are so pressed-down that they have not even this bread of oppression to eat. There are so many who are hungry that they cannot all come and eat with us tonight. Therefore we say to them, we set aside this bread as a token that we owe you righteousness, *tzedakah,* and that we will fulfill it. **(Set aside one piece of matzah.)** And to ourselves we say, not by bread alone, but by everything that is brought forth by the mouth of YHWH, lives the human; share your bread with the hungry, says YHWH.

As the tradition says, *"Ha-sha-tah ha-kha; l-sha-nah ha-ba-ah b'ar-ah d'yis'ra'el,"* this year we celebrate here, but the next year we hope to celebrate in the land of Israel, the land of God-wrestling. For even if we were sitting tonight in Jerusalem, we should still say, "Next year in Jerusalem, next year in the city of peace." For this year, not only we here

but all men and women are slaves to fear; next year we hope that all men and women shall be free. This year, not only we here but all women and men live in a city at war with itself, a city in agony; next year we hope all humankind will celebrate in "the land of Israel"—that is, in a world at peace and a world made free, a world where all can wrestle with God.

Fill the wine cups a second time. The youngest person present asks:

Why is this night different from all other nights? On all the other nights we may eat either leavened or unleavened bread, but on this night only unleavened bread; on all the other nights we may eat any species of herbs, but on this night only bitter herbs; on all the other nights we do not dip even once, but on this night twice; on all the other nights we eat and drink either sitting or leaning, but on this night we all lean.

Mah nishtanah ha-lai-lah ha-zeh mi-kol ha-le-lot? She-b'khol ha-le-lot anu okh-lin chametz u-ma-tzah, ha-lai-lah ha-zeh ku-lo ma-tzah. She-b'khol ha-le-lot a-nu okh-lin sh'ar y'ra-kot, ha-lai-lah ha-zeh ma-ror. She-b'khol ha-le-lot eyn anu mat-bilin a-fi-lu p-am a-chat, ha-lai-lah ha-zeh sh'tay f'a-mim. She-b'khol ha-le-lot a-nu okh-lin beyn yosh-vin u-veyn m'su-bin, ha-lai-lah ha-zeh ku-la-nu m'su-bin.

מַה־נִּשְׁתַּנָּה הַלַּיְלָה הַזֶּה מִכָּל־הַלֵּילוֹת. שֶׁבְּכָל־הַלֵּילוֹת אָנוּ אוֹכְלִין חָמֵץ וּמַצָּה. הַלַּיְלָה הַזֶּה כֻּלּוֹ מַצָּה:

שֶׁבְּכָל־הַלֵּילוֹת אָנוּ אוֹכְלִין שְׁאָר יְרָקוֹת. הַלַּיְלָה הַזֶּה מָרוֹר:

שֶׁבְּכָל־הַלֵּילוֹת אֵין אָנוּ מַטְבִּילִין אֲפִילוּ פַּעַם אֶחָת. הַלַּיְלָה הַזֶּה שְׁתֵּי פְעָמִים:

שֶׁבְּכָל־הַלֵּילוֹת אָנוּ אוֹכְלִין בֵּין יוֹשְׁבִין וּבֵין מְסֻבִּין. הַלַּיְלָה הַזֶּה כֻּלָּנוּ מְסֻבִּין:

Another participant says:

But these are not the only questions we could ask. Any question is a way in. And every question is an act of freedom. So let us ask new questions, our own questions.

Members of the community ask questions arising from their own life-experience about freedom, food and hunger, work and jobs, homelessness, war, etc. The more concrete the better. If possible go around the circle of the table so that everyone has the chance to ask one question. A reader responds:

Because we were slaves to Pharaoh in Mitzra-yim, and YHWH our God brought us forth from there with a mighty hand and an arm outstretched to sow seed; and if the most Holy, blessed be You, had not brought forth our ancestors from Mitzra-yim we and our children and our children's children would still be slaves to Pharaoh in Mitzra-yim. Therefore, even if we were all wise, all of us people of understanding and experience, all of us having and knowing the Torah, we would nevertheless be required to discuss the departure from Mitzra-yim, and all who go beyond telling about the departure from Mitzra-yim—all these are worthy of praise.

All sing:

Avodim hayinu, hayinu; avodim hayinu, hayinu; avodim, hayinu; atah atah b'nei chorin.

And so it is related of Rabbi Eliezer, Rabbi Joshua, Rabbi Elazar ben Azariah, Rabbi Akiba, and Rabbi Tarfon, that they once met on the night of Passover in B'nai B'rak and continued discussing the departure from

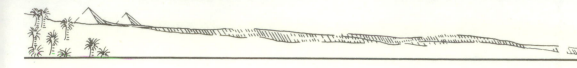

Mitzra-yim so far into the night that they forgot what time it was till their students came and said, "Teachers, it is already time to read the morning Sh'ma!"

Another member of the company interrupts:

Friends, I have heard a story about this story. It is said that when the five rabbis met that night, nineteen hundred years ago, they were stirred by the story of Passover to talk about how to throw off the tyranny of the Roman Empire. And they told their students to let them know at once if the Roman troops came into the neighborhood — to let them know by a code phrase about the morning prayer. So the story goes that they planned a rebellion that night. For when we are slaves, we must talk, but we must do more than talk.

Another participant says:

Where is this Mitzra-yim?

The reader answers:

In those days it was the land of Egypt, but it is not just the land of Egypt. Mitzra-yim means the narrow place — the place that squeezes the life out of a human soul and body. No one place is always Mitzra-yim, but any place — even our own — can be turned into Mitzra-yim. It was a close and narrow Egypt that we left to come to a broad and open wilderness where we felt free, but lonely.

A reader:

Rabbi Elazar ben Azariah said: "Look! I am like someone of seventy years, yet I never understood why the story concerning the departure from Mitzra-yim should be recited at night, until Ben Zoma interpreted it this way: It is said, 'That you may remember the day when you came forth out of the land of Mitzra-yim all the days of your life.' Had it been written simply 'the days of your life' it would have meant the days only; but '*all* the days of your life' means the nights as well."

But the other sages explain the verse differently: "Had it been written simply 'the days of your life,' it would have meant this world only; '*all* the days of your life' means that the days of the Messiah are brought in as well." *Just so we in our telling and our doing must bring in the days of the Messiah.*

Blessed be the Place who is beyond all places, blessed be You who gave us the Teaching.

The teaching invites us to meet and to teach four children: one wise and one wicked, one innocent and one who does not relate by asking.

What does the wise one say? "What are the testimonies, and the statutes, and the rules which YHWH our God has commanded us?"

So you instruct her in the detailed rules of Passover, even that one may not conclude after the Paschal meal by saying, "On to the entertainment!"

What does the wicked one say? "What is this service to you?" "To *you*," and not to him. Since he removes himself from the community, and

so plucks up the Root of Being, you in return must set his teeth on edge, and answer him: "It is because of what YHWH did for me when I came forth from Egypt." For *me*, not for him. Had he been there, he would not have been redeemed.

What does the innocent one say? "*Mah zot*, what is this?" And you shall say to her: "By strength of hand YHWH brought us from Egypt, from the house of bondage."

And with the one who does not relate by asking, you must open up to him and say: "And you shall tell your child in that day, saying: It is because of what YHWH did for me when I came forth out of Egypt."

Invite and wait for discussion on these questions: Who are the four children? Are they among us? Are they within each of us? Are these good answers? After discussion, all sing:

Go tell it on the mountain,
Over the hills and everywhere.
Go tell it on the mountain—
Let my people go!

Who are the people dressed in white?
Let my people go!
Must be the children of the Israelite—
Let my people go!

Who are the people dressed in red?
Let my people go!
Must be the people that Moses led.
Let my people go!

Who are the people dressed in black?
Let my people go!
Must be the hypocrites a-turning back.
Let my people go!

The reader:

In the beginning our forebears served as serfs to idols, but now the Place Who is beyond all places has drawn us near to God's own service, as it is said: "And Joshua said to all the people: 'Thus says YHWH the God of Israel: "Ages ago your forebears dwelt beyond the River—Terah, the father of Abraham, and the father of Nahor; and they served other gods. And I took your father Abraham from beyond the River, and led him throughout all the land of Canaan, and multiplied his seed, and gave him Isaac. And I gave to Isaac, Jacob and Esau; and I gave Esau, Mount Seir, to possess it; but Jacob and his children went down into Egypt."' "

Blessed be the One who keeps Your promise to Israel, blessed be You! For the Holy One, blessed be You, thought, spoke, and acted to end our slavery. As you said to Abraham in the Covenant between the Sections, "And God said to Abraham: 'Know for sure that your seed shall be a stranger in a land that is not theirs, and shall serve them; and they shall afflict them four hundred years; and also that nation, whom they shall serve, will I judge; and afterward shall they come out with a great deal of property.' "

The participants lift up their cups of wine and say:

And it is this promise which has stood by our forebears and by us. For it was not one only who stood up against us to destroy us; in every generation they stand up against us to destroy us, and the Holy One, blessed be You, saves us from their hand.

The cups are put back on the table. Reader says:

Search and inquire how our forebears died in the Middle Passage, in the ships of slavery that brought us to the cotton fields of slavery.

Search still further and inquire in the last generation, what Hitler intended to do; for once again he intended to destroy all Israel and enslave humankind.

And in this generation, search and demand to know about those who shape the fire of the sun to murder nations and all humankind; for at last those who rise up against us, to annihilate us, make no distinctions of race or belief, but plan to destroy us all, without exception. May the Most Holy, blessed be You, deliver us out of their hand again!

May YHWH deliver us again as in the past we celebrate; for it is said, "The Egyptians ill-treated us, afflicted us, and laid heavy bondage upon us. And we cried out to YHWH, the God of our forebears; YHWH heard our voice, and observed our affliction, our labor, and our oppression; and YHWH brought us forth from Egypt, with a strong hand and with an outstretched arm; with terror and with signs and wonders."

"And YHWH brought us forth from Egypt," not by means of an angel nor by means of a seraph, nor by means of a messenger; but the Most Holy, blessed be You, Yourself, in Your glory: as it is said, "And *I* will pass through the land of Egypt this night; and *I* will smite all the first-born in the land of Egypt, both of human and beast; and on all the gods of Egypt will *I* execute judgment; I am YHWH."

"And I will pass through the land of Egypt," I myself and not an angel; "and I will smite all the first-born," I myself and no seraph; "and on all the gods of Egypt will I execute judgment," I myself and not a messenger; "I am YHWH, I am Thou and no other."

These are the ten plagues which the Most Holy, blessed be You, brought on the Egyptians in Egypt.

All drop wine from the cup ten times while saying the ten plagues in unison:

BLOOD, FROGS, LICE, POISONOUS BEASTS, PLAGUE, BOILS, HAIL, LOCUSTS, DARKNESS, SLAYING OF THE FIRST-BORN.

A reader:

The tradition says that we spill wine from our cups in recounting the plagues because we must reduce our pleasure as we remember the sufferings of the Egyptians. And the tradition also tells us that when the angels rejoiced in the drowning of the Egyptians, the Lord our God, blessed be You, rebuked them, saying, "Are these not My people also, and the work of My hands?" Let us therefore grieve for the sufferings of our cousins the Egyptians.

A moment of silence. Then a reader says:

But let us also face the question of the plagues: Can the winning of freedom be bloodless?

The struggle was not bloodless when the people of America announced, "Whenever any form of government becomes destructive of these ends, it is the right of the people to alter or to abolish it," and when Jefferson added, "Can history produce an instance of rebellion so honorably conducted? God forbid we should ever be twenty years without such a rebellion. The tree of liberty must be refreshed from time to time with the blood of patriots and tyrants."

It was not bloodless when Nat Turner proclaimed, "I had a vision, and I saw white spirits and black spirits engaged in battle, and the sun was darkened—the thunder rolled in the heavens and blood flowed in streams— and I heard a voice saying, Such is your luck, such you are called to see, and let it come rough or smooth, you must surely bear it."

All join in singing:

When Israel was in Egypt's land,
Let my people go;
Oppressed so hard they could not stand,
Let my people go!

(Chorus)
Go down, Moses,
'Way down in Egypt's land;
Tell ol' Pharaoh,
Let my people go!

Thus saith the Lord, bold Moses said,
Let my people go;
If not I'll smite your first-born dead;
Let my people go!

No more shall they in bondage toil,
Let my people go;
Let them come out with Egypt's spoil,
Let my people go!

We need not always weep and mourn,
Let my people go;
And wear these slav'ry chains forlorn,
Let my people go!

The devil thought he had us fast,
Let my people go;
But we thought we'd break his chains at last,
Let my people go!

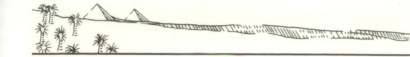

A reader:

It was not bloodless when Henry David Thoreau wrote of John Brown, "It was his peculiar doctrine that a man has a perfect right to interfere by force with the slaveholder, in order to rescue the slave. I agree with him. They who are continually shocked by slavery have some right to be shocked by the violent death of the slaveholder, but no other"; or when Lloyd Garrison burned the Constitution that protected slavery because it was "a covenant with death and an agreement with Hell"; or when Abraham Lincoln said, "If every drop of blood drawn by the lash must be paid by one drawn by the sword, still must it be said, 'The judgments of the Lord are true and righteous altogether.'"

It was not bloodless in the dark months of 1942 when Emmanuel Ringelblum wrote from the Warsaw ghetto: "Most of the populace is set on resistance. It seems to me that people will no longer go to the slaughter like lambs. They want the enemy to pay dearly for their lives. They'll fling themselves at them with knives, staves, coal gas. They'll permit no more blockades. They'll not allow themselves to be seized in the street, for they know that work camp means death these days. And they want to die at home, not in a strange place."

All present sing:

Far and wide as the eye can wander,
Heath and bog are everywhere.
Not a bird sings out to cheer us,
Oaks are standing gaunt and bare.
We are the peat-bog soldiers,
    marching with our spades to the bog.
We are the peat-bog soldiers,
    marching with our spades to the bog.

Up and down the guards are passing;
No one, no one can get through.
Flight would mean a sure death facing—
Guns and barbed wire meet our view.
We are the peat-bog soldiers,
    marching with our spades to the bog.
We are the peat-bog soldiers,
    marching with our spades to the bog.

But for us there's no complaining,
Winter will in time be past.
One day we shall cry, rejoicing,
"Homeland dear, you're mine at last!"
Then will the peat-bog soldiers march no
    more with their spades to the bog.
Then will the peat-bog soldiers march no
    more with their spades to the bog.

A reader resumes:

No, the moments of resistance have not been bloodless. The blood of tyrants and the blood of free people has watered history. But we may not rest easy in that knowledge. The freedom we seek is a freedom from blood as well as a freedom from tyrants. It is incumbent upon us not only to

remember in tears the blood of the tyrants and the blood of the prophets and martyrs, but to end the letting of blood. To end it, to end it!

As our rabbi Aaron Samuel Tamaret taught, "This message was conveyed by the Holy One, blessed be He, in connection with the last of the plagues upon Egypt, when He Himself executed the judgment of death directly by His own power: 'For I will go through the land of Egypt in that night,' I and not an intermediary. Now obviously the Holy One, blessed be He, could have given the Children of Israel the power to avenge themselves upon the Egyptians, but He did not want to sanction the use of their fists for self-defense even at that time; for, while at that moment they might merely have defended themselves against evil-doers, by such means the way of the fist spreads through the world, and in the end defenders become aggressors. Therefore the Holy One, blessed be He, took great pains to remove Israel completely from any participation in the vengeance upon the evil-doers, to such an extent that they were not permitted even to see the events. For that reason midnight, the darkest hour, was designated as the time for the deeds of vengeance, and the Children of Israel were warned not to step outside their houses at that hour — all this in order to remove them totally and completely from even the slightest participation in the deeds of destruction, extending even to watching them.

"The language itself is very precise: '... And none of you shall go out of the door of his house until the morning' — 'that there not be in your midst the plague of the destroyer.' Which means: your abstention from any participation in the vengeance upon Egypt will prevent the plague of vengeance from stirring the power of the destroyer which is in you, yourselves.

"The Children of Israel, then, must derive this lesson from the events of that Passover eve: not to put their trust in wealth, and not to put their trust in might, but rather in the God of truth and justice, for this will serve to defend them everywhere against those who would dominate by the power of the fist."

And as one of the greatest of our prophets, whose own death by violence at a time near the Passover, we remember in tears tonight — as the prophet Martin Luther King called us to know:

"The old law of an eye for an eye leaves everybody blind. It destroys community and makes brotherhood impossible. It creates bitterness in the survivors and brutality in the destroyers. But the principle of non-violent resistance seeks to reconcile the truths of two opposites — acquiescence and violence. The non-violent resister rises to the noble height of opposing the unjust system while loving the perpetrators of the system. Non-violence can reach men where the law cannot touch them.

"So, we will match your capacity to inflict suffering with our capacity to endure suffering. We will not hate you, but we cannot in all good conscience obey your unjust laws. And in winning our freedom we will so appeal to your heart and conscience that we will win you in the process."

He did not win us while he lived. Yet the night before he died he stood with Moses.

Guitar or humming voice, etc., begins the tune of "The Battle Hymn of the Republic" in the background as the reader continues:

"We've got some difficult days ahead. But it really doesn't matter with me now. Because I've been to the mountaintop, I won't mind. Like anybody, I would like to live a long life. Longevity has its place. But I'm not concerned about that now. I just want to do God's will. And He's allowed me to go up to the mountain. And I've looked over, and I've seen the Promised Land. I may not get there with you, but I want you to know tonight that we as a people will get to the Promised Land. So I'm happy tonight. I'm not fearing any man. Mine eyes have seen the glory of the coming of the Lord!"

Sing:

Mine eyes have seen the glory of the coming of the Lord;
God is trampling out the vintage where the grapes of wrath are stored;
God has loosed the fateful lightning of that terrible swift sword;
God's Truth is marching on.
Glory, glory, halleluyah; glory, glory, halleluyah; glory, glory, halleluyah,
    God's Truth is marching on.

A moment of silence. Then the reader says:

In sadness we remember death and suffering, but in joy we remember liberation. To You we raise our voices, in a song of thanks and joy.

Raise the cup.

How many are the claims of the Place beyond all places upon our thankfulness!

All sing or recite Dayenu:

Had You taken us out of Egypt,
but not executed judgments on them,
it would have been enough for us!
Had You executed judgments on them,
but not on their gods,
it would have been enough for us!
Had You executed judgments on their gods,
but not slain their first-born,
it would have been enough for us!
Had You slain their first-born,
but not given us their property which we had worked to create,
it would have been enough for us!
Had You given us their property,
but not torn the Sea apart for us,
it would have been enough for us!
Had You brought us through it dry,
but not sunk our oppressors in the midst of it,
it would have been enough for us!
Had You sunk our oppressors in the midst of it,
but not satisfied our needs in the desert for forty years,
it would have been enough for us!
Had You satisfied our needs in the desert for forty years,
but not fed us manna,
it would have been enough for us!

Had You fed us manna,
but not given us the Shabbat,
it would have been enough for us!
Had You given us the Shabbat,
but not brought us to Mount Sinai,
it would have been enough for us!
Had You given us the Torah,
but not brought us into the Land of Israel,
it would have been enough for us!
Had You brought us into the Land of Israel,
but not built us the House of Your choosing,
it would have been enough for us!

I-lu ho-tzi ho-tzi-a-nu, ho-tzi-anu mi-mitz-ra-yim, ho-tzi-a-nu mi-mitz-ra-yim dai-ye-nu.
DAI-DAI-YE-NU, DAI-DAI-YE-NU, DAI-DAI-YE-NU, Dayenu, dayenu!

I-lu na-tan na-tan la-nu, na-tan la-nu et ha-sha-bat, na-tan la-nu et ha-sha-bat, dai-ye-nu.
DAI-DAI-YE-NU, DAI-DAI-YE-NU, DAI-DAI-YE-NU, Dayenu, dayenu!

What does this mean, "It would have been enough"? Surely no one of these would indeed have been enough for us. It means to celebrate each step toward freedom *as if* it were enough, then to start out on the next step. It means that if we reject each step because it is not the whole liberation, we will never be able to achieve the whole liberation. It means to sing each verse as if it were the whole song — and then sing the next verse!

Then how much more, doubled and redoubled, is the claim the Place beyond all places has upon our thankfulness! For You did take us out of Egypt, and execute judgments upon them, and judgment on their gods, and slay their first-born, and give us their property, and tear the Sea apart for us, and bring us through it dry, and sink our oppressors in the midst of it, and satisfy our needs in the desert for forty years, and feed us manna, and give us the Shabbat, and bring us to Mount Sinai, and give us the Torah, and bring us into the Land of Israel, and build us the House of Your choosing to atone for all our sins.

But there is also work for us to do. It is our own labor that must give birth to freedom. In every generation we stand with those who first gave birth to freedom: with the midwives Shifrah and Puah. When Pharaoh chose death, they chose life. When Pharaoh proclaimed that babies must be murdered, they revered God and resisted Pharaoh. Their eyes saw God in every mother's face, their ears heard God in every baby's cry, their hands drew forth from the narrow place not only life but freedom.

All read:

How many and how hard are the tasks the Redeemer has set before us!
If we were to free the peoples of the world,
but not to beat the swords of every nation into plowshares,
it would not be enough for us.
If we were to beat the swords of every nation into plowshares,
but not to free our earth and air of poison,
it would not be enough for us.
If we were to free our earth and air of poison,
but not to share our food and end all hunger,
it would not be enough for us.
If we were to share our food and end all hunger,
but not to free the poets from their prisons,
it would not be enough for us.
If we were to free the poets from their prisons,
but not to free all women, men, and children to be persons,
it would not be enough for us.
If we were to free all humans to be persons,
but not to free ourselves to know You,
it would not be enough for us.

Then how great, doubled and redoubled,
are the claims the Redeemer makes upon our effort!
You call us to struggle, work, share, give,
think, plan, organize, sit-in, speak out, dream, hope,
and pray for the great Redemption:
to end the oppression of all peoples,
to beat the swords of every nation into plowshares,
to free our earth and air of poison,
to share our food and end all hunger,
to free the poets from their prisons,
to free all women, men and children to be persons,
and to free ourselves to know You.

All sing:

O Freedom!
O Freedom!
O Freedom over me!
And before I'd be a slave
I'd be buried in my grave
And go home to my Lord and be free!

No more killing
No more hunger
No more pollution
No more racism
No more sexism
    (etc.)

The reader says:

Rabban Gamaliel used to say: "Whoever does not explain the following three things on Passover has not fulfilled the obligation: namely, the Passover Sacrifice, unleavened bread, and bitter herbs."

The Passover Sacrifice which our forebears used to eat at the time when the Holy Temple still stood—what was the reason for it? Because the Holy One, blessed be You, passed over the houses of our forebears in Egypt. And as You redeemed our first-born from being killed, may all the children of all Your peoples be redeemed from being killed.

For it is said: "It is the sacrifice of YHWH's Passover, for S/He passed over the houses of the children of Israel in Egypt, when S/He smote the Egyptians, and delivered our houses. And the people bowed their heads and worshipped."

Another participant lifts up the matzot, showing them to the celebrants.

This matzah that we eat, what is the reason for it? Because the dough of our forebears had not yet risen when You Who Rule over all rulers, Holy One, revealed Yourself to them and redeemed them.

As it is said: "And they baked unleavened cakes of the dough which they brought forth out of Egypt, for it was not leavened; because they were thrust out of Egypt, and could not tarry, neither had they prepared for themselves any food."

Participant lifts up the bitter herbs, showing them to the celebrants.

These bitter herbs we eat, what is the reason for them? Because the Egyptians made the lives of our forebears bitter in Egypt.

As it is said: "And they made their lives bitter with hard service, in mortar and in brick, and in all manner of service in the field; in all their service, wherein they made them serve with rigor."

The reader says:

So in every generation let every human being look on himself, herself, as if we all came forth out of Mitzra-yim.

As it is said: "And you shall tell your child in that day, saying: It is because of that which YHWH did for *me* when I came forth out of Mitzra-yim."

It was not only our forebears that the Holy One, blessed be You, redeemed, but us as well did You redeem along with them.

As it is said: "And S/He brought us out from thence, that S/He might bring us in, to give us the land which S/He swore unto our forebears."

The participants lift up their cups of wine and say:

Therefore, we are bound to thank, praise, laud, glorify, exalt, honor, bless, extol, and adore the One who performed all these miracles for our forebears and for us. You have brought us forth from slavery into freedom, from sorrow to joy, from mourning to holiday, from darkness to great light, and from bondage to redemption. Let us then recite before You a new song: Halleluyah!

Sing to tune of "Michael Row the Boat Ashore."

Praise Yah in the heavens, halleluyah.
Praise God in the heights, halleluyah.
Praise God, all you angels, halleluyah.
Praise Yah, all you hosts, halleluyah.
Praise God, sun and moon, halleluyah.
Praise Yah, you stars of light, halleluyah.
Praise God, high heavens and waters above heaven, halleluyah.
Let them all praise God's Name, halleluyah.
For God spoke and they appeared, halleluyah.
God made them stand forever, halleluyah.
God gave order none can break, halleluyah.
Praise Yah from the earth, halleluyah.
You sea-monsters and all deeps, halleluyah.
Fire, hail, snow, and steam, halleluyah.
Stormy wind to do God's word, halleluyah.
Mountains and small hills, halleluyah.
Trees of fruit and cedars too, halleluyah.
Wild beasts and quiet flocks, halleluyah.
Creeping things and winged birds, halleluyah.
Kings on earth and every nation, halleluyah.
Princes, judges, in the world, halleluyah.
Young men and maidens, too, halleluyah.
Let us praise the holy Name, halleluyah.
For God's Name alone is high, halleluyah.
God's glory outshines earth and heaven, halleluyah.
And God lifts the people's hearts, halleluyah.
For all who wrestle God, halleluyah.
For all who touch God close, halleluyah.

Blessed are You, YHWH our God, Ruler of the universe, who redeemed us and who redeemed our forebears from Mitzra-yim, and have brought us to this night, to eat thereon unleavened bread and bitter herbs. In the same way, YHWH our God and God of our forebears, bring us to other festivals and holy days that come toward us in peace, happy in peace, happy in the building of Your City of Peace and joyful in Your service. There may we renew the Passover in all its fullness, with the liberation of all peoples and the redemption of all children. Then shall we give thanks to you with a new song, for our redemption and the liberation of our life-breath. Blessed are You, who redeem all those who wrestle with God.

Blessed are You, YHWH our God, Ruler of the universe, who create the fruit of the vine.	*Barukh atah YHWH elohenu melekh ha-olam, boray p'ri ha-gafen.*	בָּרוּךְ אַתָּה יְיָ אֱלֹהֵינוּ מֶלֶךְ הָעוֹלָם. בּוֹרֵא פְּרִי הַגָּפֶן:

The second cup of wine is drunk in a reclining position. The participants wash their hands and say the following benediction:

Blessed are You, YHWH our God, Ruler of the universe, who made us holy with Your commandments, and commanded us concerning the washing of hands.	*Barukh atah YHWH elohenu melekh ha-olam asher kid-shanu b'mitzvotav vitzivanu al n'tilat yadaim.*	בָּרוּךְ אַתָּה יְיָ אֱלֹהֵינוּ מֶלֶךְ הָעוֹלָם. אֲשֶׁר קִדְּשָׁנוּ בְּמִצְוֹתָיו וְצִוָּנוּ עַל נְטִילַת יָדָיִם:

A participant breaks pieces from the upper and middle matzot and distributes them; the following benedictions are recited:

Blessed are You, YHWH our God, Ruler of the universe, who bring forth bread from the earth.

Barukh atah YHWH elohenu melekh ha-olam hamotzi lechem min haaretz.

בָּרוּךְ אַתָּה יְיָ אֱלֹהֵינוּ מֶלֶךְ הָעוֹלָם. הַמּוֹצִיא לֶחֶם מִן הָאָרֶץ:

Blessed are You, YHWH our God, Ruler of the universe, who made us holy with Your commandments, and commanded us concerning the eating of unleavened bread.

Barukh atah YHWH elohenu melekh ha-olam asher kidshanu b'mitzvotav vitzivanu al akhilat matzah.

בָּרוּךְ אַתָּה יְיָ אֱלֹהֵינוּ מֶלֶךְ הָעוֹלָם אֲשֶׁר קִדְּשָׁנוּ בְּמִצְוֹתָיו וְצִוָּנוּ עַל אֲכִילַת מַצָּה:

The matzah is eaten in a reclining position.

Blessed are You, YHWH our God, who have made us holy by Your commandments and commanded us to share our bread with the hungry, as is written in the Torah: "You shall not gather the fallen fruits of your vineyard, you shall leave them for the poor and for the stranger: I am YHWH your God."

Pause and allow time for those at the table, either silently or aloud, to say: "I pledge myself to . . . [and say what he or she is prepared to do for the hungry]." Dip a slice of the raw horseradish root in the charoset and offer a piece to each participant. The following benediction is spoken before eating the bitter herbs:

Blessed are You, YHWH our God, Ruler of the universe, who made us holy with your commandments, and commanded us concerning the eating of bitter herbs.

Barukh atah YHWH elohenu melekh ha-olam asher kidshanu b'mitzvotov vitzivanu al akhilat maror.

בָּרוּךְ אַתָּה יְיָ אֱלֹהֵינוּ מֶלֶךְ הָעוֹלָם. אֲשֶׁר קִדְּשָׁנוּ בְּמִצְוֹתָיו וְצִוָּנוּ עַל אֲכִילַת מָרוֹר:

Break the bottom matzah, put some chopped horseradish sandwich-fashion between two pieces of matzah. The following is recited before eating:

In memory of the Temple, according to the custom of Hillel. Thus did Hillel when the Holy Temple still stood: he used to combine unleavened bread and bitter herbs and eat them together, to fulfill what is said: "They shall eat it with unleavened bread and bitter herbs."

The Seder platter is removed. At this point the Seder meal is eaten.

At the end of the meal the Afikoman [the piece of matzah that was hidden earlier] is redeemed from the children who have found it, since it is necessary to have this taste of matzah as the last taste at the end of the meal. Alternatively, the children may take the Afikoman and hide it themselves. If the adults cannot find it they must redeem it. The Seder platter is again placed on the table. The matzah which has been set aside for Afikoman is distributed among the Seder company, and everyone eats.

Fill the third cup, and all say:

Blessed are You, YHWH, Ruler of the universe, who feed the whole world in Your goodness, with grace, lovingkindness, and compassion. You give bread to all flesh, for Your lovingkindness is for all space-time. And through Your great goodness, food has never failed us. May we indeed never let it fail us; may we share it, to honor Your great name. For You feed and sustain all and do good to all and prepare enough food for all the creatures You created—enough if we all share it. Blessed are You, YHWH, who feed all.

A participant asks:

Why this egg, and why these flowers?

In the beginning the Passover was a festival of spring and the rebirth of all life. As is said, if we cannot enjoy the return of spring, how can we be happy in utopia? The egg we see here is the form of life and rebirth. And these flowers rise up against winter, as our forebears rose up against Pharaoh.

And these flowers remind us to sing the Song of Songs. Our forebears knew that the Departure from Egypt could teach us how to burst out of slavery to freedom when the moment comes but they also knew that there is another shape of freedom: openness in *every* moment, openness to the love that is stirred up when it pleases. That is the shape of freedom in the Song of Songs. And as the Departure from Egypt was led by a man, so the Song of Songs is led by a woman. So the tradition arose that just as at Passover we tell of the Departure from Egypt, so also we sing from the Song of Songs, of liberation through love. May we learn from both and join both together that we may be redeemed, speedily in our own day!

Woman speaks:

Come with me, my love, come away,
For the long wet months are past,
The rains have fed the earth
And left it bright with blossoms.

Birds wing in the low sky,
Dove and songbird singing
In the open air above,

Earth nourishing tree and vine,
Green fig and tender grape,
Green and tender fragrance.

Come with me, my love, come away.

Man speaks:

Of all pleasure, how sweet
Is the taste of love!

There you stand like a palm,
Your breasts clusters of dates.

Shall I climb that palm
And take hold of the boughs?

Your breasts will be tender
As clusters of grapes,

Your breath will be sweet
As the fragrance of quince,

And your mouth will awaken
All sleeping desire,

Like wine that entices
The lips of new lovers.

Woman speaks:

Turning to him, who meets me with desire—
Come, love, let us go out to the open fields
And spend our night lying where the henna blooms,
Rising early to leave for the near vineyards
Where the vines flower, opening tender buds,
And the pomegranate boughs unfold their blossoms.
There among blossom and vine I will give you my love,
Musk of the violet mandrakes spilled upon us . . .
And returning, finding our doorways piled with fruits,
The best of the new-picked and the long-stored,
My love, I will give you all I have saved for you.

Man speaks:

O women of the city,
Swear by the wild field doe
Not to wake or rouse us
Till we fulfill our love.

The reader passes a blossom from the flowers on the table — if possible on a living plant — to everyone and all say:

Blessed are You, YHWH our God, Ruler of the universe, who have made your world lack nothing, but have created in it beautiful creatures and beautiful blossoming trees, to give delight to the children of Adam.

Barukh atah YHWH elohenu melekh ha-olam shelo khisar ba-olamo davar uvarah vo briyot tovot v'ilanot tovim l'hanot bahem b'nai adam.

בָּרוּךְ אַתָּה יְיָ אֱלֹהֵינוּ מֶלֶךְ הָעוֹלָם. שֶׁלֹּא חִסַּר בְּעוֹלָמוֹ דָּבָר. וּבָרָא בּוֹ בְּרִיּוֹת טוֹבוֹת וְאִילָנוֹת טוֹבִים לְהַנּוֹת בָּהֶם בְּנֵי אָדָם:

All sniff and look carefully at their flowers. All sing:

(Chorus)
Do-di li va-a-ni lo
Ha-ro-eh ba-sho-sha-nim
(Repeat)

Mi zot olah
Min hamidbar
Mi zot olah

M'kituret mor
Mor u-livonah
Mor u-livonah
(Chorus)

Uri tzafon u-vo-i teyman
Uri tzafon u-vo-i teyman
(Chorus)

All lift their glasses and say:

Blessed be You, YHWH our God, who create the fruit of the vine.	*Barukh atah YHWH elohenu melekh ha-olam boray p'ri ha-gafen.*	בָּרוּךְ אַתָּה יְיָ אֱלֹהֵינוּ מֶלֶךְ הָעוֹלָם. בּוֹרֵא פְּרִי הַגָּפֶן:

All drink the third cup. Refill glasses, but not to the top.
Reader says:

YHWH our God, we share Your spring with all that lives and breathes. But there are still some who would crush out of us our joy in spring, in flowers, in freedom and in You. Help us to pour out our wrath against those who have oppressed us—pour it out so that we may be emptied of it.

The door is opened and the following verses are recited:

On those who pour out their hatred upon Your earth and people, let earth and heaven pour out Your wrath upon them. Yes, let Your wrath pour out on those who reject Your creation and revile Your creatures, for they are devouring Your people and laying waste their earthly dwelling place.	*Sh'foch chamatchah el ha-goyim asher lo y'da-ucha v'al mamláchot asher b'shimcha lo kara-oo. Ki achal et-yaakov v'et havey-hu heyshamu. Sh'fach aleyhem zamecha vacharon apcha yasigeym. Tirof b'af v'tashmideym mitachet shmey Adonai.*	שְׁפֹךְ חֲמָתְךָ אֶל־הַגּוֹיִם אֲשֶׁר לֹא־יְדָעוּךָ וְעַל־מַמְלָכוֹת אֲשֶׁר בְּשִׁמְךָ לֹא קָרָאוּ: כִּי אָכַל אֶת־יַעֲקֹב וְאֶת־נָוֵהוּ הֵשַׁמּוּ: שְׁפָךְ־עֲלֵיהֶם זַעְמֶךָ וַחֲרוֹן אַפְּךָ יַשִּׂיגֵם: תִּרְדֹּף בְּאַף וְתַשְׁמִידֵם מִתַּחַת שְׁמֵי יְיָ:

But we plead with You that in that day of recompense, You shield us—all who love You and love Your image in every human face and every creature.

A reader:

Now we are ready to say Your words of peace. Now we are ready to welcome Your prophet Elijah, who will come to prepare the path of Messiah by turning the hearts of the children toward the parents and the hearts of the parents toward the children, who will come to teach us truly that all the paths of Your teaching lead toward peace.

Fill Elijah's wine cup in the center of the table. All sing:

Eliyahu ha'navi, Eliyahu ha'Tishbi, Eliyahu, Eliyahu, Eliyahu ha-Giladi, Bimheyra v'yamenu, yavo elenu, im mashiach ben-David; im mashiach ben-David.

For as You have told us, are we not as the children of the Ethiopians to You? Have You not brought us up out of the land of Egypt, but also the Philistines from Kaphtor and Aram from Kir? May the day come soon when, as is written in Your Torah, Ishmael will dwell face to face with all his brothers, and when, as is written by Your prophet, "In that day Israel shall be the third with Egypt and with Assyria, a blessing in the midst of the earth; for the Lord of hosts has blessed him, saying: 'Blessed be Egypt My people, and Assyria the work of My hands, and Israel My inheritance.'"

A reader:

And may Your day come soon when swords are beaten into plowshares and spears into pruning-hooks, when nation does not lift up sword against nation, neither do they learn war any more.

All sing:

And every one 'neath vine and figtree
Shall live in peace and unafraid
(Repeat)
And into plowshares beat their swords—
Nations shall learn war no more
(Repeat)

All stand. A reader says:

Brothers and sisters, we have been remembering our slavery and our liberation. But just as it was we, not our forebears only, who were liberated in Egypt, so it is we, not our forebears only, who live in slavery. Our slavery is not over, and our liberation is not complete. The task of liberation is long, and it is work that we ourselves must do.

We will share the cup of Elijah. To each other and to You we say: "We ourselves shall be Elijah, we ourselves shall act to bring Messiah."

All say:

We may not live to complete the task, but neither may we refrain from beginning. If not now, when? We have eaten; may our food give us strength for the work ahead! We will drink; may our wine give us joy for the work ahead!

A participant pours some wine from Elijah's cup into that of the next person, who then takes Elijah's cup and does the same for the next person, and so on until the wine has circled the table, and the last person has poured wine from Elijah's cup into that of the first person. All lift their cups, and say in unison:

Blessed are You, YHWH our God, who create the fruit of the vine.	*Barukh atah YHWH elohenu melekh ha-olam, boray p'ri ha-gafen.*	בָּרוּךְ אַתָּה יְיָ אֱלֹהֵינוּ מֶלֶךְ הָעוֹלָם. בּוֹרֵא פְּרִי הַגָּפֶן:

All drink the fourth cup. Then all say:

Next year in the City of Peace!	*L'shana Haba-ah b-Yeru-shalayim!*	לְשָׁנָה הַבָּאָה בִּירוּשָׁלָיִם:

All sing:

> We shall overcome,
> We shall overcome,
> We shall overcome some day!
> Deep in my heart, I do believe,
> We shall overcome some day.
>
> We'll walk hand in hand . . . (Repeat as ''We shall overcome,'' above)
> Black and white together . . . (Repeat . . .)
> We are not afraid . . . (Repeat . . .)
> The people shall be free . . . (Repeat . . .)
> We shall live in peace . . . (Repeat . . .)
> We shall overcome!

Dance joyfully

A Note on the Names of God

The most mysterious and most intimate Name of God in Jewish tradition is יְהֹוָה , which in transliteration is YHWH. This Name is especially closely connected with the liberation from Egypt, since it was revealed to Moses at the Burning Bush as the Name of God he could give to the Israelites in preparing them for their birth of freedom.

The YHWH had no vowels, and certainly was not pronounced "Jehovah" or "Yahweh."

When the letters on the scroll or book said YHWH, Jews usually said aloud "Adonai," "my Lord," and most translations say "Lord." But this conveys a sense of God that is outside, above, dominating — and not at all a sense of God as intimate, "in here," liberating. So in our generation some Jews have struggled toward a better way of understanding and translating YHWH.

Two aspects of the Name could help us understand it better. One is that these four letters draw on the letters for the past, present, and future of the verb "to be" — so that this Name of God might mean "The One Who Was/Is/Will Be." Some translations have therefore used "The Eternal" or "Holy One of Being."

Another aspect of YHWH is that if we were to "pronounce" these four letters *without* any vowels — Y-h-w-h — the pronunciation would be simply a breath. An outbreath. In this way, we not only understand but experience bodily God as the One Who is the breath and gives the breath to us and to all life. As the prayer book says, "The breath of all that lives praises Your Name."

In accord with this aspect of the Name, we could simply pause to breathe whenever we come to YHWH, or we could translate it as "Breath of Life."

This Haggadah prints this Name as YHWH. Readers may choose, therefore, how to say these letters. We would encourage readers to pause and breathe so as to have an inner sense of God within and all around them, God Who breathes into us the urge toward freedom.

The other major Names of God in the Haggadah are:

Elohim, the Creator. This we translate as "God."

HaMakom, literally "the Place." This we usually translate as "the Place beyond all places," in accordance with the Hassidic comment that God is at no particular place *in* the world, but is rather the place *of* the world. It is especially interesting that this Name appears often in the Haggadah, which is concerned with how the people Israel may move from place to place.

Hakadosh Barchu, literally "the Holy One, Blessed be He." This we have changed into "the Holy One, Blessed be S/He" or "Blessed be You." Some readers have found that pronouncing "S/He" as "Sh'he" is especially helpful in echoing the sense that God is not only "masculine" and "feminine," but also beyond both these categories.

Notes

The "Kavvanah" (directed intention) before the blessing of the candles is based on the traditional notion of being a "light to the peoples."

"Humus-Human" is an attempt to capture in English the Hebrew pun of "Adamah" (earth) and "Adam" (human being).

"Ha lachma anya" can best be translated not "bread of affliction" but "...of oppression" or "...of pressing down" because the Aramaic "anya," like Hebrew "oni," "the poor," means literally that.

The Bergen-Belsen prayer is published in the Glatzer-Goldschmidt *Passover Haggadah* (New York: Schocken Books, 1969), p. xxiii.

The setting aside of a matzah as a symbol and promise for *tzedekah* (toward the hungry) was developed by Robert Agus and myself as a result of discussions in Fabrangen, a participatory congregation in Washington, D.C., of Jewish responsibility to deal with world hunger. The "hunger" could also be understood metaphorically as the hunger for freedom among Soviet Jews or any other oppressed people.

"Not by bread alone" comes from Deut. 8:3. At least midrashically, there is a pun in the passage: "Not by lechem (bread) but by all the motzah (what comes forth) shall a human live"; not by bread but by "matzah," and the true matzah is what comes forth from God's mouth.

"Israel" means literally, "God-wrestler"; "Jerusalem," "Yirushalayim," has been taken to mean "City of Shalom," "City of Peace." The hope of freedom, peace, and God-wrestling for all women and men is slightly revised from a passage in my *Freedom Seder* (New York: Holt, Rinehart and Winston and Micah Press, 1970). In the Talmud, Pesachim, 115 b and 116 a; Soncino English ed., Pesachim, pp. 592, 595, there are wonderful passages about how asking other questions may fulfill the function of asking "Mah nishtanah." The Fabrangen "discovered" and discussed them in Talmud classes led by Max Ticktin.

"An arm outstretched to sow seed" is a midrashic translation based on the fact that "zeroa," "outstretched arm," is based on the root meaning "seed." Thus the imagery of God's arm is not of an arm raised in violence but of one reaching out to cast the people Israel as seed upon the earth.

"Go tell it on the mountain"—a traditional Black song. The version here is the one I learned from Fannie Lou Hamer and the Mississippi Freedom Democratic Party at the Atlantic City Democratic Convention in 1968. The song is one of many cases in which the Passover has become an organic part of the liberation thought and feelings of peoples other than Jews.

The story about plotting rebellion at B'nai B'rak has been passed on orally for generations—orally for obvious reasons.

As in the psalm-phrase "min hamaytzar," "from the straits" or "narrow-places," Mitzra-yim is here interpreted as "narrowness"—a 'drash I first learned from Robert Agus. This is included partly to clarify what the spiritual-political oppressiveness of Egypt was, and partly to lessen the danger that Passover celebrants will simply identify the "Egypt" of the Exodus with modern Egypt. The identification could, if not explicitly examined, lead to feelings like those aroused in some Christians who identify references to "the Jews" in the Gospels with the Jews of their own day. "Mitzra-yim" may or may not describe modern Egypt or America, or the Soviet Union, or even—God forbid!—Israel. "Mitzra-yim" is a way of behaving, not simply a place.

The days of Messiah are "brought in" rather than "included"—a more literal translation of "l'havi," which may well originally have been intended to hint at "bringing in" not only in the telling but the doing too.

The Haggadah often uses "HaMakom," "The Place," as a word for God. Why? Some feel that this is an attempt to remind us to be sojourners—like Abraham, Isaac, and Jacob and his children who went into Egypt, as well as the generation that departs from Egypt—rather than to make an idol of any one place as Esau did of Seir. Hence the translation, "Place who is beyond all places." (I learned this from Rob Agus in Fabrangen discussions of the Haggadah.)

The midrash of the Four Children opens up many questions of its own. For example, some feel that the reply given the "wicked" child is unwise, unloving, and unjust—and least likely to reconnect him to the community. Others feel that it honors him by taking his own stance seriously. Some say that to "set his teeth on edge" is to slap him across the face; others, that it is to press upon him the taste of matzah and of bitter herb, to remind him that liberation and community are a matter not of ideas or words alone but of full bodily reality.

Some feel that all the Four Children should be viewed as aspects of every human being—evidences of the several different identities half-buried in us all. Indeed, some have said that each of the four is as necessary to wholeness as is each of the Four Questions—the wise one, with a flat question about rules, as necessary as the flat matzah; the wicked one, as necessary as the bitter herb; the innocent one, as necessary as the herb so unblemished that it must be dipped twice; the one who waits to be told, as necessary as reclining to be fed.

Some celebrants have wondered whether the order of the four children is important. Is it deliberate that they move from the most detailed questions to less and less specific questions to no question at all, but open waiting? Is the fourth child—rather than one who is too young to ask, rather than one who "does not yet know how to ask"—instead one who is *beyond* asking? Does s/he have a different way of relating—open ears and an open but unspeaking mouth, the position of the silent letter Aleph? Is the Haggadah saying that questioning is the highest form of freedom, but the highest form of questioning is not words but an open-ended silence? Or is the order of the children not orderly at all?

The traditional Haggadah says that the four children "k'neged," "stand opposite" the Torah. This could be translated "encounter," or "meet and teach."

"Four children" rather than "four sons" is in these circumstances a legitimate translation for "banim," and throughout I have in any case changed language to make clear that women as well as men are to be fully part of all aspects of Jewish life and practice.

"Innocent" rather than "simple" child because "tahm" means unblemished, pure, like a lamb fit for sacrifice.

"Does not relate by asking" is a translation of "she-ayno yodaya lishol." It is used instead of "Does not know to ask" because the Hebrew "yodaya," usually translated "know," means to make love as well as to understand; it means to have a strong relationship with either person or information.

"*Mah zot*, what is this?" There almost seems to be a pun here on *matzah—mah zot*?

The midrash on pouring wine from the cup has been passed on orally. God's rebuke to the angels is in the Talmud, Sanhedrin 39 b; in Soncino English edition, Sanhedrin, p. 251.

The dialogue of Ben Zoma and the Sages continues in the Talmud, B'rachot 12 b-13 a; Soncino English edition, B'rachot pp. 72–73, with a very powerful passage. It asks: in the days to come, the days of Messiah, will we indeed continue telling the story of the Exodus from Egypt—or will we rather tell stories of deliverance from all the earthly tyrants whose overthrow will be necessary if Messiah is to come? Both, says the Talmud—just as we remember that "Avram" became "Avraham" and "Sarai" became "Sarah." Their original names were particularist: "Father of Aram" (Syria) and "My Princess." Their later names were universalist—"Father of All Nations" and "Princess of All Peoples." Just so the Messianic redemption: when we tell the story we will remember that it began with the people of Israel leaving Egypt, and then spread to all the peoples leaving their oppression.

Rabbi Aaron Samuel Tamaret of Mileitchitz is translated by Rabbi Everett Gendler in the pamphlet *Roots of Jewish Nonviolence*, published by the Jewish Peace Fellowship, Box 271, Nyack, N.Y. The pamphlet is an excellent review of Jewish tradition and thought on peace and nonviolence.

The passage from Song of Songs—in Marcia Falk's extraordinary translation—is the result of a remarkable discussion of the Song of Songs by Fabrangen during Passover 1973. (See Chapter VI of *Godwrestling* [New York: Schocken Books, 1978] for a fuller explanation.)

For the blessing over flowers I have chosen the one traditionally set aside for first seeing a blossoming tree in Nisan—the month of Passover—because it seemed poignantly appropriate to the Seder. It is in the traditional Siddur, edited by Joseph H. Hertz, *Authorized Daily Prayer Book* (New York: Bloch, 1948), p. 961.

The 'drash on "pouring out" our and God's wrath comes from Robert Agus, who has over and over at Fabrangen Seders gathered up and poured out all our fury at oppression in the most soul-shaking chants of "Shfoch chamatcha." The English is not a translation of the Hebrew verses, but a midrashic rendering of the way the Hebrew could be understood in our generation. The Hebrew is retained for those who might want to chant it, beginning in fury and gradually letting the chant break into hurt, sadness, and peacefulness.

The "Ethiopian" passage is from Amos 9:7, the prophecy of peace with Ishmael in Genesis 16:12, and the "Assyria" passage from Isaiah 19:24.

Seder of the
Children of Abraham

" We considered it a fundamental point that in this case two vital claims oppose each other, two claims of a different nature and a different origin which cannot objectively be pitted against one another and between which no objective decision can be made as to which is just, which unjust. We considered, and still consider, it our duty to understand and to honor the claim which is opposed to ours, and to endeavor to reconcile both claims. We could not and cannot renounce the Jewish claim; something even higher than the life of our people is bound up with this land, namely, its work, its divine mission. But we have been and still are convinced that it must be possible to find some compromise between this claim and the other, for we love this land and we believe in its future; since such love and such faith are surely present on the other side as well, a union in the common service of the land must be within the range of possibility. Where there is faith and love, a solution may be found even to what appears to be a tragic opposition." [1]

Martin Buber

Dedication

This Seder is dedicated to two extraordinary people, an Israeli and a Palestinian, both of whom worked to better understanding between their peoples and both of whom died before they could see the realization of their shared dream.

Emil Greenzweig was an Israeli who lived on Kibbutz Revivim where he taught mathematics at the high school. He then worked on educational projects at the Van Leer Institute, an institute in Jerusalem which is devoted to peace. He is remembered by his friends as a man of boundless energy and enthusiasm. Emil was an activist with Peace Now. On February 10, 1983, he participated in a demonstration which called on the Israeli government to accept the recommendations of the Kahan Commission. He was killed by a grenade thrown by a member of an opposing group.

Issam Sartawi was a Palestinian born in 1935 in the town of Acre in mandate Palestine. Trained as a heart surgeon, he practiced for a time in Cleveland, Ohio. After the 1967 Arab-Israeli war, he founded a small Palestinian guerrilla group, The Organization for Action for the Liberation of Palestine, which he disbanded in late 1970 after Black September in Jordan. A member of the Palestine National Council based in Paris, Sartawi was the key Palestinian involved in contacts with Israelis. Beginning in 1976, Sartawi engaged in a series of secret dialogues with members of the Israeli Council for Israeli-Palestinian Peace, including General Mattityahu Peled and Arie Eliav. These discussions were far ranging, dealing with questions of land and national identity. Together they forged a vision of a shared future for Israelis and Palestinians, based on mutual recognition, security, and self determination for both peoples. On April 10, 1983, Issam Sartawi was assassinated while attending a socialist conference in Portugal, and a courageous voice for peace in the Middle East was stilled.

Seder of the Children of Abraham

Suggestions for the Seder

This Seder was written not to be a substitute for the traditional saga of the Exodus of the Jews from Egypt, but to be conducted on another night of Pesach. It can be celebrated with a small group of friends and family or as a large political event. In the latter case, arrange the room in tables seating eight to twelve people, and place the necessary ritual food and objects on each table. Have a facilitator at each table; this will help during those segments that call for sharing and may also serve to prevent potential disruptions. During the meal (which may be no more than a light snack), the facilitator may promote a frank discussion of people's reactions to the Seder, but he or she should discourage argument and encourage people to listen to one another.

In conducting the Seder we have found it most effective to have a few people function as overall moderators, reading the narrative sections and giving the instructions, while designating other participants to read the quotations. If at all possible, try to have Jews and Palestinians participating together in the Seder. Music is a very important part of the evening; singing helps bring about the needed spirit. A musician and a song leader can add a crucial element. The Seder is quite long, so you may decide to omit some of the readings or to do them silently. We have provided guidelines by designating some as optional readings. In addition to being an organizing and educating tool, the Seder can be a moving and uplifting experience. Our greatest wish is that events in the Middle East move closer to a peaceful sharing of the land and render this Seder obsolete.

Introduction

Optional reading

We come to this Seder as Jews committed to Jewish survival and to the survival of the State of Israel. We as Jews acknowledge that we are deeply affected by the historic pain and suffering of our people. In our own time the Holocaust as the culmination of centuries of Jew-hatred and persecution has left us scarred.

At this point in our history we feel that it is crucial for our survival to hear not only our own pain and vision but the pain of the Palestinians, the people with whom we so urgently need to effect reconciliation. We admit that it will be hard for us as Jews to hear of their anguish and suffering, yet it is in fact in our own self interest to open ourselves to listen, however hard it may be.

Listening to their story in no way negates our own—our claim and our vision remain legitimate, central to our identity and survival.

Pesach is our festival of freedom. At times we may be slaves to our own suffering, unable to call forth the strength needed to listen to the other. We hope that we can join together in this Seder to listen to both stories—ours and theirs.

Sing together:

How good and pleasant for brethren to dwell in harmony!

Hiney ma tov uma na-im, shevet achim gam yachad.

הִנֵּה מַה־טּוֹב וּמַה־נָּעִים שֶׁבֶת אַחִים גַּם־יָחַד:

This Seder is dedicated to the fulfillment of a dream and a promise—the promise made to Isaac and Ishmael, the children of Abraham, Sarah, and Hagar.[2] Isaac and Ishmael were brothers, brothers separated from each other by jealousy and animosity. Yet both were direct descendants of Abraham, and each received a Divine promise to be a great nation.

Since this separation between the two brothers, the Jewish and Arab peoples who believe themselves to be physically and spiritually descendants of Isaac and Ishmael have often come into contact with one another, appreciating and even sharing in each others' cultures. But in our century these two peoples, *our* two peoples, have entered into unprecedented, violent, and bitter conflict.

This conflict between the Israeli and Palestinian peoples is over a land that has nurtured the traditions and cultures of both peoples, a land which is deeply loved by them. This Seder is dedicated to the dream that both peoples can share this land in peace.

To understand how it is possible to share the land, we need to acknowledge the history of our relationship. In this Seder we will present threads of this history, mostly through the eyes of the actors themselves, Israelis and Palestinians. These threads of history are not offered as an authoritative, objective historical account but rather as a way of gaining an understanding of our commonalities and finding a way to move toward peace. Therefore, our history will focus on the commonalities that are shared by both people: our common love for the land, our common experience of exile, and our common oppression. We also acknowledge the tragic, destructive killing that we have inflicted on one another. We will focus special attention on those Israelis and Palestinians who have had the courage to envision a new reality, a reality of peace, sharing and mutual respect.

At the same time, part of the process of healing that must take place if Jews and Arabs are to co-habit the same land is to recognize our differences. We look at the world with different eyes. Words, the basic tool of dialogue, play a different part in each of our cultures. One emphasizes literal expression, the other hyperbole. And thus we must confront the reality of an inevitable struggle: to learn to speak that we might be heard. This must be the first step.

We believe that both peoples have a right to this land and that there can be a just settlement between the two claims. As Martin Buber said, ". . . we have been and still are convinced that it must be possible to find some compromise between this claim and the other, for we love this land and we believe in its future; since such love and such faith are surely present on the other side as well, a union in the common service of the land must be within the range of possibility. Where there is faith and love, a solution may be found even to what appears to be a tragic opposition."

For those beginning on Saturday night:
Havdalah הבדלה

Directions for Havdalah

A Havdalah candle, a wine goblet filled with wine, and a spice box are needed.

The Havdalah candle is held high. After the blessing over the wine, the wine goblet is passed around the table, and each participant takes a sip. After the blessing over the spices, the spice box is passed around, and each participant smells its aroma.

After the blessing is completed, a drop of wine is poured on a plate and the candle is extinguished in it.

We start our Seder with Havdalah. Havdalah, the ceremony of separation, is directly connected to the central affirmation of this Seder. We affirm that we are two peoples, distinct and separate, and yet we also share a common origin and common destiny. Havdalah marks the end of Shabbat, the weekly celebration of creation. The act of creation is the act of separation, light and dark, dry land and ocean, heaven and earth. All life begins with separation of cells.

Similarly, our two peoples are descendants of one man, Abraham, yet have developed as two separate peoples. We each have our own distinct way of viewing the world and of expressing what we see. Sometimes this makes it hard for us to hear and understand one another. But like the wicks of the Havdalah candle, each people needs its own light, its own fire, its own creativity, its own culture. To create the great flame of hope, we need to realize our interconnectedness and commonality.

Ei-li-ya-hu ha-na-vi, Ei-li-ya-hu ha-tish-bi; Ei-li-ya-hu, Ei-li-ya-hu, Ei-li- ya-hu ha-gil-a-di. Bi-me-hei-ra ve-ya-mei-nu, ya-vo ei-lei-nu; im ma-shi- ach ben Da-vid, im ma-shi-ach ben Da-vid. Ei-li-ya-hu. . . .

אֵלִיָּהוּ הַנָּבִיא, אֵלִיָּהוּ הַתִּשְׁבִּי;
אֵלִיָּהוּ, אֵלִיָּהוּ, אֵלִיָּהוּ הַגִּלְעָדִי.
בִּמְהֵרָה בְיָמֵינוּ, יָבֹא אֵלֵינוּ; עִם
מָשִׁיחַ בֶּן דָּוִד, עִם מָשִׁיחַ בֶּן דָּוִד.אֵלִיָּהוּ . . .

God is my deliverance; I will be confident and unafraid. She is my strength, my song and my salvation. In joy we shall drink from the wells of salvation. God will rescue and bless Her people. The God of all creation is with us, the God of Israel is our refuge. The Jews of old had light, joy, delight and honor; so may it be for us. I lift up my cup of deliverance and call upon the Holy One.

Hiney eyl yeshuatee, evtach v'lo efchad. Hee ozi v'zimrat yah Adonai va'y'hee lee lee'shua. U'sh'avtem mayiim b'sason mee-ma-aynei ha-y'shua. La-Adonai ha-y'shua al amcha veerchatecha sela. Adonai z'vaot eemanu meesgav lanu eloheh ya'akov sela. La-yehudeem haita ora v'simcha v'sason veekar. Ken t'heeyeh lanu. Kos y'shuot esah u-v'shem Adonai ekra.

הִנֵּה אֵל יְשׁוּעָתִי אֶבְטַח וְלֹא אֶפְחָד.
כִּי עָזִּי וְזִמְרָת יָהּ יְיָ יְיָ וַיְהִי־לִי
לִישׁוּעָה: וּשְׁאַבְתֶּם מַיִם בְּשָׂשׂוֹן
מִמַּעַיְנֵי הַיְשׁוּעָה: לַיְיָ הַיְשׁוּעָה עַל־
עַמְּךָ בִרְכָתֶךָ סֶּלָה: יְיָ צְבָאוֹת עִמָּנוּ
מִשְׂגָּב־לָנוּ אֱלֹהֵי יַעֲקֹב סֶלָה:
לַיְּהוּדִים הָיְתָה אוֹרָה וְשִׂמְחָה וְשָׂשׂוֹן
וִיקָר. כֵּן תִּהְיֶה לָנוּ: כּוֹס־יְשׁוּעוֹת
אֶשָּׂא וּבְשֵׁם יְיָ אֶקְרָא:

Holy One of Blessing Your Presence fills creation forming the fruit of the vine.	*Baruch atah Adonai eloheynu melech ha-olam, boray p'ri ha-gafen.*	בָּרוּךְ אַתָּה יְיָ, אֱלֹהֵינוּ מֶלֶךְ הָעוֹלָם, בּוֹרֵא פְּרִי הַגָּפֶן.
Holy One of Blessing Your Presence fills creation making fragrant spices.	*Baruch atah Adonai eloheynu melech ha-olam boray meenai v'sameem.*	בָּרוּךְ אַתָּה יְיָ אֱלֹהֵינוּ מֶלֶךְ הָעוֹלָם, בּוֹרֵא מִינֵי בְשָׂמִים.
Holy One of Blessing Your Presence fills creation forming the lights of fire.[3]	*Baruch atah Adonai eloheynu melech ha-olam boray m'orai ha-aish.*	בָּרוּךְ אַתָּה יְיָ אֱלֹהֵינוּ מֶלֶךְ הָעוֹלָם בּוֹרֵא מְאוֹרֵי הָאֵשׁ.
Holy One of Blessing Your Presence fills creation. You separate the holy from the profane light from darkness Israel from the other peoples Shabbat from the six other days. Holy One of Blessing You separate the holy from the profane.	*Baruch atah Adonai eloheynu melech ha-olam ha-mavdeel ben kodesh l'chol ben or l'choshech, ben Yisrael la-ameem, ben yom ha-sh'vee-ee l'shai-shet 'y'mai ha-ma-aseh, baruch atah Adonai ha-mavdeel ben kodesh l'chol.*	בָּרוּךְ אַתָּה יְיָ אֱלֹהֵינוּ מֶלֶךְ הָעוֹלָם הַמַּבְדִּיל בֵּין קֹדֶשׁ לְחוֹל בֵּין אוֹר לְחוֹשֶׁךְ בֵּין יִשְׂרָאֵל לָעַמִּים בֵּין יוֹם הַשְּׁבִיעִי לְשֵׁשֶׁת יְמֵי הַמַּעֲשֶׂה בָּרוּךְ אַתָּה יְיָ הַמַּבְדִּיל בֵּין קֹדֶשׁ לְחוֹל:

Ha-mav-dil bein ko-desh le-chol, cha-to-tei-nu hu yim-chol, zar-ei-nu ve-chas-pei-nu yar-beh ka-chol, ve-cha-ko-cha-vim ba-lai-la. Sha-vu-a tov...

הַמַּבְדִּיל בֵּין קֹדֶשׁ לְחוֹל, חַטֹּאתֵינוּ
הוּא יִמְחֹל, זַרְעֵנוּ וְכַסְפֵּנוּ יַרְבֶּה
כַּחוֹל, וְכַכּוֹכָבִים בַּלָּיְלָה.
שָׁבוּעַ טוֹב...

Start here if not Saturday night.
Introductions: At this point we ask that the people at each table take a moment to go around and allow everyone to introduce themselves, stating the reasons which brought them to this special Seder.

Kiddush קדש

The First Cup of Wine, The Cup of Security

"A person who does not own a piece of land is not a secure person."

Talmud

And, we might add, in the land of one's heritage.

We raise this first cup of wine in acknowledgment of the legitimate desires of each people to lead a secure life—a life free from fear—secure in the knowledge that they have a land, a land from which they cannot be driven.

We conduct this Seder in the belief that the security is attainable.

"They shall sit every person under their vine and fig tree and no one shall make them afraid."

Micah 4:4

We will now say the blessing over the wine together.

Baruch atah Adonai eloheynu melech ha-olam boray p'ri ha-gafen.

בָּרוּךְ אַתָּה יְיָ אֱלֹהֵינוּ מֶלֶךְ הָעוֹלָם, בּוֹרֵא פְּרִי הַגָּפֶן

Ur-chatz ורחץ

Directions: **A bowl of water with a cup or ladle is passed around. Each person pours water over his/her neighbor's hands, as a symbolic washing. The song "Bamboo" is sung throughout this ritual.**

BAMBOO

You take a stick of bamboo (3x), you throw it in the water
Oh oh, Hana (repeat)

Refrain

River she comes down (2x)

You travel on the river...
My home's across the river...

Wash your hands without reciting the customary blessing.

Karpas: Rebirth and Renewal כרפס

Dip a vegetable in salt water and recite:

Praised are You, Adonai our God, King of the Universe who creates the fruit of the earth.

Baruch atah Adonai, eloheynu melech ha-olam, boray p'ri ha-damah.

בָּרוּךְ אַתָּה יְיָ אֱלֹהֵינוּ מֶלֶךְ הָעוֹלָם בּוֹרֵא פְּרִי הָאֲדָמָה.

The vegetable is now eaten.

DODEE LEE

I belong to my beloved and he is mine.

Do-dee lee vaanee lo,
Ha-ro-eh ba-sho-sha-neem. (2)

Mee zote o-lah min ha-mid-bar,
Mee zote o-lah? (2)
Do-dee lee...

Lee-bav-tee-nee acho-tee cha-lah
Lee-bav-tee-nee cha-lah. (2)
 Do-dee lee...

Oo-ree tsa-fon oo-vo-ee tai-man. (2)
 Do-dee lee.

דּוֹדִי לִי

דּוֹדִי לִי וַאֲנִי לוֹ,
הָרוֹעֶה בַּשׁוֹשַׁנִים. (2)

מִי זֹאת עוֹלָה מִן הַמִּדְבָּר,
מִי זֹאת עוֹלָה? (2)
דּוֹדִי לִי . . .

לְבַבְתִּנִי אֲחוֹתִי כַלָה
לְבַבְתִּנִי כַלָה. (2)
דּוֹדִי לִי . . .

עוּרִי צָפוֹן, וּבוֹאִי תֵימָן (2)
דּוֹדִי לִי . . .

The Breaking of the Middle Matzah יחץ

Directions: **A plate with three matzot is on the table. The middle matzah is broken in two. An optional part of the Seder is to hide half of this piece, known as the *afikoman*, for a child to find and "sell" back at the appropriate time—at the end of the meal. The *afikoman* is a symbolic dessert, which allows the Seder to proceed after the meal is finished.**

The other half of this piece of matzah is raised high, as the narrative proceeds.

Note: Grapejuice can be substituted for wine in all cases.

One explanation of *lehem oni* is the "bread over which much is answered." In this spirit we break the matzah, in the hope that as we share our questions, some answers may be generated, some directions given to a more hopeful future.

Bread of Affliction

This is the matzoh, the bread of affliction which our ancestors ate in Mitzraim.

Mitzraim literally means "tight places," the time of our slavery. Today we are slaves of our fear. Jews are slaves to the fear bred of 2,000 years of Jew hatred culminating in the Holocaust; Palestinians are slaves to the fear bred of being homeless refugees and of living under an occupying power. Fear, insecurity, is the villain—our affliction.

"Let all who are in need come and partake of the paschal lamb.
This year we are here:
Next year in the land of Israel."

Israel is both a metaphor and a reality. It is a metaphor for peace: next year may we all be at peace. Israel is the reality of a land which Jews and Palestinians both want. Next year may we share the land in peace.

This year we are slaves, next year free men and women. As long as we are imprisoned in our own fears, not recognizing the rights of others, we are slaves. As long as Israel is an occupier operating from her fears, she cannot be healthy and is a slave. As long as Palestinians are not willing to recognize the rights of a Jewish homeland in Israel, they too are imprisoned in the slavery of fear. Next year may we recognize the needs of the other and be free.

MIN HAMEYTZAR
Sing together:

From the narrow straits I called to HaShem.	*Min hameytzar kah-rah-tee yah.* *ah-na-nee ba-mer-chav-yah.*	מִן־הַמֵּצַר קָרָאתִי יָהּ, עָנָנִי בַמֶּרְחַב יָהּ.
Then HaShem answered me with room to breathe.		

The Four Questions

Why is this night different from all other nights?

On all other nights we eat leavened bread or matzah, on this night we eat only matzah which reminds us of the afflictions we share.

On all other nights we eat all kinds of herbs, on this night we eat bitter herbs especially to remind ourselves of the bitter suffering and pain that have marked our relationship for more than thirty years.

On all other nights we do not dip herbs at all, on this night we dip them twice to honor the two peoples, the Palestinians and the Israelis, who must and will together find the path to mutual respect and coexistence.

On all other nights we are seated or recline when we eat, on this night we only recline, in anticipation of the day in the future when we will no longer need to brace ourselves against the stranger, and will be able truly to relax together.

The Four Children

Four children bring different questions to the Seder table tonight:

The angry child asks, "Why should I compromise?"

And we answer that we choose the route of compromise because the alternative is the mutual destruction, both moral and physical, of our two peoples. If we fail to compromise we will lose a vision of the future for our children.

The naive child asks, "Why can't we just love each other?"

And we answer that neither of us can live as if history has not happened. Unfortunately, too much blood has already been shed on both sides. It takes time to build trust.

The frightened child asks, "How can I be safe?"

And we answer that we are both afraid. "How can I be safe if my brother or sister is not safe?"

The wise child asks, "How can we share the land in peace?"

And indeed this is the question with which we will wrestle tonight.

Maggid מגיד

BIBLICAL BEGINNINGS

The rabbis were divided over the question of where to begin the telling (Maggid) of the Exodus. We too don't know where to start. So, like the traditional Haggadah, we will have two beginnings. One that begins with the story of our two ancestors and one that begins with the conflict of our two peoples in this century.

Let's start by looking at the way Isaac and Ishmael are seen in the sacred text of our two peoples.

Reader:

Abraham was childless...and he co-habited with Hagar and she conceived...and the angel of the Lord said to her,

---

Community:

I will greatly increase your offspring and they shall be too many to count.

You shall bear a son.
You shall call him Ishmael
For the Lord has paid heed to your suffering.
He shall be a wild ass of a man,
His hand against everyone
And everyone's hand against him.
He shall dwell alongside all his kinsmen.

Reader:

And God said to Abraham, "as for your wife Sarai you shall not call her Sarai but her name shall be Sarah. I will bless her; indeed I will give you a son by her. I will bless her so that she shall give rise to nations, rulers of peoples shall issue from her."

Community:

"...Sarah your wife shall bear you a son and you shall name him Isaac; and I will maintain my covenant with him as an everlasting covenant for his offspring to come. As for Ishmael, I have heeded you. I hereby bless him. I will make him fertile and exceedingly numerous. He shall be the father of twelve chieftains and I will make of him a great nation. But my covenant I will maintain with Isaac whom Sarah shall bear to you at this season next year."

Reader:

And from the Koran, the story of Ismail:

Community:

He was strictly true to what he promised and he was an apostle and a prophet. He used to enjoin on his people prayer and charity, and he was most acceptable in the sight of the Lord.

Reader:

And we gave Abraham the good news of Isaac, a prophet, one of the Righteous. We blessed Abraham and Isaac.

Community:

And remember Abraham and Ismail raised the foundations of the house with this prayer:
Our Lord! Accept this service from us for thou art the All Hearing the All Knowing....Our Lord make of us submissive bowing to thy will and of our progeny a people submissive bowing to thy will.

What questions emerge from the reading of these texts? Are there visions for reconciliation in these verses?

In Jewish tradition, Isaac is the son who is bound to be sacrificed. In Muslim tradition it is Ishmael. In our generation, both peoples, the Israeli and the Palestinian, have faced the possibility of extermination, of being sacrificed. Both sides have even talked about exterminating the other.

In the face of this prospect of mutual extermination, our only alternative is in fact mutual recognition. The urgent challenge of our time is to learn to dwell "face to face" as brothers and sisters.

OSEH SHALOM

May He who makes peace in his high places	*Oseh shalom bimromav*	עֹשֶׂה שָׁלוֹם בִּמְרוֹמָיו הוּא יַעֲשֶׂה
Make peace for us	*Hu ya'aseh shalom aleynu*	שָׁלוֹם עָלֵינוּ וְעַל כָּל יִשְׂרָאֵל וְאִמְרוּ
And for Israel	*V'al kol Yisrael*	אָמֵן.
And we say ''Amen''	*V'imru Amen*	

AND OTHER BEGINNINGS

At the beginning of the 1880's there were nearly 7 million Jews in Europe out of a total of 7.5 million in the entire world. The majority lived in Russia and the Austrio-Hungarian empire. In 1881 horrible pogroms (concentrated, planned attacks against Jewish communities) broke out in Russia, and continued with sporadic outbreaks throughout 1882. Moshe Lilienblum (1843–1910), an important Zionist thinker and writer, records in his diary the awesome shock of that experience:

> May 5, 1881. Terrible! The situation is terrible and frightening! We are virtually under siege. The courtyards are barred up and we keep peering through the grillwork of the court gates to see if the mob is coming to swoop down on us. What does the future have in store for us? Will they have mercy on the youngsters—who don't even know yet that they are Jews, that they are wretches—and not harm them?...
>
> It is not a lack of high culture that was the cause of our tragedy—for aliens we are and aliens we shall remain, even if we become full to the brim with culture.
>
> I have opened my eyes to a new ideal—all the old ideals have left me in a flash. How sweet and dear this ideal has become to me! All my life I grieved over the decline of Jewish nationality and the thought that Jewry's existence as a nation was doomed. And now there lies before me a straight and sure path to the everlasting salvation of our people and its nationhood, a path to which the imperatives of life have brought me—the ingathering of the exiles and the settlement of Eretz Israel.[4]

The dream of Israel, a dream which had remained alive in the Jewish soul through the daily worship service for 2,000 years, in which the prayer for return to Zion was recited as a metaphor for spiritual redemption, that dream took on a new dimension for a growing number of Jews—a political dimension. The messianic dream meshed with the European nationalistic spirit, to create a radical new philosophy, political zionism.

To many of these early builders, zionism and socialism were viewed as complementary world views. It seemed absurd to create a system which would duplicate in any way the inequalities of their former lives. One of the most essential ingredients in the way this philosophy was actualized by these early settlers was through their relationship to the land.

ANU BANU ARTSA

We have come to our land to build and to be rebuilt through it.	*A-nu ba-nu ar-tsa* *Liv-not oo-l'-hee-ba-not ba!* *A-nu ba-nu ar-tsa* *Liv-not oo-l'hee-ba-not.* *La, la...*	אָנוּ בָּאנוּ אַרְצָה אָנוּ בָּאנוּ אַרְצָה לִבְנוֹת וּלְהִבָּנוֹת בָּהּ! אָנוּ בָּאנוּ אַרְצָה לִבְנוֹת וּלְהִבָּנוֹת.

The great prophet of this religion of labor was Aaron David Gordon. Gordon worshipped labor; the power of the land was, to him, almost transcendent.

It all seems very clear: from now on our principal idea must be Labor. Through no fault of our own we have been deprived of this element and we must seek a remedy. Labor is our cure. The ideal of Labor must become the pivot of all our aspirations. It is the foundation upon which our national structure is to be erected. Only by making Labor, for its own sake, our national ideal, shall we be able to cure ourselves of the plague that has affected us for so many generations and mend the rent between ourselves and Nature.[5]

And slowly, with much pain and disease and death, but with even more courage and perseverance and hope, the land began to bear fruit. Villages and towns were created. The dream was nourished during the early years of British rule by Lord Balfour who, in 1917, promised a "Jewish homeland," thus paving the way for a new wave of immigrants to add support to the communities already developed, and build a new generation of kibbutzim.

SHEER HA'EMEK

Rest has come to the weary	*Ba'ah menucha layage'ah*	באה מנוחה ליגע
And calm for the worker	*Umargo'ah l'amel*	ומרגוע לעמל
A pale night spreads	*Leilah cheever mistare'ah*	לילה חיור משתרע
Over the valley of Yeezre-el	*Al sdot emek Yizrael*	על שדות עמק יזרעאל
Dew below and moon above	*Tal milmatah ulvanah me'al*	טל מלמטה ולבנה מעל
From Beit Alpha to Nahalal	*Mi'beit Alfa ad Nahalal*	מבית־אלפא עד נהלל.
Oh, what a night	*Mah, Mah? Leilah meeleil*	מה, מה? לילה מליל
Nothing stirs in the valley	*Dmamah be'Yizrael*	דממה ביזרעאל
of Yeezre-el	*Noomah emek eretz tife'ret*	נומה עמק ארץ תפארת(2×)
Sleep, oh valley, glorious land	*Anu lecha mishmeret*	אנו לך משמרת.
We shall guard you.		

And all this time there was a certain naiveté, a certain unawareness on the part of Jewish settlers, as to the effect of their policies on the already existing Arab communities. Slowly some became aware that the growing clashes between Jews and Arabs were not between natives and colonialists in the ordinary sense, but between two nationalist movements. Both were, in their own way "right" and "natural." But the two peoples, despite efforts of many individuals to bridge the growing hostility between them, were pawns

in the game of the greater nation-states of the world. Certainly, the intransigence and fear of both Jew and Arab was an important factor in the growing hostilities, both on a popular and a leadership level; but little could compare to the damage done by the insensitive policies of Great Britain. These only served to expand already existing hostilities, never to lessen them.

Never was the need for a Jewish homeland more obvious than during the period of World War II. Hitler's policies created an atmosphere of total panic on the part of European Jewry. Some—not enough, but some—managed to get out. Many came to Israel. And, after the war, when the remnants of European Jewry longed for a place to rebuild their shattered lives, Israel held out the promise of emotional peace unlike any other place on earth.

Perhaps for the thousandth time the Jewish committee in Buchenwald was holding a meeting on the question: Where to? A Polish Jew, a German, a Czech, a Hungarian—each faced the same burning problem: Where should the few surviving Jews of Buchenwald go? How could we ever have believed that at the end of the war the surviving Jews would have no more worries, that everything would be fine! The world, we had thought, would welcome our few survivors with open arms! We, the first victims of the Nazis. They would love us!

Quickly enough, we saw that the world had other things on its mind than Jewish suffering. So where to?

Comrade Posnansky put forth an idea: into our own kibbutz. To build a group of Buchenwald's youth, and find a farm where we could prepare for Palestine. A wonderful idea. There would be no lack of candidates for the kibbutz, for energy was reawakening in the survivors and seeking an outlet.

From that idea sprang Kibbutz Buchenwald.

After several days of coming and going, the Jewish committee in Buchenwald possessed a document from the American Military Government which gave it the right to make use, for a long term, of the township farm of Eggendorf, near Blankenheim.

June 3, 1945—Here we are, the first few comrades, sitting on a truck that is taking us away from Buchenwald. Finally, the Buchenwald chapter is ended. The concrete road takes us away from the barracks, the watchtowers, the SS quarters; on this straight road, which turns neither to right nor to left, we head for our new life. We are all determined to follow this road to a place of our own, a Jewish settlement where we can put our energies into something that will belong only to us, a place where we can live for the future. This road must take us to Palestine.[6]

Journal of Kibbutz Buchenwald

The Zionists believed that they were coming to a land without a people. In fact there were inhabitants with an ancient attachment to the same land. There existed a rich culture and a viable economy. Palestinian nationalism, in the European sense, was slow to develop.

To the world, the million Palestinians who had been living in their ancient homeland for centuries were merely wretched natives and not sensitive human beings whose fate in history was about to be affected. It may astonish a lot of people when I say they *were* human beings who felt pain when they suffered, laughed when they were happy, and dreamed when they contemplated the future. There were peasants working on the land, there were shopkeepers tending their merchandise, there were teachers and students in their schools, there

were housewives in their homes, there were men working on their goals. There were towns throbbing, houses building, mosques and churches being visited. There were thieves and vagabonds and lunatics, and there were poets and scholars and singers. And because I want to indulge in a return in my mind to the time when I was a child, I will add that there was a small township, near Haifa, which had a square in the middle of it where the locals gathered at evening time to play backgammon, dance the dabke, and listen to the oud. This was real to me, to us, and its intensity and poignance were not, and are not, negated by those who, thousands of miles away, smug in their seats of power, denied my existence over my pleas, and decided my fate over my head.[7]

Fawaz Turki

In 1916 Sir Henry McMahon, British High Commissioner in Cairo, negotiated with Hussein Ibn Ali, the Sherif of Mecca. The British government promised to grant one all-encompassing Pan-Arab state in exchange for support of the British war effort against Turkey. Arab nationalist hopes were boosted. And yet Britain promised a Jewish homeland in Palestine less than twelve months later in the Balfour declaration. The political wedge between Jew and Arab had been inextricably driven.

I first became aware of the Jewish-Arab conflict a little before the end of the Second World War. I was on my way to visit some close relatives in Sumeil, an Arab village in the Tel Aviv region. Rounding a bend in the road I saw a group of young people on a hill in the distance being trained in the use of weapons. After the initial shock I watched astonished as they went through various exercises, following orders in Hebrew with perfect discipline. I was eleven years old at the time and the scene made a powerful impression on me. Why were these Jewish boys and girls (who must have been about sixteen to twenty-five years old) preparing for war? Whom were they going to fight? What group did they belong to? When I told one of my teachers about it, he said they must belong to the Hagannah. That was the first time I ever heard the name, the first time I vaguely understood that we were heading toward confrontation.[8]

Abu Iyad

The Arab community in Palestine felt more and more anger and despair as Jewish immigration and land purchases increased—land the Arabs felt was theirs. This was coupled with their outrage at what they felt was British deception. What began to arise was an overwhelming, deeprooted sense of betrayal.

The anger of Palestinian Arabs became explosive. On April 19, 1936, Arab riots broke out in Jaffa which resulted in the imposition of a curfew and the enforcement of emergency regulations. This prompted Palestinian leaders to call for a general strike, and, a few days later, to form the Higher Arab Committee to coordinate political and resistance activities. This date may be taken to mark the beginning of a series of major disturbances that continued up to 1939.

The conflict between Jews and Palestinians took on the character of a Greek tragedy. Each step, renewed and intensified, followed predictably on the heels of the preceding one.

The area degenerated into chaos. Britain lost control of the situation back in the '30s. And in 1948, Britain withdrew.

The central fact in Jewish political life had always been passivity. Jewish history had consisted of what Jews suffered, endured, resisted, or survived, not what they themselves initiated or resolved. The point of reference had always been the attitudes and the policies of others. Now, for a change, the world had been waiting with curiosity and even with apprehension to see what Jews would say or do. Our history had entered a phase of autonomy.

> What a long and weary journey it had been across vast space and time since
> our nation had first been born under those very skies! There had been the
> generations in which kings and prophets flourished, and then the seeming end
> when Jerusalem crumbled before the legions of Titus Vespasianus. Across all
> the intervening centuries the beat of Jewish hearts had everywhere been
> quickened by the prospect of return. Now the hour of choice had come, and it
> had been seized. No matter what ensued, something of great moment had been
> enacted of which future Jewish generations would never cease to speak and
> dream.[9]

Abba Eban

For Jews 1948 marked the fulfillment of the dream of modern zionism, the establishment of a Jewish state in Israel. The following is an excerpt from the declaration of independence:

> The state of Israel will be open for Jewish immigration and for ingathering of
> the exiles; it will foster the development of the country for the benefit of all its
> inhabitants; it will be based on freedom, justice, and peace as envisaged by the
> prophets of Israel; it will ensure complete equality of social and political rights
> to all its inhabitants irrespective of religion, race, or sex; it will guarantee
> freedom of religion, conscience, language, education, and culture; it will
> safeguard the holy places of all religions; and it will be faithful to the principles
> of the charter of the United Nations. . . .
> We appeal—in the very midst of the onslaught launched against us now for
> months—to the Arab inhabitants of the state of Israel to preserve peace and
> participate in the upbuilding of the state on the basis of full and equal citizen-
> ship and due representation in all its provisional and permanent institutions.

FROM HAIFA TO NEAR FARAWAY CAIRO

I recall the velvet sugar-cane juice we drank together
with the smooth blue air under the open skies,
the sunflower seeds we cracked together
with jokes,
echoing laughter in the sun.
How sweet the roasted sweet potatoes were in those rainbow days
of pretty sugar dolls.

But unlike you, dear Kadreya, friend of my sunny schooldays,
I was told I was just a visiting guest—
though born in the land of the Nile.
Ordered by Egypt my Jewish wings to spread, to search for a new nest,
I have found it on Mount Carmel
and here I mean to stay.

My foremost wish today is our soldier sons to bathe in the peaceful rays
their mothers wove when younger than they,
in the near faraway rainbow days.[10]

Ada Aharoni

For the Jews the establishment of the State was the fulfillment of a dream, for the Palestinians it marked the loss of their homeland. The jubilation of the Jews stands in stark contrast to the despair of the Palestinians. Following the declaration and the war that ensued, 650,000 Arabs fled their homes to find temporary refuge in the Arab countries. Abu Iyad was one of these refugees:

May 13, 1948, is a day that will remain forever engraved in my memory. That day, less than twenty-four hours before the proclamation of the Israeli state, my family fled Jaffa for refuge in Gaza. We had been under siege; the Zionist forces controlled all the roads leading south, and the only escape left open to us was the sea. It was under a hail of shells fired from Jewish artillery set up in neighboring settlements, especially Tel Aviv, that I clambered into a makeshift boat with my parents, my four brothers and sisters, and other relatives.

Hundreds of thousands of Palestinians started for exile that day, often under tragic conditions. Not yet fifteen, I was overwhelmed by the sight of this huge mass of men, women, old people and children, struggling under the weight of suitcases or bundles, making their way painfully down to the wharfs of Jaffa in a sinister tumult. Cries mingled with moaning and sobs, all punctuated by deafening explosions.

The boat had scarcely lifted anchor when a woman started shrieking. One of her four children wasn't on board and she implored us to put back to port to look for him. Caught under the heavy fire of the Jewish guns, we couldn't turn back without risking the lives of the several hundred people, many of them children, crushed together in the small craft.

The piercing cries of the woman went unanswered.[11]

This flight to temporary refuge turned into the Palestinian Diaspora (ghourba), with a generation of Palestinians never knowing their own land, growing up in refugee camps.

Optional reading.

TENT #50 (SONG OF A REFUGEE)

Tent #50, on the left, is my new world
Shared with me by memories:
Memories as verdant as the eyes of spring,
Memories like the eyes of a woman weeping,
And memories the color of milk and love!

Two doors has my tent, two doors like two wounds
One leads to the other tents, wrinkle-browed
Like clouds no longer able to weep;
And the second—a rent in the ceiling, leading
To the skies
Revealing the stars
Like refugees scattered,
And like them, naked.

Tent #50, on the left, that is my present,
But it is too cramped to contain a future!
And—"Forget" they say, but how can I?

> Teach the night to forget to bring
> Dreams showing me my village
> And teach the wind to forget to carry me
> The aroma of apricots in my fields!
> And teach the sky, too, to forget to rain.

Only then, I may forget my country.[12]

Rashid Hussein

The Palestinians in exile did not feel at home among the Arabs. Fawaz Turki describes his feelings in his autobiography, *The Disinherited:*

> The irony of my plight was that as I grew up my bogeyman was not the Jew (despite the incessant propaganda that Cairo radio subjected us to), nor was he the Zionist (if indeed I recognized the distinction), nor was he for that matter the imperialist or the Western supporters and protectors of the state of Israel, but he was the Arab. The Arab in the street who asked you if you'd ever heard the one about the Palestinian who. . . . The Arab at the Alien's Section who wanted you to wait obsequiously for your work permit, the Arab at the police station who felt he possessed a carte blanche to mistreat you, the

Arab who rejected you and, most crucially, took away from you your sense of hope and sense of direction. He was the bogeyman you saw every morning and every night and every new year of every decade tormenting you, reducing you, dehumanizing you, and confirming your servitude. To the Palestinian, the young Palestinian, living and growing up in Arab society, the Israeli was the enemy in the mathematical matrix; we never saw him, lived under his yoke, or, for many of us, remembered him. Living in a refugee camp and going hungry, we felt that the causes of our problem were abstract, the causes of its perpetuation were real.[13]

The mirror image of the exile of the Palestinians was the ingathering of the Jews. Between 1949–52, 754,800 Jews immigrated to Israel, doubling its population. Many of these Jews came from Arab countries. Known as "Sephardim" (in contrast to the "Ashkenazim" of Europe), these Jews brought with them a special blend of Jewish and Middle Eastern tradition.

The following is a Sephardi melody.

AHAVAT HADASSAH

The love of Hadassah is tied to my heart

And my steps are sunk deep in the exile.

Ahavat Hadassah al levavi neeksherah

Va'ani betoch golah, p'amai tzol'lim.

The tragedy of the clash of the Jews and Palestinians—refugees from Europe and Palestinians from Israel—is poignantly reflected in a story told by Raymonda Tawil:

> Attending school in Haifa, I would have loved to go to visit my aunt's home. But she had fled to Lebanon during the fighting; she thought she was going for no more than a few weeks, but when the war ended, she was not allowed back.
>
> One of my schoolfriends was a Jewish girl named Dvora; she was very sweet, and I loved her. One day, she invited me home, and I went along. When we neared her house, I suddenly realized where she was taking me: her family now occupied my aunt's house! My shock was redoubled when I went inside and found my aunt's pictures still hanging on the walls; it was on my aunt's piano that Dvora practiced. I even found a doll I used to play with!
>
> It was a shattering experience to renew my acquaintance with a place simultaneously so familiar and so strange. It was now 1953, five years after the war, and I was overjoyed to see all these familiar objects and articles of furniture, all intact, precisely as they were the last time I saw them. But then I realized with despair that the house did not recognize me; it had been taken over by strangers, while my aunt and cousins were far away, beyond the Lebanese border, and unlikely to return.
>
> When I told Dvora, she was as shocked as I. "Take your doll!" she exclaimed. "Let's be friends!" She explained that her family had received this house from the government on arriving in Israel. "We came from Poland; we were also refugees. We lost everything. All our relations died in the concentration camps." Later, she showed me the Auschwitz number tattooed on her mother's arm. "I'm very sorry we took over your aunt's home," she said, "But try to understand—if we hadn't come here, we would have all ended up in the gas ovens."
>
> I bore no resentment against Dvora or her parents. I sensed that they, too, felt the injustice of occupying someone else's home. "Soon, the Arab refugees will be allowed to return to their homes," they reassured me, "and our government will build new houses for us... and then Jews and Arabs will live together in peace." They were as naive as I: neither they nor I knew the true intentions of their government. My aunt was never permitted to return, and Dvora's family remained in that house for twenty-five years.[14]

The Arab and the Israeli look at each other, but they do not really see. Their vision is blocked by centuries of fear and violence. The Israeli sees not an Arab with a deep need to understand how this all came about, but rather a Cossack plunderer or a Nazi murderer. The Arab sees not a Jew whose need for physical security runs as deep as his soul, but rather a typical European colonialist, smug and self-righteous, whose only aim is to exploit at any cost.

Both the Israeli and the Arab are victims, victims of a past full of degradation and horror. That past is so awesome as to be everpresent, in every thought, every emotion, every act.

The commonality of that oppression must be used as a key to opening up dialogue between these two peoples. Their common humiliation, common exploitation, common suffering must be realized. Its power must penetrate the walls of fear which have been built through the ages. Through the creative genius of the human spirit there is a way to knock down those walls and slowly to create an edifice of mutual respect.

On June 5, 1967, fearing an attack from its Arab neighbors, Israel launched the six day war. It moved swiftly: in hours it destroyed the air forces of Egypt, Syria, and Iraq. In a difficult battle it reunified Jerusalem, and then went on to occupy the West Bank, the Gaza strip, and the Golan Heights. Israel thus gained control over an additional one million Arabs. In the course of the hostilities another wave of Palestinian refugees was created, this time over 300,000. For Israelis, 1967 was an exhilarating victory, crowned by the reunification and control of Jerusalem.

> The paratroops dismount and rush headlong toward Temple Mount, with history in their wake. The paratroop commander pauses by the square in front of the Mosque of Omar to report on his signals communications: "Temple Mount is under my control." Somewhere the snipers are active. The paratroops run along the maze of alleys, heading for the Western Wall. How do you get there? Suddenly a hoarse yell rises above the clattering of feet. "I see the Western Wall!" They squeeze through the narrow opening, throw themselves on the large worn stones. Red-eyed, bearded paratroops weep aloud like children, embrace each other, shout "Jerusalem is ours!"
> Ten a.m., June 7, 1967. The Western Wall is again in the possession of the Jewish people.[15]

Mixed with the euphoria after victory, many Israelis felt that peace with Arabs was imminent. But for the Palestinians the 1967 war had a very different meaning. Raymonda Tawil describes the feelings of the inhabitants of the West Bank:

> After the trauma of the war, which began with such high expectations and ended in bitter humiliation, people were still numb. It was difficult to grasp what had happened—and even harder to accept it. Seeing Israeli troops and vehicles in the streets of Nablus was still a shocking experience; like a wound that refuses to heal, it has remained a source of pain.[16]

Many were uprooted and dispersed, some for the second time. For the residents of the West Bank and Gaza, 1967 marked the beginning of the occupation that continues to this day. Several Arab villages were razed in the wake of the war, bulldozed so flat that they no longer exist. Raja Shehadeh speaks of the occupation:

> It is like being in a small room with your family. You have bolted the doors and all the windows to keep strangers out. But they come anyway—they just walk through your walls as if they weren't there. They say they like your room. They bring their families and their friends. They like the furniture, the food, the garden. You shrink into a corner pretending they aren't there, tending to your housework, being a rebellious son, a strict father, or an anxious mother—crawling about as if everything was normal, as if your room was yours forever. Your family's faces are growing pale, withdrawn—an ugly grey as the air in their corner becomes exhausted. The strangers have fresh air, they come and go at will—their cheeks are pink, their voices loud and vibrant. But you cling to your corner, you never leave it, afraid that if you do, you will not be allowed to go back.[17]

After the '67 war, Palestinians realized that they had to take their destiny into their own hands and could not rely on the Arab nations to regain their land for them. The struggle over charting a new course began.

> In meeting after meeting, day after day, in a feverish climate reminiscent of the one prevailing at the 1964 meetings, we debated the options and their implications. Were we going to take up arms against the victors? Did we have even the slightest chance of holding in check Israeli military might? Didn't we risk unleashing terrible reprisals against the population of the occupied territories? And yet if we refrained from any action, wouldn't we be lumped together with the vanquished, despised, and scorned, as much as they by the Palestinian masses?[18]

> Abu Iyad

Many Palestinians wrestle with the question of the use of violence to achieve their aims. Rashid Hussein, a Palestinian who was devoted to the cause of Palestinian-Jewish reconciliation, wrote about this struggle:

OPPOSITION

I am against my country's revolutionaries
Wounding a sheath of wheat
Against the child
   any child
Carrying a hand-grenade.

I am against my sister
Feeling the muscle of a gun
Against it all
And yet
What can a prophet do, a prophetess,
When their eyes
Are made to drink
The sight of the raiders' hordes?

I am against boys becoming
   heroes at ten
Against the tree flowering
   explosives
Against branches becoming scaffolds.
Against the rose-beds turning to trenches
Against it all
And yet
When fire cremates my friends
      my youth
   and country
How can I
Stop a poem from becoming a gun?[19]

Just as Palestinians were concerned about resorting to violence, so too were many Israelis concerned about being occupiers. One soldier reported, "If I had (in this war) a clear association with the...holocaust, it was in a certain moment, when I was going up the Jericho-Jerusalem road and the refugees were streaming down (toward the River Jordan)....I felt directly identified with them. When I saw those children carried in their parents' arms, I saw myself carried by my father...(my) identification was precisely with the other side, with our enemies." Still another soldier bitterly admitted that when he entered an Arab refugee camp in order to put down a disorder, he felt "like a Gestapo man....I thought of home, I thought my parents were being led away...."[20]

The PLO became the world voice for the Palestinian people. In building a fighting organization they amplified their rhetoric and dehumanized the Israelis. Tragically, some turned to terrorism to bring their cause to the world.

LAMENT

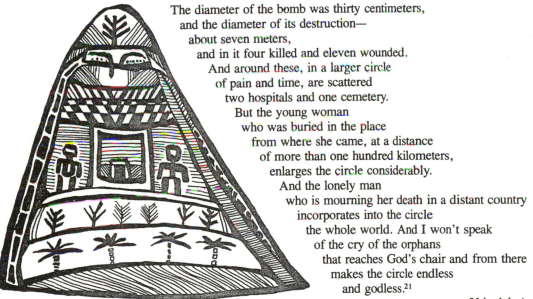

The diameter of the bomb was thirty centimeters,
and the diameter of its destruction—
about seven meters,
and in it four killed and eleven wounded.
And around these, in a larger circle
of pain and time, are scattered
two hospitals and one cemetery.
But the young woman
who was buried in the place
from where she came, at a distance
of more than one hundred kilometers,
enlarges the circle considerably.
And the lonely man
who is mourning her death in a distant country
incorporates into the circle
the whole world. And I won't speak
of the cry of the orphans
that reaches God's chair and from there
makes the circle endless
and godless.[21]

Yehudah Amichai

The Israelis in turn dehumanized the Palestinians in order to be able to deal with the difficult feelings of being occupiers. Occupier and occupied objectify the other, making negotiations difficult. The Arab nations continued to refuse recognition of the right of the State of Israel to exist. On Yom Kippur 1973 Egypt launched a surprise attack. Israel was able to defend itself but its euphoria and sense of security were shattered. The Egyptian perception of a great victory allowed Sadat to make his peace initiative.

I come to you today on solid ground to shape a new life and prepare a peace. We all on this land, the land of God, we all—Moslems, Christians and Jews— we all worship God and no one but God. God's teaching and commandments are love, sincerity, purity and peace. . . .

You want to live with us, in this part of the world. In all sincerity, I tell you we welcome you among us, with full security and safety. This in itself is a tremendous turning point, one of the landmarks of a decisive historic change. . . . But how can this be achieved? How can we reach this conclusion, which would lead us to permanent peace based on justice?

As for the Palestine cause, nobody could deny that it is the crux of the entire problem. Nobody in the world today could accept slogans propagated here in Israel, ignoring the existence of the Palestinian people and questioning even their whereabouts. The cause of the Palestine people and their legitimate rights are no longer ignored or denied today by anybody. Nobody who has the ability of judgment can deny it. . . . It is incumbent upon you to show understanding of the insistence of the people of Palestine in establishing once again a state on their land. When some extremists ask the Palestinians to give up the sublime objective, this in fact means asking them to renounce their identity and every hope for the future. . . .

Allow me to address my call from this rostrum to the people of Israel. I address myself with true and sincere words to every man, woman, and child in Israel. I tell them, from the Egyptian people who bless this sacred mission of peace; I convey to you the message of peace, the message of the Egyptian people, who do not know fanaticism and whose sons—Moslems, Christians and Jews—live together in a state of cordiality, love, and tolerance. . . . To every man, woman and child in Israel, I say, encourage your leadership to struggle for peace.

Extracts from the Knesset speech by Sadat

The Palestinian leaders took little comfort from Sadat in their struggle to regain some of their land. Israel continues to govern the West Bank using the same repressive legislation that Great Britain used against it in the Mandate period. Over one half of the men living on the West Bank have been arrested at one time in their lives.

The settlement of the West Bank by Israel, as well as the protest over this policy in Israeli society, can be viewed in the light of two distinct fears. The first is a fear of attack. The feeling of vulnerability on the part of the average Israeli on the street, who has lived through several wars, and who has lost numerous relatives and friends to the guns of the Arabs is perhaps the most powerful emotion felt in Israeli society. This person is not about to surrender what he considers to be the best insurance he has against future bloodshed— land, the only concrete buffer he has ever known between him and his family and potential disaster.

This fear of attack is offset by another fear, one which is just as deeply felt by a large number of Israelis. This is the fear of loss of vision—the vision of Israel. For Israel was to be a society based on a model of social equality and social justice, the kind of society which was envisioned by the prophets of every era of Jewish life, but which was never allowed the possibility to emerge. Many Israelis fear that the price to pay in being occupiers over 1.5 million West Bank Arabs is a loss of that vision. And that is a price too great for anything. To lose a sense of social purpose, of moral integrity, is to lose Israel. It is to lose hope. It is to mock the lives and dreams and toil of tens of

thousands of settlers, who came to Israel fired by that vision. The fear is that Israel will destroy herself through such a policy.

Israeli settlements are increasing faster than ever and Palestinian land and water rights are being expropriated. The government is engaged in a massive effort to settle the West Bank, subsidizing Jewish families at the rate of over $100,000 per family and selling lands to private developers in violation of international law treaties to which Israel is a signatory.

We are facing a critical moment in the history of Israel. The intentions of the present government are to annex the West Bank. If this happens, there are two possibilities for the Palestinian population: 1) full equality which in time would mean a Palestinian majority and a State of Israel that would no longer be a Jewish state, or 2) permanent second-class citizenship, creating a South Africa-like situation. Neither is acceptable. The only alternative is mutual recognition of the national rights of the other people.

> Israelis must somehow be convinced to accept these new Jews of the Middle East, these citizens of a land that's not a country, these Zionists with neither a Herzl nor a Ben-Gurion, these Palestinians who refuse to go away just as they refuse to renounce their country. Their crimes and mistakes are not proof that their historic claim is not right and just. If we could learn to accept their human identity, as we did with the Germans after World War II, we would know how to accent their national identity. . . . What this war has demonstrated, and continues to demonstrate with today's sad news—once more the fighting is renewed and helicopters laden with the bodies of young soldiers are returning to Israel—is that only one new opportunity has emerged: the mutual recognition of the two peoples, Israeli and Palestinian. Neither the Machiavellian dealings of the Saudi Arabians, nor the careful strategy of the Soviet Union, nor the deployment of American diplomacy, nor the swaggering of Menachem Begin and Yasir Arafat can produce any other opportunity than another variation on the endless butchery. Peace is the only opportunity.[22]
>
> Jacobo Timerman

The Ten Plagues

"When, my friends, have we last seen peace?" the poet Chaim Guri exclaimed some years ago in a short prose piece. "This soil is insatiable," he wrote bitterly. "How many more graves, how many more coffins are needed until it will cry out—enough, enough!"[23]

We remove ten drops of wine from our full cup of joy in commemoration of ten places infamous in both of our histories for the suffering which took place there. Each drop of wine we pour symbolizes our hope and prayer that these will be the last such bloody encounters between our two peoples, that beginning today we will both resolve to cast out killing and learn a new way to be together. Let us join in saying these names.

HEBRON	MAALOT
DEIR YASSIN	TEL AVIV ROAD
GUSH ETZION	NAHARIYA
KFAR KASSEM	NABLUS
BEIT NUBA	SABRA AND CHATILLA

Hebron: August 24, 1929—Police stood by while rioting Arabs killed twenty-three Jews in the upper rooms of the town inn. In all, sixty Jews including children were killed. Again, in 1983, Hebron was the scene of violence, this time Jewish and Arab lives were lost.

Deir Yassin: April 9, 1948—The Irgun, the more militant faction of the Jewish resistance, killed over two hundred people in this Arab village and then paraded the survivors in a degrading manner through the streets of Jerusalem.

Gush Etzion: May 12, 1948—For months Gush Etzion was cut off from Jerusalem. Arab Legion forces surrounded the area and launched an attack. The bloc surrendered. After the surrender many were massacred by Arab villagers from the Hebron area.

Kfar Kassem: October 29, 1956—This Israeli Arab village near the Jordanian border was placed under curfew; there was no time for anyone to inform workers returning from the fields. Forty-three were lined up and killed.

Beit Nuba: After the 1967 war—One of a number of towns levelled by bulldozers after the six day war. Its residents were forced to flee.

Maalot: May 15, 1974—Palestinian guerrillas of the PDFLP seized a school with ninety teenagers inside. Before the Israeli Defense Force stormed the school, the guerrillas machine gunned the children, killing twenty.

Tel Aviv Road: March 11, 1978—Palestinian guerrillas seized two buses filled with passengers on the Tel Aviv-Haifa road. Twenty-five people were killed, including photographer Gail Rubin.

Nahariya: April 22, 1979—Palestinians killed three people on the beach at Nahariya.

Nablus: June 2, 1980—Bombs were set in the cars of three West Bank Mayors. Two suffered serious injuries, as did a policeman defusing one of the bombs.

Sabra & Chatilla: September, 1982—Lebanese right-wing militias massacred Palestinian civilians in two refugee camps in Beirut while the area was under Israeli control: Over three hundred bodies were found, hundreds more are still missing.

DAYENU

If only there had not been mistrust	OyLa~
If only there had not been a holocaust	OyLan~
If only there had not been so many soldiers killed	OyLanu~
If only there had not been so many made homeless	OyLanu
If only there had not been so many massacres	OyLanu
If only there had not been so many terrorist attacks	OyLanu
If only there had not been so many bombings	OyLanu
If only so many children had not died	OyLanu
If only both peoples would renounce violence	Dayenu
If only both peoples would talk to one another	Dayenu
If only both peoples would recognize each other's rights	Dayenu
If only they would appreciate each other's culture	Dayenu
If only they would recognize their common origin and destiny	Dayenu
If only the descendants of Isaac and Ishmael could live face to face	Dayenu
If only they could beat their swords into plowshares	Dayenu
If only both people could share the land	Dayenu

There are possibilities for peace. The rest of the Seder will explore them.

Let the sun rise / And give the morning light,
The purest prayer / Will not bring us back
He whose candle was snuffed out / And was buried in the dust
A bitter cry won't wake him / Won't bring him back
Nobody will return us / From the dead dark pit
Here — neither the victory cheer / Nor songs of praise will help
    So—sing only a song for peace / Do not whisper a prayer
    Better sing a song for peace / With big shout

SHEER LASHALOM

T'nu lashemesh la'alot	תְּנוּ לַשֶּׁמֶשׁ לַעֲלוֹת
Laboker l'ha'eer	לַבֹּקֶר לְהָאִיר
Hazakah shebatfilot	הַזַּכָּה שֶׁבַּתְּפִילוֹת
Otanu lo tachzir	אוֹתָנוּ לֹא תַחְזִיר
Lachen rak shiru shir lashalom	לָכֵן רַק שִׁירוּ שִׁיר לַשָּׁלוֹם
Al tilcheshoo t'filah	אַל תִּלְחֲשׁוּ תְפִילָה
Mi asher kavah nero	לָכֵן רַק שִׁירוּ שִׁיר לַשָּׁלוֹם
Uve'afar nitman	בִּצְעָקָה גְדוֹלָה!
Bechi mar lo ya'iro	
Lo yachziro l'chan	מִי אָשֶׁר כָּבָה נֵרוֹ
Lachen rak shiru shir lashalom	וּבֶעָפָר נִטְמַן
Bitz'akah g'dolah!	בֶּכִי מַר לֹא יָעִירוֹ
	לֹא יַחְזִירוֹ לְכָאן

Matzah, Maror, Pesach מוֹצִיא מַצָּה מָרוֹר

**Directions: The matzah, maror, and Pesach (shankbone or beet) should be raised
high for all to see as they are being described.**

This Matzah which we eat, what is the reason? It is the bread of oppression, of being pressed down, from the Hebrew letters "nun," "tsaddi," "yud": to press down. We remember the oppression of slavery and of exile.

This maror which we eat, what is the reason? It is to remind us of the bitterness and bloodshed between our two peoples. We hope that confronting the pain of our past can free us to acknowledge one another in a new way.

This Pesach sacrifice which we eat, what is the reason? It is the offering to redeem the first-born children from being killed. May all our children be redeemed from being killed from now and forever more.

In every single generation it is one's duty to think of oneself as if one had come out of slavery.

The Second Cup of Wine, The Cup of Trust

The second cup of wine is dedicated to the need for trust between our two peoples. As we commemorate together the Ten Plagues and sing the Dayenu, we are reminded of the pain our peoples have experienced at one another's hands. We cannot erase these memories after so much bloodshed. Trust begins as we come to know our neighbor, to see him or her as a human being with fears and pain rather than as simply the reflection of our fears and suffering. It takes more courage to make peace than to make war.

Slowly, individuals in both our communities, at great personal risk, have begun to reach out, to start dialogue. Secretly, since the mid-seventies, Israelis and Palestinians have been meeting with one another, exploring ways to resolve their shared conflict. They have listened to each other's fears, known each other's anger and begun together to nurture a common vision of a shared future for their two peoples.

Arie Lova Eliav, an Israeli who served in the Knesset, was one of these people. In 1979 he spoke of his conviction that

> the conflict in the Middle East is the confrontation of two national movements. One is zionism, the movement of National Liberation of the Jewish people. The other is the movement of the national liberation of the Palestinian people. . . . What we have struggled for all these years, I repeat today: this land, from the sea to Jordan, is the land of our fathers. In this land the Jewish people were born and grew. In this land the Bible was written and the prophets had their visions. From this land our fathers were exiled and to it they began to return as a modern national movement in the last century. We have dreamed of it always. But in the same breath we proclaim that this land is also the land of the Palestinians, that on this land the Palestinian people grew and this is the land they worked. We have full rights to this land. And so do they. These are the simple words — "and so do they" — that have made us doves and made us for many years voices in the wilderness.[24]

Issam Sartawi, PLO representative in Paris, was also one of the people who dared to try trust. On the occasion of the fifth anniversary of the Israeli Council for Israeli-Palestinian Peace, he sent a telegram to his Israeli colleagues. In it he said,

> I extend to you my heartiest congratulations and best wishes. Your valiant struggle for a just peace in the Middle East and your enormous courage have earned the respect of peace-loving forces all over the world. I realize that the price which you paid for your courageous position was a heavy one, but so do all pioneers and visionaries whose sacrifices are so vital. Sooner than all our combined enemies think, peace shall and must reign between the Palestinian and Israeli states and their peoples.

Let us raise our second cup in the spirit of these two men, in honor of their courage and dedication, and let us rededicate ourselves to building trust between our two peoples.

Holy One of Blessing, Your Presence fills creation, forming the fruit of the vine.

Baruch atah Adonai, eloheynu melech ha-olam, boray p'ri ha-gafen

בָּרוּךְ אַתָּה יְיָ אֱלֹהֵינוּ מֶלֶךְ הָעוֹלָם, בּוֹרֵא פְּרִי הַגָּפֶן.

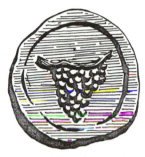

Motzi/Matzah

Matzah is the bread of faith (*lehem l'emunah*). As we eat this matzah, may it give us the faith to break out of the cycle of fear and begin to trust. May it give us the strength to reach out in peace to the other.

The uppermost of the three *matzot* is broken and distributed among the group. Then all read together:

We praise You, O Lord our God, King of the Universe, Who brings forth bread from the earth.

Baruch atah Adonai, eloheynu melech ha-olam ha-motzi lehem min ha-aretz.

בָּרוּךְ אַתָּה יְיָ אֱלֹהֵינוּ מֶלֶךְ הָעוֹלָם הַמּוֹצִיא לֶחֶם מִן הָאָרֶץ:

We praise You, O Lord our God, King of the Universe, Who hallows our lives with commandments, Who has commanded us regarding the eating of *matzah*.

Baruch atah Adonai, eloheynu melech ha-olam asher kid-shanu b'mitzvo-tav v'tzivanu al achilat matzah.

בָּרוּךְ אַתָּה יְיָ אֱלֹהֵינוּ מֶלֶךְ הָעוֹלָם אֲשֶׁר קִדְּשָׁנוּ בְּמִצְוֹתָיו וְצִוָּנוּ עַל אֲכִילַת מַצָּה:

Eat the matzah.
A bit of horseradish is placed on another piece of *matzah* and the following blessing is said.

We praise You, O Lord our God, King of the Universe, Who hallows our lives through commandments, Who has commanded us regarding the eating of *maror*.

Baruch atah Adonai, eloheynu melech ha-olam asher kidshanu b'mitzvo-tav v'tzivanu al achilat maror.

בָּרוּךְ אַתָּה יְיָ אֱלֹהֵינוּ מֶלֶךְ הָעוֹלָם אֲשֶׁר קִדְּשָׁנוּ בְּמִצְוֹתָיו וְצִוָּנוּ עַל אֲכִילַת מָרוֹר:

Eat the *maror*. Next, the leader breaks the bottom matzah and distributes it to all. Each assembles two pieces of matzah with maror in between.

We eat this sandwich in memory of our sage Hillel who ate matzah and maror together. To Hillel, slavery and freedom were merged in one historical event. In time of freedom we must not forget the bitterness of slavery; in time of oppression we must keep alive the hope of freedom.

Charoset and maror are eaten.
Dinner is eaten.

If three have eaten at a table and discussed Torah, it is as if they had eaten from the table of God.

Blessings after the Meal

Wisdom is to the soul as food is to the body.

My friends, let us praise God!

Praise God now and forever!

With your consent, then, let us praise our God
from whose abundance we have eaten.

Praise God from whose abundance we have eaten
and by whose goodness we live.

Praise God, Praise God!

Holy One of Blessing, Your Presence fills creation.
You nourish the world with goodness
and sustain it with grace, loving kindness and mercy.
You provide food for every living thing because
You are merciful. Because of Your great goodness,
the earth yields its fruits. For Your sake
we pray that we shall always have enough to eat,
for You sustain and strengthen all that lives and
provide food for the life that You created.
Holy One of Blessing, You nourish all that lives.

We thank You, God, for the good land that You gave
to our parents as a heritage; for liberating us from
the soft slavery of Egypt; for the Covenant You sealed
in our flesh; for the Torah that You teach us; for the
laws that You reveal to us; for the life that
You have given us and for the food which nourishes
and strengthens us each day; even as it does right now.

ברכת המזון

רַבּוֹתַי נְבָרֵךְ

יְהִי שֵׁם יְיָ מְבֹרָךְ מֵעַתָּה וְעַד עוֹלָם:

בִּרְשׁוּת מָרָנָן וְרַבָּנָן וְרַבּוֹתַי נְבָרֵךְ (אֱלֹהֵינוּ)
שֶׁאָכַלְנוּ מִשֶּׁלוֹ:

בָּרוּךְ (אֱלֹהֵינוּ) שֶׁאָכַלְנוּ מִשֶּׁלוֹ וּבְטוּבוֹ חָיִינוּ;
בָּרוּךְ (אֱלֹהֵינוּ) שֶׁאָכַלְנוּ מִשֶּׁלוֹ וּבְטוּבוֹ חָיִינוּ:

בָּרוּךְ הוּא וּבָרוּךְ שְׁמוֹ;

בָּרוּךְ אַתָּה יְיָ, אֱלֹהֵינוּ מֶלֶךְ הָעוֹלָם. הַזָּן אֶת־
הָעוֹלָם כֻּלּוֹ בְּטוּבוֹ בְּחֵן בְּחֶסֶד וּבְרַחֲמִים. הוּא נוֹתֵן
לֶחֶם לְכָל־בָּשָׂר. כִּי לְעוֹלָם חַסְדּוֹ: וּבְטוּבוֹ הַגָּדוֹל
תָּמִיד לֹא־חָסַר לָנוּ וְאַל־יֶחְסַר לָנוּ מָזוֹן לְעוֹלָם
וָעֶד. בַּעֲבוּר שְׁמוֹ הַגָּדוֹל: כִּי הוּא אֵל זָן וּמְפַרְנֵס
לַכֹּל, וּמֵטִיב לַכֹּל. וּמֵכִין מָזוֹן לְכָל־בְּרִיּוֹתָיו אֲשֶׁר
בָּרָא. בָּרוּךְ אַתָּה יְיָ, הַזָּן אֶת־הַכֹּל:

נוֹדֶה לְךָ יְיָ אֱלֹהֵינוּ עַל שֶׁהִנְחַלְתָּ לַאֲבוֹתֵינוּ אֶרֶץ
חֶמְדָּה טוֹבָה וּרְחָבָה. וְעַל שֶׁהוֹצֵאתָנוּ יְיָ אֱלֹהֵינוּ
מֵאֶרֶץ מִצְרַיִם. וּפְדִיתָנוּ מִבֵּית עֲבָדִים. וְעַל בְּרִיתְךָ
שֶׁחָתַמְתָּ בִּבְשָׂרֵנוּ. וְעַל תּוֹרָתְךָ שֶׁלִּמַּדְתָּנוּ. וְעַל
חֻקֶּיךָ שֶׁהוֹדַעְתָּנוּ. וְעַל־חַיִּים חֵן וָחֶסֶד
שֶׁחוֹנַנְתָּנוּ. וְעַל אֲכִילַת מָזוֹן שֶׁאַתָּה זָן וּמְפַרְנֵס
אוֹתָנוּ תָּמִיד בְּכָל־יוֹם וּבְכָל־עֵת וּבְכָל־שָׁעָה:

We thank You God, for all Your gifts
and praise You, as all who live must praise You
each day; for You teach us in Your Torah: "When you
have eaten your fill, you shall praise God for the
good land that God has given you." Holy One of Blessing
we thank You for the land and its fruit.

O God, have compassion on Israel, Your people;
on Jerusalem, Your city; on Zion, the home of Your glory
on the royal house of David, Your anointed, and
upon the great and holy Temple that was called by
Your name. Dear God, tend us, nourish us, sustain us.

May our compassionate God send Elijah, the prophet,
may he be remembered for good, to bring us the
good news of redemption and consolation.

May our compassionate God bless us and all who
are dear to us with the perfect blessing that
God bestowed on our parents, Abraham and Sarah,
Isaac and Rebecca, and Jacob, Leah, and Rachel.

May we be worthy of peace, O God, and
the blessings of justice from the God
of our salvation and may we find grace and
understanding in the sight of God and all peoples.

May our compassionate God find us worthy of
the Shabbat of life everlasting.

May our compassionate God find us worthy of
the Messiah and of life in the world to come.
You are a tower of strength to Your king
and are compassionate to Your anointed, David,
and his descendants now and forever.
May God, who makes peace on high,
bring peace to us and to all Israel.

Fear God, you holy ones,
for those who fear God will feel no want.
Even the strong may lack and hunger
but those who seek God will lack nothing that is good.
Let us thank You, O God, for You are good.
Your compassion endures forever. You open Your hand
and satisfy every living thing with favor. You, who
trust God, are blessed for God will protect you.
I have been young and now I am old, yet never have
I seen the righteous abandon those who lack bread.
God will give strength to His people.
God will bless Her people with peace.

One who has fed strangers may have fed angels.

Wisdom is to the soul as food is to the body.

וְעַל־הַכֹּל יְיָ אֱלֹהֵינוּ אֲנַחְנוּ מוֹדִים לָךְ וּמְבָרְכִים
אוֹתָךְ. יִתְבָּרַךְ שִׁמְךָ בְּפִי כָל־חַי תָּמִיד לְעוֹלָם וָעֶד:
כַּכָּתוּב וְאָכַלְתָּ וְשָׂבָעְתָּ וּבֵרַכְתָּ אֶת־יְיָ אֱלֹהֶיךָ עַל־
הָאָרֶץ הַטֹּבָה אֲשֶׁר נָתַן־לָךְ. בָּרוּךְ אַתָּה יְיָ, עַל
הָאָרֶץ וְעַל־הַמָּזוֹן:

רַחֵם יְיָ אֱלֹהֵינוּ עַל־יִשְׂרָאֵל עַמֶּךָ, וְעַל יְרוּשָׁלַיִם
עִירֶךָ וְעַל צִיּוֹן מִשְׁכַּן כְּבוֹדֶךָ וְעַל מַלְכוּת בֵּית דָּוִד
מְשִׁיחֶךָ, וְעַל הַבַּיִת הַגָּדוֹל וְהַקָּדוֹשׁ שֶׁנִּקְרָא שִׁמְךָ
עָלָיו: אֱלֹהֵינוּ אָבִינוּ, רְעֵנוּ, זוּנֵנוּ, פַּרְנְסֵנוּ וְכַלְכְּלֵנוּ
וְהַרְוִיחֵנוּ.

הָרַחֲמָן, הוּא יִשְׁלַח לָנוּ אֶת־
אֵלִיָּהוּ הַנָּבִיא. זָכוּר לַטּוֹב. וִיבַשֶּׂר־לָנוּ בְּשׂוֹרוֹת
טוֹבוֹת, יְשׁוּעוֹת וְנֶחָמוֹת.

הָרַחֲמָן. הוּא יְבָרֵךְ אֹתָנוּ וְאֶת־כָּל־אֲשֶׁר לָנוּ.
כְּמוֹ שֶׁנִּתְבָּרְכוּ הוֹרֵינוּ. אַבְרָהָם וְשָׂרָה: יִצְחָק
וְרִבְקָה. יַעֲקֹב וְרָחֵל וְלֵאָה. בַּכֹּל. מִכֹּל. כֹּל. כֵּן
יְבָרֵךְ אֹתָנוּ כֻּלָּנוּ יַחַד בִּבְרָכָה שְׁלֵמָה. וְנֹאמַר אָמֵן:

בַּמָּרוֹם יְלַמְּדוּ עֲלֵיהֶם וְעָלֵינוּ זְכוּת שֶׁתְּהִי
לְמִשְׁמֶרֶת שָׁלוֹם. וְנִשָּׂא בְרָכָה מֵאֵת יְיָ. וּצְדָקָה
מֵאֱלֹהֵי יִשְׁעֵנוּ: וְנִמְצָא־חֵן וְשֵׂכֶל טוֹב. בְּעֵינֵי
אֱלֹהִים וְאָדָם:

הָרַחֲמָן הוּא יַנְחִילֵנוּ יוֹם שֶׁכֻּלּוֹ שַׁבָּת וּמְנוּחָה
לְחַיֵּי הָעוֹלָמִים:

הָרַחֲמָן הוּא יְזַכֵּנוּ לִימוֹת הַמָּשִׁיחַ וּלְחַיֵּי הָעוֹלָם
הַבָּא: מִגְדּוֹל יְשׁוּעוֹת מַלְכּוֹ. וְעֹשֶׂה־חֶסֶד לִמְשִׁיחוֹ.
לְדָוִד וּלְזַרְעוֹ עַד־עוֹלָם: עוֹשֶׂה שָׁלוֹם בִּמְרוֹמָיו,
הוּא יַעֲשֶׂה שָׁלוֹם עָלֵינוּ. וְעַל־כָּל־יִשְׂרָאֵל. וְאִמְרוּ
אָמֵן:

יְראוּ אֶת יְיָ קְדֹשָׁיו, כִּי אֵין מַחְסוֹר לִירֵאָיו:
כְּפִירִים רָשׁוּ וְרָעֵבוּ, וְדֹרְשֵׁי יְיָ לֹא־יַחְסְרוּ כָל־
טוֹב:
הוֹדוּ לַיְיָ כִּי־טוֹב, כִּי לְעוֹלָם חַסְדּוֹ:
פּוֹתֵחַ אֶת יָדֶךָ, וּמַשְׂבִּיעַ לְכָל־חַי רָצוֹן:
בָּרוּךְ הַגֶּבֶר אֲשֶׁר יִבְטַח בַּיְיָ, וְהָיָה יְיָ מִבְטַחוֹ:
נַעַר הָיִיתִי גַּם־זָקַנְתִּי וְלֹא־רָאִיתִי צַדִּיק נֶעֱזָב
וְזַרְעוֹ מְבַקֶּשׁ־לָחֶם:
יְיָ עֹז לְעַמּוֹ יִתֵּן, יְיָ יְבָרֵךְ אֶת־עַמּוֹ בַשָּׁלוֹם:

The Third Cup of Wine, The Cup of Hope

This is the third cup—the cup of hope. After the story we have told one could easily give up in despair. But as the rabbis said, "Though the task is great we may not desist." We must have hope and vision. We have seen the commonality of the people: both have been refugees, both lived in a diaspora, both love the land, and both have experiences that could lead to a profound understanding of the plight of her neighbor.

There are concrete signs of hope: 10 percent of the Israeli population demonstrated in Tel Aviv after Sabra and Chatilla. Or consider this article from Maariv, an Israeli newspaper, dated December 28, 1982: "A first of its kind dialogue with Palestinian academicians was held yesterday evening at the Weizman Institute. A large crowd filled the hall. . . . The Arab speakers pointed out that most of the students at Berzeit University, and even most of the population in the territories, would agree today to a territorial compromise with Israel that would bring about the establishment of a Palestinian State in the West Bank and the Gaza Strip and an Israeli withdrawal from these territories."

Further, an increasing number of Israelis are refusing to serve on the West Bank.

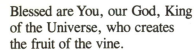

More Palestinians are willing to speak out about the need for mutual recognition and for the existence of two states living side by side in peace.

Perhaps we can attain the peace that Ishmael and Isaac attained when they came together to bury their father Abraham. In the words of Nassim D. Gaon, President of the World Sephardi Federation, in his call for mutual recognition: "It is high time that we all bore in mind the fact that we all are the Children of Abraham, whether through Isaac or Ishmael. May this call for fraternity not remain unanswered."

Let us raise the third cup in hope and recite the blessing together.

Blessed are You, our God, King of the Universe, who creates the fruit of the vine.	*Baruch atah Adonai, eloheynu melech ha-olam boray p'ri ha-gafen.*	בָּרוּךְ אַתָּה יְיָ אֱלֹהֵינוּ מֶלֶךְ הָעוֹלָם, בּוֹרֵא פְּרִי הַגָּפֶן.

At each table Elijah's cup is passed from person to person; each one while holding the cup expresses a vision of hope . . .

LO YISA GOI

Nation shall not lift up sword against nation	*Lo yi-sa goi el goi che-rev*	לֹא יִשָּׂא גוֹי אֶל גּוֹי חֶרֶב
Nor shall they learn war anymore.	*Lo yil-m'du od mil-cha-mah*	לֹא יִלְמְדוּ עוֹד מִלְחָמָה.

Open Discussion Time

The Fourth Cup of Wine, The Cup of Peace

The fourth cup is the cup of peace. With this cup we affirm a vision of a time when Palestinian and Jew shall no longer raise arms against one another but rather shall abandon war and create together a new order. We pray that this day will hasten in coming and that both our peoples will soon know true peace, a time of harmony, built on individual tranquility and the acceptance and appreciation of one another.

Let us drink together.
To peace!
To life!
L'Chaim!

You abound in blessings, Adonai, Infinite Being, Cosmic Majesty, Creator of the fruit of the vine.

Baruch atah Adonai, eloheynu melech ha-olam boray p'ri ha-gafen.

בָּרוּךְ אַתָּה יְיָ אֱלֹהֵינוּ מֶלֶךְ הָעוֹלָם, בּוֹרֵא פְּרִי הַגָּפֶן.

WHEN WILL IT COME, THE DAY

When will peace take over?
When will it come, the day?
When with armies and bombs will they do away,
When all this hostility cease,
A day on which battleships
Will become palaces of leisure and fun
Floating on the seas.

A day on which the steel of guns
Will be melted into pleasure cars,
A day on which generals will begin to raise flowers.

When peace
Will include all the peoples of these neighboring lands,
When Ishmael and Israel
Will go hand in hand,
And when every Jew
The Arab's brother will be.
When will it come, the day?[25]

Mahmud Abu Radj, Age 12, Kfar Sachnin (Arab Village)

TO DREAM OF PEACE

Peace is like dreaming
    of something eternal,
A fairy tale both old and new;
With its heroes—the good and the evil,
The love of life and of death, too.
To dream of Peace is like thinking of a world
With sorrow, anger and hate.
There's a marvelous ending
    to this story of blood,
Although it's far away beyond the gate...

To dream of Peace in the evening glow
And in the morning, early to rise,
To dream of Peace and suddenly to know
That such it will be, not otherwise.[26]

                Nitsa Sha'shua, Age 13, Tel Aviv

ISHMAEL

O Ishmael...
Listen.
It is Isaac speaking.
Too long have we crossed swords over Sinai,
Too long has there been desert between us,
Where nothing grows.
Only Death.
Let there be peace.

One night,
At the foot of Sabbath,
I waited for you.

You said you would come to Jerusalem,
And meet me face to face.
I watched you, Ishmael,
As you rode above the desert sand,
On a strange, colossal camel,
With smoking hooves,
Across a cloudless sky.
You alighted,
And I ran to meet you,
And held out both my hands.
I have waited for this moment
Countless generations.
We wept and embraced.

O Ishmael,
How long shall we wage war with one another?
How long must there be rancor and mistrust?
How much more blood must still be spilled
Before the final epic?
How many shall we shovel in the sand?

O Ishmael,
Let us be reconciled at last,
In the field of the dead,
By the gravestones of our beloved sons,
As we were once long ago
By the field of Ephron,
In the cave of Machpelah,
When we buried
Our father,
Abraham.

O Ishmael,
My Brother.[27]

                         Amy Azen

Footnotes

1. "A Letter to Gandhi" by Martin Buber first appeared as an open letter in *The Bond*, Jerusalem, 1939. It has been reprinted in many places, first in *Israel in the World: Essays in a Time of Crisis* (New York: Schocken Books, 1948).

2. The title we have chosen for the Seder—the Children of Abraham—is intended not to slight their mothers but to emphasize their common lineage and their connection with both the Islamic and Jewish traditions.

3. This and all other translations of traditional Hebrew prayers are from *V'tahere Lebanu*, Congregation Beth El of the Sudbury River Valley, Sudbury, MA, 1980. Reprinted by permission.

4. Moshe Leib Lilienblum, quoted in Arthur Hertzberg, *The Zionist Idea* (New York: Doubleday, 1959).

5. Aaron David Gordon, quoted in Hertzberg, *The Zionist Idea.*

6. *Homecoming in Israel: Kibbutz Buchenwald*, written collectively by members, quoted in Leo W. Schwarz, ed., *The Root and the Bough, The Epic of an Enduring People* (New York: Rinehart and Co., 1949), pp. 310-11. Reprinted by permission.

7. Fawaz Turki, *The Disinherited: Journal of a Palestinian Exile* (New York: Monthly Review Press, 1972), p. 19.

8. Abu Iyad, *My Home, My Land* (New York: New York Times Books, 1981), p. 6.

9. Abba Eban, *Abba Eban: An Autobiography* (New York: Random House, 1977), p. 116.

10. Ada Aharoni, *From the Pyramids to the Carmel* (Tel Aviv: Eked Publications).

11. Iyad, *My Home, My Land*, p. 3.

12. Kamal Boullata and Mirone Ghossein, eds, *The World of Rashid Hussein* (Detroit: American University Graduates, 1979), p. 159.

13. Turki, *The Disinherited*, p. 53.

14. Raymonda Tawil, *My Home, My Prison* (New York: Holt, Rinehart, and Winston, 1979), pp. 44-45.

15. "To the Western Wall," based on Army press releases, quoted in *Mission Survival*, edited and compiled by Ruth Bondy, Ohad Zmora, and Raphael Bashan (New York: Sabra Books, 1968), p. 278.

16. Tawil, *My Home, My Prison*, p. 115.

17. Raja Shehadeh, *The Third Way* (London: Quartet Books, 1982), p. 133.

18. Iyad, *My Home, My Land*, pp. 51-52.

19. Kamal Boullata and Mirone Ghossein, eds., *The World of Rashid Hussein.*

20. Quoted from *Siach Lochamim* (Kibbutz interviews with Israeli soldiers after the Six Day War) in Amos Elon, *Founders and Sons* (New York: Holt, Rinehart, and Winston, 1971), pp. 343-44.

21. Howard Schwartz and Anthony Rudolph, eds., *Voices Within the Ark* (New York: Avon Books, 1980), p. 32. This translation is by Howard Schwartz and Shlomo Vinner. Reprinted by permission of Howard Schwartz.

22. Jacobo Timerman, *The Longest War* (New York: Alfred A. Knopf, 1982), p. 114.

23. Elon, *Founders and Sons*, p. 301.

24. Arie Lova Eliav, "If We Choose Peace Then We Will Have Chosen Life," *New Outlook*, November-December, 1979, XXII, #8, pp. 41-42. Reprinted by permission.

25. *My Shalom, My Peace* (Tel Aviv: Sabra Books, 1975), p. 78.

26. Ibid., p. 24.

27. Amy Azen, "Ishmael," *Israel Horizons*, February 1978, vol. 26, no. 1, p. 19.

A Haggadah of Liberation

A Haggadah of Liberation

Shabat b'zman cheruteynu

Begin here for a Friday evening Seder (erev Shabat).

Shalom. On this wonderful night we have two mitzvot to celebrate, Shabat and Pesach. (A mitzvah is a special obligation that confers blessings on those who fulfill it.) On Shabat we say "Shabat shalom"; we feast, study, and sing songs of peace, rest, and joy. On Pesach we say "Chag ha'Matzot ha'zeh, z'man cheruteynu"—"this feast of unleavened bread, the Season of our Freedom"—and we remember times of slavery when Shabat was not respected, and we were forced to labor seven days and seven nights with no rest.... But it is written, "Heaven and Earth were finished, and all of their inhabitants, and on the seventh day, when the work of creation was complete, a time of rest was blessed and made holy, perfect, and special."

As the world was created, so was the six-day work-week and the mitzvah of Shabat. It was and still is a revolutionary concept that in order to work effectively for a better world, we must take the time to heal ourselves, to rest, and to welcome the Shabat. By participating in Shabat we become equals in perfection and joy. We are part of a cycle. Without rest, we are incapable of working for justice. We must rejuvenate ourselves. This is our heritage: tikkun olam, "making the world whole" in times of strife, oppression, and exile as well as in times of peace and plenty.

Shabat begins at sunset with the candlelighting. As our senses rejoice in the warmth of the flame, let our hearts and minds open to welcome our special guest, She who rests with us and within us—Shabat ha'Malkah—the Sabbath queen, the womanly aspect of creation, who is named Shechinah. Let us remember our mothers and sisters, our daughters and friends, who have kindled the lights of Shabat for thousands of cycles, thousands of years.

Everyone say together the blessing over the Sabbath candles, then light them.

Shechinah, we welcome you tonight! Blessed is the miracle of the universe and of life, in whose honor we kindle the lights of Shabat, in this, the season of our freedom.

Boruch atah Adonai, eloheynu melech haolam, asher kidshanu b'mitzvotav, v'tsi-vanu l'hadlik ner shel shabat, b'zman cheruteynu.

בָּרוּךְ אַתָּה יְיָ אֱלֹהֵינוּ מֶלֶךְ הָעוֹלָם, אֲשֶׁר קִדְּשָׁנוּ בְּמִצְוֹתָיו וְצִוָּנוּ לְהַדְלִיק נֵר שֶׁל שַׁבָּת בַּזְּמַן חֵרוּתֵנוּ.

SHABAT SHALOM
"Sabbath peace, Sabbath greetings"
Shabat shalom, Shabat shalom! (2x)
Shabat, Shabat, Shabat, Shabat Shalom!

HEYVENU SHALOM ALEICHEM
"Peace to everyone"
Heyveynu shalom aleichem (2x)
Heyveynu shalom, shalom,
    shalom aleichem!

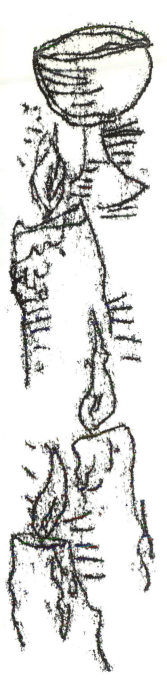

Begin here for a Saturday evening Seder.

Havdalah is the name of a short service which takes place during sunset on Saturday, at the very end of Shabat (the Sabbath). Havdalah means division or separation; it stands between the Sabbath, the holiest time of the week, and the rest of the working week. The Havdalah rituals are meant to ease the transition out of Shabat with a final fling of Shabat joy.

The three main Havdalah rituals are the lighting of more than one candle or fire, the smelling of herbs and spices, and the drinking of wine. We bless the wine, filling the cup until it overflows onto the floor of the house. In this way we celebrate the traditional holiness and sweetness of the wine and of Shabat; it spills over, and we are thankful for the abundance we enjoy. Tonight, we will have four more opportunities to say Kiddush (to bless the wine) and to drink. Our cup already runneth over, so at this time we will bless the spices and the candles and say the Hamavdil (the prayer that ends Shabat).

Bless the spices, breathing in the fragrance as we read:

Your plants are an orchard of
    pomegranates
With precious fruits—
Henna with spikenard plants
Spikenard and saffron
Calamus and cinnamon—
With many trees of frankincense,
    myrrh and aloes
With all the favorite spices.
You are a fountain of gardens
A well of living water and
    flowing streams from Lebanon.

Awake, o North wind, cleanse the air.
Come thou, South, to warm and ripen.
Blow upon my garden
That the spices thereof may flow out.
    Shir ha-Shirim (Song of Songs) 4:13

We are thankful for the world's abundant spices and for our ability to savor them; they exhilarate our senses and enhance our lives.

Boruch atah Adonai, eloheynu melech ha-olam, boray meenay b'sameem.

‎. . . בּוֹרֵא מִינֵי בְשָׂמִים

Bless the candles, saying the blessing as we light them:

We bless all the fires of the earth, the many flames of beauty which come together to reflect the shining light of the soul.

Boruch atah Adonai eloheynu melech ha-olam, boray moray ha-aysh.

‎. . . בּוֹרֵא מְאוֹרֵי הָאֵשׁ

75

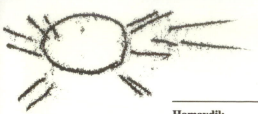

Hamavdil:

Blessed is the separation between light and darkness, between the seventh day, Shabat, and the six days of work.

Boruch atah Adonai, eloheynu melech ha-olam, hamavdil beyn kodesh l'chol, beyn or l'choshech, beyn yom ha-sh'vee-ee l'shay-shet y'may ha-ma-ah-seh. Boruch atah Adonai, hamavdil beyn kodesh l'chol.

בָּרוּךְ אַתָּה יְיָ אֱלֹהֵינוּ מֶלֶךְ הָעוֹלָם הַמַּבְדִּיל בֵּין קֹדֶשׁ לְחוֹל בֵּין אוֹר לְחוֹשֶׁךְ בֵּין יִשְׂרָאֵל לָעַמִּים בֵּין יוֹם הַשְּׁבִיעִי לְשֵׁשֶׁת יְמֵי הַמַּעֲשֶׂה בָּרוּךְ אַתָּה יְיָ הַמַּבְדִּיל בֵּין קֹדֶשׁ לְחוֹל:

Extinguish the candles.

Welcome to our Passover Seder. This Haggadah, which reflects a secular approach and collective style, has evolved over many years. It challenges us to connect our history with our present and to act. Let us celebrate our freedom and strengthen ourselves to join the fight against injustice wherever it exists today. For as long as one person is oppressed, none of us are free.

The first Pesach was celebrated 3,000 years ago when the People of Israel liberated themselves from the oppression of the Egyptian slavemasters and began their march toward freedom. We honor all people who have struggled or are struggling for their freedom as we share the aspirations of our liberated ancestors.

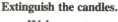

For it is said:
Every person, in every generation,
must regard his or her self
as having been personally freed from
bondage in Mitzraim, the biblical land
of Egypt.

This week, Jews all over the country and the world are observing Pesach at their own Seders. The word "Seder" means "order," and "Haggadah" means "the telling." The orthodox Haggadah contains very specific things to do and say. Our Haggadah has retained the basic order but has adapted much of the content. This follows in a long tradition.

For it is said:
"Whoever enlarges upon
the telling of the exodus from Egypt,
those persons are praiseworthy."

Please join in these blessings as we light the holiday candles:

Blessed is the spirit of freedom in whose honor we kindle the lights of this holiday, Passover, the season of Freedom.

Boruch atah Adonai, eloheynu melech ha-olam asher kidshanu b'mitzvotav v'tsi-vanu l'hadlik ner shel yom tov pesach b'zman cherutaynu.

בָּרוּךְ אַתָּה יְיָ אֱלֹהֵינוּ מֶלֶךְ הָעוֹלָם, אֲשֶׁר קִדְּשָׁנוּ בְּמִצְוֹתָיו וְצִוָּנוּ לְהַדְלִיק נֵר שֶׁל יוֹם טוֹב בַּזְּמַן חֵרוּתֵנוּ.

Blessed is the force of life that brings us to this year's spring, to this renewal of our quest for freedom.

Boruch atah Adonai, eloheynu melech ha-olam she-heh-chi-anu v'ki'manu, v'hig-ianu la-z'man ha-zeh.

בָּרוּךְ אַתָּה יְיָ אֱלֹהֵינוּ מֶלֶךְ הָעוֹלָם, שֶׁהֶחֱיָנוּ וְקִיְּמָנוּ וְהִגִּיעָנוּ לַזְּמַן הַזֶּה.

It is spring again! The flowering magnolia and cherry trees are in full bloom and the daphne scents the air. Pesach has its roots in the ancient spring festivals of farmers and shepherds who celebrated the sacred season of rebirth. The early Hebrews were an agricultural people who shared these customs and carried them forward (Kadima) into the Diaspora, adapting and interpreting them in new ways.

The First Cup of Wine—To Spring!

Let us fill our cups and toast the first of the four traditional cups of wine. At this time we fill a special cup for Elijah, who may join us later tonight.

We dedicate this cup of wine to Spring, a time of rebirth.

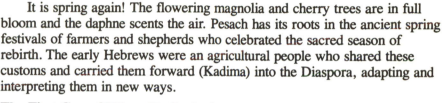

Rise up, my loved ones, my dear friends
    and come away...
For the winter is past
The rain is over and gone
The flowers appear on the earth
The time of singing has come
The voice of the turtle dove is heard in our land
The fig tree puts forth her green figs
and the vines in blossom give forth their fragrance
Arise, and come with us!

    Shir ha-Shirim (Song of Songs) 2:10

We raise our cups in a blessing:

Bless all these good things and rejoice!
Bless all the people we have touched,
Bless the gardens we have tended,
and the battles we have won.
Bless the steps we have taken, the decisions we have made.
Bless our friends and allies.
Bless this night of reflection and remembrance, as we celebrate,
each of us, the liberation from Egypt, the liberation
of each and all of us, and
Bless our work for the liberation of all peoples!

Amen. So be it!

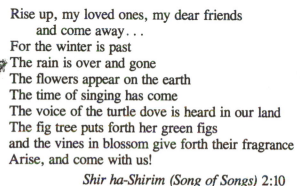

Blessed are you, world maker, who brings forth the fruit of the vine.	*Boruch atah Adonai, eloheynu melech ha-olam boray pree ha-gafen.*	בָּרוּךְ אַתָּה יְיָ אֱלֹהֵינוּ מֶלֶךְ הָעוֹלָם, בּוֹרֵא פְּרִי הַגָּפֶן.

Drink the first cup of wine.

LO YISA GOY

And everyone 'neath their vine and fig tree (2x) Will live in peace and unafraid And into plowshares turn their swords (2x) Nations shall learn war no more!	*Lo yisa goy el goy cherev, lo yil-m'du od mil-cha-mah*	לֹא יִשָּׂא גוֹי אֶל גּוֹי חֶרֶב, לֹא יִלְמְדוּ עוֹד מִלְחָמָה.

Now we wash our hands as we prepare ourselves for the Passover rituals. A bowl of water and a towel are passed around.

Symbols of the Seder:

Matzah. Hold up the matzah:

This is matzah, the bread of liberation, of rebellion, that our foremothers baked and ate in a time when they had to be organizing more and cooking less. It is traditional to open our door at this time and say:

"May all who are hungry come and share our matzah; may all who struggle for freedom come and share our spirit!"

We eat the matzah later in the Seder, but now we will hide the afikomen! We take one piece of matzah and wrap it in a napkin and hide it. When we find the afikomen it will remind us that what is broken off is not really lost to our people, so long as our children remember and search.

Eggs:

The eggs are a symbol of springtime, fertility, and the giving of life. We are reminded of Pharaoh's threat to kill newborn Jewish babies, and of the courageous midwives who refused to carry out his orders. The egg also tells us, "the longer things are in hot water, the tougher they become." Such is the case in the "oppression cooker" of life.

We dip the eggs in salt water to taste the tears which accompany birth and death in times of slavery and freedom.

Dip eggs in salt water, pass to everyone, and eat.

The Shankbone:

Tradition directs us to hold up a roasted lamb bone, (z'roa), which is symbolic of the animals sacrificed during the exodus. The doorposts of the Jewish homes were marked with the blood so that the angel of death would "pass over" and not take their first-born children. Also, our ancestors ate the paschal lamb as a spring sacrifice.

This year, we will not sacrifice a lamb for our ritual; instead we invited a baby lamb to our Seder as a guest. Unfortunately she couldn't trust us and didn't come. Maybe next year.

The Maror:

The bitter herbs symbolize the bitterness of slavery.

The salt water:

This represents the tears of our ancestors in slavery.

Charoset:

Charoset is a mixture of apples, nuts, wine and spices made into a paste. It symbolizes the mortar that our ancestors used to build the pyramids. The sweet taste of the Charoset also reminds us that in the most bitter times of slavery, our people have always remembered the sweet taste of freedom.

Parsley, in Hebrew "karpas."

The parsley and the salt water remind us that both the tender greens of the earth and the salt of the sea are joined together to sustain life.

Bless the karpas, fruit of the earth: כַּרְפַּס

Blessed is the force of life, the strength of farmworkers, that brings forth the fruits, grains, and vegetables from our bountiful earth.

Boruch atah Adonai, eloheynu melech ha-olam boray pree ha-adamah.

בָּרוּךְ אַתָּה יְיָ אֱלֹהֵינוּ מֶלֶךְ הָעוֹלָם,
בּוֹרֵא פְּרִי הָאֲדָמָה.

Dip the parsley in salt water, pass to everyone, and eat.

Songs of Work, Farming, and Food (choose one)

From Woody Guthrie

PASTURES OF PLENTY©

It's a mighty hard row that my poor hands have hoed
My poor feet have travelled a hot dusty road
Out of your dustbowl and westward we rolled
And your deserts was hot and your mountains was cold

> I work in your orchards of peaches and prunes
> And I sleep on the ground 'neath the light of your moon
> On the edge of your city you'll see us and then
> We come with the dust and we go with the wind

California, Arizona, I make all your crops
Then it's up north to Oregon to harvest your hops
Dig beets from your ground, cut the grapes from your vine
To set on your table your light sparkling wine

> Green pastures of plenty from dry desert ground
> From the Grand Coulee Dam where the waters run down
> Every state in the union us migrants has been
> We'll work in this fight and we'll fight 'til we win

It's always we rambled that river and I
All along your green valleys I'll work 'til I die
My land I'll defend with my life if need be
'Cause my pastures of plenty must always be free

From Zionist tradition

In Europe, restrictive laws prevented Jews from farming. Jewish settlers in Palestine have taken up farming with spirit and determination.

ZUM GALI GALI

"The pioneer is for her work,
work is for the pioneer.
The pioneer is for his friends,
friends are for the pioneer."

zum gali gali gali
zum gali gali

] (2x)

chalutza le'man avoda
avoda le'man chalutza

zum gali gali gali
zum gali gali

] (2x)

hechalutz le'man chaverav
chaverav le'man hechalutz

זוּם גַּלִי גַלִי,
חֲלוּצָה לְמַעַן עֲבוֹדָה,
עֲבוֹדָה לְמַעַן חֲלוּצָה.

הֶחָלוּץ לְמַעַן חֲבֵרָיו,
חֲבֵרָיו לְמַעַן הֶחָלוּץ.

Four Kinds of Children and Four or Five Questions
The sages speak of four kinds of children who view the Seder in four different ways and so ask different questions.

- The wise child asks: What does this all mean?

  This child should be taught about the details of the Seder. Talk with this child about the nature of freedom and justice and about the need to act to transform the world.

- The isolated child asks: What does this mean to all of you? and in so doing isolates him or herself from the community of the Seder.

  This child should be answered by saying: Join us tonight. Be fully *here*. Listen closely. Sing and read and dance and drink. Be with us, become a part of us. Then you will know what the Seder means to us.

- The simple child asks: What is this?

  This child should be told: We are remembering a long time ago in another land when we were forced to work for other people as slaves. We became a free people and we are celebrating our freedom.

- Then there is the child who is too young to ask.

  We will say: Sweetheart, this wondrous evening happens in the spring of every year, so that we may remember how out of death and sorrow and slavery came life and joy and freedom. To remember the sorrow we eat bitter herbs; to remember the joy we drink sweet wine. And we sing of life because we love ourselves and each other and you.

We are thankful for the questions that children ask—for growth and strength and courage and safety and love and warmth and fun and friends; for games and work and pets and teachers, for sisters and brothers, parents and grandparents and all the favorite relatives in the world; for trees, ducks, bunnies, and raisins, peanut butter, clean pajamas, bicycles, dolls, and bathtubs. For you, the young people here tonight; for all that you love and for your futures.

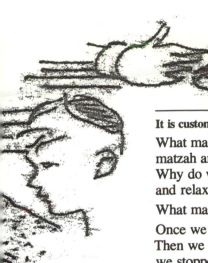

It is customary for a young person, or one learning the tradition, to ask the questions:

What makes this night different from all other nights? Why do we eat only matzah and no bread on this night? Why do we eat bitter herbs on this night? Why do we dip our food in salt water two times on this night? Why do we sit and relax when we eat on this night?

What makes this night different from all other nights?

Once we were slaves in Egypt. The rulers made us do whatever they wanted. Then we refused to be slaves any more. Tonight we tell the story about how we stopped being slaves, and we celebrate that we are on our way to freedom.

1) Why do we eat only matzah and no bread on this night? When we left Egypt to escape from being slaves, we were in a hurry. We didn't have time to wait for the bread to rise. So we baked flat bread called matzah to take with us.

And why do we call it matzah? Well, it has little holes like matzah, and it smells like matzah, and it tastes like matzah...

Ma nish-ta-na ha-lai-la ha-zeh mee-kol ha-lay-lot? Sheh-b'chol ha-lay-lot a-nu o-ch'leen cha-maytz u-ma-tsah, ha-lai-la ha-zeh ku-lo ma-tza

מַה נִּשְׁתַּנָּה הַלַּיְלָה הַזֶּה מִכָּל הַלֵּילוֹת.

שֶׁבְּכָל הַלֵּילוֹת אָנוּ אוֹכְלִין חָמֵץ וּמַצָּה, הַלַּיְלָה הַזֶּה כֻּלוֹ מַצָּה.

2) Why do we eat bitter herbs on this night? The bitter taste helps us to remember how we felt when we were slaves, and how people feel when they get hurt by other people.

Sheh-b'chol ha-lay-lot a-nu o-ch'leen sh'awr y'ra-kot ha-lai-la ha-zeh mahror

שֶׁבְּכָל הַלֵּילוֹת אָנוּ אוֹכְלִין שְׁאָר יְרָקוֹת, הַלַּיְלָה הַזֶּה מָרוֹר.

3) Why do we dip our food in salt water two times on this night? The first time, the salty taste reminds us of the tears we cried when we were slaves. The second time, the salt water and the greens help us to remember the ocean and green plants and the earth, where we get air and water and food that help us to live.

Sheh-b'chol ha-lay-lot ayn a-nu mat-bee-leen a-fee-lu pa-am e-chod, ha-lai-la ha-zeh sh'tay p'ah-meem

שֶׁבְּכָל הַלֵּילוֹת אֵין אָנוּ מַטְבִּילִין אֲפִילוּ פַּעַם אֶחָת, הַלַּיְלָה הַזֶּה שְׁתֵּי פְעָמִים.

4) Why do we sit and relax when we eat on this night? A long time ago, free people sat down to eat, but slaves weren't allowed to sit and relax. Tonight we sit and eat slowly, so we'll remember that we don't have to be slaves any more. We and our friends and our children can be free.

Sheh-b'chol ha-lay-lot a-nu o-ch'leen bayn yosh-veen u-vayn m'su-been, ha-lai-la ha-zeh ku-lah-nu m'su-been

שֶׁבְּכָל הַלֵּילוֹת אָנוּ אוֹכְלִין בֵּין יוֹשְׁבִין וּבֵין מְסֻבִּין, הַלַּיְלָה הַזֶּה כֻּלָּנוּ מְסֻבִּין.

Four or five questions—are there only four or five questions? There are countless questions. In the spirit of this night, we invite questions.

Here are some we thought of:

Why does oppression exist in the world?

Why have Jewish women, with their strength and influence, often been excluded from a leadership role in the Jewish community?

Why do people poison the water they drink, pollute the air they breathe, and spoil the land which sustains them?

Why do we not have peace when so many people want it?

A song!

AVADEEM HAYEENU

"We were slaves, now we are free people"

Avadeem hayeenu, hayeenu
Atah beney chorin, beney chorin
Avadeem hayeenu
Atah, Atah beney chorin,
beney chorin

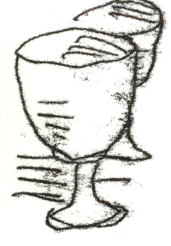

Second Cup of Wine—To Liberation!

As we recall the liberation from slavery of our own people we are able to empathize with the plight of other peoples. This continent was built in part through the enslavement of blacks who were wrenched from rich strong cultures of their own. All physical slavery involves a spiritual slavery as well. We Jews know that we have often been robbed of a sense of dignity and pride. We dedicate ourselves tonight to a freeing of body and soul of all human beings.

_____

Bless the wine:

_____

Drink the wine.

L'chaim! To life.

Boruch atah Adonai, eloheynu melech ha-olam boray pree ha-gafen!

בָּרוּךְ אַתָּה יְיָ אֱלֹהֵינוּ מֶלֶךְ הָעוֹלָם,
בּוֹרֵא פְּרִי הַגָּפֶן.

The Story

The Hebrew People came to Egypt from their land to get provisions during a famine. They became a favored group in Egypt and prospered and multiplied there. According to the Bible, our ancestor Joseph, who was sold into slavery by his brothers, became valuable to Pharaoh for his astute economic predictions and ability to administer before and during the famine, and his people were welcomed. When new rulers came to power the Hebrews fell out of favor and were enslaved. Vineyards and fields were confiscated, work quotas were increased, families separated and wages dropped to nothing. Despite these hardships, the Hebrew people survived and grew in numbers. The new Pharaoh became concerned that they would unite with Egypt's enemies.

Tonight's story is about the liberation of our people from their enslavement under Pharaoh in Egypt.

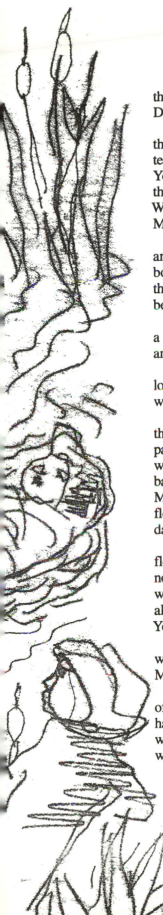

Miriam was four years old when Pharaoh said, "There are too many of those Jews—I'm scared of them—they'll take over soon. Kill all their sons! Drown them in the Nile!"

Amram, Miriam's father, said to Yochevet, Miriam's mother, "Dear, there is only one solution. We mustn't make any more babies, and we must tell our people to do the same. If no sons are born, no sons will be killed." Yochevet sighed, but strong, young Miriam cried: "No! You shall not do that! Pharaoh's decree kills only the boys—your decree kills the girls as well. We will find another way." Amram and Yochevet listened to their daughter, Miriam, and Jewish babies continued to be conceived and born.

Pharaoh then summoned the Jewish midwives whose names were Shifra and Pu-ah and ordered that the boy babies be killed as soon as they were born. Slyly, they responded "No way! We mean, sir, there is no way because the strong Jewish mothers birth their babes so quickly that they are hidden before we arrive."

Miriam was five years old when Yochevet became pregnant. Miriam was a prophet and she said, "Yochevet will give birth to a son who will survive and help our people."

Ah Moses, now comes Moses. . .teeny-tiny baby boy, cute, but makes a lot of noise, "Whaa, whaa. . . ." What shall we do? If the baby is found, we will all be punished.

The baby must be saved! Think Miriam, think; a basket of reeds, one that will float. She said to her brother, "Aaron, we must weave a basket of papyrus reeds," and they did. Smart young people. All night long they worked together. In the morning, tired, hopeful, the family took the new baby, kissed him all over, patted his "tuchas," and tucked him in his basket. Miriam took the basket to the river and while she hid in the tall grasses, floated her new brother downstream past the very place where Pharaoh's daughter went swimming every morning.

And there she was, ready to dive in, when a beautiful woven basket floated by. And in the basket? A tiny perfect Jewish baby, cute and very noisy: Whaa, whaa! Pharaoh's daughter drew him from the water and said with love, "I will raise you, but who will *feed* you?" Miriam, delighted, alert, piped up from her hiding place and said: "I know a good woman, Yochevet, who will nurse him."

"Perfect," said the daughter of Pharaoh. "Bring him to me when he is weaned; he will be as my own son for I have no other. Moses, I will call him Moses because I brought him from the river's water."

History tells us that Moses grew up in the palace and had no awareness of himself as a Jew. But we know that Moses was nursed by Yochevet and had played with Aaron and Miriam and his father Amram, and though he left when he was weaned, the memory of their warmth, their love, their plight, was in his head and heart.

Growing up, Moshe is growing up
Restless, very restless
Not at ease in his palace home
Not at peace with the Pharaoh
He goes walking, is often out
Watching and listening. . .
He's learned all his teachers
Have to offer

Lonely, this upper class boy,
With no peers, heir to the Pharaoh,

Honest and compassionate,
Moshe tries to ease the burdens
Of the workers

He has questions
"Who are these Jews to me?
Who are these workers, these slaves,
So driven in toil
That the quarries, the cities, the roads,
And the tombs are built with the blood
Of the Jews in their bricks?
Why the Jews?

I must speak out
I can't bear this
Don't you beat him!
He is dying! She is starving!
You overseer,
Why must you be so brutal?

The Taskmaster says to Moses,
You mind your own business.
Young Pharaoh-son!
A slave who can't work here
Is useless, is guilty, is worthless.
The whip is master.

But *no*! You can't kill them
Tho' slaves
We're all people!
My just heart is breaking
My reason is shattered. . . .

And in fury, in pain and confusion, young Moses killed the taskmaster who beat the slave. And then he fled to the desert, through barren hills and lands, to think, to wait, to grow, and to follow the flow of the dry lands to Midian on the far shore of the Dead Sea, beyond the Jordan River.

Moses stayed many years in Midian. He married Tsipporah and had children. He tended flocks in the wilderness. Life there was good, and yet he never forgot Mitzraim and the good people enslaved there under Pharaoh.

One day, while grazing his flock and gazing on the vastness of the desert, he envisioned a bush that burned and burned and did not burn up. And he heard a voice, saying to him what he knew in his heart to be true—that the people in his memories were his own people, that he should return to them, and together they would find a way to be free. Perhaps Pharaoh would negotiate. Perhaps they would have to use force, threats, or magic, or perhaps they would flee, as he himself had done, into the desert 'til the ways of slavery were lost and a new homeland found.

Moses left his life and family in Midian and returned to Mitzraim.

Meanwhile, what's happening back in Mitzraim, in Egypt?

The Jews are hungry.
The Jews are tired.
The Jews are angry.
The Jews are talking with each other.
The Jews are beginning to organize!
Talk of rebellion, talk of escape
debate argue struggle
unity struggle unity NO struggle unity struggle—community!
New unity—and a plan evolves:
    first, negotiate with Pharaoh, and if that doesn't work
    then, threaten with powerful magic, and if *that* doesn't work
    then, split from Mitzraim

After all, Pharaoh is not likely to choose to free his entire exploitable labor force just like that! (Snap the fingers.)

Did ya hear?
Hear what?
He's back in town.
Who's back in town?
Moses. Remember Moses?
Never expected to see him again.
How does he look?
Older and wiser and . . .
He's come out as a Jew!
He wants to work with us, says he has ideas about
    how we can all get out of here . . .

So, a new committee was formed—the "how-to-get-out-of-here" committee. They met every Tuesday and Thursday night for two months; and at the end of two months, people weren't sure that much had been accomplished. Some preferred to remain in slavery rather than face the perils of committee life.

They debated questions of violence and non-violence: is property damage acceptable? Causing enemies to suffer? What about the innocent bystanders? What about revenge?

They also debated questions of leadership: "I think Moses has taken too much power. Let's try rotational leadership—after all, we don't want him to have a distorted role in history. We're *all* working very hard for our liberation!"

And they were. But Moses had an "in" with the Pharaoh, and the time for negotiation had arrived. Armed with the best speech the propaganda committee could prepare and several support people, Moses proposed that Pharaoh free the Jews, with as little fuss as possible. And we sing:

LET MY PEOPLE GO

When Israel was in Egypt land
    Let my people go
Oppressed so hard they could not stand
    Let my people go
Chorus
Go down, Moses, way down in Egypt land
Tell old Pharaoh, "Let my people go"
We need not always weep and mourn
    Let my people go
And wear these chains of slaves forlorn
    Let my people go
(Chorus)

Pharaoh, of course, said "No," and the peaceful negotiation was ended.
Then Miriam spoke for the women:
In sadness we must proceed with our plans,
Pharaoh, do you hear us?
Great suffering will come to the land of Mitzraim.
We'd rather our freedom be gained without hurting the
    people of this land.
One plague at a time we will bring you,
And each time we will say again: "Let my people go!"

The Ten Plagues

Reader:

		All respond:
BLOOD	Oh Pharaoh, you have wasted the lives of our people	Let my people go!
FROGS	You cast our infants to perish in the river Nile, yet required us to fish for food in the Nile's water	Let my people go!
LICE	for the years of crowded ghetto living; poverty, filth, despair	Let my people go!
GNATS & FLIES	swarming pests that sting like the slavedrivers' whips and cruel words	Let my people go!
MURRAIN	We worked as the yoked beast is made to work. Soon neither human nor beast will slave for you. A sickness on your herds will come	Let my people go!
BOILS	from the wounds of anger, long denied, an ache, like the aching of our souls	Let my people go!
HAIL	Our tears, unheeded, frozen by your greed, will bruise your land	Let my people go!
LOCUSTS	will devour every spring green plant like the hordes of bad thoughts, born of exhaustion and lack of trust	Let my people go!
DARKNESS	yes, darkness, that we cannot smile upon one another as friends, and may not for thousands of years	Let my people go!
DEATH	At midnight, your loss will equal our own, the death of the first born child	Let my people go!

And Pharaoh didn't listen.

The Jews marked their doorposts and death "passed over" their homes, taking only the children of the people of Pharaoh. And hearing the awful cries of mourning, the grief of all the parents and brothers and sisters, Pharaoh ordered the Jews to leave.

And they did, very quickly, taking only their journey food, matzah. Yet Pharaoh had a change of heart, and mobilized his forces to recapture the fleeing slaves. The chariots reached the Jews when they were nearing the shores of the Red Sea. They turned around to see the army of the Egyptians bearing down upon them, and were filled with fear. They turned on Moses for bringing them to this impasse.

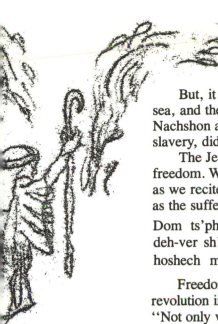

But, it is said that one man, Nachshon, took a risk and walked into the sea, and the waters divided. In doing this he acted as a free man. Only after Nachshon and those who followed him had made their first break with slavery, did the waters divide and drown the army of Egyptians.

The Jews never forgot the price that the Egyptians paid for their freedom. We remember tonight by spilling out a drop of wine from our cups as we recite the plagues one by one. In this way we diminish our pleasure, as the suffering of others diminished our joy.

Dom ts'phar-day-ah keeneem orov
deh-ver sh'cheen bah-rad ar-beh
hoshech mah-kat b'cho-rote

דָּם, צְפַרְדֵּעַ, כִּנִּים, עָרוֹב, דֶּבֶר,
שְׁחִין, בָּרָד, אַרְבֶּה, חֹשֶׁךְ, מַכַּת
בְּכֹרוֹת.

Freedom from a slaveholder was only the first step to liberation. A revolution in the Jews' consciousness was the second step. Our sages said, "Not only was it necessary to take the Jews out of Egypt; it was also necessary to take Egypt out of the Jews." The minds of the Jews remained enslaved through forty long years in the desert. Every time there was a crisis the Jews forgot the bitterness of slavery and remembered only the security. For this reason, it wasn't until a new generation of Jews grew up, a generation born in freedom, that the people were allowed to enter the land of Israel.

It would be comforting to end this story here. But in fact there is no land of milk and honey until we live in a world where all people are free. To that world and to all those who wander, a song!

ERETZ ZAVAT CHALAV

"The land flows with milk and honey!"

Er-etz za-vat cha-lav, cha-lav oo-d'vash! (4x)
Er-etz za-vat cha-lav, za-vat cha-lav oo-d'vash! (2x)

The Dayenu is a rousing song of praise and thanksgiving. "Dayenu" means, "it would have been sufficient"; we are reminded to be grateful and proud of each success as it is achieved.

Sing:
Day, Dayenu, day, dayenu, day, dayenu, dayenu, dayenu dayenu (2x)
   (Repeat chorus after each verse)
Ilu ilu hotsianu, hotsianu mi-Mitsraim, hotsianu mi-Mitsraim...
Ilu ilu natan lanu, natan lanu et ha-Shabat, natan lanu et ha-Shabat...
Ilu ilu natan lanu, natan lanu et ha-Torah, natan lanu et ha-Torah...

If we had freed ourselves from slavery
   and not passed through the sea in safety...dayenu
If we had passed through the sea in safety
   and not learned to survive in the desert...dayenu
If we had survived our sojourn in the desert
   and not had the mitzvah of Shabat...dayenu
If we had learned to rest on Shabat
   and never knew the stories and laws of the Torah...dayenu
If we had studied the stories and laws of the Torah
   and never entered the land of Israel...dayenu
If we had settled in the land of Israel
   and never built a temple there...dayenu

If we had built the temple
and had no wise people to share their vision with us. . .dayenu
If we had wise people who saw truth and spoke it to us
and we were not wise enough to take it to heart. . .dayenu
If we were wise enough to take it to heart
and never lifted a hand to make it happen. . .dayenu?
We would probably still be in Egypt!

So let's bring Dayenu into the present, tonight. We have a vision, we take it to heart, and we work hard to make it happen. We are grateful, and yet what miracles and accomplishments would be sufficient (Dayenu) in today's world for us to be truly satisfied?

When all the workers of the world receive just compensation and respect
for their labors, enjoy safe, healthy, and secure working conditions,
and can take pride in their work. . .Dayenu
When governments end the escalating production of devastating weapons,
secure in the knowledge that they will not be necessary. . .Dayenu
When technology for the production and conservation of energy and our other
natural resources is developed so that we can maintain responsible
and comfortable lifestyles—and still assure a safe environment
for our children. . .Dayenu

When the air, water, fellow creatures and beautiful world are protected
for the benefit and enjoyment of all, and given priority over development
for the sake of profit. . .Dayenu
When all people live freely in their own countries, practicing their beliefs
and cultures without interference or persecution. . .Dayenu
When all women and men are allowed to make their own decisions on
matters regarding their own bodies and their personal relationships
without discrimination or legal consequences. . .Dayenu
When people of all ages, sexes, races, religions, cultures and nations
respect and appreciate one another. . .Dayenu
When all children grow up in freedom, without hunger, and with the love
and support needed to realize their full potential. . .Dayenu
When all children, women, and men are free of the threat of violence,
abuse and domination; when personal power and strength are not used
as weapons. . .Dayenu
When all people have access to the information and care they need for
their physical, mental, and spiritual well-being. . .Dayenu

When food and shelter are accepted as human rights, not as commodities, and are available to all. . .Dayenu

When no elderly person in our society has to fear hunger, cold, or loneliness. . .Dayenu

When the peoples of the Middle East, and all peoples living in strife, are able to create paths to just and lasting peace. . .Dayenu

When people everywhere have the opportunities we have to celebrate our culture and use it as a basis to work for progressive change in the world. . .Dayenu

If tonight each person could say, ''this year I worked as hard as I could toward my goals for improving this world, so that one day all people can experience the joy and freedom I feel sitting with my family and friends at the Seder table. . .Dayenu Dayenu

---

Bless the matzah: מוֹצִיא מַצָּה

Blessed is the labor which has brought us this bread from the earth. It is a mitzvah, a blessing, to partake of this matzah.

Boruch atah Adonai, eloheynu melech ha-olam ha-motsee le-chem min ha-aretz

Boruch atah Adonai, eloheynu melech ha-olam asher kidshanu b'mitzvotav v'tsivanu al ah-cheelat matzah

בָּרוּךְ אַתָּה יְיָ אֱלֹהֵינוּ מֶלֶךְ הָעוֹלָם, הַמּוֹצִיא לֶחֶם מִן הָאָרֶץ.

בָּרוּךְ אַתָּה יְיָ אֱלֹהֵינוּ מֶלֶךְ הָעוֹלָם, אֲשֶׁר קִדְּשָׁנוּ בְּמִצְוֹתָיו וְצִוָּנוּ עַל אֲכִילַת מַצָּה.

Eat the matzah.

Bitter herbs, in Hebrew,"maror."

Tonight we taste the bitter herb and recognize the bitter consequences of exploitation—the loss of lives, the waste of the sweet, powerful potential greatness of all children, of all peoples.

Bless the maror: מָרוֹר

It is a mitzvah, a blessing, to partake, to taste the bitter herb.

Boruch atah Adonai, eloheynu melech ha-olam asher kidshanu b'mitzvotav v'tsi-vanu al acheelat mahror

בָּרוּךְ אַתָּה יְיָ אֱלֹהֵינוּ מֶלֶךְ הָעוֹלָם, אֲשֶׁר קִדְּשָׁנוּ בְּמִצְוֹתָיו וְצִוָּנוּ עַל אֲכִילַת מָרוֹר.

We eat the maror dipped in Charoset.

The Hillel sandwich:

Now we eat a sandwich of matzah and maror together.

A TOAST OF THANKFULNESS TO US

to where we've each come from
to where we're going and how we're changing
to being where we are and who we are

to what we can share
to what we can't share. . .yet

to our joys and our struggles
which in full times we know are connected
which in hard times isolate us

to process, and the times when we lose sight of process
to pain, to growth
to painless growth, to painful growth

to our efforts, our faith, our determination
to our fears, tears, laughter, hugs, and kisses

to wisdom, to study, alone and in groups
to our books and tools, to toys
to materials, raw and fine
to work, to meetings, to sleep
to our eyes, which fortunately read Haggadahs
and see mountains
and faces
and flowers and bodies
and occasionally sunshine

to our ears, hands, noses, mouths, toes, breasts
to caresses, to touch, to our senses
to our knees
to the times we fall down and pick ourselves up
and the times friends help us up

to the shoulders we cry on
to the arms that hold us
to the strength in each of us, alone

to our work
to our play
to our loving
to our growth
to life itself . . . l'chaim

Shulchan orech: It's time to eat dinner

Dessert:

At the end of the meal the Afikomen is found, ransomed, distributed, and eaten.

Is everyone finished with the Seder dinner? We will say grace and then eat no more tonight.

Grace after Meals   Beer-kaht Ha-mazone

Friends, let us sing
and give thanks for the food we
   have eaten
through whose goodness we
   live
Let there be food for all,
   abundant and healthful

*Boruch atah Adonai, eloheynu
   melech ha-olam
hazan et ha-olam coo-loh b'too-
   voh,
b'chen b'chesed oo-v'racha-
   mim.
Hoo no-tain le-chem l'kol bah-sar,
Kee l'olam chas-doh.*

בָּרוּךְ אַתָּה יְיָ אֱלֹהֵינוּ מֶלֶךְ
הָעוֹלָם, הַזָּן אֶת־הָעוֹלָם, כֻּלּוֹ בְּטוּבוֹ,
בְּחֵן בְּחֶסֶד וּבְרַחֲמִים, הוּא נוֹתֵן לֶחֶם
לְכָל־בָּשָׂר, כִּי לְעוֹלָם חַסְדּוֹ.

Let us have the wisdom to choose to eat only that which enhances our precious energy and sustains us through our labors and our rest	*Oo-v'too- voh ha-gadol tah-meed loh cha-sar lah-noo, V'al yech-sar lah-noo mazone l'olam va-ed ba-avoor sh'moh ha-gadol.*	וּבְטוּבוֹ הַגָּדוֹל תָּמִיד לֹא־חָסַר לָנוּ, וְאַל־ יֶחְסַר לָנוּ מָזוֹן לְעוֹלָם וָעֶד, בַּעֲבוּר שְׁמוֹ הַגָּדוֹל.
	Kee hoo ale zan oo-m'far-nais lah-kol,	כִּי הוּא אֵל זָן וּמְפַרְנֵס לַכֹּל,
	oo-may-teev lah-kok, oo-may-cheen mazone l'chol b'ree oh-sav	וּמֵטִיב לַכֹּל, וּמֵכִין מָזוֹן לְכָל־ בְּרִיּוֹתָיו
	asher boh-roh. Boruch atah Adonai, ha-zan et ha-kol.	אֲשֶׁר בָּרָא. בָּרוּךְ אַתָּה יְיָ, הַזָּן אֶת־הַכֹּל.

To sing of love is one of this night's traditions. Here are two songs from the passionate biblical *Song of Songs (Shir ha-Shirim)*:

ANA PANA DODECH

Where has your beloved gone, o dearest one? Where has your beloved turned? . . . to the garden, to the flowerbeds of balsam (with the flocks) to pasture in the gardens, and to gather wild lilies.	*Ana halach dodech, ha-yaffah ba-na-shim* *Ana pana dodech oo-n'vashey-nu ee-mach* *Dodi yarad l'gano, yarad l'gano* *l'aroogote ha-bo-sem*	אָנָה הָלַךְ דּוֹדֵךְ, הַיָּפָה בַּנָּשִׁים; אָנָה פָּנָה דוֹדֵךְ, וּנְבַקְשֶׁנּוּ עִמָּךְ. דּוֹדִי יָרַד לְגַנּוֹ, לַעֲרוּגוֹת הַבֹּשֶׂם

DODI LI

My beloved is mine and I am my beloved's, a shepherd in the wild roses. Who is this, coming up from the wilderness, perfumed with myrrh and frankincense? You have captured my heart, my sister, my bride . . . Awake, northwind, and come, southwind . . .	*Dodi Li, Va-ani lo, ha ro-eh ba-shoshanim (2)* *Mi zote olah, min ha-midbar, mi zote olah* *Meh-ku-teret mor, mor u'leh-va-nah, mor u'leh-va-nah* *Dodi Li . . . (2)* *Li bav-ti-ni ah-cho-ti chalah, li bav-ti-ni chalah (2)* *Dodi Li . . . (2)* *Oo-ri, tsafon, oo-vo-ee tey-mahn (2)*	דּוֹדִי לִי, וַאֲנִי לוֹ, הָרֹעֶה בַּשּׁוֹשַׁנִּים. מִי זֹאת עוֹלָה מִן הַמִּדְבָּר מְקֻטֶּרֶת מֹר וּלְבוֹנָה לִבַּבְתִּנִי, אֲחוֹתִי כַלָּה עוּרִי צָפוֹן, וּבוֹאִי תֵימָן

Remember

As we retell the story of the Jews' enslavement to Pharaoh, we remember other times in history when a leader wished to annihilate our people. The story of the Holocaust is a story too recent and too painful for many to comprehend. It is our story. We are not free to ignore it or to forget. From Terezin Concentration Camp have come poems composed by children. This one symbolizes the tragedy. It is touched with grace and hope.

The Butterfly

The last, the very last butterfly
  so richly brightly dazzlingly yellow.
Perhaps if the sun's tears
  would sing against a white stone...
Such, such a yellow
  is carried way on high.
It went away I'm sure because
  it wished to kiss the world goodbye
For seven weeks I've lived in here.
Penned up inside this ghetto
But I have found my people here
The dandelions call to me
And the white chestnut candles in the court.
Only I never saw another butterfly
That butterfly was the last one,
Butterflies don't live in here,
    in the ghetto.

Let us recite the names of some of the death camps in which six million Jews and five million other people were killed:

AUSCHWITZ
MAIDANEK
TREBLINKA
BUCHENWALD
MAUTHAUSEN
BEIZE
SOBIBOR
CHELMO
PONARY
THERESIENSTADT
WARSAW
VILNA
SKARZYSKO
BERGEN-BELSEN
JANOW
DORA
NEUENGAMME
PUSTKOW

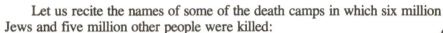

"Never to forget, never to forgive."
—An appeal from the Jewish Resistance Fighters to posterity

It is our tradition to say Kaddish, a prayer of praise and peace, for a loved one who has died. During the Holocaust many died with no one to remember them; tonight we remember. Tonight we recite the Kaddish for those people. Please stand.

MOURNERS' KADDISH
Read the translation silently, if desired.

Magnified and sanctified is the name of God throughout the world, which is created according to God's will. May the kingdom of God be established during the days of our lives and during the life of all the house of Israel. Speed-

ily, yes, and soon. And we say Amen. May God's great name be blessed for ever and ever. Exalted and honored is the name of the holy one, blessed in glory, transcending all praises, hymns and blessings we can offer. And we say Amen. May there be abundant peace from heaven and life for us and for all Israel. And we say Amen. As there is peace in the heavens, grant there be peace for us and for all Israel and for all the peoples of the world. And we say Amen.

Yis-gadal v'yis-kadash sh'mey rabah.

B'almah di-v'rah khir-usay, v'yamlikh mal-khusay.

B'khai-yeykhon uv-yo-meykhon uv-khai-yey d'khol beys Yisrael ba-agalah u'vizman kariv. V'imru Ameyn.

Y'hey sh'mey rabah m'vorakh, l'olam ul-almey al-mayah.

Yis-borakh v'yis-tabakh, v'yispo-ar,
v'yis-romam, v'yis-nasay, v'yis-hadar,
v'yis-aleh, v'yis-halal sh-mey d'kudeshah.

B'rikh hu. L'elah u-l'elah min kol
bir-khasah v'shirasah, tush-b'khasah
v'nekheh-masah, da-amiran b'almah.

V'imru Ameyn.

Y'hey sh'lamah rabah min sh'maya
v'khayyim aleynu v'al kol Yisrael.

V'imru Ameyn.

Oseh shalom bim-romav, hu ya-aseh shalom,
aleynu v'al kol Yisrael,
v'al kol amim ba-olam.
Vimru Ameyn.

יִתְגַּדַּל וְיִתְקַדַּשׁ שְׁמֵהּ רַבָּא. בְּעָלְמָא דִּי בְרָא כִרְעוּתֵהּ. וְיַמְלִיךְ מַלְכוּתֵהּ בְּחַיֵּיכוֹן וּבְיוֹמֵיכוֹן וּבְחַיֵּי דְכָל בֵּית יִשְׂרָאֵל בַּעֲגָלָא וּבִזְמַן קָרִיב. וְאִמְרוּ אָמֵן:

יְהֵא שְׁמֵהּ רַבָּא מְבָרַךְ לְעָלַם וּלְעָלְמֵי עָלְמַיָּא:

יִתְבָּרַךְ וְיִשְׁתַּבַּח, וְיִתְפָּאַר וְיִתְרוֹמַם, וְיִתְנַשֵּׂא וְיִתְהַדָּר, וְיִתְעַלֶּה וְיִתְהַלָּל שְׁמֵהּ דְּקֻדְשָׁא, בְּרִיךְ הוּא, לְעֵלָּא (וּלְעֵלָּא) מִן כָּל בִּרְכָתָא וְשִׁירָתָא תֻּשְׁבְּחָתָא וְנֶחֱמָתָא, דַּאֲמִירָן בְּעָלְמָא. וְאִמְרוּ אָמֵן:

יְהֵא שְׁלָמָא רַבָּא מִן שְׁמַיָּא וְחַיִּים עָלֵינוּ וְעַל כָּל-יִשְׂרָאֵל. וְאִמְרוּ אָמֵן:

עֹשֶׂה שָׁלוֹם בִּמְרוֹמָיו הוּא יַעֲשֶׂה שָׁלוֹם עָלֵינוּ וְעַל כָּל-יִשְׂרָאֵל. וְאִמְרוּ אָמֵן:

"Pesach 1943 is a historic date in modern Jewish history. On that day began the revolt against the Nazis who had come into the ghetto of Warsaw to complete the deportation of the remaining Jews. Few conflicts in history can compare with the fantastically unequal battle of the Warsaw ghetto. On one side was the tremendous power of the German army and the gestapo. On the other side was the remnant of Warsaw's starving Jews—40,000 civilians led by the Jewish Fighting Organization, several hundred poorly armed young women and men. Confined in a small area of the ghetto, they were unable to maneuver beyond a few city blocks. Nevertheless, the Jews fought back for forty-two days.

"A shot on Malevki street at dawn of April 19, 1943, the first day of Pesach, was the signal for the revolt. The fighting units, concealed in nearby bunkers, attics, and cellars, began firing at Nazi patrols. The Germans retreated. On that day Mordecai Anielevitch, the commander of the Jewish Fighting Organization, wrote: 'The dream of my life has come true. I have had the good fortune to witness Jewish defense in the ghetto in all its greatness and glory.'"*

Each Jewish fighter knew in her/his heart that it was an unequal struggle, that the odds were too great. But they hoped against hope and kept on fighting. As the days passed, the situation grew more and more desperate. One by one, the defense positions were wiped out. On May 8th the leadership of the Jewish resistance perished in the bunker at 18 Mila Street. No one surrendered. But for weeks thereafter small groups battled the Nazis from behind rubble and wreckage. And although the Germans were certain that not one Jew would escape from the ghetto, several hundred did succeed in making their way through the underground sewers and eventually joined the Partisan bands in the woods and forests. Similar acts of resistance took place in Minsk, Vilna, Bialystock, and in cities and towns in Poland. And in the concentration camps, too, there were countless acts of resistance.

We were slaves in Egypt and slaves in fascist Europe. We resisted and we fought back. We remember the heroism of the Jews and our allies—men, women, and children who fought in the ghettos, in the camps, in the forests, on the war fronts. We will be true to their memory by being fighters for freedom and justice in our land and throughout the world.

We have much to remember.

The Third Cup of Wine—To Resistance

Let us drink our next toast to those who have resisted, who have fought back; to those who are resisting, who are fighting back; to those who will resist, who will fight back.

Tonight we particularly remember our glorious and brave sisters who fought so courageously against the Nazis. We remember Hannah Senesh and Haviva Reik, who parachuted behind enemy lines in Hungary and Slovakia to organize resistance and rescue Jews. We remember Vladka Meed, and Chaika and Frumka Plotnitski, who served as couriers and smuggled arms for the ghetto fighters. We remember Rosa Robota, who organized the smuggling of dynamite to blow up a crematorium in Auschwitz. Chaika Grossman, Gusta Drenger, Zivia Lubetkin, Gisi Fleishman, Tosia Altman, Zofia Yamaika, Niuta Teitelboim—these are but a few of the names we know.

Boruch atah Adonai, eloheynu melech ha-olam boray pree ha-gafen.

ZOG NIT KEYNMOL, by Hirsh Glik

Hirsh Glik wrote this song while imprisoned in a concentration camp. It was inspired by the Warsaw Ghetto uprising. It was immediately chosen as the official hymn of the Jewish underground Partisan Brigades.

Never say that there is only death for you,
Tho' leaden, skies may be concealing days of blue
Because the hour that we have hungered for is near,
Beneath our tread the earth shall tremble: We are here!

---

*Reprinted by permission of Sholom Aleichem Club, Philadelphia, 1975. Originally appeared in *Haggadah for a Secular Seder.*

From land of palm tree to the far off land of snow,
We shall be coming with our torment and our woe.
And everywhere our blood has sunk into the earth,
Shall our bravery, our vigor blossom forth.

We'll have the morning sun to set our day aglow,
And all the yesterdays will vanish with the foe.
And if the time is long before the sun appears,
Then let this song go like a signal through the years.

This song was written with our blood and not with lead;
It's not a song that birds sing overhead.
It was the people amidst toppling barricades,
That sang this song of ours with pistols and grenades.

(Repeat first verse)

Yiddish:

Zog nit keynmol az du geyst dem letstn veg,
Chotsh himlen blayene farshteln bloye teg;
Kumen vet noch undzer oysgebenkte sho,
S'vet a poyk ton undzer trot—mir zaynen do!

ELIJAH'S CUP

We open the door to beckon the spirit of Eliyahu, the prophet Elijah. In the ninth century, B.C., a farmer arose to challenge the domination of the ruling elite. In his tireless and passionate advocacy on behalf of the common people, and his ceaseless exposure of the corruption and waste of the court, Elijah sparked a movement and created a legend which would inspire people for generations to come.

Before he died, Elijah declared that he would return once each generation in the guise of any poor or oppressed person, coming to people's doors to see how he would be treated. By the treatment offered this poor person, who would be Elijah himself, he would know whether the population had reached a level of humanity making them capable of participating in the dawn of the Messianic age.*

Eliyahu ha-navi	אֵלִיָּהוּ הַנָּבִיא.
Eliyahu ha-tishbi	אֵלִיָּהוּ הַתִּשְׁבִּי
Eliyahu, Eliyahu	אֵלִיָּהוּ, אֵלִיָּהוּ,
Eliyahu ha-giladi	אֵלִיָּהוּ הַגִּלְעָדִי.

Bimheyrah b'yameynu	בִּמְהֵרָה בְיָמֵינוּ
Yahvoh elehnu	יָבֹא אֵלֵינוּ
Im moshiach ben David	עִם מָשִׁיחַ בֶּן דָּוִד
Im moshiach bat Sarah	עִם מָשִׁיחַ בֶּן דָּוִד.

Tonight we acknowledge our parents and ancestors and political leaders as well. We vow that we will not allow their stories, their experiences, their wisdom to be stolen from us. It is our legacy and we will study it and teach it to our friends and children.

*Adapted from *A Radical Haggadah* by Marcia Prager.

Anne Frank:

"It's really a wonder that I haven't dropped all my ideals, because they seem so absurd and impossible to carry out. Yet I keep them, because in spite of everything, I still believe that people are really good at heart. I simply can't build up my hopes on a foundation consisting of confusion, misery, and death. I see the world gradually being turned into a wilderness, I hear the ever-approaching thunder, which will destroy us too; I can feel the sufferings of millions and yet, if I look up into the heavens, I think that it will all come right, that this cruelty too will end, and that peace and tranquility will return again. In the meantime, I must uphold my ideals, for perhaps the time will come when I shall be able to carry them out."

Ethel and Julius Rosenberg:

"Eventually, too you must come to believe that life is worth living. Be comforted that even now, with the end of ours slowly approaching, that we know this with a conviction that defeats the executioner! Your lives must teach you, too, that good cannot really flourish in the midst of evil; that freedom and all things that go to make up a truly satisfying and worthwhile life must sometimes be purchased very dearly. Be comforted then, that we were serene and understood with the deepest kind of understanding, that civilization had not as yet progressed to the point where life did not have to be lost for the sake of life, and that we were comforted in the knowledge that others would carry on after us."

I.L. Peretz, one of the three founders of modern Yiddish literature:

DON'T THINK THE WORLD IS A TAVERN

Don't think the world is a tavern—created
For fighting your way, with fists and with nails
To the bar, where you gorge and you guzzle, while others
Swooning from hunger and swallowing spit
Drawing their swollen cramped bellies in tighter.
Oh, don't think the world is a tavern.

Don't think the world is a market—created
So the stronger can prey on the tired and weak
And purchase from destitute maidens their shame,
From women, the milk of their breasts, and from men
The marrow of their bones, from the children their smiles
That infrequent guest in the innocent face.
Oh, don't think the world is a market.

Don't think the world is a wasteland—created
For wolves and for foxes, for spoils and for booty
The heavens a curtain, so God shall not see!
The mist—so that no one might look at your hands
The wind—just to muffle the sound of wild crying
The earth is to soak up the blood of the victims.
Oh, don't think the world is a wasteland.

HO CHI MINH:

The wheel of the law turns without pause.
After the rain, good weather in the wink of an eye.
The universe throws off its muddy clothes.
For ten thousand miles the landscape
    spreads out like a beautiful brocade.
Light breezes, smiling flowers.
High in the tree, among the sparkling leaves
    all the birds sing at once.
People and animals rise up reborn.
What could be more natural?
After sorrow comes joy.

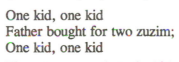

Rabbi Tarfon in *Pirkei Avot (Sayings of the Fathers)*:

It is not your obligation to complete the task [of creating a better world] but neither are you free to desist from it.

Rabbi Hillel:

''If I am not for myself, who will be for me? But if I am only for myself, what am I? And if not now, when?''	*Im eyn ani li, mi li?* *Uch'she-ani l'atzmi, ma ani?* *V'im lo achshav, ey-matai?*	אם אין אני לי מי לי וכשאני לעצמי מה אני אם לא עכשו אימתי.

ONE BABY GOAT (Chad Gadya)

(This nursery rhyme implies that ''you get back what you give....'')

One kid, one kid
Father bought for two zuzim;
One kid, one kid

Chad gadya, Chad gadya!
Deez-van abah beetray zoozay
Chad gadya, chad gadya

The cat came and ate the kid
That father bought for two zuzim;
One kid, one kid.

V'atah shoonrah v'achal l'gadya
Deezvan abah beetray zoozay, chad...

The dog came and bit the cat
That ate the kid
That father bought for two zuzim;
One kid, one kid.

V'atah chalbah v'nashach l'shoonrah
D'achal l'gadya,
Deezvan abah beetray zoozay, chad...

The stick came and beat the dog
That bit the cat
That ate the kid
That father bought for two zuzim;
One kid, one kid.

V'atah chootrah v'heekah l'chalbah
d'nashach l'shoonrah, d'achal l'gadya
Deezvan abah beetray zoozay, chad...

The fire came and burned the stick
That beat the dog
That bit the cat
That ate the kid
That father bought for two zuzim;
One kid, one kid.

V'atah noorah v'saraf l'chootrah
d'heekah l'chalbah, d'nashach l'shoonrah
d'ahchal l'gadya, deezvan abah...

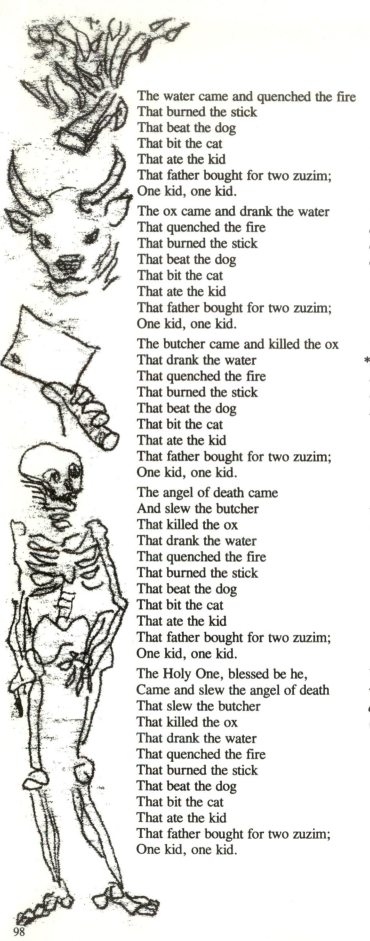

The water came and quenched the fire
That burned the stick
That beat the dog
That bit the cat
That ate the kid
That father bought for two zuzim;
One kid, one kid.

*V'atah mayah v'chavah l'noorah
d'saraf l'chootrah, d'heekah l'chalbah
d'nashach l'shoonrah, d'achal l'gadya
Deezvan abah beetray zoozay, chad...*

The ox came and drank the water
That quenched the fire
That burned the stick
That beat the dog
That bit the cat
That ate the kid
That father bought for two zuzim;
One kid, one kid.

*V'atah sorah v'shatah l'mayah
d'chavah l'noorah, d'saraf l'chootrah
d'heekah l'chalbah, d'nashach l'shoonrah
d'achal l'gadya, deezvan abah...*

The butcher came and killed the ox
That drank the water
That quenched the fire
That burned the stick
That beat the dog
That bit the cat
That ate the kid
That father bought for two zuzim;
One kid, one kid.

*V'atah ha-shochet v'shachat l'sorah
*d'shatah l'mayah, d'chavah l'noorah
d'saraf l'chootrah, d'heekah l'chalbah
d'nashach l'shoonrah, d'achal l'gadya
Deezvan abah beetray zoozay, chad.***

The angel of death came
And slew the butcher
That killed the ox
That drank the water
That quenched the fire
That burned the stick
That beat the dog
That bit the cat
That ate the kid
That father bought for two zuzim;
One kid, one kid.

*V'atah ha-malach ha-mavet
v'shachat l'shochet d'shachat l'sorah
(Repeat preceding verse from *)*

The Holy One, blessed be he,
Came and slew the angel of death
That slew the butcher
That killed the ox
That drank the water
That quenched the fire
That burned the stick
That beat the dog
That bit the cat
That ate the kid
That father bought for two zuzim;
One kid, one kid.

*V'atah ha-kadosh boruch hu
v'shachat ha-malach hamavet
d'shachat l'shochet d'shachat l'sorah.
(Repeat from * to **)*

EHAD MI YODEA

Who knows *one?* I know *one!*
One is our God in heaven
and earth.

Who knows *two?* I know *two!*
Two are the tablets of the covenant;
One is our God in heaven and earth.

Who knows *three?* I know *three!*
Three are the fathers of Israel;
Two are the tablets of the covenant;
One is our God in heaven and earth.

Who knows *four?* I know *four!*
Four are the mothers of Israel;
Three are the fathers of Israel;
Two are the tablets of the covenant;
One is our God in heaven and earth.

Who knows five? I know *five!*
Five are the books of the Torah;
Four are the mothers of Israel;
Three are the fathers of Israel;
Two are the tablets of the covenant;
One is our God in heaven and earth.

Who knows *six?* I know *six!*
Six are the parts of the Mishnah;
Five are the books of the Torah;
Four are the mothers of Israel;
Three are the fathers of Israel;
Two are the tablets of the covenant;
One is our God in heaven and earth.

Who knows *seven?* I know *seven!*
Seven are the days of the week;
Six are the parts of the Mishnah;
Five are the books of the Torah;
Four are the mothers of Israel;
Three are the fathers of Israel;
Two are the tablets of the covenant;
One is our God in heaven and earth.

Who knows *eight?* I know *eight!*
Eight are the days to *brith milah;*
Seven are the days of the week;
Six are the parts of the Mishnah;
Five are the books of the Torah;
Four are the mothers of Israel;
Three are the fathers of Israel;
Two are the tablets of the covenant;
One is our God in heaven and earth.

• *Echod mi yodea? Echod ani yodea. Echod eloheynu*
Eloheynu (4) sheh bashamayim oo-va-aretz.

Shnayim mi yodea? Shnayim ani yodea
• *Shney luchos ha-bris . . .*

Shloshoh mi yodea? Shloshoh ani yodea
• *Shloshoh avos . . .*

Arba mi yodea? Arba ani yodea
• *Arboh imahos . . .*

Chameeshah mi yodea?
Chameeshah ani yodea
• *Chameeshah Chumshay torah . . .*

Sheeshah mi yodea? Sheeshah ani yodea
• *Sheeshah seedray mishnah . . .*

Sheevah mi yodea? Sheevah ani yodea
• *Sheevah y'may shabatot . . .*

Shmonah mi yodea? Shmonah ani yodea
• *Shmonah y'may meelah . . .*

Who knows *nine?* I know *nine!*
Nine are the months to childbirth;
Eight are the days to *brith milah;*
Seven are the days of the week;
Six are the parts of the Mishnah;
Five are the books of the Torah;
Four are the mothers of Israel;
Three are the fathers of Israel;
Two are the tablets of the covenant;
One is our God in heaven and earth.

Teeshah mi yodea? Teeshah ani yodea
• *Teshah yarhay laydah . . .*

Who knows *ten?* I know *ten!*
Ten are the divine commandments;
Nine are the months to childbirth;
Eight are the days to *brith milah;*
Seven are the days of the week;
Six are the parts of the Mishnah;
Five are the books of the Torah;
Four are the mothers of Israel;
Three are the fathers of Israel;
Two are the tablets of the covenant;
One is our God in heaven and earth.

Ahsarah mi yodea? Ahsarah ani yodea
• *Ahsarah Deeb'rayah . . .*

Who knows *eleven?* I know *eleven!*
Eleven are the stars in Joseph's dream;
Ten are the divine commandments;
Nine are the months to childbirth;
Eight are the days to *brith milah;*
Seven are the days of the week;
Six are the parts of the Mishnah;
Five are the books of the Torah;
Four are the mothers of Israel;
Three are the fathers of Israel;
Two are the tablets of the covenant;
One is our God in heaven and earth.

Achad ohsor mi yodea? Achad ohsor ani yodea
• *Achad ohsor coch'vayah . . .*

Who knows *twelve?* I know *twelve!*
Twelve are the tribes of Israel;
Eleven are the stars in Joseph's dream;
Ten are the divine commandments;
Nine are the months to childbirth;
Eight are the days to *brith milah;*
Seven are the days of the week;
Six are the parts of the Mishnah;
Five are the books of the Torah;
Four are the mothers of Israel;
Three are the fathers of Israel;
Two are the tablets of the covenant;
One is our God in heaven and earth.

Shnayim ohsor mi yodea? Shnayim ohsor ani yodea
• *Shnayim ohsor sheev'tayah . . .*

Who knows *thirteen?* I know *thirteen!*
Thirteen are the divine qualities;
Twelve are the tribes of Israel;
Eleven are the stars in Joseph's dream;
Ten are the divine commandments;
Nine are the months childbirth;
Eight are the days to *brith milah;*
Seven are the days of the week;
Six are the parts of the Mishnah;
Five are the books of the Torah;
Four are the mothers of Israel;
Three are the fathers of Israel;
Two are the tablets of the covenant;
One is our God in heaven and earth.

*Shloshoh ohsor mi yodea? Shloshoh ohsor
ani yodea*
• *Shloshoh ohsor meedayoh . . .*

The Fourth Cup of Wine—To the Future!

We dedicate the final cup of wine to our hopes and dreams for the future.
We dream of a world not threatened by destruction.
We hope for a time when Jerusalem will be a beacon of brotherhood and sisterhood.
We dream of a world in which Jews and all other people are free to be themselves.
We dream of a world at peace.

Boruch atah Adonai, eloheynu melech ha-olam, boray pree ha-gafen. Amen.

We drink the last cup of wine.

Next year may Jerusalem be at peace.

New Jewish Agenda is a national
multi-issue organization committed
to Jewish peoplehood and to fostering a
progressive voice in the Jewish
community and in society at large.
Founded in December, 1980 Agenda has
chapters in 40 cities. For more
information write to New Jewish
Agenda, 149 Church Street, Suite 2N,
New York, New York 10007.

Book design by Dennis Sheheen.

"The Rainbow Seder" cover by Beth Haber.

Illustrations from *The Prague Haggadah, 1526*
(New York: The Shulsinger Brothers, 1964)
and *Haggadah and History* (Philadelphia: The
Jewish Publication Society of America, 1975).

"Seder of the Children of Abraham"
cover and illustrations by Amnon Danziger.

"Haggadah of Liberation"
cover and illustrations by Irwin Rosenhouse.

Additional illustrations by John Opulski and
Nina Raab.

1 The Old Testament

The Story of God's Boundless Love

The Bible can be thought of as a love letter from God.

A woman prays from the Scriptures at the Western Wall in Jerusalem, a site that is sacred to Jews.

Imagine that you have just received a letter from someone who loves you deeply. This person knows you inside and out, has stood by you through the best of times and the worst of times, believes in you, challenges you, forgives you when you are hurtful or neglectful of your relationship with her or him. The one who sent you this letter loves you more than anyone else in the world has ever loved you.

Eagerly you open the envelope, unfold the letter, sink into a chair, and begin to read. You not only read words on a page; you also soak up the deeper meaning of what was intended by them. Through this letter you encounter the person who sent it to you. Across the distance of time and space, your heart meets the heart of the one who loves you like no one else does.

The Bible: A Love Letter from God

The Bible can be thought of as a love letter from God. It is the expression, through human words and ways of communicating, of his boundless love for us and his longing for our happiness.

The Bible is a love letter like no other. It tells the Story of God's love for us, but is not only a human account. It is the **word of God**, inspired by the Holy Spirit. The Bible's ultimate source is God. Thus the Scriptures can nourish and transform the lives of those who approach them with an open heart. In the Bible we can encounter not just words on a page but the living God.

The Great Story

As you probably know, the Bible consists of both the **Old Testament** and the **New Testament.** (*Testament* is another word for "covenant.") Taken as a whole, these two testaments tell the great Story of God's love. Here, in the briefest outline, is that Story:

1. God created the world and humankind out of infinite love.
2. God offered hope and a promise of salvation when human beings rejected that love.
3. God chose a people and formed a covenant, or special relationship, with them and promised that through them the whole world would be saved. *1*
4. God molded and fashioned this people, the Israelites, during the ups and downs of their history. He offered them liberation, challenged them to live justly and faithfully, took them back when they

strayed, consoled them in sorrow, and saved them when they got into trouble. The people of Israel—eventually called the Jews—looked to a future day when God's Reign of justice and peace would fill the whole world.
5. God sent the divine Son, Jesus, the long-awaited Messiah, as the human expression of his love and the fulfillment of his promises to Israel. Jesus is the fullness of God's revelation.
6. By his life, death, and Resurrection, Jesus brought salvation to all the world.
7. The Holy Spirit was sent by God the Father and Jesus Christ to nourish, sustain, and renew the followers of Christ, who carry on his work and message until the end of time. In the end Christ will return in glory as Lord of all, and God's universal Reign of justice and peace will finally be complete.

This course considers the Old Testament, the first part of the Bible, which tells the great Story through the time just before Jesus. You will probably study the New Testament in another course.

A note on terminology: For Christians the word *old* in Old Testament does not imply "outdated" or "no longer in effect," and *new* in New Testament does not imply that it replaces or substitutes for the Old Testament. Rather, the New Testament is the fulfillment of the Old Testament. Both form a unity that is the inspired word of God. We cannot understand the New Testament without understanding the Old Testament. Both are the sacred Scriptures; both are inspired by God.

1

Promise is a major theme throughout the Bible. What is the most important promise you ever made? Write about what that promise has meant to you and what difficulties, if any, you have faced in keeping it.

The Inspired Word of God

What does it mean to say that the Bible is the inspired word of God?

First, we need to clear up any misconceptions about the meaning of divine inspiration. To say that the Bible is inspired by God does not mean that he dictated the words to the writers, who simply recorded what was whispered to them! Nor does it mean that everything in the Bible is factually correct or scientifically valid.

Instead, to say that the sacred Scriptures are inspired means that God ensured they contain *all the truth that is necessary for our salvation*. This is the truth about our relationship to God and all creation and the destiny meant for us, union with God forever. This is *religious truth*, which is not the same as historical accuracy or scientific explanation.[2]

In inspiring the Bible, God worked through human beings who wrote the sacred Scriptures. They, like us today, were subject to the cultural and intellectual limitations of their own eras; they had many customs and ways of thinking that are not our own, and they wrote in languages that most of us English-speaking people do not understand—Hebrew, Greek, and Aramaic.

Furthermore, these authors used various literary forms (some of which may seem strange to us) in ways that met the needs of their audiences. The Old Testament includes ancient myths and legends, royal court histories, letters, poems, songs, genealogies, sermons, liturgical instructions, laws, accounts of visions, and stories passed down orally for generations before being written down. The process of writing the Old Test-

A Jewish boy reads in Hebrew from the Torah, the first five books of the Bible, as part of his bar mitzvah, a ceremony that celebrates his reaching the age of religious duty and responsibility.

ament spanned about a thousand years, whereas the New Testament was written over a period of about fifty years.

So the Bible was created by a kind of collaboration of God with human beings. God inspired the Biblical writers and guided the Church as it selected which writings would be collected in the Bible. The listing of the books of the Bible is called the canon of the Scriptures. Just as Jesus is both divine and human, the Bible itself shows the hands of both God and human beings.

2

List five *facts* about your family. Then list five *truths* about them. How have you come to understand these truths?

Each person is invited to know the living, loving God through the Scriptures.

For Review

☐ In what sense can the Bible be thought of as a love letter from God?

☐ Give a brief outline of the great Story of God's love as told in the Bible.

☐ What does it mean to say that the sacred Scriptures were inspired by God? Explain how the Bible can be thought of as the result of a collaboration of God and human beings.

This parchment scroll containing scriptural writings is from fifteenth-century Germany, but it is constructed like those used by the ancient Israelites.

Studying the Scriptures

Why *Study* the Bible?

Why do we *study* the Bible? If it is God's truth, can't we just read the words and immediately "get" what they mean?

The fact is that some of the Bible can be quite puzzling to modern ears. We may not understand the circumstances in which the texts were written or the meaning originally intended by the authors. Some of the material may seem contradictory. This is particularly so for the Old Testament, whose origins are complex.

Let's go back to the image of the Bible as God's love letter to us. It is as if the letter has come to us in a foreign language, and we need to translate it before we can really understand its message and meet the living God behind the message. In a literal sense, the Bible *has* been translated from the Hebrew and Greek into a number of English versions. But we are speaking here of a different kind of translation—the study aimed at discovering the original intent of an author in writing a given scriptural text. Once we see what the author meant—and this takes some understanding of the circumstances in which the Scriptures were written and handed down—we can appreciate what God is saying to us today through these texts.

The Treasured Scrolls

The Scriptures of ancient Israel were first written in the Hebrew language on sheets of goatskin or sheepskin called parchment. These leather sheets were sewn together to make one continuous strip. Each end of the strip was fastened to a dowel, and then the strip was rolled up from both ends to make a scroll. One or more of these scrolls made up a book of the Bible.

Scripture scholarship

Scripture scholars do much of that "translation" for us—not just the obvious kind from the ancient Hebrew and Greek to modern languages, but the even more challenging kind that tries to get at what the authors really meant. Scholars delve into the history, archaeology, literary forms, and culture surrounding the development of the texts to help us understand their intended meanings. Of course, even the best Scripture scholars disagree on their findings and theories, and many questions are still open to debate (such as when a given scriptural text was written or who wrote it). By and large, though, Scripture scholarship has shed great light on modern understanding of the Bible.

The Church's guidance

The Catholic Church provides help and guidance in understanding the theological meaning of the sacred Scriptures. This guidance comes through the Church's passing on of its **Tradition.** Like the Scriptures, the Church's Tradition comes from God's revelation—his self-communication with us. While the sacred Scriptures were written down, the Church's Tradition is the oral preaching of Jesus' followers, the Apostles, that has been handed down to the bishops and expressed in the Church's doctrines, teachings, and worship. Tradition is closely connected to the sacred Scriptures but

distinct from them. Both are ways that the truth of God's revelation—God's self-communication—is made known to us.

The Church's **magisterium,** its official teaching voice or office, consists of the world's bishops together with the pope. The magisterium, guided by the Holy Spirit, has been entrusted with the task of interpreting the Scriptures and Tradition in every era. This is to ensure that the authentic faith handed down by the Apostles since the time of Jesus is preserved, passed on, and understood from age to age. Since the 1940s the magisterium has affirmed and promoted the use of modern methods of biblical scholarship as a help in interpreting the Scriptures.

The purpose of studying the Scriptures is not simply that we might know a lot of things about the Bible or even its theological meaning. Knowledge is important and useful but not enough. Rather, the deeper intent of Scripture study is that we might "fall in love" with the Bible, and with God, who is its source and inspiration.

Why the Old Testament?

Why, some might wonder, do we study the Old Testament in particular? Isn't it enough for a Christian to study and appreciate the New Testament? As said earlier, Christians cannot understand the New Testament and

In 1947 a library of Hebrew scriptural scrolls dating back almost two thousand years were discovered in these limestone caves near the Dead Sea.

The Dead Sea Scrolls

Modern Scripture studies can be greatly affected by discoveries such as the Dead Sea Scrolls.

Possibly before the Roman invasion of Palestine in the first century A.D., a Jewish community called Qumran hid its library of scrolls in caves near the Dead Sea. There they remained until 1947, when shepherds discovered them.

Before the discovery of the Dead Sea Scrolls, the earliest manuscripts in Hebrew came from the ninth century A.D. The scrolls from Qumran date back almost a thousand years before that and serve as a check on the accuracy of later manuscripts. These scrolls confirm that Jewish scribes copied their manuscripts with great care and precision.

Jesus without understanding the Old Testament. But in itself—and not just because it points to the New Testament—the Old Testament has permanent value. It contains profound teachings, beautiful prayers, and some of the greatest literature ever created. Most important, in the Old Testament we encounter God, its inspiration.**3**

Why This Course?

This course provides you with a "guided tour" of the Old Testament. It walks you through all the books, considering the circumstances in which they were composed, describing their contents, and offering insights into their meaning from the perspectives of contemporary Scripture scholarship and Catholic Tradition.

The course directs you to read key passages from each book of the Old Testament, and that reading is the heart of this course.

No textbook can substitute for reading the word of God. So you are invited to plunge into the Scripture passages themselves, which have the power to touch our life in a way that summaries of them do not.

Numbered activities throughout this textbook can help you relate what is in the Bible and this course to your own life and experiences. You will also find several types of sidebars in the chapters:

 World Happenings tells of developments that were going on around the world at the same time as the biblical events covered in a given chapter.

 I-Witness gives a point of view on biblical times by a fictional young character.

 The Prayer of Israel offers a prayer from the Old Testament that is related to an event described in a given chapter.

3

Spend some time exploring your Bible. Find a passage in the Old Testament that you think is beautiful, powerful, or inspiring. Write out the passage and explain why you chose it. What does it have to say to you (what is the *truth* it offers you)?

This course provides you with a "guided tour" of the Old Testament, a tour in which you are encouraged to plunge into the Scripture passages themselves.

Other informational sidebars explain aspects of the culture and history surrounding the people of Israel and the development of the Bible. Maps and timelines will help you situate the biblical events in terms of geography and chronology.

Once you are equipped with a Bible, this textbook, and a willingness to participate in this course, you are ready to discover the meaning of the Old Testament, and to encounter God in the process.

For Review

- ☐ How does Scripture scholarship help us get in touch with the intended meanings of the scriptural texts?
- ☐ What is the relationship of the Scriptures to the Church's Tradition?
- ☐ Why do Christians need to understand both the Old Testament and the New Testament?

A God Who Acts in History

The God revealed in the Old Testament is not aloof or distant from human affairs. He acts within human history. The Story of God's actions and the people's responses over many centuries is called **salvation history.**

It will help to keep the big picture of that history in mind as we set out to discover the meaning of the Old Testament because the history and the Scriptures of ancient Israel were intertwined. (Notice that the history on pages 16 to 19 is actually a fuller explanation of the great Story outlined at the beginning of this chapter.) Do not be concerned about memorizing names and events at this point; they will come up again many times in this course. Instead, simply try to recognize the broad pattern of history.

First, referring to the timelines on pages 14 to 15, note the time period in which the biblical events happened. As you can see, humankind existed for many thousands of years before the biblical era; most of that time is called prehistory because no historical records of those ancient peoples exist. (The time period of the Creation and the earliest stories of humankind appearing in the Old Testament fall into the category of prehistory.) About 3000 B.C., history as we know it

The Prayer of Israel: "Lead Me in Your Truth"

To you, O Lord, I lift up my soul.

. . . .

Make me to know your ways, O Lord;
    teach me your paths.
Lead me in your truth, and teach me,
    for you are the God of my salvation;
    for you I wait all day long.

(Psalm 25:1–5)

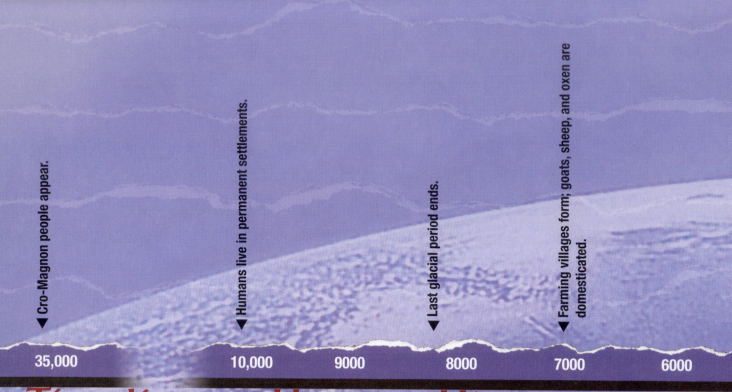

Cro-Magnon people appear.

Humans live in permanent settlements.

Last glacial period ends.

Farming villages form; goats, sheep, and oxen are domesticated.

| 35,000 | | 10,000 | 9000 | 8000 | 7000 | 6000 |

Timeline of Human History

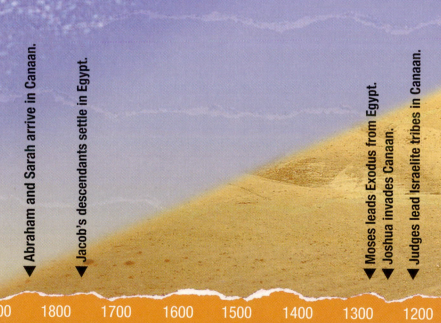

Abraham and Sarah arrive in Canaan.

Jacob's descendants settle in Egypt.

Moses leads Exodus from Egypt.

Joshua invades Canaan.

Judges lead Israelite tribes in Canaan.

| Prehistory | 2000 | 1900 | 1800 | 1700 | 1600 | 1500 | 1400 | 1300 | 1200 | 1 |

Timeline of Biblical History

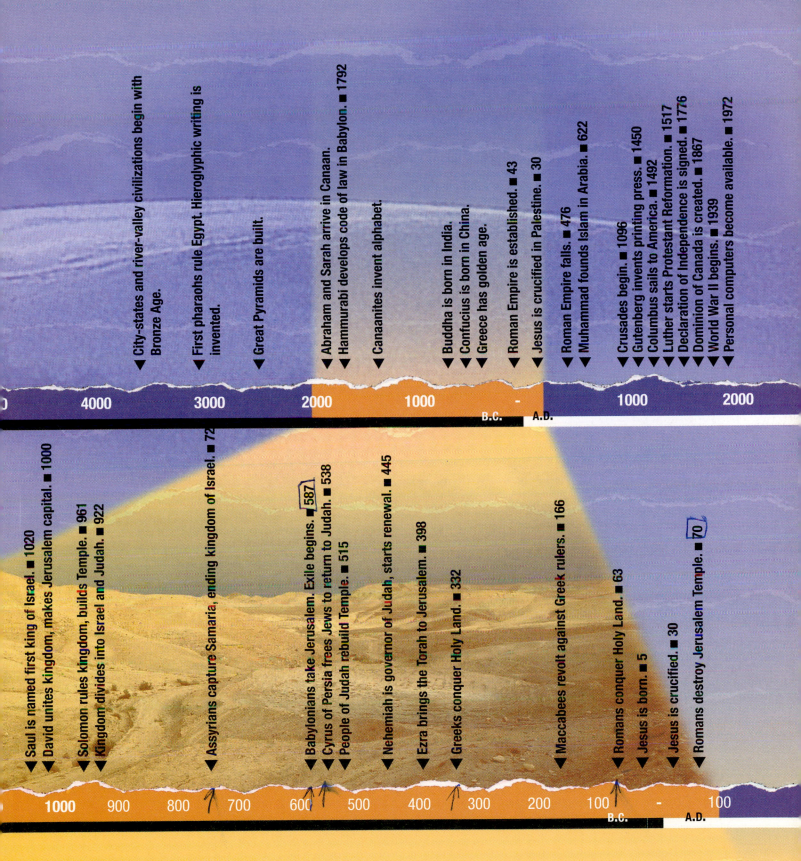

Top timeline (B.C. / A.D.):

- City-states and river-valley civilizations begin with Bronze Age.
- First pharaohs rule Egypt. Hieroglyphic writing is invented.
- Great Pyramids are built.
- Abraham and Sarah arrive in Canaan.
- Hammurabi develops code of law in Babylon. ■ 1792
- Canaanites invent alphabet.
- Buddha is born in India.
- Confucius is born in China.
- Greece has golden age.
- Roman Empire is established. ■ 43
- Jesus is crucified in Palestine. ■ 30
- Roman Empire falls. ■ 476
- Muhammad founds Islam in Arabia. ■ 622
- Crusades begin. ■ 1096
- Gutenberg invents printing press. ■ 1450
- Columbus sails to America. ■ 1492
- Luther starts Protestant Reformation. ■ 1517
- Declaration of Independence is signed. ■ 1776
- Dominion of Canada is created. ■ 1867
- World War II begins. ■ 1939
- Personal computers become available. ■ 1972

Scale: 4000 — 3000 — 2000 — 1000 — B.C. | A.D. — 1000 — 2000

Bottom timeline (detail, B.C. / A.D.):

- Saul is named first king of Israel. ■ 1020
- David unites kingdom, makes Jerusalem capital. ■ 1000
- Solomon rules kingdom, builds Temple. ■ 961
- Kingdom divides into Israel and Judah. ■ 922
- Assyrians capture Samaria, ending kingdom of Israel. ■ 72
- Babylonians take Jerusalem. Exile begins. ■ 587
- Cyrus of Persia frees Jews to return to Judah. ■ 538
- People of Judah rebuild Temple. ■ 515
- Nehemiah is governor of Judah, starts renewal. ■ 445
- Ezra brings the Torah to Jerusalem. ■ 398
- Greeks conquer Holy Land. ■ 332
- Maccabees revolt against Greek rulers. ■ 166
- Romans conquer Holy Land. ■ 63
- Jesus is born. ■ 5
- Jesus is crucified. ■ 30
- Romans destroy Jerusalem Temple. ■ 70

Scale: 1000 — 900 — 800 — 700 — 600 — 500 — 400 — 300 — 200 — 100 — B.C. | A.D. — 100

The Old Testament   **15**

began, with the development of early forms of writing. The biblical period—from the beginnings of Israel as a people through the time of Jesus and the earliest years of the Church—went from about 1850 B.C. until about A.D. 100. It lasted almost two thousand years. And that is about the same amount of time as has elapsed from the time of Jesus until today.

What follows is a brief overview of the events of the biblical period. You may also refer to the map entitled "Israel and the Empires of the Ancient Western World," on page 20 of this text.

The Founders and the Promise

The history and the religion of the Israelites began with Abraham. Abraham was a wandering herdsman, or nomad, who lived in the region now called Iraq, around 1850 B.C. According to the Book of Genesis, God made an agreement with Abraham. God promised to make Abraham's descendants a blessing to the world and to give them the land of Canaan, later known as Palestine. The Promise, as this is called, was that Abraham's descendants would reveal the one God to the world. Christians believe that this Promise reached its fulfillment in the coming of Christ.

Abraham's descendants and their families inherited the Promise. Abraham, his son Isaac, and grandson Jacob would be called the patriarchs, or founders, of the Jewish faith. Their wives—Sarah, Rebekah, and Rachel—would be called the matriarchs. *4*

The Exodus of the Israelites and the Covenant

At the close of the Book of Genesis, the descendants of Abraham are living in Egypt, having traveled there from Canaan in order to survive a famine. Yet as the Book of Exodus opens, we find them enslaved by the Egyptians. Practically nothing is known about the Israelites in Egypt from about 1700 to 1290 B.C.

Moses, the main character in the story of the Exodus, was one of the greatest religious leaders in history. About 1290 B.C. the understanding that one God was above all other gods came to Moses when God revealed his name—Yahweh, meaning "I am the One who is always present." With God's power the Israelites, led by Moses, made a daring escape from Pharaoh's army through the sea—the Exodus—and were thus freed from slavery.

After a dramatic encounter between Moses and God on Mount Sinai, a covenant, or agreement, between Yahweh and the Israelites was confirmed. The Israelites' part of the Covenant was to keep the Ten Commandments, which God had presented to Moses. God's part was to make the Israelites "the people of God" and to be with them as long as they kept the Covenant. Once again God promised that they would be given the land of Canaan. But before they entered Canaan, they wandered for forty years in the desert as they learned to trust God's care for them. *5*

4

Who are the patriarchs and matriarchs in your family tree? What legacy have they left your family? If you are unsure about this, interview your parents, grandparents, aunts, or uncles. Ask them to tell you stories about your ancestors, and write down one of them that you find interesting or inspiring.

5

Do you find it easy or challenging to trust that God is taking care of you? Write a paragraph or two explaining your thoughts on this. If you wish, offer an example of a time you felt deep trust in God, or a time you faltered in your trust.

The Nation and the Temple

Around 1000 B.C. Israel became recognized as a nation, with David as its anointed king and Jerusalem as its capital city. God made a promise to David that his royal line would endure forever. (Later Jews put their hopes in a descendant of David to save them from oppression.)

David's son Solomon built the Temple in Jerusalem, and it became the principal place of worship for the nation. As both a political and a religious capital, Jerusalem became a great and holy city.

The Kings and the Prophets

After Solomon's death in 922 B.C., the nation divided, with the kingdom of Israel in the north and the kingdom of Judah in the south. Heavy taxes and forced service in both kingdoms created hardships for the people. In addition, the kings often practiced idolatry—the worship of idols (images of other gods).

Prophets spoke out against both kingdoms' injustices to the people and infidelity to God. They questioned the behavior of the kings and called them and their people back to the Covenant. Yet the kingdoms continued to oppress the poor and worship pagan gods until eventually both kingdoms were crushed by powerful conquerors. The Assyrians obliterated the northern kingdom of Israel in 721 B.C. and took its people into exile. In 587 B.C. the Babylonians destroyed Judah, including the city of Jerusalem, and took its people to Babylon as captives.

The Babylonian Exile and the Jewish Dispersion

While the people were exiled in Babylon, still other prophets encouraged them to repent of their sins and turn back to God. During this time the prophet known as Second Isaiah proclaimed that God was the one and only God. Monotheism, the belief in one God, was now the revelation of this people to the world, their blessing to the nations.

The Promised Land of Canaan offered the Israelites the chance to settle down into agricultural life, planting vineyards and raising crops.

Taking Over the Promised Land

After Moses' time the Israelites, led by Joshua, entered Canaan. Over the next centuries—from about 1250 to 1000 B.C.—they fought against the people who lived in that region. In these battles the Israelites were led by military leaders called judges. During this time the Israelites abandoned their nomadic ways for the more settled agricultural life that was native to the region.

The Greek Empire, with its capital in Athens, ruled the Jews for nearly three hundred years.

More Oppressors

The Persian Empire was conquered in 330 B.C. by the armies of Alexander the Great, leader of the Greek Empire. This made the Greeks overlords of the Jews for nearly three hundred years, with the exception of a brief period of independence after a revolt led by the Maccabees family. The Greeks were followed by the Romans, who captured Jerusalem in 63 B.C. Although tolerant of other cultures and religions, the Roman Empire severely punished its subjects for revolts.

It was a dark time for the people of the Promise, who longed for release from oppression and for the day when all their hopes for a good and peaceful life would be fulfilled. Many Jews looked toward the coming of a messiah, one sent by God to save them; some expected this messiah to be from the family line of David.

It is at this point in the history of Israel that the Old Testament accounts end. We will return shortly to see what became of the religion of Judaism.

After fifty years in Babylon, the exiles were released from captivity by the conquering Persians and allowed to return home. Judah, no longer a politically independent kingdom, had become a district within the Persian Empire, and the returned exiles became known as Jews, from the word *Judah*. They rebuilt the Temple, and under Ezra and Nehemiah, they re-established the Law and restored Jerusalem. That city became the religious capital for the Jews who had resettled all over the world—that is, the Jews of the Dispersion.

During the exile the Jewish leaders had begun collecting and reflecting on their ancestral writings, forming the core of what would later become their Bible, known to Christians as the Old Testament.

Jesus, the Savior

Into a situation of defeat and darkness for the people of Israel, Jesus was born, one of the house, or family line, of David. Christians see Jesus as the long-awaited Messiah—the fulfillment of all God's promises to Israel and the Savior of the world. With his death and Resurrection, Jesus' followers recognized that he was the Son of God. The community of believers began to grow, first among Jews but later among Gentiles, or non-Jews. The story of Jesus and the growth of the early Church is told in the New Testament.

Judaism After the Biblical Period

Most of the Jews of the first century A.D. did not become Christian. Judaism went on, and it has carried the light of faith in the one God into our contemporary age.

Still the Chosen People: Catholic Teaching on Judaism

Catholic teaching is that Christians are forever linked with the Jewish people, who were the first to hear the word of God. God's Covenant and special relationship with the Jews still stand, "for the gifts and the calling of God are irrevocable" (Romans 11:29). The words of Saint Paul about the Jews express this: "To them belong the adoption, the glory, the covenants, the giving of the law, the worship, and the promises; to them belong the patriarchs, and from them, according to the flesh, comes the Messiah" (9:4–5).

In spite of great suffering and persecution (often at the hands of Christians), Jews have remained faithful to God through the centuries since biblical times. Like Christians, Jews work toward and await in hope the coming of God's Reign of peace and justice. But whereas Judaism looks for an unknown messiah to come, Christianity recognizes Jesus Christ as the Messiah who has already come and who will return in glory.

In a historic gesture, Pope John Paul II visited Rome's Jewish synagogue in 1986, meeting with Rome's chief rabbi, Elio Toaff.

The history of Judaism in the time after Jesus began with a crushing blow. In A.D. 70 a Jewish revolt against the Roman Empire led to the Roman destruction of Jerusalem and the second Temple. The surviving Jews fled to Africa, Asia, and Europe. The Jewish Dispersion, sometimes called the Diaspora, became the central fact of Jewish history.

The dispersion of Jews all over the empire spurred the definition of an official set of scriptures to guide Jewish religious life. This would ensure the Jews' sense of identity as a people set apart and bound by the Covenant with God; it would help them keep separate from the surrounding cultures that worshiped other gods and had immoral practices.

By the end of the first century A.D., this official set of the Hebrew Scriptures was defined. In A.D. 90 Jewish religious leaders met to agree on the *canon*—that is, the list of books recognized as divinely inspired and thus the primary source and guide for religious belief and practice. In translations this canon became known as the Bible, literally meaning "the book." The Jewish Bible was organized into three main parts: the Torah, the Prophets, and the Writings.

For Review

☐ List the events in salvation history as given in the timeline of biblical history in this chapter.

☐ How do Christians see Jesus Christ in relation to the promises made by God to Israel?

☐ Summarize Catholic teaching on Judaism.

Israel and the Empires of the Ancient Western World

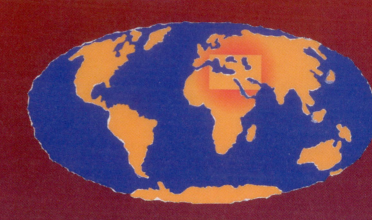

Rome ruled Israel beginning in 63 B.C. and destroyed the Temple in Jerusalem in A.D. 70. In A.D. 135, the Romans forbade all Jews to enter Jerusalem.

Alexander the Great conquered the Persian Empire in 330 B.C. The Greek rulers of Egypt and Syria, successors of Alexander, controlled Israel for nearly three hundred years.

EUROPE

ASIA

• Rome

GREECE

Black Sea

Caspian Sea

1 inch = 600 miles

ASSYRIA

Mediterranean Sea

ISRAEL
• Jerusalem

• **Babylon**

PERSIA

Indus River

EGYPT

Persian Gulf

INDIA

AFRICA

Red Sea

Nile River

Arabian Sea

From 2000 to 1200 B.C., Egypt frequently dominated the land known as Canaan.

Assyria destroyed the capital of the kingdom called Israel in 722 B.C.

Babylon destroyed Jerusalem in 587 B.C. and took many of its citizens into exile.

Persia replaced Babylon as ruler of the Near East in 538 B.C.

What Are the Scriptures of the Old Testament?

For the Jews: Letters from Home

We have already seen that the Old Testament, and the Bible as a whole, can be thought of as a letter from God—a message conveying God's truth that enables us to encounter God, who inspired it. It is not simply an ordinary human document.

The Scriptures, though, can also be considered under their human aspect. They were written by flesh-and-blood men (and perhaps women) for real audiences who needed to hear what these writers had to say in their own time and place. And so, for the Jews of the Dispersion, flung around the ancient world of the Mediterranean by war and persecution, their Hebrew Scriptures must have seemed like letters from home.

Imagine what a letter from home might mean to a group of refugees. Even a brief note in their own language would be treasured as a source of deep joy. The Hebrew Scriptures were like that for the Jews of the Dispersion. They were words from their families, from their homeland, and from their ancestors. They told the Jews in their own language how best to live a faithful life in unfamiliar surroundings. Most important, the Scriptures told them that their people still loved them and that the God of their people would be with them always.[6]

These "letters from home" took the form of many types of writing: stories, legends, histories, oracles, conversations, letters, novels, lists, biographies, laws, speeches, poems, proverbs, and prayers.

The Catholic Canon of the Old Testament

The Hebrew Scriptures were sacred to the early Christian communities because Christianity's religious roots were in Judaism. Christians thus adopted the sacred writings of Judaism as their own; they were always considered part of the Scriptures of Christianity.

The sacred Scriptures of Judaism became part of the Scriptures of Christianity.

6

List five experiences you have had of being a stranger or of being *with* strangers: for example, moving to a new city or trying to communicate with a foreigner. Next to each experience, write the emotions you felt.

So the Bible of Judaism contains the same Scriptures as what Christians call the Old Testament, with the exception of a few more texts in the Catholic canon. (These other texts—some of them originally written in Greek and others translated from Hebrew or Aramaic into Greek—often appear in Protestant Bibles under the category of apocryphal writings; they are not part of the Protestant or the Jewish canon.)

The **Catholic canon** of the Old Testament consists of forty-six books, grouped in the following major sections:
- the Pentateuch
- the historical books
- the wisdom books
- the prophetic books

The Pentateuch

The heart of Israel's story is told in the first five books of the Bible, called the Pentateuch, which means "five books." The Jews refer to these books as the Torah, a Hebrew word that means "instruction" but is sometimes translated as "the Law." In the Jewish faith, these books are the primary scriptural authority in matters of belief and practice.

The Pentateuch's opening stories about the Creation, Adam and Eve, Cain and Abel, Noah, and the Tower of Babel show us God as a loving Creator and reveal the effects of disobedience. Following these stories are the tales of the patriarchs and the matriarchs— Abraham and Sarah, Isaac and Rebekah, Jacob and Rachel, and Joseph.

Next we are told of Israel's slavery in Egypt, its escape under the leadership of Moses, the Covenant at Mount Sinai, and the forty years in the wilderness, ending on the eve of Israel's entry into the Promised Land.

The Pentateuch is called the religious masterpiece of the Old Testament, and its five books are Genesis, Exodus, Leviticus, Numbers, and Deuteronomy.

The historical books

The historical books tell of Israel's conquest of the land of Canaan—including stories of Joshua, of the judges, and of Israel's first kings (Saul, David, and Solomon). These books also describe the breakup of the nation Israel, the reigns of the later kings, and the prophets' attempts to warn those kings of coming disaster.

In spite of the prophets' warnings, the kings disobey, disaster comes, and exile follows. Fifty years later a remnant of the people returns to Jerusalem, rebuilds the Temple, and struggles again with foreign powers and the people's own weaknesses. Through it all Israel's prophets remind the people of their Covenant with God and of their call to be a blessing to all the nations of the world. In addition to Joshua and Judges, the historical books include Ruth, 1 and 2 Samuel, 1 and 2 Kings, 1 and 2 Chronicles, Ezra, Nehemiah, Tobit, Judith, Esther, and 1 and 2 Maccabees. (The phrase *1 and 2* before a book name indicates "the First and Second Books of.")

The wisdom books

The wisdom books are usually listed as Job, Psalms, Proverbs, Ecclesiastes, Song of Songs, Wisdom, and Sirach (also called Ecclesiasticus).
- The Book of Job explores the problem of good versus evil. Job demands a reason from God for the calamities that overcome him, and God answers in a speech of matchless splendor.
- The Book of Psalms is a collection of religious songs once attributed solely to David but now to a number of authors. Some psalms were written for liturgical occasions, others for private prayer.
- The Book of Proverbs is a collection of writings filled with practical advice about living ordinary life in the spirit of godliness.

The Books of the Old Testament

In the Mass, Catholics hear readings from the Old Testament proclaimed.

Catholic Christians accept the following books as their canon of the Old Testament:

The Pentateuch

Genesis
Exodus
Leviticus
Numbers
Deuteronomy

The historical books

Joshua
Judges
Ruth
1 Samuel
2 Samuel
1 Kings
2 Kings
1 Chronicles
2 Chronicles
Ezra
Nehemiah
Tobit
Judith
Esther
1 Maccabees
2 Maccabees

The wisdom books

Job
Psalms
Proverbs
Ecclesiastes
Song of Songs
Wisdom
Sirach

The prophetic books

Isaiah
Jeremiah
Lamentations
Baruch
Ezekiel
Daniel
Hosea
Joel
Amos
Obadiah
Jonah
Micah
Nahum
Habakkuk
Zephaniah
Haggai
Zechariah
Malachi

- The author of the Book of Ecclesiastes was a questioner who, in the end, saw that life was a mystery for which he had no answers. It is wise to live life as well as possible and to enjoy it, he decided.
- The Song of Songs is a collection of love songs in the form of dialogue, the speakers being bride, bridegroom, and attendants.
- The Book of Wisdom was meant to strengthen the faith of Israel and spoke for the first time in Israel's history about life after death.
- The Book of Sirach was written to show that true wisdom had been revealed by God to Israel.

The prophetic books

The early prophets—such as Samuel and Nathan, Elijah and Elisha—are known for their life stories rather than for their recorded words. Often called the nonwriting prophets, these figures appear in the historical books.

The writing prophets, each of whose teachings are a book of the Bible, can be thought of in three groups, named in reference to the exile in Babylon:
- The *pre-exilic* prophets are Hosea and Amos (who spoke to the northern kingdom of Israel) and Isaiah, Jeremiah, Micah, Nahum, Habakkuk, and Zephaniah (all of whom spoke to the southern kingdom of Judah).
- The *exilic prophets* are Ezekiel (who went to Babylon with the deportees), Second Isaiah (the second part of the Book of Isaiah), and the unknown author of the Book of Lamentations.
- The *postexilic* prophets include Haggai, Zechariah, Malachi, Third Isaiah (the third part of the Book of Isaiah), Joel, Obadiah, and Baruch.

Containing some of the most powerful religious writing in the world, the prophetic books tell us about men who loved Israel and who warned it that to depart from fidelity to God would lead not only to moral blindness but to destruction as a nation—which is what happened. The Books of Jonah and Daniel are also listed with the prophetic writings. Isaiah, Jeremiah, and Ezekiel are called major prophets because their books are long, and the others are called minor prophets because their books are short.

This course covers all the books of the Old Testament (some only briefly). However, it does not treat the books in the same order that they appear in the Bible, which is by categories. This is so that the course can follow roughly the history of Israel. For example, historical and prophetic books are treated together in some chapters because in a given chapter they relate to the same biblical period.

A full listing of the books of the Old Testament by main categories appears on page 23.

For Review

- [ ] How many books are in the Catholic canon of the Old Testament? Into what main sections are they divided?
- [ ] Name three books in each of the main sections of the Old Testament.

Begin . . .
at the Beginning

With all this in mind, open the first book of the Old Testament—the Book of Genesis, which tells the story of the Creation and of the first people on earth. As you proceed keep in mind the words of the great modern Jewish thinker Martin Buber. Referring to the Hebrew Scriptures, Buber addressed these words to Christian readers:

> To you, the book is a forecourt;
> to us, it is the sanctuary.
> But in this place,
> we can dwell together,
> and together listen to the voice
> that speaks here.[7]
> (*The Writings of Martin Buber*, page 275)

7

In your own words, write a paragraph explaining the meaning of Martin Buber's statement.

Your word is a lamp to my feet and a light to my path.

Psalm 119:105

2 Beginnings
Stories of God's Creation and Promises

"God saw everything that he had made, and indeed, it was very good" (Genesis 1:31). The ancient Jews must have marveled at the beauties of God's Creation, such as this oasis in Israel.

Much of the Old Testament, including the **Book of Genesis,** was written down and put into final form around the period of the Babylonian exile, in the sixth century B.C. Imagine what that period must have been like for the exiles:

The exile is a time of great crisis for the Israelite people. They have lost their beloved homeland, Judah. Their holy city, Jerusalem, has been conquered, and their sacred Temple, the center of their life, has been destroyed. Here they are, a defeated people forced to live among their captors in Babylon. Babylonian culture and religion, with their strange ways and belief in many destructive, warring gods, feels like a horrendous assault on everything the exiles hold dear.

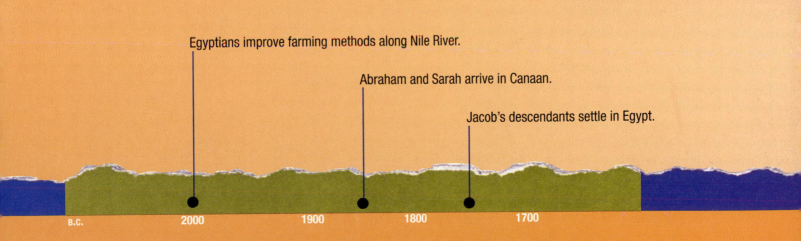

Egyptians improve farming methods along Nile River.

Abraham and Sarah arrive in Canaan.

Jacob's descendants settle in Egypt.

| B.C. | 2000 | 1900 | 1800 | 1700 |

Flowers bloom in the Judean desert.

Disturbing questions gnaw at the exiles: Has God abandoned us? We thought we were the Chosen People of an all-powerful God. Or are the Babylonians right after all? Could the chaotic, competitive gods of the Babylonians really be superior to the one God we worship? Is that why we have been defeated, humiliated, and brought here to this strange, unfriendly land—because our God failed?

In the midst of their doubts and feelings of despair, the exiles desperately need to hear the liberating truth: Our God is in charge—of *everything in the world,* including the Babylonians. God is all good and creates only goodness. We can count on that. Even when we mess things up through our weakness and sin, God brings goodness out of that. Defeat? Nonsense! God can turn even our failures to good if we trust in him with all our heart. We are God's people, and he will never abandon us.

That message of hope and trust in God's goodness did reach the discouraged exiles and their offspring, who after about fifty years were released from Babylon to go back and build a new life in their home country, Judah. The Book of Genesis, put together in its final form during and after the exile, strengthened and lifted the hearts of the returning Israelites (by that time called the Jews, which comes from *Judah*). It helped remind them that from the beginning their God had been in charge, bringing forth goodness out of everything, even out of nothingness! Genesis helped them understand their origins, who they were, and why they should have hope.

Stories of the Origins

The first part of Genesis (which means "beginning"), chapters 1 to 11, is a kind of prehistory of Israel. Various versions of the stories in it were first told by folksingers and storytellers early in Israel's history, as they wove together accounts of "where we came from." The stories are filled with fragments of myths from the ancient Near East. But over the centuries and especially around the time of the exile, the stories were transformed by the Scripture writers, who were guided by the Holy Spirit. The stories became powerful, God-inspired religious tales that expressed Israel's beliefs about God and the world's origins, in stark contrast to the beliefs of their Near East neighbors. Those eleven chapters of Genesis contain the marvelous stories many of us recall from childhood:

- Creation (how the original goodness of Creation came from the one God)
- Adam and Eve and the Fall (how sin entered the world)
- Cain and Abel, Noah and the Flood (how the evil of sin spread)
- the Tower of Babel (how humanity, in terrible condition, was unable to save itself from its own sinfulness)

By the end of Genesis, chapter 11, the stage is set for the great drama that follows, the story of God's relationship with a special people through whom the world would be saved. The rest of Genesis tells of how one man, Abraham, and his descendants down to Joseph became that Chosen People, the Israelites.

But let's begin at the very beginning: "In the beginning . . ."

Creation: Original Goodness

Where did we come from? Why are we here at all? Are we meant to be happy or miserable? Ancient peoples turned these questions over in their minds, as human beings have continued to do right down to today. You may find yourself wondering about them at times.

Many people in the ancient Near East, including the Babylonians, had rather pessimistic answers to these questions. They were **polytheistic** (worshiping many gods) and believed that the world had come from those gods—self-serving, violent, and destructive deities that had made the earth for their own pleasure, and humankind for their slaves. This was a chaotic world where human beings were caught in the middle of the gods' wars, trying to please first one bad-tempered god, then another, to avoid their wrath.

But the ancient Jews had quite a different answer to the question of why we are here at all. Contrast the Babylonians' frightening worldview with the Jewish view in the Book of Genesis of a wonderful world created by God: Out of chaos, the one God brings forth goodness—order, beauty, and

An ancient stone relief depicts magical gods of the Babylonians.

The Prayer of Israel: Praise!

Praise the LORD!

. . . . . .

Praise him, sun and moon;
　　praise him, all you shining stars!
Praise him, you highest heavens,
　　and you waters above the heavens!

. . . .

Praise the LORD from the earth,
　　you sea monsters and all deeps,
fire and hail, snow and frost,
　　stormy wind fulfilling his command!

Mountains and all hills,
　　fruit trees and all cedars!
Wild animals and all cattle,
　　creeping things and flying birds!

Kings of the earth and all peoples,
　　princes and all rulers of the earth!
Young men and women alike,
　　old and young together!

Let them praise the name of the LORD,
　　for his name alone is exalted;
　　his glory is above earth and heaven.

(Psalm 148:1–13)

abundant forms of marvelous life. It is all meant to be wondered at, enjoyed, and cared for by human beings, who are made partners with God in loving all Creation. *1*

1

What difference do a people's beliefs about their origins make to their attitudes about life? Make two columns, one headed, "Babylonians' Attitudes" and the other, "Ancient Jews' Attitudes." In each column, list the attitudes toward life you might expect to see in each group because of the beliefs its members held about how the world and humans came about.

In this first story, the sun and the moon and the stars are not gods that rule humans (as the Babylonians believed them to be) but are *created by* God as good and then are calmly set in their proper place in "the dome" (Genesis 1:7) of the sky. God is in charge. The great sea monsters, perceived as evil demons by many ancient peoples, are shown to be what they are—good, innocent creatures that God loves. When he creates man and woman, they are godlike, made in God's image—full of dignity, not slaves of the gods.

You can sense God's delight in such handiwork: "God saw everything that he had made, and indeed, it was very good" (Genesis 1:31).

Read Genesis 1:1–31; 2:1–4.

A love for life and the world

The beautiful story of Creation underlies a basic attitude in the Judeo-Christian heritage: God is good, we are good, and life is good. He cares about us and all Creation, and wants us to be happy. We are to uphold the inherent dignity and worth of each human being because all are created in God's image. And God has entrusted us with this amazing world to be caretakers, not destroyers, of Creation. He wants full life for every person and intends for us to preserve and watch over the environment.

The Sabbath: A gift of rest

The Creation story tells of God "resting" on the seventh day after such a flurry of creative work. This might seem a curious detail to include: why would God need to rest?

Remember that the story was written during the exile. Keeping the **Sabbath,** a day of rest each week, was a sacred custom the Jews had carried with them to the exile. It marked them as unique among their neighbors. In Babylon the Sabbath took on much importance as a constant reminder for the Jews that they were God's people, not the Babylonians' or their gods'. So the Creation story writer included God's own resting on the seventh day to emphasize the importance of keeping the Sabbath holy as a day to rest, praise God, and be refreshed together— a gift from God, not to be turned down.

I-Witness: Deborah

Lord, I'm Deborah, daughter of Simon, the best carpenter in Babylon. The men in our family have been carpenters since the time of our ancestor Abraham, my father says.

I want to shout my thanks for life! Our Babylonian neighbors don't pray like this, I know. Their gods seem cold and calculating, and their prayers like frightened begging.

My sister married today, and the celebration filled our street with singing and music. We filled our bellies with food and wine, and danced until evening. I couldn't get to sleep, with all the excitement. So I want to share my joy with you.

And to share some sadness too. My older sister and I have been close all our life; she has been almost a mother to me. Now she is leaving for her new husband's town, which is days distant from Babylon. I will miss her greatly.

And it's easy for me to forget what a great gift you have given me. What if I had never had a sister? Her care for me has given me a soft smile and a light heart, and has lighted my path in life this far. Thank you for all that! Amen.

The Garden of Eden, a seventeenth-century painting by Jan Brueghel the Elder

Jews today celebrate the Sabbath from Friday sunset to Saturday sunset. Christians observe a day of rest on Sunday, the day they recall the Resurrection of Jesus Christ. For Christians, the obligation to rest on Sunday replaces the obligation to rest on the Sabbath. *2*

Is it science?

The Creation account in Genesis has stirred up controversy among believers, both Christian and Jewish, especially in the last century. You may have heard of arguments by **creationists,** who insist that the account in Genesis is factually true—that is, God created the world in just seven days, in the order given in the story. On the other side are **evolutionists,** who argue that the uni-

verse has evolved over millions of years, with humankind as a recent part of that evolutionary process. Evolutionists claim that the Bible's Creation account was never intended by its biblical writer to be a factual explanation. Developed in the literary form of a myth, it was meant to convey religious truth, not scientific fact.

The Catholic understanding of the Creation account is that no contradiction exists between the biblical story and the theory of evolution. The Genesis story is about the religious meaning of the origins of the universe, not the scientific facts of those origins. The Church affirms that much scientific evidence supports the evolution theory. But in no way does that shake the religious truth of the Creation account—the truth that God is the source of all goodness, including our own existence as humans made in God's image.

In the story of Creation, we can see the magnificence of God's truth. It is expressed through the inspired poetic genius of its writer, probably a member of the priestly class, who with few words put everything in place.

Adam and Eve: Sin Enters the World

Genesis moves on to another account of Creation, which focuses on the story of **Adam and Eve.** Do not be concerned if some of the

2

"[God] rested on the seventh day" (Genesis 2:2). When was the last time you rested? Create a chart of your typical week, noting how much time is given to schoolwork, school activities, job, family, friends, sleep, and other things you're involved in. Write a paragraph or two about how much time you spend relaxing and unwinding, and how you use that time. If you could say no to one "extra" activity in your life so that you would have more room for relaxing, what would you give up?

details are inconsistent with the first account. Remember, the biblical writers had the job of weaving together a number of different strands from their oral tradition. Sometimes, when inconsistencies arose, they didn't worry about them but let both accounts stand. No doubt they figured that each one contributed some valuable religious truth that they did not want to leave out. From our vantage point, we can see God's inspiration at work in the writers' decisions of what to include.

In the story Adam and Eve are created to enjoy the delightful garden and be intimate companions for each other. They are also privileged to be on walking and talking terms with their Creator. But soon the man and the woman are caught up in disobedience and guilt. They have eaten the forbidden fruit, and feeling naked, they try to cover themselves. When they hear God approaching, they hide. God calls Adam, and his excuse for hiding is his nakedness. Yet earlier Adam was naked and unashamed. God asks if he has eaten the fruit of the tree of knowledge, and Adam, unwilling to take the blame, tries to shift it to Eve. Eve, just as unwilling, accuses the serpent of tricking her.

Thus sin has done its work and ruined Adam and Eve's relationships—with God, between themselves, and with Creation. Now God foretells the consequences of their sin: Man's work will not give him perfect pleasure but will be difficult and will weary him, and woman will be subject to her husband and bear children in pain.

Read Genesis 2:4–25; 3:1–24.

The sin of trying to be equal to God

This story of Creation tells of the **Fall** —that is, the first sin of humankind—termed by Christians **Original Sin.** The "knowledge of good and evil" (Genesis 2:17)—so alluring to Eve and Adam—is the knowledge of all things, and this is God's alone. Adam and Eve are not satisfied with being what they are, finite creatures loved by God and destined for happiness. No, they want to be equal to God. That desire is an illusion, for no one can be God but God. So Adam and Eve choose to rebel against the divine command that human beings should not try to be equal to God. Their sin reminds us of what sin essentially is—the refusal to acknowledge God as God and ourselves as dependent on him. *3*

The Fall of humanity into sin is the source of human suffering. Here, a shopkeeper in Baghdad, Iraq, in 1991, copes with the suffering caused by the Persian Gulf war.

3

In the Fall, Adam and Eve try to be equal to God. List three situations in the world today where human beings are trying to be equal to God and refuse to acknowledge their dependence on him. Write about one of them that you find interesting or inspiring.

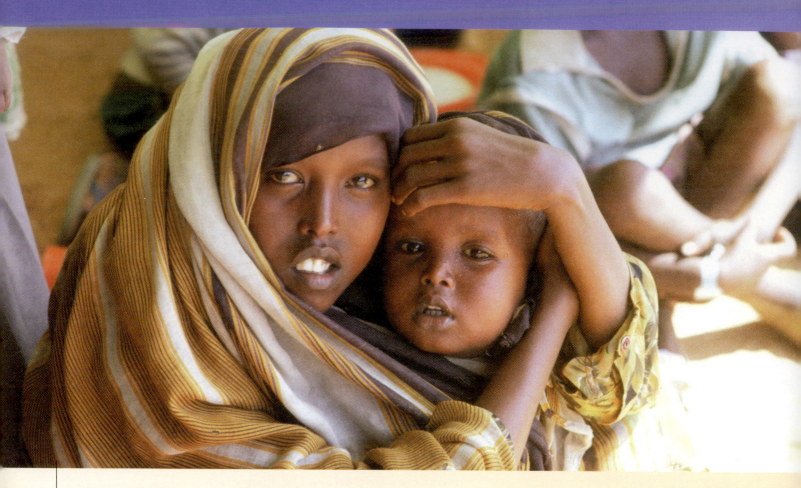

A mother with her baby seeks help during a famine and a civil war in Somalia.

Human freedom and suffering

We must not miss the crucial message that God wanted to convey through the ancient Jewish storytellers: It was free human beings who screwed up life in the garden, not God. Created with freedom, humans can choose to rebel against God. The misery that follows results from free human choice. Thus God does not create injustice in the world; human beings do by their own bad choices. In Catholic Tradition all suffering—even that from natural disasters, illness, and death—stems from the sin of Adam and Eve, not from God.

One might argue that Adam and Eve were tricked by the serpent, so how can we say they were really free? Oddly enough, the trickery in the story is not so different from what most of us experience when we sin. Like the serpent deceiving Adam and Eve, we delude and trick ourselves into thinking that the bad we choose is really good for us, that we know better than God. Then are we really free? Yes, the biblical storytellers would say, because such self-deception and rationalizing for the purpose of going against what God wants is itself a free choice. We don't *have* to be tricked by our own desires—we choose to be!

Sin's Spread: Cain and Abel

Like ripples in a pond, sin will spread out over the ages and touch everyone. Genesis describes sin's spread first with a story about hatred between brothers that ends in murder, then with a story about depravity in society, and finally with one about arrogance among the nations.

The story of **Cain and Abel** tells of two brothers, sons of Adam and Eve—the first a farmer, the second a shepherd—offering gifts to God in sacrifice. God blesses only Abel's sacrifice and encourages Cain to rise above his jealousy. Angry, Cain murders Abel. So the first sin has begun to affect the human family, in the form of another sin, murder. As if that were not enough, in response to God's inquiry about Abel's whereabouts, we hear Cain's insolent, hypocritical reply, "Am I my brother's keeper?" (Genesis 4:9). Those familiar words are echoed even today in the responses of people who want to deny they have any responsibility toward others. *4*

Read Genesis 4:1–16.

More Sin and a Promise: Noah and the Flood

The account of the **Flood** tells of how bad things can get once sin spreads its ugliness. There is such depravity on the earth that God regrets creating the human race.

Only one man, **Noah,** finds favor with God and is instructed to build an ark to protect himself, his family, and some animals from destruction. Noah does as God com-

Through the story of Noah and the Flood, the rainbow has become a sign of the covenant, reminding us of God's love for every creature on earth.

mands, the Flood comes, and the ark safely rides the waters until they recede. All other creatures are destroyed.

Leaving the ark, Noah offers a sacrifice of thanksgiving. The story of Noah ends with God's first **covenant,** or solemn promise—with Noah because he obeyed.

Read Genesis, chapters 6 to 8; 9:1–17.

God's word saves us

The story of Noah is probably related to other similar flood stories found in ancient literature. The tale's authors were not interested in figuring out historical causes of the flood, if indeed such a flood occurred, but in teaching the powerful truth that whoever hears and obeys God's word will be saved and whoever does not, will be lost.

"Saved from what?" is the question. We know that devout people are not necessarily saved from disaster. Even those who Jesus says will live forever are not saved from calamity in this life.

4

"Am I my brother's keeper?" What does it mean to be responsible for another person? Perhaps someone in your school, neighborhood, family, or workplace, or some group in your community is at risk or in trouble. Is it *your* job to help them? Share your thoughts on this in a one-page essay.

The story of Babel points to the contemporary tendency to hustle through life seeking power, wealth, and dominance—without a thought for God.

The answer is that hearing and keeping God's word save us from forgetting how to love and serve. When we *do* forget how to love, something happens inside us, where it is unseen. We turn hard and cold, perhaps not instantly but gradually. Our warm, fleshy heart eventually turns to cold stone without our even being aware of it. *That* is the awful fate that God wants to save us from.

The rainbow: A sign of a promise

The end of the Flood is marked with a rainbow as a sign of God's love for every creature on the earth, and a promise that the world will never again be destroyed by a flood. This promise is the first instance in the Bible of a covenant, or solemn agreement, between God and human beings.

The next time you see a rainbow, allow yourself to feel the hope that rainbows seem

to nurture in us human beings. Remember how dearly God loves the earth.

An Arrogant World: The Tower of Babel

The last of the prehistory stories in Genesis is the tale of **Babel**. Once again humankind tries to carve out a destiny of its own making. Here the presumptuous ambition of Adam and Eve to be equal to God is projected on a grand scale when the nations try to build a tower with its summit in the heavens so they can "make a name for themselves." God comes down to see the tower, is appalled by the nations' arrogance, and stops them by confusing their language and dispersing the peoples. [5]

Read Genesis 11:1–9.

The presumption of the nations

The story of Babel is not about how the earth's people came to have different languages or be dispersed. Rather, it shows how sin has spread to affect even the behavior of the nations, who seek glory in power, might, wealth, superiority, and dominance—without a thought for God. Today the nightly newscasts are filled with stories of such attempts, as well as stories of the pain, corruption, and devastation they beget. [6]

Thus the first eleven chapters of Genesis tell about God's good purpose for the world, but then how things went wrong when human beings arrogantly chose to try to be God's equal and how this sin spread over the world. These prehistory chapters come to a close with the world in a terrible state, desperately in need of God's salvation.

5

In a paragraph, compare the story of Babel, which illustrates the effect of sin, to the story of Pentecost (Acts 2:1–21), which illustrates the effect of the Holy Spirit. Find a newspaper clipping showing the effect of sin in our society, and another that shows the effect of good.

6

Create a story that shows the destructive nature of sin, especially how one act of sin can lead to another and another.

If the first part of Genesis explains why things went wrong in the world, the second part tells how God chose a people to start setting things right again. This latter part of Genesis, the focus of the remainder of this chapter, tells stories about the founders of the Israelites, the people chosen as the instrument through whom God would save the world.

For Review

- [ ] How did the Book of Genesis lift the hearts of the exiles as they returned to their homeland, Judah?
- [ ] Summarize the difference between the Jewish view of the origins of the world and the Babylonian view.
- [ ] In the Creation story, why is it said that God rested on the seventh day?
- [ ] What is the Catholic understanding of how the biblical Creation account relates to the theory of evolution?
- [ ] What do Adam and Eve desire by eating of the tree of the "knowledge of good and evil" (Genesis 2:17)?
- [ ] According to the story of the Fall, who is responsible for suffering and injustice in the world—God or human beings?
- [ ] Which Genesis stories tell about the spread of sin after the first sin?
- [ ] To whom does God offer the first covenant? Why is it offered, and what is the sign of that event?

7

Identify someone you know of who left behind all that was familiar to him or her in order to follow the call of some good purpose. If possible, ask the person what the experience was like and write it up in one page.

Abraham: The Father of Biblical Faith

Like the stories about Creation, the stories of the founders were remembered and told for centuries before they were written down. Unlike the stories of Creation, the stories of the patriarchs and the matriarchs take place in historical times. Their setting is a period about four thousand years ago (2000 to 1700 B.C.).

The first of these stories tells about **Abraham,** the father of biblical faith, and his wife, **Sarah**. Through Abraham and his descendants, God would establish a people, a "nation," through which he would save the world. It all begins with the story of a man who is willing to follow God's call wherever it leads him. Abraham and Sarah first appear in the Book of Genesis with the names **Abram** and **Sarai.**

The Call of Abram and God's Promise

Among the Semitic nomads wandering the highlands of the Near East is a man named Abram. (The word *Semites* refers to a number of ancient peoples of the Near East, from whom the Israelites descended.) Abram travels from the city of Ur to the city of Haran (see the map on page 42), and it is in Haran that he hears God's call. God bids Abram to take his family away from all that is familiar and go to a land "that I will show you" (Genesis 12:1). And God promises that from Abram's offspring will come a great nation, a blessing for the world. This is the first mention of God's **Promise** to the people who would become Israel. Abram takes Sarai, his nephew **Lot,** and all his possessions, and goes, not knowing where God is leading him or what to expect. In faith he follows a God he does not yet know to the land called **Canaan.** *7*
Read Genesis 12:1–9.

let God lead him—and became the father of the faith of the Jews, the Christians, and the Muslims. Recall the story of Babel, where human beings close themselves off to God in the illusion that they are "on top," in control. Their arrogance brought disaster! Abram, on the other hand, was humble before God. He was open to God's purpose for his life, and was willing to leave behind all that was familiar to follow God's call. He knew he was not in control; God was. Thus God was able to accomplish great things through Abram.

Count the Stars If You Can

Years pass, and Abram and his family travel to other lands and arrive back in Canaan. But still there are no children. Having waited faithfully and grown older, Abram begins to doubt that he will have a son. Imagine him sitting in his tent one night, gently complaining to God in prayer. He has no child; Sarai is barren, apparently unable to bear children. Is he to adopt a son?

In answer God tells Abram to look up at the stars and count them if he can. God promises that Abram's descendants will outnumber the stars. And Abram believes, despite the apparent impossibility of it all.

Read Genesis 15:1–6.

By *descendants* God refers to all who believe or will believe because Abram believes. It is a beautiful story for a starry night or for a time when faith burns low and discouragement seems to press the spirit. In the Christian faith, this promise is ultimately fulfilled when God sends his only son, Jesus Christ, to live with humans.

An Alternative Plan: Hagar

Sarai continues to be childless. She finally proposes that Abram take her Egyptian maid, **Hagar,** as a concubine and beget a child by her, which would legally belong to Sarai. (As we will see later, God still intends for Sarai to bear a child. God's plans cannot be foiled that easily by human tinkering with

A new God

The story of Abram's call is about Abram's struggle to understand the mystery of the gods—until it comes to him that one God is above all other gods. Abram's call probably came the way that God's call comes to anyone: silently, subtly, during the search for answers that we call prayer.

Abram may not have understood God as the *only* God, but as the God he would worship above all others. Even though belief in the one God is the cornerstone of Judaism, it was not yet clear to the people of Abram's time. But from a later perspective, Jews recognized the God of Abram as *the* one and only God.

Abraham humble

Letting God lead

Abram, an old man whose wife was childless and beyond her childbearing years,

God told Abraham that his descendants would be more numerous than the stars. Today, Jews from around the world gather at the Western Wall in Jerusalem.

destiny.) This idea works, but not without a lot of bad feeling between the two women. At one point the pregnant Hagar runs away to flee the harshness of her mistress. In the wilderness a messenger of God appears to her. At his command she returns to submit to Sarai, fortified by the promise that her unborn son, **Ishmael,** will grow to manhood wild and free.

Read Genesis 16:1–16.

Concubines and polygamy

The customs in early biblical times of taking concubines and of practicing **polygamy**—that is, taking more than one wife—need some explanation: If a wife was barren, a female servant might become a surrogate childbearer, a concubine to the husband. Or the husband might take a second wife in order to give the family children. Both of these practices helped to assure the survival of the tribe. The story of Adam and Eve suggests, however, that **monogamy**—taking only one wife—was the biblical ideal.

The Sign of the Covenant

God establishes with Abram a covenant, a solemn pledge on both sides. This repeats the covenant made previously with Abram—the Promise that he will bring forth a multitude of descendants, and that all the land of Canaan eventually will be his people's. The sign of the covenant between God and the people is a ritual for all males, **circumcision** (the removal of the foreskin of the penis), which identifies Abram's people as God's people. To reflect this new status and identity, Abram's name is changed to Abraham and Sarai's to Sarah.

Read Genesis 17:1–22.

Visited by Strangers

Abraham is sitting at the entrance to his tent in the heat of the day when he is approached by three strangers—who, we later learn, represent God. In a beautiful display of graciousness, Abraham offers them refreshment, water for bathing, and a place to rest.

According to the custom of the time, Sarah, as a woman, is not present in this scene, but she is listening behind the flap of the tent. When she hears one of the visitors say that in a year she will bear a son, she laughs out loud. The visitor answers her laugh with, "Is anything too wonderful for the LORD?" (Genesis 18:14). The story, rich in color and detail, repeats God's promise to Abraham that one day he will be a father of nations. *8*

Read Genesis 18:1–15.

Hospitality: "Entertaining angels"

The story of the visit to Abraham highlights a solemn obligation of biblical times: the giving of **hospitality.** For a traveler in the wilderness, hospitality was a matter of survival, and to be refused hospitality was sometimes a death sentence.

Abraham and Sarah offer generous hospitality out of pure kindness, without any inkling that these mysterious guests represent God and have something marvelous to tell them. The Letter to the Hebrews in the New Testament hints at this story, which would have been quite familiar to readers of the letter, with these words: "Do not neglect to show hospitality to strangers, for by doing that some have entertained angels without knowing it" (13:2). *9*

"Laugh"

Both Abraham and Sarah laugh when told they will have a son of their own (Genesis 17:17; 18:12). These verses contain a bit of wordplay: **Isaac,** the name that God gives to their son-to-be, means "laugh" in Hebrew.

Pleading with God

As the story continues, God reveals to Abraham a plan to destroy the wicked cities of **Sodom and Gomorrah** if the complaints against their inhabitants are found true. Abraham pleads for the safety of his nephew Lot, who lives in Sodom, and again and again presses God not to destroy the just people along with the wicked in this infamous city—even if they number only a few. God graciously agrees. It is amusing but also touching to hear the dialogue as Abraham bargains, successfully, with his God. *10*

In Sodom the wicked inhabitants propose the rape of some young men (or angels) to whom Lot has given shelter. Rape is evil at

8

"Is anything too wonderful for the LORD?" Sarah laughs when she hears she will have a child in her old age. But with God nothing is impossible, nothing is too wonderful! Write about a wonderful event from your life. What were the circumstances? Did you expect it to happen?

When Abraham said yes to God's call, he received the gift of *expectant faith*—knowing, with all his heart and soul, that God would take care of him, bless him, *amaze* him. This journey would be a wonder-filled, God-filled adventure. We, too, can *expect* that God is with us every moment of our life.

9

Usually we associate hospitality with physical needs being met, like Abraham and Sarah did for the desert travelers. But more than offering food, drink, or rest, hospitality is about offering friendship and a safe presence. Think about a person with whom you feel *safe.* Perhaps it is someone who listens to you without judgment, or doesn't attach strings to your relationship. Maybe she or he is a good secret keeper, or is always encouraging you. In writing, describe that person and the effect she or he has in your life. Then consider simple ways you can show warmth, safety, and care—hospitality—to the people who make up the fabric of your life.

any time but doubly heinous considering the life-giving hospitality required by guests. Lot offers his own daughters in order to protect his guests—to no avail. So the cities will be destroyed, except for Lot and his family, the only just people remaining in those wicked places. The angels rescue Lot and his family. In the well-known ending to the story, Lot's wife, curious about the fate of the cities, looks back to check out the destruction and turns into a pillar of salt—a famous but unimportant biblical detail.

Read Genesis 18:16–33; 19:1–29.

Enter Isaac, Exit Ishmael

Isaac is born, and now Sarah's laughter is of a joyful kind. Hagar is expelled because Sarah fears that Ishmael might threaten Isaac's inheritance. Again we must admire Hagar's behavior. Alone in the wilderness with no water left and thinking that her boy will die, she walks some distance away from him because she cannot bear to watch his suffering. Then, aided by an angel of the Lord, Hagar finds a spring and saves her son. Ishmael goes on, with God's blessing, to live in the wilderness and eventually take a wife. The story is a tribute to Hagar's perseverance and faith.

Read Genesis 21:1–21.

10

Expecting God's goodness to prevail, Abraham does not give up. Abraham *pleads* with him to protect Lot and his family. Who is someone you care about so much that you would plead with God on his or her behalf? Is it someone who is in trouble? hurting? lost or confused? angry? Write a conversation between you and God about this person dear to your heart.

Abraham's hospitality to strangers in the wilderness illustrates the obligation to welcome and care for those in need.
Vietnamese children wait at a refugee camp in Hong Kong to be settled into countries that will accept them.

The Founders' Journeys

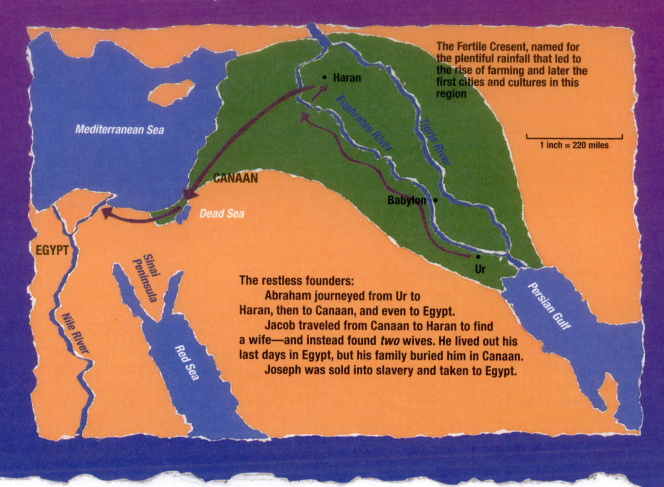

The Fertile Cresent, named for the plentiful rainfall that led to the rise of farming and later the first cities and cultures in this region

Mediterranean Sea

Haran

Euphrates River

Tigris River

1 inch = 220 miles

CANAAN

Dead Sea

Babylon

EGYPT

Sinai Peninsula

Nile River

Ur

Red Sea

Persian Gulf

The restless founders:
Abraham journeyed from Ur to Haran, then to Canaan, and even to Egypt.
Jacob traveled from Canaan to Haran to find a wife—and instead found *two* wives. He lived out his last days in Egypt, but his family buried him in Canaan.
Joseph was sold into slavery and taken to Egypt.

A God who chooses imperfect people

Curiously, Hagar emerges from the Genesis story more noble than the ancestral heroes Abraham and Sarah. Hagar is portrayed very sympathetically, even though Sarah's son, not Hagar's, is the one God intends to be the ancestor of the Chosen People.

11

How do you define *hero?* Make a list of your "heroic ancestors," including family heroes as well as national ones. Pick three and write a brief reflection for each about what makes him or her a hero. Be sure to include the hero's imperfections as well as his or her good points. How has he or she made a difference in your life?

The Jews did not try to whitewash their heroes. Instead they showed that God had chosen a people far from perfect. Yet in spite of their faults, God was able to make them a light to the world. And that says something encouraging to all of us imperfect people. *11*

What of poor Hagar? Does God love her any less than Sarah? Is that why her son is not chosen to be an ancestor of the Israelites? The story makes it clear that God holds her and her offspring in the most tender care. Being chosen does not necessarily mean being more worthy, as the Israelites will be reminded over and over in their checkered history with their God.

Ishmael's destiny

Tradition has made Ishmael a **bedouin,** that is, a nomadic Arab, and the **father of the Arab peoples.** The religion of the Muslims, **Islam,** developed many centuries after biblical times among the Arabs. Thus Muslims claim Abraham as their father in faith through the line of Ishmael. So Abraham is considered the ancestor of all three great **monotheistic** (worshiping one God) religions in the world today: Judaism, Christianity, and Islam.

Abraham's Sacrifice

The next story is often called **Abraham's test.** In it, God bids Abraham to take Isaac, the son he loves with all his heart, to a place on a mountain and sacrifice him as a holocaust— that is, a burnt offering. Abraham responds by immediately setting out for the mountain with the boy. In answer to Isaac's question about what they will sacrifice, Abraham can only say, filled with faith, that God will provide a lamb. At the last moment, an angel of God stops Abraham from killing his son, and instead provides a ram for the sacrifice. *12*

Read Genesis 22:1–19.

A story of faithfulness

Most modern readers strongly object to the idea that God would ask anyone to kill his or her child. But that is not the point of the story for the biblical writer, who wants us to focus on the faithfulness between Abraham and God.

Think for a moment about how much Isaac must have meant to Abraham. He and Sarah had longed for a child for years. Moreover, it was supposed to be through Isaac that God's promise to Abraham would be fulfilled. And we can imagine that most parents would rather die themselves than see their children die. In a way then, by asking Abraham to give up his only son, God is asking Abraham to give up more than if he had asked him to give up his own life! God seems to be asking, "Are you willing to give up everything for me?"

Abraham's unhesitating obedience to God's command dramatically demonstrates the extent of his faithfulness and his complete trust in God's goodness. Abraham knows that everything—even human life—comes from and belongs to God. But he also trusts that "God himself will provide" (Genesis 22:7) what is good.

Abraham's faith and trust in God are not in vain. Abraham entrusted everything to God, who responded by giving it all back to him, plus much more. Because of his great faith, Abraham became the father of all people who place their trust and faith in God.

This story has special significance for Christians, who see in it a foreshadowing of Jesus' saving death and Resurrection. Just as Abraham was willing to give his only son to God, God was willing to give his only Son, Jesus Christ, to humanity. Just as God provided a ram in order to save Isaac's life,

When Hagar finds a spring in the wilderness, she understands God's tender care for her and her son.

12

Write your own reactions to the story of Abraham's test. What questions does that story raise for you?

God provided Jesus—whom Christians call the "lamb of God"—in order to save all humanity from sin and death.

Some readers still wonder whether this story shows God approving of child sacrifice. But notice that God prevented Abraham from carrying out the sacrifice of his son. While child sacrifice to the gods was not uncommon among the cultures of the time, many Scripture scholars believe that the story of Abraham's test confirms that God forbids human sacrifice, as do other passages in the Old Testament (see 2 Kings 16:3 and Micah 6:7).

Isaac and Rebekah: Best Biblical Romance

Abraham returns home and at Sarah's death buys a field in which to bury her, the first piece of ground that his people possess in a land that will one day be theirs.

Isaac grows up, and Abraham, facing his own death, instructs his steward to find a bride for Isaac from among their tribe back in Haran. Now we have a novella—a little masterpiece of storytelling. Rich detail, exotic marriage customs, and the loveliness and generosity of **Rebekah** are woven together in the most beautiful of all the biblical romances. We see Rebekah's adventurous spirit

World Happenings from 2000 to 1700 B.C.

Africa
The Egyptian pharaohs no longer build pyramids as their tombs. Instead they are buried in tombs deeply tunneled into the walls of the hills on the western side of the Nile River.

America
The Eskimo culture begins on the Bering Strait. Pottery is made in Mexican villages.

China
The potter's wheel is introduced. Pigs, dogs, oxen, goats, and sheep are domesticated.

Europe
Early cultures begin using bronze to make tools and weapons. The Stonehenge circle in England is used for religious and astronomical ceremonies. Culture on the island of Crete is at its height; the bull-god is worshiped at the city of Knossos.

India
Chickens and elephants are domesticated. Sacrifice is offered in the worship of a mother-goddess.

The Near East
Around 2000 B.C. the destruction of Ur, the Near East's major city, results in the decline of the dominant culture.

when she agrees to leave Haran immediately, over the protests of her kin. The story ends with the bride glimpsing Isaac as she approaches her new home and Isaac taking her to his tent, where he marries her. In Rebekah he finds comfort after the death of his mother.

Abraham marries again and has many children by another woman. When he dies—at the age of one hundred and seventy-five—Isaac and Ishmael bury him next to Sarah in the family's field.

Read Genesis 24:1–67.

Abraham's great age

Abraham's unbelievable age at his death is an exaggeration common in biblical stories. It is a way of saying that Abraham was wise and blessed.

And so the story unfolds. Through many ins and outs, heroic moments, laughter, sinfulness, and sadness, God is at work. First through Abraham and Sarah, then through Isaac and Rebekah, God is keeping the Promise to fashion a people who will be God's own, and a blessing for all the nations. After the disaster of the Fall and the rampant spread of sin and depravity over the earth, it looks as though God is beginning to put the world back together again.

But the drama is just getting started. . . .

For Review

☐ Who is called the father of biblical faith?

☐ What does God promise to Abram as the covenant? What is the sign of that covenant for Abram's people?

☐ Why are Sodom and Gomorrah destroyed?

☐ Who is traditionally known as the father of the Arab peoples?

☐ What is emphasized as a forbidden act in the story of Abraham's test?

☐ Which of Abraham's sons is destined to become an ancestor of the Israelites? Whom does that son marry?

Jacob: A Man Named Israel

Once again, in the stories about Isaac and Rebekah's son Jacob, the biblical writer shows God at work building a people—making sure, by hook or by crook, that the divine purposes are accomplished. And in the case of Jacob, a bit of the "crook" is definitely involved.

A Birthright Stolen, a Blessing Ripped Off

From the time of her pregnancy, Rebekah knows that the younger of the twins she will bear (the one to be born second) is destined to be the principal heir to Isaac's goods and, most important, heir to his leadership of the tribe. By rights, the elder, the firstborn of the twins, should succeed his father. But Rebekah is convinced that God's purpose is otherwise, and she devotes herself to maneuvering the younger twin into the position of heir. This move will entail some deception, which Rebekah seems quite ready to engage in.

The twins are born—first **Esau,** the shaggy redhead, and then **Jacob,** following close behind, grasping Esau's heel as if trying to get ahead of him. Clued in about his destiny by his mother as a child, the young man Jacob manages to trick Esau into swearing over his birthright to him.

In time, father Isaac, old and failing in his eyesight, wants to give his dear elder son, Esau, his blessing to seal his right to head the clan. Rebekah, ever alert on Jacob's behalf, stages an elaborate deception of her husband so that Jacob, not Esau, will get Isaac's blessing. In a scene that would make a hilarious charade, Jacob puts goatskin on his neck and wrists so as to feel like hairy Esau to his near-blind father. Sure enough, the little drama works, and Jacob gets the prized blessing. Aghast, Isaac realizes he has been deceived, but he cannot take back his blessing once given. The furious Esau vows to kill Jacob one day.

Read Genesis 27:1–41.

Rebekah's good intent

For all her presumption, Rebekah sincerely believes that the will of God in this affair is in her hands. She strives to obey it at great personal risk. *13*

Jacob Journeys to Haran

To escape Esau's fury, Jacob suddenly must flee to Haran, where Abraham first heard his call from God so many years before. The young man can also find a suitable wife there, not a Canaanite that his mother would frown upon. Jacob—young, feisty, and self-satisfied—sets off with Isaac's blessing. Camping the first night, he dreams of angels ascending and descending from heaven (have you ever heard the old spiritual "Jacob's Ladder"?). He hears the voice of God repeat the Promise made to Abraham, and names the place **Bethel,** meaning "the house or abode of God."

Read Genesis 27:42–46; 28:1–5,10–22.

A brash young man

In the final scene of this episode, Jacob seems to choose the terms of the relationship with God (Genesis 28:20–21). But God, not people, initiates covenants. Jacob sounds like a brash young man who feels that it is his right to bargain with God.

Life in Haran

Arriving in Haran, Jacob stays at the home of his uncle **Laban.** He is so good at helping with the flocks that Laban would like to keep him there, and marry off both of his daughters to Jacob as well. Jacob is in love with the younger, **Rachel.** But Laban tricks him into marrying the older sister, **Leah,** after seven years and then has him wait seven more years before giving him Rachel in marriage.

The years pass, and Jacob is older and wiser, although no less conniving. He has two wives, two concubines, and many children, and is totally fed up with Laban. In a kind of midlife crisis, he remembers the land of Canaan and God's Promise and wants to return home. So he and his substantial household of wives, slaves, and flocks set off for Canaan.

A Strange Encounter on the Way to the Promised Land

Midway to Canaan, Jacob remembers Esau. Fearful of his brother's anger, Jacob sends herdsmen ahead with large flocks of animals to be given as gifts to placate him. In his fright Jacob reminds God, to whom he was almost flippant many years before, of the promise of protection, which he now desperately needs.

Reaching the border of Canaan, Jacob shepherds his family and flocks across a river

13

In the Israelites' understanding, things would work out the way God wanted them to—no matter what or who tried to get in the way. God could bring good out of situations that were weird, puzzling, unfair, or evil. Write a one-page reflection on this idea, including examples from your own life, if possible.

and, staying alone on the other side, has a strange encounter, the meaning of which continues to puzzle biblical commentators.

The mysterious being who meets Jacob in this story has been called by translators a stranger, a man, an angel—some even suggest a demon. This "someone" wrestles with Jacob until the break of day, when Jacob, refusing to let go, asks for a blessing. In reply the stranger asks his name, and when he says that it is Jacob, he is told that from now on he will be known as **Israel,** meaning "one who has contended with divine and human beings." Left alone as the sun rises, Jacob marvels that he has seen God face-to-face and has not died. *14*

Read Genesis 32:23–32.

A curtain-raising story

In the context of biblical history, this is a curtain-raising story. Jacob is returning to the destiny long ago promised, to the land of Canaan, and to his place among the people chosen to be a blessing to the nations. He has been named Israel by God, and his descendants, the chosen ones, will be known as the Israelites.

Family Worship of God

Jacob continues on to meet and make peace with Esau. He then goes to Bethel and builds an altar on the spot where he heard God's promise on his outward journey. He orders his family to rid themselves of the trappings of their pagan religion—not only the household gods but also their ornaments, earrings, even clothing—in a purification rite that initiates the family into the worship of the

14

Imagine a young person "wrestling" with God. What issues might he or she be struggling with? Write a story describing the situation.

Jacob and his family returned to Canaan to settle, perhaps at a desert oasis like this bedouin sheepherding settlement.

God of Israel. Again God transfers to Jacob the blessing given to Abraham and Isaac, the Promise of the land of Canaan and a royal line that is to be a blessing to the nations.

In a short passage, we are told of the death of Rachel at the birth of her second son, **Benjamin.** Jacob returns home and finds Isaac still alive. At his death Jacob and Esau bury their father in the field where Abraham and Sarah lie.

Read Genesis 35:1–29.

For Review

☐ Why does Rebekah try to maneuver Jacob into the position of principal heir of Isaac?

☐ What strange encounter does Jacob have on the way back to Canaan? What new name is he given then, and what does it mean?

☐ How does Jacob initiate his family into the worship of the God of Israel?

Joseph: Treachery, Triumph, and Forgiveness

The stories about Joseph are also about his father, Jacob, because God is not finished with Jacob yet. These famous tales also drive home the message that keeping God's word brings rewards far beyond anything imaginable—and that he can bring good out of even the most wicked of deeds and desperate of circumstances.

Sold into Slavery

Joseph, Rachel's first son, is seventeen years old and Jacob's favorite. Some of his brothers—Dan, Naphtali, Gad, and Asher—however, dislike Joseph because after he tended flocks with them, he told his father tales about their behavior. The others resent him for being his father's favorite, the son of Jacob's beloved Rachel. Jacob has a long, flowing tunic made for Joseph—the garb of tent dwellers, not shepherds, and unlike the short, coarse garments that his brothers wear. Worse, Joseph's dreams contain portents that one day he will lord it over his family. When he rashly recounts these dreams, even Jacob rebukes him. The scene is set for his undoing.

One day the brothers are tending the flocks some distance away from home, and Jacob sends Joseph to see if things are well with them. As the brothers watch him approach wearing his long, flowing coat—hardly the clothing for a hike in the country—they plot to kill him and throw his body down a well. But **Reuben** has no heart for such a deed and suggests that instead they put Joseph into a dry well, for Reuben plans to return later to rescue him. The brothers do this and then sit down to eat—the writer's comment on their callousness.

Seeing traders on the way to Egypt, **Judah** suggests that they sell Joseph instead

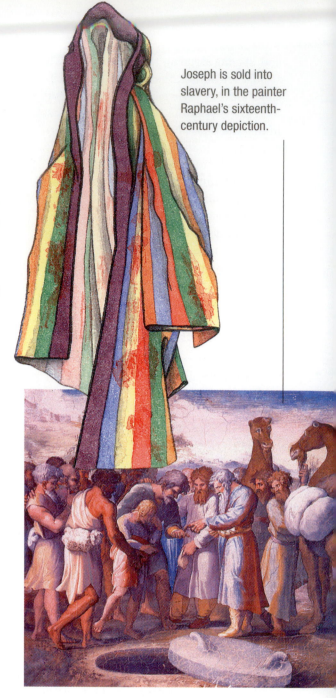

Joseph is sold into slavery, in the painter Raphael's sixteenth-century depiction.

and avoid having his blood on their hands. The deed is done, and the brothers hide it by showing Joseph's coat, which they have dipped in goat's blood, to Jacob. Seeing the bloody coat, Jacob believes that Joseph has been killed by a wild animal. Jacob tears his own garments and mourns the loss of Joseph for many days. *15*

Read Genesis 37:1–35.

A melodrama

Here are all the elements of a family saga. Consider the parts of this melodrama:

- Jacob's favoritism
- Joseph's talebearing and boastfulness
- the brothers' envy and betrayal
- the brothers' deception of their father, Jacob (they seem to have inherited some of his traits)

The wonder is that sinful and guilty as they are, God will lead these men to self-knowledge and remorse, some even to heroism and holiness.

Joseph's Fate in Egypt

Once in Egypt Joseph does quite well for himself. Though a slave, he is given considerable responsibility under the pharaoh's chief steward. But Joseph lands in prison, falsely accused of rape by the steward's lustful wife, who has tried unsuccessfully to seduce the handsome young man.

Even in prison, though, Joseph is singled out as special. The knack for interpreting dreams that got him in such trouble with his brothers comes in handy when Joseph is asked to explain the pharaoh's dreams to him. He does so well at it that he gains the pharaoh's favor.

By the age of thirty, Joseph has been made governor of Egypt, second only to the pharaoh in power. He has married a beautiful Egyptian woman, and they have two sons, Manasseh and Ephraim.

Then severe famine strikes the whole Near East, including Egypt. But years earlier Joseph had predicted the famine through the pharaoh's dreams, and fortunately he has been storing up grain supplies for just such a

15

Do you identify with the feelings of any of the characters in the beginning of this story: the favorite son? the brothers? Reuben? Write a paragraph describing how families can be harmed by jealousy or favoritism.

disaster. People from all over the Near East go to Egypt to buy grain from the Egyptian surplus.

Read Genesis, chapters 39 to 41.

The Brothers on Joseph's Turf

You can probably imagine what comes next. Back in Canaan, Jacob sends ten of his sons to Egypt to buy grain for the family's survival. And who is in charge of grain sales? Governor Joseph, of course.

Joseph's brothers, however, do not recognize him, and so Joseph takes the opportunity to toy with them a bit. He pretends to think they are spies and puts them in prison, refusing to sell them grain. Then he decides to let them go with the grain on condition they will return with their younger brother, Benjamin (as Jacob's dearest child after Joseph, Benjamin has not been allowed to come along on the trip). And they must leave one of the brothers, Simeon, as a pledge until they return.

Back home, the brothers plead with Jacob to let them take Benjamin to Egypt so they can rescue the brother they left behind. Reuben even offers his own sons as a pledge for Benjamin's safety. But Jacob is adamant: they may not take his beloved Benjamin.

Read Genesis 42:1–38.

Jacob's Sacrifice

Eventually Jacob's clan needs grain again, but without Benjamin the brothers cannot go back to Egypt for it. After bemoaning the terrible price he must pay, Jacob finally consents to part with Benjamin because his people must live. The sacrifice will take him to his grave, he cries—surely plucking out his beard—but he will do it.

Read Genesis 43:1–14.

The great Jacob

We want to shout, "Hooray, Jacob!" Up until this point we have not seen a lot to admire in Jacob's character. Consider his

And he kissed all his brothers and wept upon them; and after that his brothers talked with him. Genesis 45:15

lifelong deceit, craft, and greed. Not until the moment when he agrees to sacrifice Benjamin (as Abraham was willing to do with his own son generations before) does Jacob reach heroic heights and become one of the great saints of the Scriptures.

Return, Reunion, Reconciliation

Back the brothers go to Egypt, and on arriving they are invited to Joseph's house for a banquet—still unaware that he is the brother they sold into slavery. When Joseph sees Benjamin, he leaves the room to weep. Later, when Joseph sits down to eat, he sends tidbits from his own plate to share with Benjamin as a gesture of royal favor.

When the brothers prepare at last to leave with their grain, the steward hides Joseph's own goblet in Benjamin's sack as a plant. Once they are on their way, Joseph sends servants after them. The cup is found, and Joseph orders Benjamin to stay behind as a slave. Now Judah steps forward and, in a beautiful speech, pleads with Joseph to consider the aged father who will die if Benjamin fails to return. Judah pledges his own life in

Benjamin's place, and Joseph, close to tears, sends everyone but the brothers from the room.

Weeping so loudly that the others hear him in the hall, Joseph finally reveals his identity, forbidding his brothers to blame themselves for their past misdeeds. Everything was allowed to happen, he says, so that when they were in danger of starving, someone would be there to feed them. Joseph's story is a tale of reconciliation and redemption. *16*

Read Genesis 43:15–34; 44:1–34; 45:1–28.

Everyone grows

Not only does Jacob get a bigger heart in this story; Joseph and his brothers do as well. Joseph, who in his youth was boastful and proud, has the heart to forgive his brothers their wicked deed of selling him into slavery. The brothers have grown, becoming ready to make sacrifices for the well-being of those they love. The whole family has developed from bitterness and hate to tender appreciation of one another.

Happy Ending

So all ends happily. The brothers return home, fetch Jacob and his family, journey back to Egypt, and settle there. Jacob is rewarded for his sacrifice of Benjamin by seeing all his sons reunited. In his old age, Jacob adopts Joseph's two sons, Manasseh and Ephraim—which is why they are listed as two of the twelve tribes of Israel. When Jacob dies, Joseph takes his body back to Canaan for burial. Joseph also lives to an old age and makes his brothers swear that whenever their

16

In Joseph we find a beautiful example of forgiveness: Joseph forgives his brothers for the extremely hostile and jealous act of selling him into slavery and abandoning him. Write about a person or group in our world who is in need of forgiveness. What was the wrongdoing? Describe any obstacles to forgiving. What could be the outcome of forgiveness in this situation? What might happen if forgiveness is withheld?

people return to the land of God's Promise, his bones will be taken there to be buried in the field where Abraham, Sarah, Isaac, and Jacob lie.

The stories of the patriarchs are all tales with happy endings—astonishingly so. Joseph's last request reveals, however, that the saga of ancient Israel is not over.

Stories Jesus heard

The personalities in the stories of Joseph are so alive and believable and the events drawn in such detail that they seem to be eyewitness accounts. These are the tales that Jesus heard—tales told to him by Mary and Joseph, by the rabbi at the synagogue school, or on feast days at worship. The blood of Joseph and his family flowed in Jesus' veins, and he must have loved them with all his heart.

For Review

- [ ] What do Joseph's brothers do to him as a young man, and why?
- [ ] How does Joseph gain the pharaoh's favor?
- [ ] How does Jacob become a hero?
- [ ] In what ways do Joseph and his brothers grow through the story?

Nourished Spirits

Imagine how the Genesis stories must have bolstered the spirits of the exiled Israelites in Babylon. They could see in these stories the pattern of God's work: *God worked with simple, flawed human beings to bring about his Promise, that we would become a "light to the nations," the people through whom he will save the world. Our all-powerful God makes good happen, in spite of our sin and weakness.* This hopeful message reached the exiles, who needed to recognize God's loving hand at work in the midst of their tragic failure.

By the end of the Book of Genesis, the descendants of Jacob Israel are living in Egypt. The stage is set for telling the story of the greatest event in the unfolding of God's plan among the Israelites—the Exodus.

Semitic tribes (in colored stripes) arrive in Egypt, requesting permission to enter, in a painting copied from a mural in an Egyptian pharaoh's tomb.

3 Freedom
The Exodus and the Covenant of Sinai

The Israelites were enslaved in Egypt, the land of the
Great Pyramids. The story of the people's liberation
from the Egyptians is told in the Book of Exodus.

Right at the heart of the Old Testament, the **Book of Exodus** proclaims the great truth that God freed the descendants of Abraham, Isaac, and Jacob from oppression and slavery in Egypt, then formed them into a chosen nation, Israel, and created an everlasting bond with them through the Covenant of Sinai.

The Exodus stories, like those of Genesis and the other books of the Torah, were collected and edited into the Book of Exodus around the time of the exile in Babylon (seven hundred or so years after the Exodus took

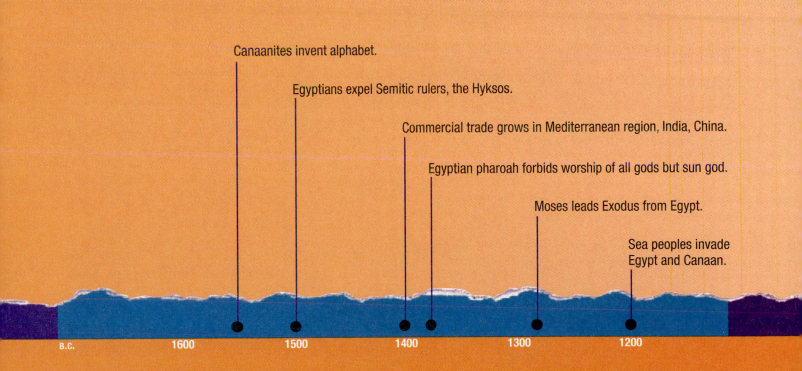

Canaanites invent alphabet.

Egyptians expel Semitic rulers, the Hyksos.

Commercial trade grows in Mediterranean region, India, China.

Egyptian pharoah forbids worship of all gods but sun god.

Moses leads Exodus from Egypt.

Sea peoples invade Egypt and Canaan.

B.C.   1600   1500   1400   1300   1200

Reeds grow along the Nile River in Egypt.

place). These accounts were close to the hearts of the exilic and postexilic Jews for many reasons:

- At the beginning of the story of the Exodus, the Israelites were living as slaves in a foreign land, Egypt. The Jews of the exile had a similar experience, living in Babylon as captive subjects of a mighty empire.

- The people of the Exodus struggled in a frightening and hostile wilderness. Similarly, the exiled Jews made a long, painful journey to Babylon, and back again to Judah some fifty years later.

- Most important for the Jews was God's revelation to their ancestors in the wilderness. Through Moses the people of Israel discovered the identity of their God, and through the Covenant, they found their own identity as his people. Similarly, in Babylon, after repenting of their sins, the exiles rediscovered their true identity as God's beloved.

The Exodus: Freed from Slavery

The Book of Exodus begins about four hundred and fifty years after the death of Joseph. The reigning pharaoh, or king, of Egypt, unlike the Semitic pharaohs of Joseph's time, hates and fears the people of Israel and orders them enslaved. Then comes the royal command: All Israelite males must be slain at birth.

Young Moses

The story of **Moses** begins when his mother, to save her infant son from being slain by Pharaoh's orders, puts him in a basket and floats it on the Nile River, where he is discovered by Pharaoh's daughter. A little girl darts out of the reeds with the information that a Hebrew woman nearby could nurse the baby. The princess hires the woman to care for the child among the Hebrews until he is old enough to be returned to the royal household. Because the little girl is Moses' sister, **Miriam,** and the nursing woman is his mother, he grows up knowing that he is really an Israelite—although he is raised by Pharaoh's daughter as an Egyptian prince. [1]

Reaching manhood, one day Moses sees an Egyptian slave driver beating a Hebrew. He is outraged at the injustice done to one of his own kinsfolk, so he attacks the slave driver, kills him, and buries his body in the sand. When he finds out the next day that the murder is known to others, Moses fears Pharaoh's anger and flees Egypt eastward to the land of the nomadic Midians. There he meets a priest, marries one of his daughters, and becomes a shepherd.

Read Exodus 1:6–22; 2:1–15.

A form of slavery persists globally today in sweatshops, where people are forced to work in unsafe conditions for extremely low wages. Here Burmese refugees work in a sweatshop.

1

Miriam and her mother risk their lives when they defy the pharaoh's orders, but Israel eventually is freed because they had the courage and ingenuity to save Moses' life. Write a one-page essay about someone you know whose courageous act brought about a change for the good. Include a picture of the person, if possible.

The Burning Bush:
In the Presence of the Holy

Life goes on miserably for the Israelite slaves; one cruel pharaoh replaces another. Though the Israelites have forgotten about the God of their ancestors Abraham, Isaac, and Jacob, they cry out in agony. God is mindful of their suffering.

One day while tending sheep in Midian, Moses sees a strange sight—a bush aflame but not consumed. Drawing near, he hears God telling him to remove his sandals, for he is standing on holy ground. Moses is awed by the mysterious presence, then alarmed to hear the command that he return to Egypt and order **Pharaoh** to let the Israelites go. Moses protests that he is unsuited for such a task, but God insists. Again Moses protests: he does not know God's name. Who will he tell the people that their God is? God reveals the sacred name to be **Yahweh**—interpreted within the scriptural text as "I am who am" or "I am who I am." Once again Moses excuses himself: the people will not believe

him. God gives him two miraculous signs by which to convince the people—or at least himself. Still Moses argues: he is slow of speech and tongue (perhaps having a speech impediment). Finally, God becomes angry and says that Moses' brother, **Aaron,** will accompany him and do the talking—but Moses is to go! [2]

Read Exodus 3:1–22; 4:1–17.

The name Yahweh

"I am who I am" might better be expressed as "I am the One who is always present." For centuries people had believed that they were the slaves of the gods. A God who was not only supreme but also a constant and caring presence was a revolutionary idea.

Scholars suggest that worship of the God named Yahweh was, in fact, unknown before the time of Moses. Although the early Israelites began to worship Yahweh within their own group, they did not necessarily see their people's God as the one and only God or as the God of all the nations. This belief came later on. The concerns of Moses' people probably did not extend much beyond their own families and tribes.

For Jews the name Yahweh stresses the unutterable mystery of God, and out of reverence they have preferred not to pronounce it. Instead they substitute titles such as Adonai, meaning "the Lord." Many Christian versions of the Bible have adopted the word *Lord* in their translations, meaning

2

How does it feel to accept someone's help? Is that easy or difficult for you? Perhaps you have a task in front of you that you believe you cannot accomplish on your own. Is there a friend, a family member, a teacher, a neighbor, or someone else who can help you? Imagine a conversation you might have about this with such a person, and write it down.

"Remove the sandals from your feet, for the place on which you are standing is holy ground." **Exodus 3:5**

A depiction of a slave being beaten, a detail of a wall painting from an ancient Egyptian tomb

"divine sovereignty." This text will follow the same practice. [3]

"Let My People Go!"

In Egypt Moses and Aaron give God's message to the Israelites, who exult because the Lord has seen their affliction. Yet Pharaoh, when told of God's command to "let my people go" (Exodus 5:1), is unmoved: Why should he heed a God of slaves? Isn't he, Pharaoh, a god also—son of the great god Ra? Besides, freeing his workforce would upset the system! Accusing Moses of luring the Israelites from their work, Pharaoh doubles their burden. The people cry out that Moses' promise of the Lord's protection has not freed them but only increased their sufferings. They want no more to do with the Lord. Now God promises to take action.

Read Exodus 4:27–31; 5:1–23; 6:1.

The forgotten God

Notice that the Israelites have to be convinced of God's presence by miracles. They have been in Egypt for over four hundred years, and they no longer know their God. Yet God knows them. [4]

Pharaoh: Plagued by Plagues

Moses and Aaron return to Pharaoh and repeat their demand, Pharaoh ignores them, and then the ten plagues begin. Water turns to blood, frogs overrun the land, and gnats and flies torment the Egyptians. Sickness afflicts their cattle, boils plague the people, hail destroys the crops, and locusts eat what is left. Darkness covers the land, and Moses proclaims the final plague—death for the firstborn of Egypt. Now Pharaoh will beg them to leave, Moses says— but Pharaoh is still adamant.

Read Exodus 6:28–30; 7:1–25; 8:1–11; 11:1–10.

3

Consider the "unutterable mystery of God." Describe in writing one aspect of God that you think you understand. How have you come to know that about him? Find or create a picture or other artwork that represents to you the mystery of God.

4

The people of Israel no longer knew their God. But God knew them. No matter how long we stay away from God, even if it is so long that we forget who he is . . . God never forgets us. Find a song or a poem that speaks of his abiding presence to us and bring it to class.

A farm family celebrates the Passover seder in Israel.

Pharaoh's hardened heart

Pharaoh's performance reads like that of a character in a TV soap opera. Note the following passages in Exodus:

- Pharaoh's arrogance in 7:22–23
- his bargaining and going back on his word in 8:4–15
- his wavering in 8:21–28
- his pretended repentance in 9:27–28
- his craftiness in 9:33–35
- his ransom plan in 10:8–11
- his hypocrisy in 10:16

Did God harden Pharaoh's heart, or was he naturally stubborn? The Scriptures say both things, ten times each, and both may be true. The human heart is hardened by flinging itself against the will of the loving God, and proud, powerful rulers do not give in easily, especially to slaves. The God of the lowly Israelites was in Pharaoh's way.

Preparation for the Passover

God gives Moses instructions in preparation for the journey out of Egypt. Every family is to slay and roast a yearling lamb or kid, eat it with unleavened bread—a yeast dough would take too long to rise—and be ready to leave. Then they are to smear the top and posts of their doorway with the blood of the lamb so that the angel of God will *pass over* their home when striking down the firstborn of Egypt. The Israelites are to celebrate this meal every year as a perpetual reminder of the **Pesach,** or **Passover.**

Read Exodus 12:1–14.

Jesus' Last Supper

The memorial meal of the Israelites became the Passover **seder,** or ritual meal, of the Jewish people. The **Last Supper,** Jesus' meal with his disciples the night before he died, was a seder. Jesus used the language, food, and ritual of the Passover to help his disciples understand the meaning of his own death in the context of their history. The Jewish seder celebrates freedom from slavery in Egypt and the longing for freedom everywhere in the world. It was at the Last Supper that Jesus instituted the Christian Eucharist, which celebrates freedom from the power of sin and death through Jesus' life, death, and Resurrection. [5]

Unleavened bread

At subsequent Passovers the Israelites rid their households of all leaven—that is, fermented dough kept from one baking to another, a form of yeast—and all leavened bread. Starting afresh with new dough symbolized a new life of freedom. Jewish families today do this during the Passover season and serve only unleavened bread, called matzo. From this custom came the Catholic use of unleavened bread in Communion.

"Go and Good Riddance!"

The Exodus account continues: At midnight a loud cry rises up over Egypt as the firstborn of every household is discovered dead. As Moses has foretold, Pharaoh summons him and cries out that Moses and his people must go, that it will be a blessing to be rid of them!

At last the people of Israel leave—a ragtag crowd of slaves, foreigners, men, women, and children, unarmed and on foot, leading their milking animals, and carrying all their belongings—including the bones of their ancestor Joseph, who wanted to be buried in the **Promised Land,** the land of Canaan first promised to Abraham.

Read Exodus 12:29–39.

Again, the point of the story is *that* God freed the Israelites, not *how* God freed them. The slaying of the Egyptians' firstborn is not described.

Matzo, eaten during Passover, reminds Jews of their escape from Egypt to freedom.

The Great Escape: Crossing the Sea of Reeds

God, in a pillar of cloud by day and a pillar of fire by night, leads the Israelites. Hardly have they left when Pharaoh, in a rage, starts after them. The Israelites see his chariots in pursuit, are terrified, and cry out to Moses accusingly: "Were there not enough graves in

5

Passover and the Last Supper, which is celebrated in the Eucharist, are ways to remember how we have been freed by God. Have you ever had an experience of being liberated or set free? Perhaps you were released from a dangerous situation, a hurtful friendship, a destructive habit that enslaved you, an illness, or suffering of another kind. Write your story and think about the ways God might have been involved in freeing you.

Egypt? Is that why you brought us out to the desert to die?" (adapted from Exodus 14:11). Moses bids them to wait to see what the Lord will do. The cloud moves to the rear of their camp and hides them from the Egyptians.

Then the wind blows all night, parting the Sea of Reeds (called the Red Sea in the biblical accounts), and in the morning the Israelites cross safely—just ahead of the Egyptians. The water returns, and Pharaoh's troops drown. Moses and his sister, Miriam, together with their people, sing a *canticle*, or song, praising God for the victory. Scholars believe that the oldest parts of the Old Testament might be found in two verses of Moses and Miriam's canticle (15:1,21). [6]

Read Exodus 13:17–22; 14:1–31; 15:1–21.

A modern story of a crossing

A modern story of a similar crossing offers a perspective on the miraculous nature of this event:

During the struggle of black people for civil rights in the United States—on the Easter Sunday in 1965 following the jailing of Dr. Martin Luther King Jr.—a crowd of two thousand people marched to the Birmingham, Alabama, jail to pray and sing outside under the windows. Police officers with dogs and firefighters with hoses awaited them. Blocked from reaching the jail, the people dropped to their knees to pray, and after five minutes someone jumped up and cried: "The Lord is with this movement! We're goin' on

6

On their journey the Israelites were protected by God in the pillars of cloud and fire. Reflect on something or someone who has given you a sense of direction in your life. Express your thoughts in writing, or in a drawing or painting.

Civil rights protesters at the Birmingham jail offer a modern story of a miraculous crossing.

60   Freedom

to the jail!" Everyone rose and started walking. To their astonishment, the police officers, firefighters, and dogs simply stood still and let them go past. Bull O'Connor, the sheriff of Birmingham, yelled, "Turn on the hoses!" But no one moved as the people slowly marched to the jail, singing. Both this story and the ancient one of the crossing were the work of the saving God.

Miracles are not just works of overcoming natural phenomena, like parting the sea. Perhaps the most wonderful miracles are those in which hearts that seem hard and unmovable are turned around by the power of God. *7*

7

"Perhaps the most wonderful miracles are those in which hearts that seem hard and unmovable are turned around by the power of God." Write about an example of this kind of miracle that you have seen in your own life, in the life of someone you know, or in the course of history.

The Prayer of Israel: Moses and Miriam's Song

"I will sing to the LORD, for he has triumphed gloriously;
    horse and rider he has thrown into the sea.
The LORD is my strength and my might,
    and he has become my salvation.

. . . .

"Pharaoh's chariots and his army he cast into the sea;
    his picked officers were sunk in the Red Sea.
The floods covered them;
    they went down into the depths like a stone.

. . . .

At the blast of your nostrils the waters piled up,
    the floods stood up in a heap;
    the deeps congealed in the heart of the sea.
The enemy said, "I will pursue, I will overtake."

. . . .

You blew with your wind, the sea covered them;
    they sank like lead in the mighty waters.

"Who is like you, O LORD, among the gods?
    Who is like you, majestic in holiness,
    awesome in splendor, doing wonders?
You stretched out your right hand,
    the earth swallowed them.

"In your steadfast love you led the people whom you redeemed;
    you guided them by your strength to your holy abode.

. . . .

The LORD will reign forever and ever."

(Exodus 15:1–18)

Murmuring and Grumbling in the Wilderness

The people of Israel have hardly finished celebrating their new freedom when they begin to complain about the hardships of the journey. When the water is bitter, the Lord sweetens it. When they lack food, the Lord sends manna and quail. When again they need water, Moses strikes a rock and water gushes out.

Read Exodus 15:22–27; 16:1–36; 17:1–6.

Manna: Bread from heaven

Scholars are not sure what the food was that the Israelites called **manna.** Whatever it was, the Israelites depended on it as their "daily bread" throughout the forty years of their wandering in the wilderness.[8]

An Exodus Perspective for the Exiles

The Israelites were freed from slavery and oppression by the power of God and then led into the wilderness, where they had to learn over and over to keep trusting in God's care for them. Reflecting on that reality centuries later, the Jewish exiles in Babylon understood what that meant for them in their oppressed situation: "The Lord will save us! The Lord will free us! And when we are tempted to give up in despair, the Lord will go on looking after us, giving us everything we need to keep going. *Trust the Lord.*"[9]

For Review

☐ Why were the accounts of the Exodus close to the hearts of Jews during and after the exile?

☐ What is the interpretation of the Hebrew name Yahweh given in the scriptural text in Exodus? What is a better expression of the meaning of that name?

☐ What is the final plague proclaimed by Moses?

☐ What does the Passover seder celebrate?

☐ What image of God is given in Moses and Miriam's canticle?

8

Throughout their difficult journey, God provided for the Israelites. When it seemed that they would starve, they discovered manna; right before their eyes was nourishment that would sustain them for forty years. Do you recognize the nourishment—the manna—that is sent to you? Reflect in writing on three things you typically take for granted, without which you could not survive. Where do these things come from? Who or what provides them? What do you have to do to get them? Do you know of people who go without these things? Find and copy a psalm that expresses how God takes care of us.

9

Consider a person or people who have been forced to flee from their home or country because of war, famine, or persecution. What challenges and fears might they face as they search for a new home? Imagine a teenager in this situation and write a prayer or a poem from his or her perspective about the difficulties of exile, longing for home, and hoping for a better life.

The Covenant of Sinai: An Offering from God

When the Israelites arrive at Mount Sinai, Moses goes up the mountain. There God bids him to tell the people that the Lord has brought them safely to this place and that if they will keep the Covenant, they will be the Lord's holy nation, dearer than all other peoples. Moses returns to the people and repeats this message, and the people say they will do everything the Lord asks of them. *10*

On the third day, as the people prepare themselves for God's coming, a great storm breaks on the mountain. Lightning flashes, thunder peals, and dense clouds cover the peaks. Moses leaves the people behind to go up the holy mountain and receive God's message. Then the Lord gives Moses the Ten Commandments.

Read Exodus 19:1–11,16–19.

Liturgical flourishes?

Some scholars speculate that the writer may have embellished this account of divine visitation with details from Israel's later liturgical celebrations. The trumpet blasts and clouds of smoke that were included to symbolize the Lord's arrival could have been part of the celebration of the great event in the centuries that followed it.

10

A relationship is understood as a covenant when both parties promise to be faithful to each other, and genuine love and care is shared between them. Do you know of any relationships that you believe are truly covenants? Find two people who are in such a relationship and interview them to discover what makes their relationship so special, and what each of them contributes to it. Write up the results of your interview.

These inscribed stone pillars, reminiscent of the traditional tablets of the Ten Commandments, were discovered in the Sinai region on the site of an Egyptian temple.

The Ten Commandments

The **Ten Commandments,** or the **Decalogue,** had a long history of development beginning in the time of Moses (1290 B.C.). Many other laws were added to them over the years and are included in Exodus—as well as in the Books of Leviticus, Numbers, and Deuteronomy. These later laws will be treated in the next chapter. Here we will look at the Ten Commandments in their historical context.

Read Exodus 20:1–26.

No other gods

The first commandment did not say that no other gods existed, but it did declare that there was only one God of the Israelites and that they should worship no other. This commandment also prohibited idolatry. In the Near East at the time, people commonly worshiped idols that represented gods—for example, a statue of a bull or a sun symbol. The first commandment stated that such human efforts to depict God were bound to fail and should not be attempted.

The meaning of the first commandment for Christians today includes the following:

- People are called to believe in God, to love God, and to place their hope in God.
- People are called to worship God and follow his ways through the practice of religion, both publicly and privately.
- Anything that rejects God, such as idolatry, superstition, or speaking of God disrespectfully, violates the first commandment.
- Idolatry is not just about worshipping other gods. At another level idolatry can be understood as "making a god" out of something that is *not* God—for instance, treating popularity or money or even school grades like God, as deserving our total allegiance and "worship."

God's name

The second commandment forbade the use of God's name in irreverent, sacrilegious ways. As mentioned earlier, devout persons rarely spoke God's name, but those less devout sometimes abused it in the belief that using the name Yahweh in prayer or when swearing an oath would magically force him to do their will.

I-Witness: Rivka

I'm Rivka the slave. "Freed slave" since I left Egypt with my husband and family. Some stayed behind; they didn't believe what Moses said about his God providing for us in the wilderness. My mother says better to die in the desert than to live as a slave. It's true: now I wake up under a starry sky instead of in a slave's shack.

Moses expects a lot from us, but his God gave us freedom. Publicly my family worships his God. But in our tent, we often pray to images of the goddess Isis. My mother says, "Why take chances with blessings from only one god?" A god, she reminds me, whose commandments promise neither long life nor wealth.

I tell my mother that if we keep praying to Isis, then we are hypocrites when we join into worship with Moses, of his God. She says it's a private, family matter, and I will understand that once I start a family—meaning the sooner the better. I think in their hearts some people are still slaves to the past.

This commandment speaks to the great reverence that is owed to God, and thus to his name. Today Christians understand it as forbidding every disrespectful use of God's name (or the names of other holy figures, such as the Virgin Mary)—including swearing, making false promises in God's name, and perjury.

The Sabbath

The third commandment called upon the Israelites to keep Saturday, their seventh day, as the Sabbath—free for worship in honor of God's rest on the seventh day in the story of the Creation.

For the Israelites, keeping the Sabbath holy and restful was one way of saying, "We belong to God, not to any human authority." The Sabbath helped them remember *who* they were, and *whose* they were. It was especially important for the Jews in exile, when, as a powerless minority in a strange land, they were trying to preserve their religious identity. *11*

Later Christians chose Sunday as their holy day in honor of the Resurrection, which they believed signaled the first day of the New Creation. Today this commandment obliges Christians to keep Sunday holy:

- For Catholics, keeping Sunday holy means worshipping God at Mass.
- It also means resting from work in order to nourish the family, social, cultural, and religious aspects of our lives—and allowing others to rest, too.

Parents

Today we associate the fourth commandment, "Honor your father and your mother" (Exodus 20:12), with children and obedience. Originally the law addressed adults and sought to protect aging parents, who needed their adult children to care for them. The humanity of a society, it has been said, can be judged by how that society treats its youngest and its oldest citizens. Christians today understand the fourth commandment in the following ways:

- Family life is meant to support the good of *all* family members; society should do everything possible to support families.
- Though children are called to respect their parents, the commandment also obliges parents to care for their children by providing for their physical and spiritual needs, as well as their education.
- For Catholics, the commandment has implications for the way citizens relate to public authorities. Citizens are obliged to work with public authorities to build a just and peaceful society, as long as those authorities do not violate God's law. Civil authorities, in turn, have a responsibility to respect the dignity, rights, and freedom of each person.

Murder

The fifth commandment, sometimes translated as "You shall not kill" (Exodus 20:13), is more accurately translated as "You shall not murder." In nomadic groups a person's life and dignity were protected only by

Protesters against the death penalty ask this question: Why do we kill people to show that killing people is wrong?

11

The first three commandments pertain to loving and respecting God. Describe in writing how young people can show their respect for God.

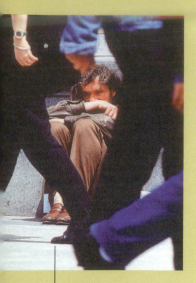

When persons with abundance ignore the needs of those who go without the necessities of life, the seventh commandment is violated.

the assurance that kinsfolk would revenge any injury or insult. Acts of revenge often escalated to bloody feuds and sometimes resulted in the extinction of entire family groups. At the time of the Exodus, the purpose this commandment was to lessen the violence arising from hatred, malice, and the taking of the law into one's hands.

Much later, speaking of this commandment, Jesus denounced other forms of destructiveness—for example, anger, slaying with words, contempt, and vicious gossip. Today this commandment speaks to a variety of threats to human life that were not obvious to the Israelites:

- Every human life is sacred from the moment of conception until natural death because every human is made in the image of God and loved by him. As a result, abortion, euthanasia, and suicide are prohibited by the fifth commandment.

- People have a right to defend their lives, even if they must kill an aggressor as a last resort.

- Capital punishment and war should be avoided whenever possible.

- The spread of weapons, especially in the arms race, violates the spirit of the fifth commandment.

- Scandal—an attitude or behavior that leads someone else to sin—is like murder because it can cause spiritual death.

- Society must work to promote the health of its members.

Adultery

The sixth commandment, "You shall not commit adultery" (Exodus 20:14), had as its purpose the protection of marriage and the family. In ancient times the well-being of the family took precedence over the individual's desires because the stability and even the survival of the community depended on it. Adultery, a married person's having sexual relations with someone other than her or his marriage partner, often led to vengeance and feuds. It was held in great horror among the Israelites, and its punishment was death.

Later laws of ancient times addressed other wrongful sexual relationships. In Catholic understanding today, the term *adultery* in the sixth commandment covers sexual relationships that do not take place within the bond of marriage:

- Everyone is called to live a life of chastity, which means living out one's sexuality in ways that are appropriate to one's life situation. Married people practice chastity by having sexual relations with only their spouses, while single people practice chastity by abstaining from all sexual activity.

- Masturbation, pornography, and contraception violate the sixth commandment because they do not respect the goodness of human sexuality as God meant it to be expressed.

Stealing

"You shall not steal" (Exodus 20:15) says the seventh commandment. Stealing is a sin that accuses God of caring for us inadequately as well as a sin against the neighbor whose goods are stolen. Today Catholics have a broader understanding of what this commandment implies not only for individuals but whole societies:

- God meant the world's goods and material resources to benefit all people, not just a few.

- Although we have a right to own property, we must recognize that God is the ultimate "owner" of everything, and therefore we have a responsibility to share what we have for the well-being of others. Stealing can be defined as people with abundance not sharing with others who go without necessary food, shelter, or employment.

- The seventh commandment forbids slavery of all kinds—including unjust labor practices.

- Because the earth is God's, we are called to respect and care for all creation and the environment. Animals should be treated with kindness. *12*

False witness

The eighth commandment forbids giving false testimony, especially in cases being judged by elders or in courts. At the time the Commandments were given, when a liar intended to bring about a sentence of death for an accused person, the penalty for false witness could also be death. Some of the implications of the commandment against "false witness" for Christians today include the following:

- People are called to be truthful in everything they say and do.
- Christians are called to share the truth that has been revealed in Jesus Christ.
- People should not use words to harm the reputations of others.
- society has a right to information based on truth.
- People are called to seek truth in all its forms, including art.

Coveting a married woman

The ninth commandment, "You shall not covet your neighbor's house; you shall not covet your neighbor's wife" (Exodus 20:17), was later divided, and the first half was made into the tenth—which is how they are treated here. Both commandments have to do with covetousness, or greediness, and both reveal a profound understanding of the path of sin. Sin begins in the mind and the heart. Entertaining the idea of a sin leads to the act. For example, coveting a neighbor's wife can be the first step toward adultery. Today this commandment reminds us that the intent in our heart is very important. It warns us against lust and calls us to keep our hearts pure through prayer, modesty, and discretion. At times an intent to do wrong can be as sinful as the deed itself.

Greed for a neighbor's property

The tenth commandment relates to coveting a neighbor's goods, an envious craving that is the first step toward injuring one's neighbor. Such greed leads not only to "keeping up with the Joneses" but also to trying to surpass them, and life can become a nightmare in which people are possessed by their possessions. The tenth commandment calls people to trust in God more than wealth. *13*

Other Laws of Israel

The Book of the Covenant, which follows the Ten Commandments in Exodus, treats laws of worship, civil laws, and laws controlling morality. Many of these laws were radical steps forward for the time, creating a relative degree of fairness in situations where previously violence or greed held sway.

Other laws in the Book of the Covenant strike us today as clearly unjust, such as the law that was quoted at one time to justify owning slaves. This law said that if the owner of a slave struck the slave but did not kill him or her, the owner would go unpunished because the slave was property.

Read Exodus 21:20–21.

The Israelites saw the Commandments as rules that free people by giving them lines or boundaries that everyone in a community pledges not to cross.

12

The last seven commandments are directed toward loving one another. Keep a journal for three days, noting instances when these commandments are upheld and when they are disregarded by you or others. Avoid judging other persons; simply observe.

13

Which of the Ten Commandments is most challenging for you? for our society? Explain in a one-page essay.

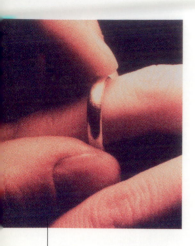

The Covenant bound the people to God in a kind of marriage.

What about slavery?

The other laws of Israel were not solely divine ordinances; they were the customs of many cultures of the time. In the ancient world, few undertakings could be completed without human power, and the use of slaves, bought or captured in war, was a universal practice. However, slavery has always been a violation of human rights; and when, in time, people saw this, they either freed their slaves or refused to own them. Much later, Western society began to see that slavery was a hideous custom, and with the arrival of the Industrial Revolution, machines and hired workers could do the work of slaves.

A Law That Frees

The Israelites perceived the Ten Commandments and the other laws not as burdens that dragged them down but as mutual understandings that enabled them to live in freedom and peace with one another. For instance, once vengeful killing is ruled out in a community and everyone agrees to follow that, people no longer have to live in fear. Once it is understood that people are not allowed to lie about one another, they can trust one another's word. Once stealing is outlawed, people are free to share with one another.

For the Israelites, keeping the Commandments was a sacred pact with one another as well as with God. They recognized that rules can actually free people by giving them lines or boundaries that everyone in a community pledges not to cross. *14*

For Review

☐ Why did the first commandment prohibit idolatry?

☐ Why was adultery held in great horror among the Israelites?

☐ Explain the understanding of sin revealed in the ninth and tenth commandments.

☐ In what sense did the Israelites consider the Law as freeing them, not restricting them?

Sealing the Covenant

In preparation for ratifying the **Covenant of Sinai,** Moses builds an altar with twelve pillars representing the twelve tribes of Israel. He has young bulls sacrificed for offerings, dividing their blood into two bowls. Half of the blood he splashes on the altar as a symbol of the Lord's presence, and the other half he sprinkles on the people as a sign of the binding of God and the people in a kind of marriage. Doing so, Moses proclaims the Covenant of Sinai. Then God bids Moses to ascend the mountain again to receive the stone tablets on which the Law has been written.

Read Exodus 24:3–8.

The symbol of blood

For the ancient Israelites, blood was the sign of life itself. In fact laws of the time prohibited the consumption of animal blood because life was God's dominion, not humans'. In the ancient world, blood rituals such as the one described above were practiced as a way to seal covenants or agreements between kings.

The Covenant of covenants

The sealing of the Covenant of Sinai is the high point of Israel's story. You have read about other blessings, promises, and covenants that God made with Adam, Noah, Abraham, and Jacob. Other covenants (solemn agreements) made between human parties are also mentioned in the Old Testament. The Covenant of Sinai, however, surpassed all others in the minds of the

14

When you try to live out a pledge that you have made to someone, what difficulties can arise? Think of a commitment or pledge that you have struggled with. Why was it a struggle? Write a letter to that person (you decide if you want to mail it) expressing how you feel about it.

biblical editors. At Sinai the Lord proclaimed for all time that the people of Israel were the people of God.

In Judaism the Covenant of Sinai is a never-to-be-repeated event—the testament (which means covenant) that gave its name to what Christians now call the Old Testament. This event is also of profound importance to Christians, who as believers in God are also children of Abraham and the people of Israel.

Something else is worth remembering: By the time the finishing touches were put to their Scriptures, the Jews better understood what it meant to be the people of God. Theirs was a privileged role but not an easy one. To be called as witnesses to the one God for all the world was an extraordinarily difficult mission.

Infidelity, Then Forgiveness

The story of Exodus continues with an account of immediate and shocking infidelity. When Moses returns to the mountaintop and remains for forty days and nights with God, the people think that he has left them. They grow bored and hunger for diversion, and astonishingly, they ask Aaron to make them an idol. More astonishingly, he does.

Gathering the gold ornaments of the women and children, Aaron melts them, fashions a golden calf, and proclaims that it is the Lord, the God who brought them out of Egypt (or, some scholars surmise, the animal on whose back God's throne rests). The people offer sacrifices to the golden calf, deluding themselves into thinking that this is not a problem.

Read Exodus 32:1–6.

Miles of commentaries have been written on this ageless tale—about the human heart, its wavering and faltering, and the need for redemption. When God seems to be absent, we quickly make gods of things that seem more real to us—or that at least are more visible.

The Tablets Destroyed

The Lord, knowing what the people have done, vows to destroy them, but Moses intercedes. Moses descends the mountain, discovers their revelry, and breaks the tablets of the Law, which has already been broken by the people. Angrily, Moses confronts Aaron, orders the idolators slain (but spares Aaron), and returns to beg God's forgiveness for the rest of the people.

At first the Lord refuses to accompany the Israelites, but orders them to continue

on their way to the land flowing with milk and honey. However, upon further pleading by Moses, God agrees to be present in a pillar of cloud before the **tent of the meeting** (a portable tent where Moses meets God in prayer throughout the journey), but only when they halt.

Read Exodus 32:7–20; 33:1–11.

The Love Between Moses and God

One of the most moving passages in the Scriptures is a conversation between the Lord and Moses that is like two lovers talking. Moses begs the Lord to go with the Israelites so that all the world will know that they are God's people. The Lord agrees. Then in a burst of

15

Moses knew that God was closer to him than his most treasured friend. And God is just that close to each of us, as well. List some of the kinds of heartfelt things that most people would share only with their best friend.

longing, Moses begs, "Show me your glory, I pray" (Exodus 33:18). The Lord replies that no one can look upon the glory of God's face and live, but that the Lord will pass by and shield Moses so that he can safely see God from the back. [15]

Read Exodus 33:12–23.

The Covenant Renewed, the Tablets Rewritten

The Lord tells Moses to bring new tablets, and before engraving the Commandments on them, the Lord reveals what God is like. (The Jewish teachers called this scriptural passage The Thirteen Attributes of God.) God then renews the Covenant, promising to work marvels for Israel that the world has never seen before—if Israel keeps God's word.

Descending from the mountain, Moses is radiant with the glory of God. Because the people are afraid to approach him, Moses covers his face with a cloth, removing it only when he goes to speak with the Lord.

The Prayer of Israel: Longing for God

As a deer longs for flowing streams,
    so my soul longs for you, O God.
My soul thirsts for God,
    for the living God.
When shall I come and behold
    the face of God?

. . . .

Why are you cast down, O my soul,
    and why are you disquieted within me?
Hope in God; for I shall again praise him,
    my help and my God.

(Psalm 42:1–6)

Following God's instructions, the people fashion a dwelling place for the **ark of the Covenant**—the container for the stone tablets of the Law. Aaron and his sons are ordained as priests—those who may offer sacrifice to God on behalf of the people. The cloud indicating the presence of the Lord settles over the ark's dwelling place (the tent of the meeting) and fills it. When the Lord moves, as a cloud by day and as fire by night, the people of Israel follow. Where the Lord stays, the people stay. Thus the Israelites resume their journey.

Read Exodus 34:1–35; 40:1–38.

What is God like?

The thirteen attributes of God are briefly described in the following list of phrases drawn from Exodus 34:6–7:

- *1, 2. "The LORD, the LORD."* This repetition indicates that the Lord is the God of all things and all creatures and is the beginning and end of all time.

- *3. "A God"*

- *4. "Merciful."* The Hebrew word for *merciful* is the same as that for *womb,* which suggests that God possesses a mother's tender understanding of a child's weakness.

- *5. "Gracious."* The Hebrew word for *gracious* suggests kindness for its own sake, not as a means to some other goal.

- *6. "Slow to anger"*

- *7. "Abounding in steadfast love."* This phrase refers to God's fidelity to the Covenant even when Israel has disobeyed.

- *8. "Faithfulness."* God is not only present but always offering love to us. In the New Testament, the term that comes closest in meaning is probably *grace.*

The Ark of the Covenant, the Tent of the Meeting

According to the Exodus account, the ark of the Covenant, which contained the stone tablets of the Law, was a small wooden box, about the size of an orange crate, kept within a tent sanctuary while the people of Israel were in the wilderness. On top of the ark was a plate of gold called the mercy seat, the throne where God met the people of Israel. Thus the sanctuary itself was called the tent of the meeting. The ark was carried at the head of the column when the people traveled through the desert, and before the army in battle.

Later, when King Solomon built the Temple in Jerusalem, he established the sanctuary within it. In English versions of the Bible, the sanctuary is called the **tabernacle,** which simply means "tent."

Jews still celebrate the **feast of Tabernacles,** known as **Sukkoth,** commemorating God's providence during the time in the wilderness. During this weeklong autumnal feast, many Jewish families put up simple booths, decorate them with harvest fruits, eat their meals there, and sleep under the stars. It is a beautiful way to remember God's constant care.

" The LORD the LORD a God merciful

**"The LORD, the LORD,
a God merciful and gracious,
slow to anger,
and abounding in steadfast love
and faithfulness"** **Exodus 34:6**

- *9. "For the thousandth generation."* The word *thousand* implies endless. Think of the faith that for thousands of years contributed to Christian faith today, starting with Abraham and Israel, reshaped by Jesus and the Apostles, carried on by missionaries, reaching the recent history of your grandparents and parents.

- *10, 11, and 12. "Forgiving iniquity and transgression and sin."* The literal translation of these attributes is "bearing crookedness and rebellion and failure." The implication is that God's love and goodness are stronger than evil.

- *13. "Yet by no means clearing the guilty, / but visiting the iniquity of the parents / upon the children / and the children's children, / to the third and fourth generation."* God forgives those who want forgiveness. The greatest sin is believing that we have no need to be forgiven.

    This attribute sounds extremely harsh, but it needs to be considered in light of the ninth attribute, describing God's graciousness to the "thousandth generation." The intention of the thirteenth attribute is to suggest that God does not let wrongs go unpunished. Remember that belief in personal punishment in an afterlife developed later in Jewish history. So if an individual died without being punished for injustices, it was believed that the punishment must then have fallen on his or her children.

    People who see "the God of the Old Testament" as angry and vengeful should ponder Exodus 34:6–7 in order to see in it the God whose attributes are made present to us in Jesus. God's self-revelation to Moses in this portrait well matches the Gospel portrait of the father in the story of the prodigal son, the parable told by Jesus in Luke 15:11–32. [16]

For Review

☐ What did blood symbolize for the ancient Israelites?

☐ Why did the Covenant of Sinai surpass all other covenants in the minds of the biblical editors?

☐ Explain what the last attribute of God means and the intention behind it: "Yet by no means clearing the guilty, / but visiting the iniquity of the parents / upon the children / and the children's children, / to the third and fourth generation" (Exodus 34:7).

More Than Miles to Go

You have completed the Book of Exodus, but the people of Israel have only half completed their journey to the Promised Land. The rest of the journey is more than simply a matter of miles. The Israelites cannot enter the land of Canaan until they comprehend more fully the Law and the Covenant. So the people have more to learn in the wilderness.

16

Choose one of the thirteen attributes of God that strikes you as significant and write a brief reflection on it. How would you like to see this attribute expressed in yourself or others?

4 The Law
Living Out the Covenant

A road stretches across a mountainous part of the Sinai desert. The Israelites traveled over land such as this on their way to the Promised Land.

Central to the Book of Exodus are the Ten Commandments, which establish the terms of the Covenant of Sinai. The next three books—Leviticus, Numbers, and Deuteronomy—tell of other laws that spell out more precisely how Israel is to keep the Covenant. These laws, expressing the spirit of the Ten Commandments, deal with relationships, rituals, and matters of daily life.

Many of the laws in these three books address situations that the Israelites would not experience until long after their period of wandering in the desert. Laws about land ownership, houses, vineyards, and how to perform Temple rituals probably grew out of their life in the Promised Land. But the biblical writers and editors set these laws within the great story of Moses leading the Israelites through the desert for forty years, thus emphasizing how important the laws were. So significant were they to the people that, taken together, the whole collection of laws from Exodus through Deuteronomy is called the **Law of Moses,** the **Mosaic Law,** or simply **the Law.**

Leviticus: Holiness and Ritual

The writer of the **Book of Leviticus** was probably an Israelite priest in the time after the exile, when the Temple was rebuilt in Jerusalem. **Priests** were members of the tribe of **Levi,** who led worship in the Temple. The Book of Leviticus can be thought of as a handbook of instructions for Israel's worship.

Community worship was crucial in the life of the Israelites: it expressed *who they were*—God's own beloved people—and bound them together as one family pouring out its faith and trust in him. Therefore, ritual was not to be treated lightly. It had to be done with great reverence and care, according to precise instructions. To stress the solemnity, the writer presented the regulations for rituals in the form of direct statements from God to Moses or the Israelites in the wilderness, in the style of the Covenant of Sinai. Scripture scholars point out that these instructions were written centuries after the wilderness period and were meant for worship in the second Temple.

For the writer of Leviticus, the grateful, reverent, humble attitude toward God that characterizes true worship was meant to be woven together with everyday concerns and actions to form one whole, holy life. The writer wanted the Jews to see their worship in the Temple as related to their life in the community. This priest knew that worship is genuine only if it is expressed in how people treat one another. So besides ritual instructions, the Book of Leviticus includes teachings and directives on how to live out the holiness of their worship in their relationships. Leviticus encourages its readers to honesty, reverence, respect, tolerance, compassion, and generosity—virtues that are as needed now as they were at the time of its writing. [1]

Sacrifices of Atonement

Leviticus treats the rituals of the Temple, which included different kinds of prayer and sacrifice. Like many other ancient peoples who offered sacrifices to their gods, the Israelites believed that when they sinned against God, they needed to do something to atone for it, to repair the damaged relation-

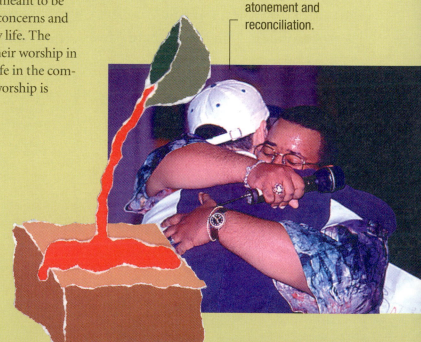

The sacrifice of animal blood in the Temple was meant to symbolize atonement and reconciliation.

[1] Write a brief reflection on this question: *If someone goes to church each Sunday and keeps the rules of his or her religion but shows little or no concern for justice and peace—as reflected in the virtues listed here—can that person be considered a good Christian?*

ship. So they sacrificed an animal as an atonement. The blood of the animal, poured out on the altar, signified life itself given to express the offerer's sorrow; the altar signified the presence of God.

The rituals described in the first half of Leviticus are **sacrifices of atonement** that took place in the Temple. In addition, once a year, on the **Day of Atonement**—called **Yom Kippur** by Jews—a very special ritual took place. The high priest entered the Temple sanctuary called the holy of holies, where God was believed to dwell, and offered first incense, then the blood of a bull and the blood of a goat. The sacrifice of blood was meant to represent the life of the people, offered to God to reconcile them with him. *2*

During the **Dispersion**—when Jews began to be sent or forced by circumstances to live in foreign lands away from Jerusalem and their Temple—Jews continued, as they do today, to celebrate Yom Kippur as their holiest day of the year, a day to atone for the sins of the past year. Beginning with the Dispersion, the day no longer included animal sacrifice.

The sacrifice of Jesus

The unknown author of the New Testament's Epistle to the Hebrews, writing to Jewish Christians, used the familiar sacrificial rituals of atonement to give meaning to the death and Resurrection of Jesus. He called Christ the true high priest— the one who not only offers the victim but is himself the victim, whose blood is spilled for the people, and who reconciles humankind to God with his perfect sacrifice. It is enlightening to see that much of the vocabulary that Christians have used to describe how Jesus Christ redeemed the world comes from the Book of Leviticus.

Read Hebrews 8:1–2; 9:11–15.

2

In writing, describe a time when you felt the need to be forgiven by someone.
- Were you conscious of being sorry for your wrongdoing?
- Were you aware of the need to admit your fault and take responsibility for it?
- Did you have a desire to make up for the offense?

Catholic Tradition includes these concerns as part of the elements of a good confession in the sacrament of reconciliation: contrition, confession, and satisfaction.

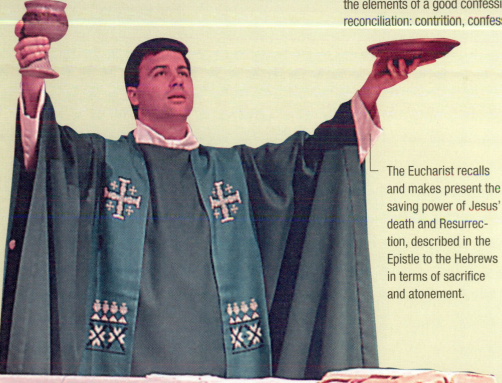

The Eucharist recalls and makes present the saving power of Jesus' death and Resurrection, described in the Epistle to the Hebrews in terms of sacrifice and atonement.

You shall love your neighbor as yourself. Leviticus 19:18

The Holiness Code

A section of Leviticus—chapters 17 to 26—contains many remarkable teachings. Known as the **Holiness Code,** these teachings were collected and put in the book by the priest-writer not because they focus on worship in itself, but because they show how true worship is expressed in a person's everyday life, in just and compassionate relationships. Some of the code indicates a remarkable sensitivity to the poor and a keen sense of what builds a just society. For example, Israel is told the following:

- Leave some of the harvest for gleaning by the poor.

- Do not withhold the wages of a laborer until the next day.

- Do not curse the deaf or put a stumbling block in the way of the blind.

- Do not take vengeance or bear a grudge; "love your neighbor as yourself" (19:17).

- Do not oppress foreigners; treat them as you would your own people.

- Do not fashion dishonest weights and measures (devices used for determining prices).

- Every fifty years there will be a **jubilee**—that is, debts are to be canceled, and those who have lost their property are to have the opportunity to redeem it.

  Read Leviticus 19:9–18,33–35; 25:1–23. **3**

Leviticus reminds us that holiness is not simply a matter of going through all the right prayers and rituals, although those are important. Love for God, the essence of true worship, is shown in love for one's neighbor.

For Review

- ☐ List three names given to the whole collection of laws that spell out the terms and specifics of the Covenant.
- ☐ What kind of handbook is the Book of Leviticus?
- ☐ Why did the Israelites offer animal sacrifices?
- ☐ What is Yom Kippur today?
- ☐ What are three moral teachings found in the Holiness Code in the Book of Leviticus? Why does Leviticus include moral teachings along with instructions for worship?

3

Create and write down a holiness code for your school, family, workplace, or community. Name at least six "musts" for expressing love of neighbor. How might you apply the concept of jubilee to your holiness code?

Numbers: Priestly Regulations and Inspiring Stories

The **Book of Numbers** is a complex work by many authors and editors. Its present title comes from the census mentioned in the first part of the book, which reports exaggerated numbers of Israelites as well as lists of priestly regulations. The original Hebrew title, "In the Wilderness," describes the second part of the book, which tells of Israel's wandering in the wilderness on the way to Canaan. This second section contains a number of stories about jealousy, rebellion, and greed.

More Complaining and Grumbling

The second part of Numbers begins with another version of the tales in Exodus of the people's grumbling. Here the people complain about the food in the wilderness, lam-

enting loudly for the cucumbers, melons, onions, and garlic they had in Egypt rather than "nothing at all but this manna" (11:6). Moses, distraught, asks God to let him die. Instead God promises that the people will eat the meat they want—until it comes out of their noses! A strong wind drives flocks of quail in from the sea, and the people gorge themselves so greedily that some of them die.

The lesson for the Israelites is that *God will provide*, especially when things look bleak. He will give us far more than we ever dreamed of. *4*

Read Numbers 11:1–23,31–34.

4

Providence means that God provides us with what we need, when we need it—sometimes through an event or a person. What are the things you need in your life that are provided for you? Where do they come from? Write a poem or a prayer reflecting an experience of providence and your feelings about it.

World Happenings from 1700 to 1250 B.C.

Africa
The Egyptians extend their empire eastward into Asia and southward into the Sudan. By 1600 B.C. the cat has taken up residence in Egyptian homes.

America
Agricultural villages, where people grow corn and other crops, become numerous in Central America.

China
A system of writing, in which each word is a picture, is used to communicate with the spirit world. Armies use chariots and wooden bows, reinforced by horn and sinew.

Europe
The Greeks lay siege to the city of Troy in what is now modern Turkey, giving rise to the legend of the Trojan War.

India
Hindu priests collect the religious hymns of the Rig-Veda. One of these hymns praises "the unknown god," who is lord of all that exists.

The Near East
After 1500 B.C. the warlike Assyrians from northern Iraq become a leading power in the region. Their kings trade gifts with the pharaohs of Egypt.

Jealousy and Rebellion

Even though God provides for the people in the wilderness, jealousy raises its ugly head, and some challenge Moses' authority. First Moses' own sister and brother, Miriam and Aaron, claim that they have authority equal to Moses'! "Does Moses think he's the only prophet around? What about us?" they imply. Angrily, God rebukes them, saying that other prophets have visions, but only Moses sees the Lord face-to-face, that is, intimately. At the end of God's denunciation, Miriam's skin has turned white with a disease referred to as leprosy. A week spent outside the camp for purification is required for her healing. The people cannot start out again until she is brought back.

In another story someone challenges Moses and Aaron's authority, and others incite a political rebellion, accusing Moses of leading Israel out of Egypt on a wild-goose chase. But the rebels, with their families, are all destroyed. Then God gives a sign—almond blossoms growing from Aaron's staff—to confirm that Aaron's tribe has been chosen for the priesthood and is not to be challenged.

Read Numbers 12:1–16; 16:1–35; 17:1–11 (or 17:16–26 in NAB or NJB).

The sinning, healing community

In some ways the story of Israel resembles the story of the Church; after all, both are communities of people gathered together by God. (In fact, Christians believe that the gathering together of the People of God in Israel prepared for the gathering together of the People of God in Christ, the Church.) Israel was made up of people who were, like people today, weak and sinful, and sin took its toll. In the story of Aaron and Miriam's jealousy of Moses, the people cannot continue their journey until Miriam has been healed and restored to them. In the same way today, sin hinders the journey of the Church, yet repentance and God's healing forgiveness get it back on its way.

It horrifies us to think that God might destroy whole families as punishment for one member's sin. However, we need to understand that the destruction may have been the result of some natural disaster. In the Israelite culture, such disasters were commonly assumed to be punishment from God.

The Israelites looked forward to the abundance of food the Promised Land would yield. On a modern-day communal farm in Israel, cantaloupes are harvested.

Exploring the Land of Canaan

At one point, as the people draw nearer to the Promised Land, God has Moses send a man from each tribe to cross the border and explore Canaan. They return with tales of a land flowing with milk and honey but, they fearfully add, occupied by giants, next to whom the Israelites would seem like grasshoppers. Two of the scouts, Caleb and Joshua, want to enter the land nevertheless, but the people begin to mutter. Forgetting that God has broken the might of Egypt for them, the people complain that it would be better to have died in Egypt or to die now in the desert than to go into Canaan and be slaughtered.

God takes the people at their word and declares that for each of the forty days spent scouting Canaan, they will spend a year in the wilderness, until every member of the generation brought from Egypt has perished. Only Caleb and Joshua, who trusted in the power of God to protect them in Canaan, will live to see the land, along with the offspring of the first generation. Immediately the people change their tune. They *will* enter Canaan! Moses warns them not to disobey God; but the people go anyway, are defeated, and return disheartened.

Read Numbers 13:1–3,17–33; 14:1–45.

Faith without risk?

The story above is about faith and risk taking. Here a frightened Israel again forgets the generosity and mercy of God. The people choose instead the fragile security of the desert—and they get to stay there. They will be lost and wander for forty years because they did not trust in God's care for them. *5*

5

Find a psalm in which the writer describes how God is with us (or pleads for God to be with us) when we are frightened or in trouble. Identify the number of the psalm and write a few paragraphs reflecting what that psalm means to you. Apply it, if possible, to a risk you have taken in your life or a dangerous situation you found yourself in.

Water from a Rock

In the next story, the people settle at a place in the wilderness called Kadesh, more often called Kadesh-barnea. Again they quarrel with Moses, complaining about the hardship of the wilderness compared to the lush life in Egypt. God bids Moses to strike a rock with his staff so the rock will produce water for the parched Israelites and their livestock. Moses and Aaron gather the people, but sarcastically berate them as rebels before striking the rock. Water gushes forth from the rock, but the Lord is angry about the brothers' outburst at the people. God punishes Moses and Aaron, saying they will die without entering Canaan because they have not shown forth his holiness in how they treated the people.

Read Numbers 20:1–13.

God wants faith, not fear

Why do Moses and Aaron deserve such a harsh penalty? The explanation seems to be that time and again, when the people's faith has weakened, God has shown unfailing care and has inspired them through a mastery of nature. This time Moses and Aaron have resorted to angry sarcasm,

The Book of Numbers tells of how God provided water from a rock. In Tanzania, Africa, villagers rejoice over the clean water flowing from a newly installed water pump, part of a project begun by a Maryknoll mission priest.

I-Witness: Abigail

I'm Abigail, a servant to Seth the herder. After we left Egypt, times were hard. We didn't know how to live in the wilderness. Food and drinkable water were scarce. My parents wore down and then died of illness. I think they mostly died of broken hearts when we turned away from Canaan. They wanted to enter with Caleb and Joshua, but many of the elders were fearful and faithless.

I have no other kin, so Seth and his wife took me in. They are a quarrelsome couple, and often they take their resentments out on me—especially at evening meal. During the days I spend my time working with the other young women—hauling water jars, sewing skins, preparing food. My friends make my life tolerable. And I believe I will live long enough to enter the Promised Land, as the Lord promised us young people.

> ## "A star shall come out of Jacob, and a scepter shall rise out of Israel."
>
> **Numbers 24:17**

A star shines over Bethlehem.

changing the people's experience from one of renewed faith to one of fear. They have not dealt with the people in a reverent way, conveying God's sanctity. **6**

A Soothsayer Predicts Victory for Israel

As the Israelites journey through lands occupied by others, they are forced to bypass or sometimes do battle with other peoples—at which they are successful. So the king of Moab, desiring to protect the Moabites from being overcome by the Israelites, asks for the services of a soothsayer, Balaam, to tell him what to do. But to the king's horror, the words that come from Balaam's mouth in the form of an oracle are actually blessings for Israel! A final blessing lists the nations that Israel will overcome and includes a passage referring to a star that will come from Jacob.

Read Numbers 24:14–17.

Jacob's star

The passage about the star coming from Jacob was probably interpreted by Jews of the exile as a prediction of the reign of David or of the great destiny of Jacob's descendants. For the early Christians, however, the oracle was seen as a prophecy of Christ's coming. The nativity story in Matthew's

Gospel also mentions a star that the wise men followed to find the child who was king of the Jews. No doubt Matthew's reference to the star and the wise men helped the first Jewish Christians understand that Jesus was the Promised One.

6

Explain in writing what this story tells us about the ways God wants us to treat one another. Think of a situation in your school, city, country, or the world where people are not being treated in a way that reflects God's holiness. Describe the causes of the mistreatment and what needs to happen for change to come about.

Out of Egypt to the Wilderness and Promised Land

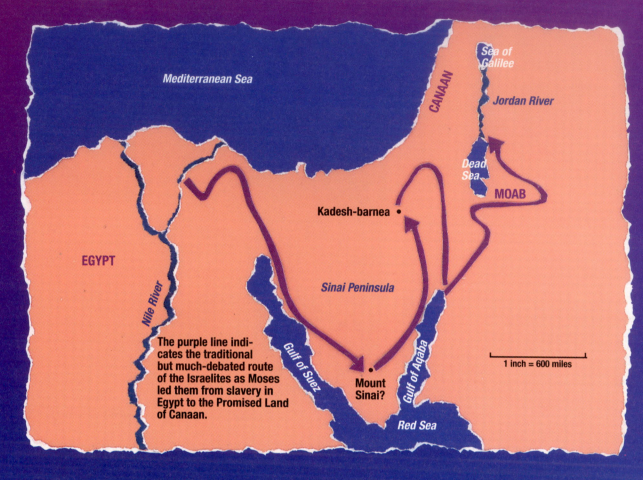

The purple line indicates the traditional but much-debated route of the Israelites as Moses led them from slavery in Egypt to the Promised Land of Canaan.

1 inch = 600 miles

A Summary of Numbers

Saint Paul provided a Christian interpretation of the Book of Numbers in his First Letter to the Corinthians. Once again we see how much is missing for Christians if, in reading the Gospels and the Epistles, Christians do not have an acquaintance with the writings in the Old Testament.

Read 1 Corinthians 10:1–13.

For Review

☐ What is the lesson for the Israelites and us in the story of the quail in the desert?

☐ Name two instances of rebellion against Moses' authority in the desert.

☐ According to Numbers, why will Caleb and Joshua be allowed to enter the Promised Land, but Moses and Aaron will not?

☐ How did the early Christians understand the oracle of Balaam about a star from Jacob?

Deuteronomy: The Law and Love

As you are reading from the **Book of Deuteronomy,** you may wonder, Haven't I heard all this before? And the answer is yes. In some fashion you have heard much of this before, in the Books of Exodus and Numbers. But the writer or editor of Deuteronomy used a different device to tell the story of Israel's liberation, Covenant with Yahweh, and wanderings in the desert. He set the story into the framework of three sermons by Moses to the Israelites as they stand on the plains of Moab poised to cross the Jordan River and enter the Promised Land. ("The hill country of the Amorites" is often used to describe Canaan, the Promised Land.)

So the opening of Deuteronomy sets the scene for Moses' sermons. The book closes with Moses climbing a mountain to take a final look at Canaan, which he will not be able to enter. He blesses the tribes of Israel, dies, and is buried and mourned by the people. Moses' assistant, **Joshua,** filled with wisdom because of his great love for God and his long apprenticeship under Moses, becomes Israel's new leader as they prepare to cross the Jordan and take the land of Canaan.

Read Deuteronomy 1:1–8; 34:1–12.

Moses' Passionate Message to His People

The sermons that make up most of Deuteronomy give a kind of last will and testament of Moses. They are Moses' passionate, often touching messages to the people he has loved and guided. He tries to inspire them to be faithful in this new land where many temptations await them—temptations to idolatry, to wealth, to trusting in their own power instead of God's.

These sermons retrace the wilderness journey of the Israelites in several retellings, reminding the people over and over of how God has been with them all along. Even though they have complained, rebelled, and not trusted, God has loved them and cared for them in their journey from slavery in Egypt, to the sealing of the Covenant at Horeb (another name for Sinai), through the forty years in the wilderness, to the brink of entering the Promised Land. 7

Read Deuteronomy 1:22–33.

The words of Moses?

Did Moses actually preach the sermons that make up most of the Book of Deuteronomy? Probably not. In biblical times it was common for followers of a great leader, even centuries after his death, to compose speeches or writings and attribute them to that

Before he was assassinated in 1968, civil rights leader Martin Luther King Jr. preached that he had been to the mountaintop and seen the "Promised Land"—a United States in which there is freedom and justice for all—but that (like Moses) he would not live to enter it.

7

In writing, share a story that is told and retold in your family. What special meaning or message does the story hold?

leader. They could do this because their leader's authority had been passed down to them and they could speak for him to people of their own era, in the spirit of his teaching if not in the details.

So the sermons of Moses probably were composed and edited by later teachers who, under God's inspiration, relied on various sources in Israelite tradition. This is one explanation of why the sermons contain many references to events or customs that came long after Moses.

Keeping the Law

In the midst of the storytelling and retelling, Moses' sermons repeatedly urge the people to keep the Law, the terms of the Covenant, faithfully and diligently. Moses recounts the giving of the Law, including a somewhat different version of the Ten Commandments than in the Exodus account. (*Deuteronomy*, incidentally, is a Greek word meaning "second law.")

Read Deuteronomy 5:1–21.

Specifics of the Law

Deuteronomy gives many other refinements of the Law, with applications to daily life as varied as what to eat, how to treat slaves justly, how to ensure that the poor are not trapped in their poverty, what festivals to celebrate, and how to carry out war so that the Israelites are not tainted by the idolatrous nations they rub shoulders with.

Deuteronomy shows a remarkable sensitivity to the poor and the oppressed. Here are some examples of laws having to do with justice:

- Every seven years debts must be forgiven, although the approach of the "release year" must not deter one from lending money to a poor neighbor.

The Prayer of Israel: Delight in the Law

Happy are those whose way is blameless,
    who walk in the law of the LORD.
Happy are those who keep his decrees,
    who seek him with their whole heart,
who also do no wrong,
    but walk in his ways.
You have commanded your precepts
    to be kept diligently.
O that my ways may be steadfast
    in keeping your statutes!
Then I shall not be put to shame,
    having my eyes fixed on all your commandments.
I will praise you with an upright heart,
    when I learn your righteous ordinances.
I will observe your statutes;
    do not utterly forsake me.

. . . .

Let your mercy come to me, that I may live;
    for your law is my delight.

(Psalm 119:1–8,77)

A scene of despair in Port-au-Prince, the capital of Haiti. One of the poorest countries in the Western Hemisphere, Haiti is burdened by its obligation to pay off its debts to rich lenders. Justice for the poor and oppressed, including periodic forgiveness of their debts, is commanded in the Book of Deuteronomy.

- Slaves who have served six years must be released in the seventh.
- Interest on a loan may be demanded of a foreigner but not of an Israelite.
- Israelites may not be sold into slavery. Anyone who does so can be punished by death.
- Millstones owned by the poor may not be taken in pledge for a loan, for without their millstones they cannot grind flour.
- Parents and children may not be punished for one another's crime. [8]

Josiah's reform movement

Those who composed the Book of Deuteronomy, called by modern scholars the **Deuteronomists,** were probably part of a vigorous reform movement in Judah that began about thirty years before the exile— **Josiah's reform.** Josiah, king of Judah, began the reform after an old "Book of the Law" was discovered in the Temple during repair work. Its scrolls contained a code of religious laws that forbade the corrupt, unjust, and idolatrous practices that had become rampant in Judah as the people polluted their Yahwistic religion with their neighbors' worship of false gods.

King Josiah was determined to call the people back to the Covenant they had broken by insisting on strict adherence to the extensive code of laws. This newly discovered code was probably the principal source for the Deuteronomists in composing the Book of Deuteronomy.

Josiah's reform movement did not succeed in heading off the disastrous exile, which came about twenty years after Josiah's

8

Find a newspaper or magazine article that depicts a situation where sensitivity and care are being shown to a person or group who is oppressed or poor. Write your reactions to the article.

death. In the Deuteronomists' view, the exile was inevitable because of the people's continuing hard-heartedness, cockiness and confidence in their own (not God's) might, and idolatry. The Deuteronomists believed that the people prosper on the land when they are good and obey the Law, but their life and land is doomed to failure when they defy God.

The Deuteronomists, before and during the exile, had a profound effect on the formation of the Bible and on the future of Judaism. Along with the Book of Deuteronomy, a number of the historical books of the Bible were written or edited by the Deuteronomists. We shall consider them in later chapters of this text.

The Prayer of Israel: The Shema

The central prayer of Jewish life, the Shema, is recited every morning and evening:

Hear, O Israel: The LORD is our God, the LORD alone. You shall love the LORD your God with all your heart, and with all your soul, and with all your might. Keep these words that I am commanding you today in your heart. Recite them to your children and talk about them when you are at home and when you are away, when you lie down and when you rise. Bind them as a sign on your hand, fix them as an emblem on your forehead, and write them on the doorposts of your house and on your gates. (Deuteronomy 6:4–9)

Mezuzah and phylacteries

Rabbis of biblical times interpreted the words of the Shema quite literally. So it is customary for many Jews to fasten to the doorpost of their dwelling a scroll on which are inscribed the verses of the Shema. This scroll, called the **mezuzah** (meaning "doorpost"), reminds Jews of God's holy presence as they enter and leave their home.

In addition, the verses of the Shema are kept in two small square leather boxes called **phylacteries.** In the Orthodox observance of Judaism, these boxes are strapped onto a person's forehead and left arm when the verses are recited. A Jew's daily act of binding the boxes to head and arm and wearing them heightens the awareness of God's nearness in all the thoughts and actions of daily life.

A mezuzah (top). A young man in Jerusalem prepares for prayer by putting on his phylacteries.

Hear, O Israel: The LORD is our God, the LORD alone. You shall love the LORD your God with all your heart, and with all your soul, and with all your might. Deuteronomy 6:4–5

Love at the core of the Law

At the heart of all the laws in Deuteronomy is the great prayer called the **Shema** (from the Hebrew word that begins the prayer, meaning "hear"). This prayer has been called the essence of Judaism. Repeated daily by Jews from biblical times up to the present, this profession of faith constantly reminds them that God is one, and the one whom they are to love with their entire being—heart, soul, and strength. In the time before the exile, the unfaithful Judahites desperately needed to hear that wake-up call, to remember the essence of the Covenant with Yahweh: God loves us, and we must love him above all else. After the exile and ever since, Jews have cherished the Shema as a prayer expressing what their life as God's people is all about.

The Shema includes the beautiful plea to the people to keep the command of love in their hearts wherever they are, to teach it to their children over and over, and to bind it to themselves so they will never forget it. [9]

Read Deuteronomy 6:4–9.

Jesus and the Great Commandment

Being thoroughly Jewish, Jesus and his parents would have recited the Shema daily. It must have been at the top of Jesus' consciousness, because he quoted Deuteronomy 6:5, about love of God, to the Pharisees who tried to trip him up with their question about which commandment of the Law was the greatest. Knowing that love of God cannot be separated from love of others, Jesus also added the command from Leviticus 19:18, "You shall love your neighbor as yourself."

9

In the Shema the Jews attempt to express and pass on their burning love for God. Has someone in your life passed on a sense of God's love to you? If so, write about this person and the ways she or he has taught you about God's love. Also reflect on any opportunities you have taken to pass on a sense of God's love to another.

A satellite photo shows the Sinai Peninsula, which was crossed by the Israelites on their way to Canaan.

In another Gospel passage, the story of Christ's temptation in the desert, Jesus like-wise used verses from Deuteronomy three times to respond to the devil's temptations. He was obviously formed and inspired by God's word in the Book of Deuteronomy. *Read Matthew 22:34–39; 4:1–11.*

For Review

- ☐ What device or style of writing was used as a framework for the Book of Deuteronomy?

- ☐ Give three examples of laws in Deuteronomy.

- ☐ What is the Shema? Explain its importance in Judaism.

- ☐ Which Gospel stories show that Jesus was inspired by God's word in the Book of Deuteronomy?

On the Brink of the Promised Land

At the closing of the Book of Deuteronomy, the Israelites are poised to enter Canaan, the abundant land promised by God to their father, Abraham, and his descendants. Moses has died, and now Joshua will lead them as they take over the land.

The Jews of the exile must have delighted in hearing about how their ancestors finally reached the Promised Land, with God's love and power protecting them all along the way. The exiles must have imagined that, like their ancestors, they would someday make it back home to their own land, if they would only stay faithful to God.

With the end of Deuteronomy, we have completed our study of the Pentateuch (Torah), the five books that Jews consider the most essential of the Jewish Bible.

- The first book, Genesis, taught us about the origins of the people of Israel.

- Exodus showed us how God freed the Israelites from slavery in Egypt and made the Covenant of Sinai with them.

- Leviticus showed us the great concern that the Jews held for reverent worship and holiness.

- Numbers took us on the journey with the Israelites through the wilderness in search of the Promised Land.

- And Deuteronomy gave us insight into the essential spirit of Judaism, which is whole-hearted love for God. This last book of the Pentateuch also brought the story of Israel to the brink of the Promised Land, with Joshua as God's chosen one in charge of the Israelites.

Now we, and the Israelites, are ready to launch into the Promised Land. **10**

10

Compose an essay, a cartoon, a poem, or a song that retells one of the stories about ancient Israel's journey through the wilderness. Use a modern setting and modern characters.

5 The Land

Finding Hope for the Future in God's Gift

A field of poppies in Israel. The Israelite tribes saw the Promised Land as God's gift to them.

Our study moves on in this chapter to the Books of Joshua, Judges, and Ruth. These Scriptures tell stories about the beginnings of the Israelites' life in the Promised Land, covering the period from Moses' death to just before Israel became a nation with a king—the period dating from about 1250 to 1030 B.C.

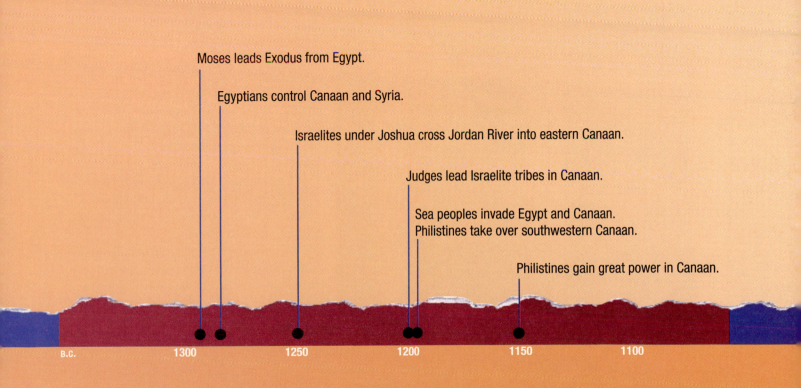

Moses leads Exodus from Egypt.

Egyptians control Canaan and Syria.

Israelites under Joshua cross Jordan River into eastern Canaan.

Judges lead Israelite tribes in Canaan.

Sea peoples invade Egypt and Canaan.
Philistines take over southwestern Canaan.

Philistines gain great power in Canaan.

B.C. 1300   1250   1200   1150   1100

Let's step back from the Old Testament for a bit to put ourselves into another frame of mind, which will help us understand the next several books of the Bible.

The View from the Pits

Imagine that you are an eighteen-year-old in the midst of what seems the most disastrous event of your life. You are picked up on the street in the middle of the night, utterly wasted. Being wasted is not something new for you, but getting picked up for it as an adult is. You are so drunk and stoned that you slug a cop just before you pass out. You are taken to the detox unit at the hospital, and when you finally wake up, you get the bad news. You've been charged with public drunkenness, possession of illegal drugs, disorderly conduct, and assaulting a police officer.

Your parents are there, looking terribly wounded and disappointed in you. This is a new low on the downhill track you've been taking since junior high. You feel like a complete failure. There's talk of pulling you out of your last semester of high school to go to treatment. But first you have to face the charges, and you could end up in jail for a while. Which you do.

As the days and weeks go by in jail, you spend a lot of time thinking. It's a bad place to be, but it's the first time you've ever had a chance to take a hard look at yourself—not with your usual pose of bravado ("Hey, I'm fine—I can handle anything") but with simple honesty. You begin to ask: "How did I end up here? I had so much going for me. Now I'm totally wrecked. What happened? Where did I go wrong?"

In the months that follow jail—in residential treatment, then in a halfway house, you look back on your personal life history. This experience has sobered you up like nothing else ever did. You move past blaming everybody else for what you've become, and you begin to look within. You think about the poor choices you've made over the years, and the opportunities you've passed up. You remember how you refused to listen to anything you didn't want to hear. You were so sure of yourself, confident you didn't need any help. Now you realize what an illusion that was.

You've made big mistakes, but life isn't over. In this time away from home and your usual life, a kind of "captive" situation, you are trying to learn from your past. From those lessons, you begin to squeeze out some hope for a future where things will be different.

A History in the Midst of Exile

What does the above imagination exercise have to do with the books of the Bible that we will study in the next few chapters of this course? Recall again that much of the Old Testament was edited and rewritten during the exile in Babylon. The Jews were "in the pits." They had just suffered a terrible disaster, losing their homeland and freedom. They had thought they could never be defeated, but here they were, humiliated subjects of a foreign king. Their self-assurance evaporated as they came face-to-face with their own failure. They wondered: "What went wrong? How did we end up here?"

During this period the Deuteronomists (recall from chapter 4 that they promoted King Josiah's reform before and during the exile) tried to answer that question by composing a history of the Israelites from their entry into the Promised Land (about 1250 B.C.) up through the monarchy to the time of the exile (587 B.C.), a span of almost seven hundred years. They used many old oral and written sources, compiling, editing, and rewriting them into several books of the Bible, which are now called the **Deuteronomic history:** Joshua, Judges, the First and Second

Books of Samuel, and the First and Second Books of Kings. The Book of Deuteronomy was a kind of introduction to that history, laying out the story of God's Covenant with Israel before they reached the Promised Land.

This history was as a **self-examination** for the people of Israel. They had gotten themselves into this terrible state of affairs, the exile, through their unfaithfulness to God and their self-delusion that they would never be overcome. The Deuteronomists knew that the people would need to own up to the mistakes of their past if they were to have any hope for the future. The people could not blame the Babylonian Empire or God or bad fortune for their plight. Their hope lay in recognizing all they had been given by God, how they had betrayed him, and his call to commit themselves to a new, faithful way of life.

So the Deuteronomists helped the people of Israel turn the disaster of the exile into a time of reflection and transformation

Self-examination and reflection can bring forth transformation.

that would ready them for the return one day to their homeland, full of hope in their hearts. The experience for the exiles was somewhat like that of our fictional eighteen-year-old at the beginning of this chapter, who uses the "captive" time to build hope for a new life.

The Books of Joshua and Judges can be read as part of the examination of conscience that is the Deuteronomic history. [1]

For Review

☐ Which biblical books are considered part of the Deuteronomic history?

☐ What purpose did this history serve for the Jews in exile?

1

Over and over in the Old Testament, we hear about the mistakes of the Israelites and the people and events that helped them get back on track. God offers us *unlimited* chances to turn from our mistakes—no matter what we have done—and to start over. It's always *our* choice, however, to make a fresh start. Have you ever had the opportunity to pause and examine your past? What did you discover? As a result of your reflecting, did you choose to make any changes? Describe in writing what it feels like to be given another chance, and the transformation and hope that can accompany that moment.

Joshua: Sweeping into the Promised Land

The **Book of Joshua** tells about one of Israel's greatest heroes, the man chosen by Moses to lead the Israelites into Canaan. It offers miraculous accounts of how Israel enters and takes the land under Joshua's command and settles there. This book, as well as the Book of Judges, contains accounts of battles and victories in which the Israelites pillage whole cities and slaughter their inhabitants. This may surprise us, or even shock us. Our study may help give perspective on why these accounts are included, and what meaning they could have for us today.

Joshua Is Sent

The book opens with God's sending Joshua to take the land of Canaan, urging him to be brave and steadfast, and reminding him to keep the Law. Joshua says that in three days the Israelites will cross the Jordan River from the east, an ideal position from which to launch an invasion of Canaan.

Read Joshua 1:1–18.

"Be strong and courageous; do not be frightened or dismayed, for the LORD your God is with you wherever you go." Joshua 1:9

Turning to God

The story of Joshua reminded the exiled Jews in Babylon centuries later of their need to turn to God again. Joshua represented everything that Israel was supposed to be—completely faithful and trusting in God. As these verses remind the reader, Israel's exile was the result of ignoring the Law of Moses and rejecting the love of God. *2*

Rahab and the Spies

Joshua sends two spies to scout Jericho, the first city across the Jordan. Entering it without trouble, they go to a lodging house run by a prostitute named **Rahab,** who recognizes that they are Israelites. When the king's men come to question her about the visitors, she sends the spies to hide under the flax drying on her roof and misdirects the search party to the countryside. After dark, Rahab bargains with the spies. She will help them escape if they will promise safety for her family when Jericho is invaded. The men give her a red cord to hang in the window of her house, which is built into the city wall, and they promise not to harm anyone in the house marked by the cord. The spies return to Joshua with news of the city's terror as it awaits invasion.

Read Joshua 2:1–24.

Doing the will of God

We might criticize Rahab for her betrayal of the city. Is she a traitor in choosing the survival of herself and her family? The biblical writers seem undivided in their opinion that she is doing the will of God.

Rahab reappears in a surprising passage in the Christian writings. The biblical writers, including those of the New Testament, had no trouble acknowledging the worthiness of this woman who was not only a prostitute but a Canaanite. They saw her divinely given role in the history of Israel, and even in the ancestry of Jesus. God's way, it seems, is to choose the most unlikely persons to accomplish his purposes in the world.

Read Matthew 1:1–6; James 2:24–25.

An excavation at the site of what is thought to be the ancient city of Jericho

Crossing the Jordan River

Now comes another story of a miraculous crossing, reminding us of Moses leading the Israelites through the Sea of Reeds. Joshua orders the march; and as soon as the feet of the priests touch the riverbed of the **Jordan,** the waters cease to flow—piling up to the north and disappearing to the south. The people cross over, and one man from each of the twelve tribes carries a stone from the

2

Reminders to keep God's Law can sound like "how to keep God happy." But morality, far from being something we must do to *please God,* is meant to *protect us.* Write a brief essay about some law that irks you. Argue both its pros and its cons, in separate paragraphs.

I-Witness: Zeb

I'm Zeb. My family has wandered with Moses for many years—more years than I've been alive. We live as herders, moving our stock from pasture to pasture. This land is hard-scrabble and sometimes our tribe must split up into small groups to find enough forage and water for our animals.

Joshua tells us it's time to band together and make a place for ourselves in Canaan—which is our birthright, the land of Abraham and Sarah. The people living in Canaan are the trespassers, not us, Joshua says. We are not warriors by tradition, but a hard life has toughened us.

No god of Canaan will stand against our God, the God of Moses, who has kept us alive in the wilderness all this time, and promised us the land of milk and honey. Imagine living long enough in one place to keep bees!

---

riverbed to build a memorial at the new camp. They call it Gilgal, meaning "circle" and referring to a circle of stones. [3]

Read Joshua 3:1–17; 4:1–24.

God's doing, not the Israelites'

The ancient stories of the crossing, worked into the Deuteronomic history, were intended to impress on the Israelites that their arrival in Canaan was a gift from God, not something they had accomplished on their own. The land was God's gift to them, and he would be on their side fighting for them in the struggle to claim the land. This theme comes through over and over in the Book of Joshua's accounts of amazing victories that could only be attributed to God's mighty hand.

Israel in the Promised Land

Once in Canaan the people eat for the first time the produce of the Promised Land. The manna—the breadlike substance from the heavens that had sustained them through their years in the wilderness—disappears. They have their first celebration of the Passover in the land of the Promise.

In a mysterious encounter, Joshua meets the captain of the army of the Lord (captain of a host of angels), and like Moses in Exodus 3:5, Joshua is told to remove his sandals because he stands on holy ground. This encounter is a sign that God will be with Joshua in the coming battle at Jericho. [4]

Read Joshua 5:10–15.

The abundance of the land

No longer wilderness people, sustained by miraculous manna, the Israelites were able to eat from the abundance of the land God had given them. They had a place to call their own. From now on their happiness and well-being would be associated with the land. For them, the land was not just a place to live but, as God's gift to them, the source

---

[3]

Read Psalm 114. This psalm was written long after the events described in Joshua. Write your reactions to the language used by the writer.

[4]

Even though Joshua was a great leader, he was humble before God. Taking off his sandals—as Moses did when he encountered God in the burning bush—was a sign of his awe and respect. List five things that cause you to feel awe and explain why.

of life, blessing, joy, and security. Here they would know **shalom,** the deep peace of God. There would be struggles ahead to attain the land from the local inhabitants. But the Israelites never doubted that God wanted them to have that land as the place they would grow and prosper. *5*

Jericho: "And the Walls Came Tumblin' Down"

Joshua's soldiers lay siege to **Jericho,** surround the city, and cut off its supplies. Then early each morning for six days, seven priests carrying rams' horns lead the Israelites out of camp. Behind these priests come other priests carrying the ark of the Covenant.

Troops march before and behind the priests. The entire company, silent except for the blaring of the rams' horns, marches once around the city. At dawn on the seventh day, the Israelites circle the city seven times, and at a signal they begin to storm the wall and shout. Jericho falls, and only Rahab and those in her house are saved from the slaughter of the people and animals in the city.

Read Joshua 6:1–21.

The walls of Jericho

The details of the procession to Jericho, the circling of the city seven times, the blowing of horns, the shouting as the people storm the walls, sound much like a liturgical ritual. Some scholars think that these descriptions may have been instructions for regular rituals of commemoration at the ruins of Jericho years after the Israelites' victory there. These instructions could have then found their way into the written account of the battle.

The story of the collapse of Jericho's walls reminds us of a 1990 "miracle"— the dismantling of the Berlin Wall in Germany, a barrier that symbolized the great divide between the Communist-controlled countries of Eastern Europe and those of the democratic West. Here, teenagers chip away at the Berlin Wall.

5

In writing or in art, create something that reflects what shalom means to you.

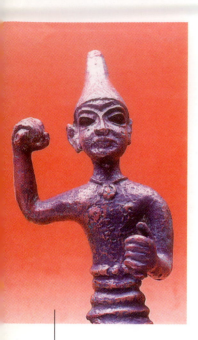

The Canaanite god Baal

The ban:
"Devotion to God for destruction"

In the Jericho account, we read of a practice called **the ban,** in some translations termed "devotion to God for destruction." The practice first comes up as God's command in the Book of Deuteronomy. It was essentially an order to destroy everything in a conquered town—all its inhabitants, their possessions, and their animals—and to take nothing for one's own. It is worth considering why such apparently savage behavior was written into the accounts as fulfilling God's command.

What About Those Battles?

The violent imagery of the battles in the Book of Joshua, and especially the practice of the ban, is hard to understand in light of our concept of God as compassionate and merciful, as the one who commands us not to kill. How can this type of warfare, which aims at total destruction, be justified by the scriptural writers as God's will, even as a sort of devotion to him?

First of all, we need to recognize that stories of such destruction were not intended to give us moral direction about war. Nor is it likely that the ban was ever really carried out in the total way that the Book of Joshua describes it. However, we know that ancient warfare involved much brutality, as it often does today, and the scriptural accounts reflect that.

A theological lesson:
Exclusive devotion to God

One way to look at these accounts is to see them as having a theological purpose, teaching the people how totally and exclusive-ly they were to devote themselves to God. The Deuteronomists, living among their fellow Jews in Babylon at the time of the exile, knew that Israel's history through the centuries before the exile was full of infidelity to God. This took the form of worshiping the idols of the Canaanites and engaging in horrible prac-tices as a way of trying to get the Canaanites' gods to do what the Israelites wanted.

These Canaanite practices included fer-tility rites, which involved the use of male and female prostitutes at the Canaanite temples. The Canaanites imagined this would encour-age their fertility gods, **Baal** and Ashtarte, to produce a good crop on the land. The Israel-ites, trying to master the techniques of farm-ing, often gave in to the temptation to do whatever the successful locals did to ensure a plentiful harvest—so they, too, would visit the temple prostitutes. Another practice was that of child sacrifice to the gods as a way of appeasing them when they were angry. Even that atrocity some Israelites practiced, includ-ing some of their kings through the centuries.

The Deuteronomists knew that God wanted the Israelites to have nothing to do with such immorality. If it meant they must get rid of everything Canaanite, so be it. Thus the ban was a practice included in the scriptural accounts partly as a warning to later Jews against having anything to do with other religions and their terrible practices. *6*

God can bring good out of evil

Beyond the theological point of the ban, we have to acknowledge that the Israelites' taking over the land did probably involve much brutality, and that this was the reality of warfare in that era. But was God truly in favor of that? Was God really on the side of the Israelites as they slaughtered women and children?

We must answer that God would never will the destruction of innocent people, in ancient times or today. However, God's will was that the Israelites possess the land. Their claiming the land was accomplished partly through the methods the people of that time knew—brutal warfare. The people may have

6

In our culture, worshiping idols takes on various forms, such as spending excessive time and energy to accumulate wealth. Think of four other kinds of idol worship around us that could inter-fere with a person's devotion to God.

7

Interview three people about the meaning of *obedience:* a parent or a grandparent, a priest or a religious sister or brother, and a peer. Explore with them the meanings that go deeper than our typical understanding of "doing what someone else tells you to do." Report your findings in an essay and include your own thoughts on the topic. How does this relate to the Israelites' understanding of obedience?

thought their means of warfare were God's will, but they were conditioned by the prevailing practices of the time. God, however, can bring good out of the strangest circumstances, even situations of great evil.

In the accounts of Jericho and other battles, the overriding message is that when the people put their trust entirely in God, they are victorious. The Deuteronomists emphasized again and again that trust in God and obedience to the Law will bring rewards. Pride in one's own power and disobedience to God will bring disaster, as is illustrated in the next story. *7*

Breaking the Ban: Defeat at Ai

After Jericho's destruction Joshua's men scout the town of **Ai** and predict an easy conquest. Yet Israel is defeated. Demoralized, Joshua prays to God, who tells him that someone has broken the ban by taking loot from Jericho (the valuables should have been destroyed). Joshua assembles the tribes and discovers that a man named Achan is the culprit.

Achan is executed by stoning, and his loot is burned and buried. He failed to trust in God by honoring the ban. His disobedience and greed, shown in his taking loot from Jericho, have brought defeat to Israel at

Ai. The point of the story is that the Israelites must hold nothing back, giving their obedient devotion entirely to God.

Read Joshua 7:1–26.

The Sun Standing Still

Local Canaanite kings become terrified of the Israelites. One group some distance away, the Gibeonites, makes a protective alliance with Israel. When the five local kings learn that the Gibeonites are allied with Israel, they put Gibeon under siege. Its citizens cry to Joshua for help. Joshua's army marches under cover of darkness, takes the besiegers by surprise, and routs them. In the midst of battle the next day, Joshua asks God to stop the sun in the sky, and the storyteller marvels at his obeying a human. The attacking kings—lumped together as "the Amorites" in some versions of the Bible—are found by Joshua and executed.

Read Joshua 10:12–14.

A gift from God

Joshua's request that the sun stop in the sky is a fragment of an ancient song of victory from the lost Book of Jashar—apparently a book of poems celebrating Israel's heroes.

A 1994 refugee camp in Rwanda, Africa, for tribal people seeking safety from persecution by another tribe

The spectacle of the sun standing still helps to underline the point of the story—that the victory of Joshua and the Israelites on that day was a marvelous gift from God, not something they achieved on their own.

Conquests, Tribal Divisions, and Cities of Refuge

The remainder of the Book of Joshua gives a simplified account of the conquest of Canaan, claiming that Joshua captures all the land and subdues all Israel's enemies. The division of the land among the tribes of Israel is reported—along with the setting aside of the cities of refuge, or asylum.

Read Joshua 20:1–6; Deuteronomy 19:1–13.

The twelve tribes of Israel

Twelve, the number of the tribes, became symbolic for the Israelites—and later for Christians. In Acts of the Apostles 1:15–26, for example, we read that the Apostles choose Matthias to replace Judas in order to complete "the Twelve," whom Jesus said would sit on twelve thrones to judge the twelve tribes of Israel.

Joshua's military successes

The writer's claim of a quick conquest of Canaan cannot be accurate because in the next book, Judges, we will see Israel living side by side with Canaanite tribes—sometimes dominating them, sometimes as their vassals, or subjects, even intermarrying with them.

The Deuteronomists do not seem troubled about telling the story inconsistently in the two books. That is because the purpose of the Joshua account is theological, not historical. It is meant to show that God was with Joshua, the faithful, obedient leader, and had given the land of Canaan to the Israelites as a miraculous gift.

The cities of refuge

Places of refuge probably came later than the time of Joshua, perhaps during the time of King David. The idea behind them was to protect people guilty of accidental or unintentional killing from being attacked by the victims' families for blood vengeance. Down through the centuries, Egyptians, Jews, Greeks, Romans, and Christians all have followed similar practices of **sanctuary**—so called because the refuge was often at a religious shrine. Sanctuary remains a universal custom, offering aid to the persecuted and the homeless. *8*

The Death of Joshua

In a solemn farewell, Joshua begs his people never to forget the one God who has done so much for them, and he warns them of the consequences if they do forget. The Israelites renew the Covenant at a place called **Shechem,** and Joshua's work is done. He dies and is buried in his tribal land.

Read Joshua 24:1–33.

8

Sanctuary was originally given to accidental murderers to protect them from the vengeance of the victim's survivors. Ironically, today sanctuary is often denied to innocent people from war-torn countries who are trying to escape being murdered. Find and read a newspaper or magazine article about refugees seeking sanctuary. Write your thoughts on the story and include your reaction to this question: *Do we have a moral obligation to offer sanctuary?*

Joshua: A model for Israel

Joshua was one of Israel's greatest leaders—strong, courageous, careful, honest, unshaken by failure, a keeper of treaties, and an upholder of the Law. Joshua was an inspiration to his people; his heart was on fire with love for God, and by obeying him, he brought Israel into the Promised Land.

An Israeli soldier takes time for prayer.

The Prayer of Israel: Choosing Whom We Will Serve

Before his death Joshua gathered the Israelites at Shechem and gave them the chance to pledge themselves either to the Lord or to the illusions of other gods. He said:

"Choose this day whom you will serve; . . . but as for me and my household, we will serve the LORD."

Then the people answered, "Far be it from us that we should forsake the LORD to serve other gods; for it is the LORD our God who brought us and our ancestors up from the land of Egypt, out of the house of slavery, and who did those great signs in our sight. He protected us all along the way that we went, and among all the peoples through whom we passed; and the LORD drove out before us all the peoples, the Amorites who lived in the land. Therefore we also will serve the LORD, for he is our God." (Joshua 24:15–18)

"Choose this day whom you will serve, . . . but as for me and my household, we will serve the LORD." Joshua 24:15

For the Deuteronomists, who constructed their history of Israel centuries after Joshua's time, Joshua was an ideal figure. Their portrayal of Joshua gave the exiles a model to follow. After the wondrous era of Joshua's divinely given victories, however, the story of the Israelites in the Promised Land takes a downward slide, as we will see in the Book of Judges. **9**

For Review

☐ What was the practice known as the ban? Explain a lesson that the scriptural accounts of the ban contained for the Jews.

☐ What characteristics of Joshua made him a model for the exiled Jews to follow?

9

Joshua was a born leader—and Hitler was also. Write a paragraph about how to choose leaders who are worth following and how to avoid those who are not.

Spring in Galilee, Israel

Judges: Saving Israel from Itself

The **Book of Judges,** which has nothing to do with legal matters, might be better called the Book of Deliverers. That is because its stories tell how God raises up deliverers to save Israel when, after settling in Canaan, the Israelites are unfaithful and overwhelmed by enemies.

The book spans the years between the death of Joshua and the beginning of the First Book of Samuel (about 1200 to 1025 B.C.), but was put together long afterward during the exile as part of the Deuteronomic history.

A Cycle of Sin, Disaster, Repentance, and Merciful Deliverance

With Joshua gone, the tribes fall into self-indulgence and idol worship, which repeatedly leads to their downfall. When Israel forgets its call to reveal the one God to the nations, it becomes selfish, timid, and self-delusional, and ends up being dominated by idol-worshiping neighbors. However, each time this happens, the people eventually repent of their infidelity, and then God brings forward a hero, a tribal leader called a **judge,** through whom God delivers the people from destruction. Here is how the pattern goes with each story of a judge:

1. The Israelites fall into sin, worshiping idols and abandoning God.
2. Their sin leads to their own calamity. They are assaulted and persecuted by their enemies, the Canaanites.
3. The Israelites repent of their sin and cry to God for help.
4. God has mercy on the people and raises up a judge to deliver them from disaster, and they triumph over their enemies.

After the victory the people are faithful to God and live in peace for a time, but soon the **cycle of sin, disaster, repentance, and deliverance** starts up again. *10*

People Called by God

The stories of the judges are derived from early songs and poems of Israel's heroes. These heroes, however, are not nobles but peasants. Nor is their behavior particularly noble. Rather, they are people called by God to deliver Israel—regardless of their personal weaknesses.

Twelve judges are mentioned in the Book of Judges itself: six minor judges, barely mentioned, and six major judges—**Othniel, Ehud, Deborah, Gideon, Jephthah,** and **Samson.** Their stories are quite entertaining to read, full of adventure, trickery, betrayal, and courage. Like the Book of Joshua, they are full of violence, at times horrifyingly graphic. We will study three of the major judges here: Deborah, Gideon, and Samson.

Israel Settles In with the Canaanites

The Book of Judges opens with a description of Israel in Canaan that is very different from the picture given in the Book of Joshua. In Joshua we read that all Canaan was captured and its people overpowered. But in Judges,

10

Write a short story about a young person that illustrates the cycle of sin, disaster, repentance, and deliverance.

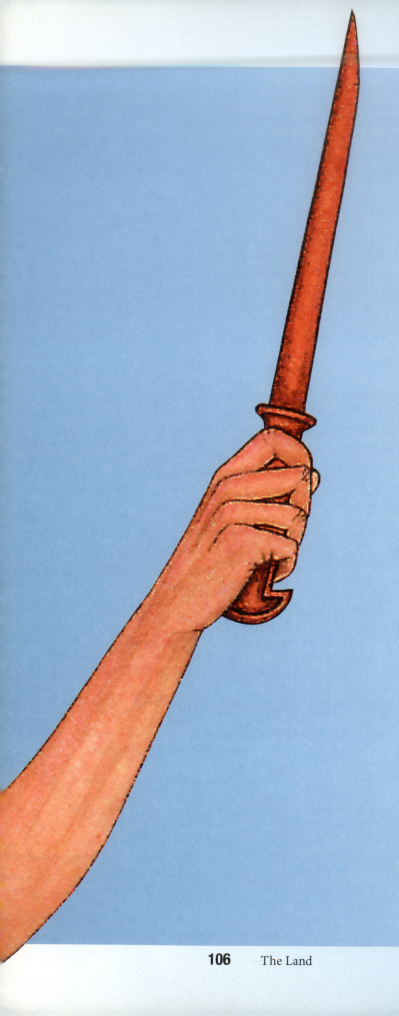

the Israelites not only settled down among the Canaanites but even intermarried and worshiped with them.

Read Joshua 21:43–45; Judges 1:21–36; 3:1–7.

Deborah: Victory with a Gruesome Touch

Deborah, referred to as both a judge and a prophet, is a magistrate of the tribe of Naphtali, deciding local disputes for her people. Her tribe has done "what was evil in the sight of the Lord" (Judges 4:1). As is the pattern in the stories of the judges, the tribe thus has fallen under the domination of the Canaanite king Jabin, whose army, with its nine hundred iron chariots, has kept the people subject for twenty years. The people cry out for help to the Lord, and God chooses Deborah as an instrument of the divine rescue. Deborah reveals to Barak, the commander of the Israelite militia, that God wants him to lead an army against Jabin's general Sisera. Barak fearfully agrees to go if Deborah will accompany him, and she consents but says that he will lose the credit for the victory.

When the Canaanite Sisera assembles his army in the valley, torrential rains render his chariots useless, and he and his troops are routed. Sisera deserts his troops and flees to the tent of his friend, whose wife, Jael, welcomes him, serves him refreshment, and bids him to rest while she stands guard.

Though she behaves hospitably, Jael is actually outraged at Sisera's desertion of his troops. So while he sleeps, she hammers a tent peg through his skull. Ever after Jael is glorified in the savagely triumphant **Canticle of Deborah.** Defeat at the hands of a wo-man—even in this case a woman who breaks her word and betrays the sacred law of hospitality—is the ultimate disgrace for a warrior. A final sarcastic touch to the story is the glimpse of Sisera's mother and wives waiting in the harem to divide the spoils that he will never bring.

Read Judges 4:1–24; 5:1–31.

A bit of gloating and glee

The purpose of the story of Deborah and Jael is not to document God's approval of hammering sharp objects into people's skulls! It is to recount the many ways that God helped Israel become free of its enemies. The Jewish exiles who later listened to this story certainly needed a victory to gloat over—needed to believe that someday, somehow, they too would be freed.

When the story of Deborah and Jael was in its early form, it was probably told at gatherings as great entertainment, with the audience's glee rising as the familiar story was recounted all the way to its gruesome climax. Such violence just added to the story's entertainment value, giving a kind of emotional release: "Yeah, we sure got 'em that time!" Perhaps everyone joined in singing the Canticle of Deborah as a sort of cheer for "our team." It is not terribly different from some films and TV shows today that use violence to capture their audience and build to a violent climax in which the "good guys" convincingly beat the "bad guys." Such violence in entertainment may not be very admirable, but it is not so different from the stories of the judges.

For all the gruesomeness of the tale of Deborah and Jael, the story surely nurtured hope in the exiles' hearts that they too, with God fighting for them, would one day overcome their oppressors.

Deborah's canticle is one of the oldest writings in the Bible, dating back almost to the time of the events it describes.

Gideon the Lowly

After forty years of "rest" for the land (that is, peace), the Israelites again fall into evil practices of worshiping Canaanite gods.

Gideon's tribe, Manasseh, together with all Israel, then comes under oppression by Midianite desert dwellers, who raid the tribe's land and ruin its crops. The Israelites cry to God for mercy, and though he is clearly unhappy with their disobedience, he decides to save the people through the young man Gideon.

We first glimpse Gideon secretly threshing wheat in his family's winepress, when an angel calls him to save his people. Gideon protests that as the youngest of the lowliest family in Manasseh, he is hardly a candidate for such a heroic task. Yet God assures Gideon of victory and consumes Gideon's sacrificial offering with fire as a sign of favor.

Read Judges 6:1–24.

Gideon Destroys the Altar of Baal

In a dream Gideon is told to destroy the altar of the Canaanite god Baal, built by unfaithful Israelites. When he does, the outraged townspeople order Gideon's father, Joash, to slay Gideon. Joash cunningly suggests that if Baal is a god, Baal should kill Gideon himself. No doubt to mock the god, Gideon is given the nickname **Jerubbaal,** meaning "Let Baal contend against him."

Gideon asks for another sign that God has chosen him to save Israel. Placing a sheepskin outdoors on the threshing floor, he asks God that dew fall on it and not on the ground—which it does. When Gideon reverses the request, the wool remains dry overnight, though the ground becomes dewy.

Read Judges 6:25–40.

The Tribes of Israel in Canaan

DAN

ASHER

ARAMAEANS

PHOENICIANS

Mediterranean Sea

NAPHTALI

ZEBULUN

Sea of Galilee

ISSACHAR

MANASSEH

Shechem

According to the Bible, the Israelites entered Canaan by crossing the Jordan River from the east side to the west near Jericho. Later they settled in tribal clusters among the Canaanites.

EPHRAIM

Ai • Gilgal
Jericho

Jordan River

GAD

AMMONITES

BENJAMIN
• Gibeon

DAN
• Jerusalem

REUBEN

Bethlehem •

Dead Sea

PHILISTINES

Hebron •

JUDAH

SIMEON

MOABITES

EDOMITES

ASHER	Tribes of Israel
EDOMITES	Other peoples in Canaan

Fearful heroes?

The worship of Baal has to be wiped out among Gideon's people before he can expect a victory over the Midianites. But even after he has accomplished that by tearing down the altar to Baal, Gideon still is not confident. The sign with the sheepskin assures him. Insecurity and fear were frequent companions of the judges, and later the prophets, when answering God's call. *11*

Gideon's Victory Is God's

Gideon gathers a large army, but is rebuked by God for doing so. God points out that with such a huge force, the Israelites would probably credit any victory they win to their own might, not to God's power. Gideon must send some men home. Under God's direction Gideon whittles down his troops to three hundred men. He divides them into companies, and each man is given a horn and an empty water jar in which is hidden a lighted torch.

On a dark, moonless night, the three hundred Israelites surround the Midianite camp, break their water jars, reveal the torches, and blow their horns. The Midianites believe Israel's attack force to be much larger than it is because in the Midianite army, only the officers (each officer commanding ten men) carry torches. In the dark the Midianites begin fighting each other, and the survivors flee in terror. Gideon's men seize the Jordan ford and slay all of the enemy who attempt to cross.

The grateful Israelites beg Gideon to be their king, but he insists that God alone is their king. However, he will erect a cultic object to celebrate the victory. Collecting the Israelites' golden ornaments, he creates an ephod—a receptacle for use in seeking oracles. Unfortunately, the people slip back into their old ways and begin to worship the object as an idol; in the end it spells the ruin of Gideon's family. Following Gideon's death his son Abimelech murders all but one of his own brothers.

Read Judges 7:1–8, 16–22; 8:22–35; 9:1–6.

The best-laid plans

God inspired Gideon to execute the brilliant bit of psychological warfare that brought him victory. The Deuteronomists passing on the story wanted to make it clear that God, not Gideon or his scaled-down army, was responsible for the Israelites' triumph. But Gideon's own scheme to erect the ephod—without consulting God—was his undoing.

Although Gideon's son Abimelech was proclaimed king, the biblical writers did not recognize him as such. His savage behavior excludes him from most lists of the judges as well.

Samson: Foe of the Philistines

The stories about Samson were probably first told around campfires in the days when the Philistines dominated the Israelite tribes of Dan; they convey the religious truth that God was with the Israelites.

11

Gideon destroyed the altar of Baal because it symbolized the worst offenses of the surrounding culture. If you could destroy something that represents evil in our society—and it would cause people to be outraged at you—what would it be?

Modern-day rebel soldiers in Ethiopia, Africa, are not unlike the fierce Philistines and the opposing Israelite guerrilla bands of the biblical era.

The **Philistines** were one of the sea peoples who had invaded Canaan from the Mediterranean Sea and were expanding into the interior, where they clashed with the Israelites. With their metalworking skills and their superior iron weaponry, the Philistines posed a severe threat to everyone in the region.

As time went on and Israel lost even more territory to Philistia, the people found comfort in these tales of Samson, a village hero and one-man war machine who had started the Israelites' resistance to the dreaded Philistines. In both life and death, Samson proved to be too much for the hated enemies of his people—but he did not ultimately conquer them.

When the story of Samson opens, the Philistines have dominated Israel, which had again fallen into unfaithfulness to God, for forty years. Samson's birth to a barren woman is foretold by an angel, who says that Samson is to be a **Nazirite**—a man consecrated to God from birth, never to touch strong drink or cut his hair or his beard.

Read Judges 13:1–25.

Some good advice

Notice that the angel advises Samson's mother not to consume wine or strong drink during her pregnancy—a recommendation that we think of as quite modern.

Samson: Strong Man and Victim of Himself

Several stories tell of Samson's exploits against the Philistines, all of which involve amazing strength and disastrous relationships with women. Samson falls in love with a Philistine woman, and there follow the famous tales of his great strength. He kills a lion barehanded, slaughters thirty Philistines, discovers that his wife has been given to another, and in a rage sets three hundred foxes afire in the Philistines' fields. Captured, Samson breaks his bonds and kills a thousand Philistines with the jawbone of a donkey.

Eventually Samson becomes infatuated with Delilah, a woman bribed by the Philistines to find out the secret of his strength. Ever unable to resist the enticements of women, Samson finally tells her of his consecration to God and that the secret of his strength is the length of his hair. He falls asleep, she has the Philistines enter and cut his hair, and he is captured.

Samson's eyes are gouged out, and he is put to grinding grain like a beast at the mill wheel. But his hair grows again, and his strength returns. When the Philistines make sport of him in the temple of their chief god, Samson stands between two pillars and pushes them over. The temple collapses, killing Samson and all the Philistines at the scene. *12*

Read Judges 14:1–20; 15:1–20; 16:1–31.

Strong back, weak character

Samson has little to recommend him. He is a violent man with an uncontrolled passion for women—like a host of undisciplined, self-destructive characters in both fiction and history. His story is the tragedy of a physically strong, morally weak man who might have been great if he had used his gifts for good.

The details of Samson's birth—including the angel and the Nazirite calling—are probably late additions to justify how such an unsavory character could be a judge.

Samson's personality, marked by rages and lusts, is familiar to us through other historical and literary characters. When finally he is the cause of his own downfall, the story becomes a classic yet familiar human tragedy. No wonder Samson has inspired so many operas, writings, movies, and paintings.

Why such a judge?

Given Samson's character, why did the Deuteronomists list him among the judges? Perhaps their purpose was to marvel at the kind of people God can make use of. That may be why God inspired the Deuteronomists to include Samson as a judge. Then too the wild adventure of the stories would have delighted the exiles, who needed to hear of larger-than-life exploits to boost their flagging spirits.

Perhaps Samson also reminded the exiles of how their nation, blessed by God with land and wealth, had also become

12

Research and write about a person or group from history whose weakness ultimately led to destruction.

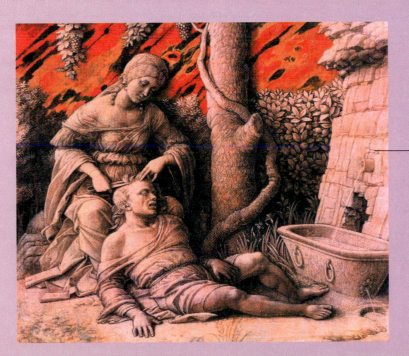

A Renaissance painting of Delilah cutting Samson's hair

The Land **111**

deluded and morally weak. Israel had brought ruin upon itself. It was plain to the exiles that Samson as a leader fell far below the ideal of Joshua, the righteous, obedient, prayerful one who had swept the Israelites into Canaan by relying totally on God. The Deuteronomists, and God, could use Samson to bring the point home strongly: Be like Joshua, not like Samson. *13*

For Review

- [ ] Describe the fourfold pattern that occurs repeatedly in the Book of Judges.

- [ ] In the Bible what was the role of the judges? List the six major judges.

- [ ] How would the story of Deborah and Jael have given the exiled Jews a sense of hope?

- [ ] Why does God tell Gideon to reduce the size of his forces?

- [ ] Describe Samson's character. Why was such a character included among the judges?

13

In writing, compare and contrast the characters of Joshua and Samson. What can you learn about leadership from them?

Ruth: An Israelite Foreigner with a Great Destiny

The story in the **Book of Ruth** is set in the time of the judges, and so it is included in this chapter. However, the story could not sound more different from the tales of the judges. In it we find no battles, but selflessness, patience, loyalty, and gentle kindness. In addition, within the story is the notion that a foreign woman could become a devoted member of the Israelites, not a theme found in Judges.

The Book of Ruth had its beginnings in Israel's oral tradition in the period of the early kings (about 800 B.C.) and was probably told by storytellers who appeared in villages and towns at the popular festivals. Its final written version was from the period after the exile; it is not part of the Deuteronomic history. Its purpose was twofold:

The Prayer of Israel: Tender, Deep Fidelity

Ruth said to her mother-in-law, Naomi:

"Do not press me to leave you
    or to turn back from following you!
Where you go, I will go;
    where you lodge, I will lodge;
your people shall be my people,
    and your God my God.
Where you die, I will die—
    there will I be buried.
May the LORD do thus and so to me,
    and more as well,
if even death parts me from you!"
                    (Ruth 1:16–17)

- to teach how God could create a blessed ending out of a difficult situation
- to tell how it came about that Israel's noble King David had a Gentile (a non-Jew) as his great-grandmother

In Ruth's concern for the survival of her mother-in-law, her strength of character far exceeds that of some of the judges.

A Family Faces Calamity

When famine strikes Israel during the period of the judges, a man from Bethlehem journeys with his wife, **Naomi,** and their two sons to start life again on the plain of Moab, a foreign land. Soon after their arrival, the man dies, leaving Naomi to raise their sons alone. When the sons are grown, each of them marries a Moabite woman—one named Orpah and the other **Ruth.** After ten years the young men die, and Naomi, grief stricken, plans to return to her homeland because she has heard that the famine is over.

Naomi starts out, and the two young widows accompany her for a distance. Then she stops, bids them good-bye, and asking God's blessing on each one, urges them to return home to find new husbands. But Ruth and Orpah want to stay with her. Naomi tries to convince them not to throw in their lot with her because her life will be miserable back in Israel. All three women weep, and after affectionate farewells, Orpah returns to Moab, but Ruth remains with Naomi.

Read Ruth 1:1–18.

The generosity of Naomi

Naomi's love for the young women is evident in her insistence that they return to Moab, marry, and bear children. She resigns herself to seeing the end of her husband's family line, an unhappy possibility for any Israelite to face. She could have urged the young widows to come with her to Israel and marry members of her dead husband's clan, but she knows that would be a great sacrifice for them.

The Book of Ruth highlights the virtues of lifelong loyalty and faithfulness.

Ruth's famous pledge

The Book of Ruth is most famous for its portrait of the beautiful relationship between Ruth and Naomi. Ruth's magnificent speech (1:16–17) pledges her not only to Naomi but to God. In her selfless commitment to Naomi, her God, and her people, Ruth makes a covenant with the God of Israel. She is a foreigner who is as worthy of the Covenant as any Israelite. *14*

14

Have you ever had a friend who stuck by you in difficult times? Write an essay about friendship, including the qualities of a friend you believe are most important.

Destitution and Generosity

As Naomi anticipated, she and Ruth face destitution when they get back to Israel. As widows they are unprovided for, and Naomi expresses her bitterness to God.

However, it is the time of the barley harvest, and Ruth decides to glean the barley fields because the two women need food. By chance Ruth goes to the field of a farmer named **Boaz,** who is a kinsman of Naomi's late husband and a man of wealth and influence.

Boaz has already noticed Ruth and learns that through Ruth's marriage to Naomi's son, he is distantly related to her. He invites Ruth to glean in his field, instructs the young men not to bother her, and bids her to follow close to the women as they harvest. Ruth, astonished, throws herself on the ground and asks why a foreigner should be treated so generously. Boaz reveals that he knows of her, and he praises her loyalty to Naomi. When he asks the blessing of the God of Israel upon her, he reveals his knowledge of her conversion. [15]

Boaz continues his kindness, offering Ruth special attention and help throughout the harvest season and asking his workers to treat her respectfully. When Naomi becomes aware of Boaz's concern for Ruth, she is delighted. Perhaps there is hope for Ruth's future after all, because by Israelite law, this generous man, being kin to Naomi's husband, may be claimed for marriage by the widowed Ruth.

Read Ruth 1:19–22; 2:1–23.

15

Think about someone you know who is truly kind. Write a speech about that person that you might give if a party was held in his or her honor.

Gleaning, *right,* and winnowing, *below,* in Israel

Harvesting in Ancient Israel

The story of Ruth uses harvesting terms that might be unfamiliar to you.

Gleaning means gathering the grain left by those who reap, or cut down the stalks of, the field.

Once cut, the grain must be loosened from the stalks. The stalks are spread on the *threshing floor* outside and are beaten, walked on, or loosened with a studded board pulled by an animal. Next, the husk, or thin outer covering of the grain, is broken by a heavy wooden sledge pulled over the grain by an ox or an ass. The threshed grain is then winnowed—tossed into the air with winnowing shovels on a windy day. The breeze carries away the paper-thin husks, or chaff, while the heavy grain drops to the ground, ready to be stored in the barn.

The Law, not theft

Ruth and Naomi are examples of "the poor and the alien," of whom the Law, and later the prophetic and wisdom books, speak. Gleaning is not theft, nor is it begging. Ruth has a right to glean because the Law requires that gleanings be left for the poor.
Read Leviticus 23:22.

Naomi Makes a Match

Naomi, seeing what good things God has in store, does a bit of matchmaking. She bids Ruth to bathe, perfume, and dress herself in her best attire. Then Ruth is to go to the threshing floor, where Boaz and his men are working late into the evening, and stay out of sight. When the men have eaten and drunk and lain down to sleep, Ruth is to go where Boaz lies, uncover a place beside his feet, lie there, and wait for Boaz to tell her what to do.

Ruth does as Naomi bids, and when Boaz awakens and finds her, she asks him to cover her with his cloak. Boaz understands that by this request, Ruth is proposing to him, invoking the claim to marry him under Israelite law, and he blesses her. He will do all he can to arrange the marriage, although first a kinsman with closer ties to Ruth must be consulted. If this man does not want her, Boaz does! He tells her to sleep but to rise before the workers awaken so that there is no suspicion of scandal.

In the morning when Ruth returns and tells Naomi what happened, Naomi assures her that Boaz will not rest until he has settled the matter.
Read Ruth 3:1–18.

Boaz's honor

Up to now Boaz has viewed Ruth as praiseworthy but not as a potential wife. Naomi's plan is for Boaz to see Ruth as a wife. Naomi must be sure of his character; someone less honorable might take advantage of Ruth. But Boaz takes precautions to protect Ruth's reputation and, aware of the meaning of her actions, plans to marry Ruth in a way that is proper and legal. (Consider Boaz's character in contrast with Samson's.)

Guests at a wedding in Israel dance around the bride and groom.

Boaz Marries Ruth

Boaz clears his right to marry Ruth with a man who is a closer kin to her. That man gives up his right, and so Ruth and Boaz marry. In time Ruth bears a son, whom they name Obed, who becomes the father of Jesse, who in turn becomes the father of David, king of Israel.
Read Ruth 4:1–22.

The valley of the Jordan River in Israel. Joshua and the Israelites entered the Promised Land by crossing the Jordan from the east.

Ruth: David's Moabite ancestor

That Ruth eventually becomes great-grandmother to David is highly significant. Being Moabite, Ruth is one of a foreign nationality that is expressly excluded from membership among the Israelite community, according to a law in Deuteronomy 23:3–6. Yet here is a Moabite woman, according to this story, who is recognized as an honored ancestor of the greatest king in the history of Israel! The postexilic author of Ruth evidently wrote to answer the question about whether it was right or good that a Gentile be welcomed by marriage into the community of Israel. The question was long debated among the Jews and was controversial after the exile. But this story of the famous and much-loved Moabite Ruth reveals the Lord's choice of a Gentile as forebear to their great king David—and a far nobler person she was than some of the other Israelites. *16*

For Review

☐ What were the two purposes of the Book of Ruth?

☐ What does Ruth pledge in her famous speech to Naomi?

16

What lessons does the Book of Ruth teach about foreigners? Find a newspaper or magazine article that describes the experiences of a person or group who has immigrated to our country. Read the article, summarize it in writing, and if possible, connect it to the lessons presented in Ruth.

A God of Surprises

A reader of the Scriptures might wonder how books like Joshua and Judges wind up in the same Bible with Ruth. What do these books share in common? What is the core biblical message present in these quite different books?

Despite their apparent differences, these books all speak a message of total trust in and fidelity to God. God is the one who brings about good, turning disastrous situations into opportunities for fullness of life, peace, and abundance on the land. In Joshua, God miraculously clears the way for the Israelites to take over the land promised to Abraham. God can do anything, even using the apparently unworthy to accomplish his purposes. So a Canaanite prostitute, Rahab, is God's instrument for the first victory in the Promised Land. In Judges, God turns around the Israelites' infidelity and failure, raising up leaders—some of them rather unsavory characters—to fight the oppressors and bring a measure of security to the Israelites on the land. And in Ruth, God blesses the simple faith and loyalty of a foreign woman, giving her a line of descendants that includes the revered King David.

Again and again God surprises. He overturns mere human plans to bring about something more wonderful, to transform even the darkest of times and dimmest of characters. What a message of hope for the exiles, for Jews and Christians down through the ages, and for us today.

"Where you go, I will go;
where you lodge, I will lodge;
your people shall be my people,
and your God my God."

Ruth 1:16

6 The Kings

Becoming a Nation

Before becoming king, David spent years hiding in the region of Judea—seeking refuge in places like this hillside settlement in the Judean desert.

Considered in this chapter are the two Books of Samuel and the beginning of the First Book of Kings. These biblical writings are part of the history edited by the Deuteronomists during the Babylonian exile. Recall that the Deuteronomic history attempted to answer the questions gnawing at the exiled Jews: How did we end up captured by our enemies, forced into exile far from home with our Temple and our beloved city destroyed? Has God abandoned us? Is there any hope for the future? What have we learned from this disaster?

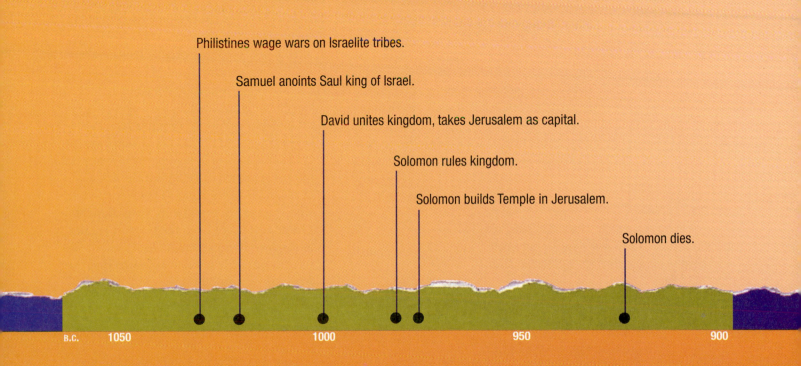

Philistines wage wars on Israelite tribes.

Samuel anoints Saul king of Israel.

David unites kingdom, takes Jerusalem as capital.

Solomon rules kingdom.

Solomon builds Temple in Jerusalem.

Solomon dies.

B.C. 1050   1000   950   900

An Egyptian stone carving depicting Philistine warriors wearing crested helmets. The mighty Philistines threatened the fragmented tribes of Israel in Canaan, making it necessary for the Israelites to unite under one strong leader and government.

Stories of Transition to Nationhood

To answer the exiles' disturbing questions, the Deuteronomists had to explain how, after the era of the judges in the Promised Land, the Israelite people became a nation "like other nations" (1 Samuel 8:20). How did they come to have a king, a capital city, wealth, military power, a palace, and a magnificent Temple to their God? And even more important, what effect did nationhood have on them?

The Need for Unity

The Book of Judges, considered in the previous chapter, ends with this simple statement: "In those days there was no king in Israel; all the people did what was right in their own eyes" (21:25). In other words, by the end of the era of the judges, no central leader like Moses or Joshua had been able to

unite the tribes into one people under God's Law. Judges like Deborah, Gideon, and Samson had arisen among the tribes as they were needed. Filled with God's spirit, they had won victories in the struggles with the Canaanites for the land. However, that temporary kind of leadership, coming in bursts, was not stable or strong enough to build unity across the tribes. It could not keep the people from disintegrating into separate groups and clans that simply went their own way, deciding what to do for themselves. Morally and spiritually, things were going rapidly downhill. This state of affairs was far from the ideal of God's Chosen People united in keeping the Covenant faithfully. *1*

The lack of unity also threatened the very existence of the Israelites: The tribes of Israel, fragmented and going their own way, did not stand a chance against the onslaught of the mighty Philistines. These "sea people" with their chariots and iron weapons were pressing eastward from the seacoast regions to threaten Israelite territories. Without the security of nationhood, it appeared that the Israelites were doomed.

1

Imagine living in a society where everyone "did what was right in their own eyes." What would that be like? Write a short story describing this kind of society.

Mixed Feelings About Nationhood

The **Books of Samuel** and the beginning of the **First Book of Kings** describe the transition to nationhood—in the decades around 1000 B.C. They tell stories of Israel's first three kings—**Saul, David,** and **Solomon.** The accounts show the new nation of Israel not only surviving the Philistine onslaught but growing in success and power.

The Deuteronomists, though, saw the whole process of becoming a nation from the perspective of four hundred or so years later. They understood that some features of being "like other nations" (1 Samuel 8:20), though attractive, were the seeds of destruction that had led to the nation's downfall. So they had mixed feelings about Israel's being a nation with a king. [2]

The story of David, Israel's greatest king, introduces God's promise that David's line of descendants, the royal house of David, would endure forever as leaders of Israel. Eventually, as we will see in other books of the Bible, this became the basis for the prophecy that from the line of David would come a great leader, the Messiah, who would save the Jews from oppression and bring in a reign of peace and justice. Christians believe that this promise of a Messiah is fulfilled in Jesus Christ.

In putting together the history of Israel's transition to nationhood, the Deuteronomists used sections of the ancient Court History of David (no longer in existence). Dated at about 1000 B.C., the court history may have been the oldest written history in the world. David is at the center of that history, but as we now have the story in the First Book of Samuel, it begins with the great judge and prophet for whom two Old Testament books are named—**Samuel.**

For Review

- [ ] Why did the tribes of Israel need to become a nation?
- [ ] Who were the first three kings of Israel?
- [ ] Why did the Deuteronomists have mixed feelings about Israel's becoming a nation with a king?

The U.S. Capitol in Washington, D.C. Nationhood implies having a central government and a capital city.

2

You have probably heard this: The grass is always greener on the other side of the fence. Sometimes we look at what other people have—their families, houses, possessions, bodies, and so on—and we believe our life would be better if we had what they have. But have you ever considered what challenges those other people face with what they have? Write a paragraph giving an example of one such challenge. In a second paragraph, write how this relates to the Israelites' desire for a king.

Samuel: Anointer of Kings

A Special Birth and Call

The baby Samuel, like a number of other important figures in the Bible, is born to a woman who had not before been able to bear a child. Once Hannah weans the child, in joy and gratitude she offers him to God as a Nazirite (meaning he had a special dedicated status like Samson the judge had) and leaves him in the care of the priest Eli at the shrine at Shiloh. **3**

Samuel grows up serving God faithfully. Eli's two sons, however, are a different story. As priests, they behave sacrilegiously—in spite of Eli's warnings. God announces through a holy man that Eli's family line will end.

One night, while sleeping in the sanctuary near the ark of the Covenant (the box that held the stone tablets of the Covenant and that was meant to be the throne, or resting place, of God), Samuel hears his name called. He goes to Eli, who merely sends him back to bed. A second and third time this happens. Finally, Eli realizes that God is calling Samuel and tells the young man to respond, "Speak, for your servant is listening" (1 Samuel 3:10). God tells Samuel of the coming fall of Eli's family. Samuel reluctantly tells Eli God's message, and Eli accepts this news. Eventually this and other prophecies reveal to the people of Israel that Samuel is a prophet to whom God speaks.

Read 1 Samuel 3:1–21.

The Cry for a King

As priest and judge, Samuel goes on to lead the Israelites for many years, rebuking them when they follow false gods and promising them victory over the Philistines if they obey God. The Philistines are finally defeated, and Israel lives in peace as long as Samuel is its leader. **4**

The sons of Samuel are unfit to take his place as judge when he grows old, so the people cry out to Samuel to "appoint for us, then, a king to govern us, like other nations" (1 Samuel 8:5). God tells a displeased Samuel that "they have not rejected you, but they have rejected me from being king over them" (8:7).

3

Read 1 Samuel 2:1–10 and Luke 1:46–55. Mary's Magnificat is said to have been modeled after Hannah's hymn of praise when she gives Samuel to the Lord. List the similarities. Then write a brief essay on the meaning of these songs for our times.

4

Samuel is described as both a judge and a priest, implying that in Israel, politics and religion were inseparable. Why was that? Do you see issues of poverty, injustice, and corruption as being primarily political or religious? Write a paragraph explaining your stance.

Even though the people prefer in some way to put their trust in a king rather than God, he tells Samuel to go ahead and give them what they want. But Samuel must warn the people of what trouble lies ahead if they have a king: A king will draft their sons to make arms, build chariots, and reap harvests; their daughters to make perfumes, cook, and bake. A king will also take their fields, vineyards, olive groves, and a tithe of their grain—that is, one-tenth of it. He will then take their menservants, maidservants, donkeys, and sheep. Finally, a king will make the Israelites into slaves. When at last they cry out to God, it will be to no avail.

Even with Samuel's warning, the people insist that they want to be "like other nations" (8:5) and have a king who will "go out before us and fight our battles" (8:20). Samuel has no choice but to follow God's command and give the people what they are clamoring for.

Read 1 Samuel 8:1–22. **5**

In hindsight

In this exchange over whether to have a king, we can see the view of the Deuteronomists. For them and for the prophets, only God is the king of Israel. From the hindsight of four hundred years after Samuel, the Deuteronomists knew what would happen

with most of the kings: they would be disasters! In fact the oppressive king described in Samuel's speech sounds much like Solomon, the third king.

Like other nations or a nation apart?

The Israelites felt pulled toward the success-and-power model of other nations, with their kings, huge armies, and vast territories. Yet the question for them always was whether to follow that model or to be a nation apart, a different kind of nation that

5

Is it possible for God to rule over us today even though we have elected officials in our local and national government? Share your reflections on how that might or might not be possible.

The Israelites wanted to be like other nations, which had powerful military forces.

The Meanings of *Israel*

The term *Israel* has already been used in several ways. Let us take a moment to clarify its numerous meanings.

- The Hebrew meaning of the word *Israel,* though uncertain, is probably "may God rule."
- After his nightlong struggle with the stranger, Jacob is given the name Israel.
- Later, the people who claim descent from Jacob and the other founders call themselves the people of Israel.
- In the Second Book of Samuel, the ten tribes in the north are called Israel. The two tribes in the south are called Judah.
- When David unites the tribes, the nation is called Israel.
- When the kingdom is divided after Solomon's death, Israel is the formal name given to the northern kingdom. This kingdom is the first one to be conquered, and it is conquered by the Assyrians.
- When the exiles return from Babylon to the province of Judah, they are called Jews; the nation is called Israel.
- From that time on, *Israel* means the land and the people as a nation.
- To some Jews the modern state called Israel is a religious continuation of the ancient nation. To others the state is primarily a political entity.

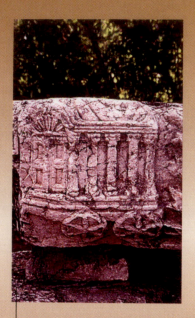

An image of the ark of the Covenant, a symbol of the people of Israel, found among synagogue ruins at Capernaum, Israel.

would be a light to all the others. This question still confronts Jews today as they struggle with the meaning of the modern state of Israel. **6**

Saul Is Anointed

Samuel is guided by God to find a king for the Israelites. He meets Saul, an unassuming farmworker searching for his father's donkeys. Samuel anoints Saul king and presents him to the tribes—even though Saul, a shy man for all his tall stature and good looks, tries to hide at the last minute.
Read 1 Samuel 9:1–27; 10:1–27.

6

What does it mean for a nation to be a "light to all the others"? Do you think our country is like this? Find a newspaper or magazine article that reflects your opinion and write a paragraph about it that answers these questions.

The lowliest and least

The theme of this story about Saul is familiar: God chooses the lowliest and least. Although tall and handsome, Saul is hardly the regal type. He is from an ordinary family background, and is afraid of attention. Yet God chooses him. We will soon see, however, that Saul has other personal characteristics that make even God think twice about the choice!

For Review

☐ What does Samuel warn will happen if the people have a king?

☐ Whom does Samuel anoint as first king?

Saul and David in Conflict

An Unsuitable King

Once he is king, Saul pulls himself together and wins a stunning victory for Israel over the Ammonites. Afterward Samuel warns both the king and the people that the key to their success will be fidelity to God. **7**

Yet Saul soon breaks faith with God. He disobeys God's Law twice. First, under pressure from his frightened soldiers who are about to be attacked by the Philistines, he offers a prebattle sacrifice instead of waiting for Samuel to do so (only priests are allowed to offer sacrifice). Then, in another battle, Saul fails to carry out the ban against a defeated enemy: he takes the enemy king and the best livestock as spoils of war instead of destroying them for God. Saul shows himself to be unfaithful, swayed by his own anxieties, and subject to the pressures of those around him. He does not truly trust in God and follow God's commands. He is inconstant—in other words, wishy-washy.

Samuel declares that Saul will now be rejected by God as king of Israel. The crown will be given to a more faithful, constant man. As the scriptural passage notes, "And the LORD was sorry that he had made Saul king over Israel" (1 Samuel 15:35).

Read 1 Samuel 11:11–15; 12:13–18; 13:5–14; 15:1–35.

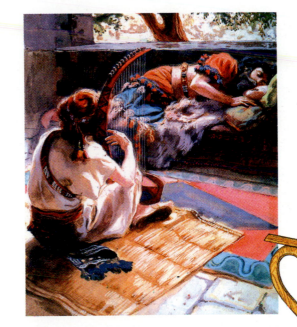

Another Choice for King

Samuel is led by God to search for another king for Israel. The theme of God's choice of the weakest and lowest is repeated in the story of David. God sends Samuel to Bethlehem, where he meets Jesse's sons. God instructs Samuel to overlook the older, taller sons that seem to have obvious regal potential—"for the LORD does not see as mortals see; they look on the outward appearance, but the LORD looks on the heart" (1 Samuel 16:7). So Samuel chooses the youngest son, David, who has been tending sheep in the hills, and secretly anoints him king. David will not be publicly declared king until later. **8**

Two biblical traditions tell of Saul's meeting David. In one David is brought to play the harp for Saul to lighten his dark moods. In the other, the well-known, marvelously told story of David and Goliath,

David played the harp. According to one biblical story about how he met King Saul, David was brought in to relieve the king's dark moods by playing music for him.

7

"The key to their success will be fidelity to God." Comment on this notion as it applies to your life, to someone you know, or to a group of people.

8

Do you know of someone who possesses far more inner beauty and strength than he or she might show on the outside? How did you come to know what he or she was really like? Write an essay about this person, including your thoughts on 1 Samuel 16:7.

young David, armed only with a slingshot, prevails against the Philistine giant. In both stories Saul likes David, finds him gifted, and decides to keep him at court. But of course Saul does not realize that David has secretly been anointed king by Samuel and is destined to take his place!

Read 1 Samuel 16:1–23; 17:1–58.

The Bethlehem connection

Recall from the account of Jesus' birth in Luke's Gospel that Joseph and his pregnant wife, Mary, make a journey to Joseph's hometown for the census ordered by the Roman emperor. Because Joseph is of the house of David—one of David's line—the couple must go to David's place of origin, Bethlehem. And that is where Jesus is born.

Read Luke 1:26–33; 2:1–5.

Saul's Jealousy of David

David's popularity, attractiveness, and skill begin to arouse jealousy in the insecure and emotionally unstable Saul, until at last he tries to kill David. Both Saul's son **Jonathan** and his daughter **Michal**—who is also David's wife—help David escape Saul's murderous traps. Convinced of the king's irrational hatred, David finally bids farewell to Jonathan and Michal. He leaves the court as a fugitive, knowing that he is God's choice to be king but also that he must not rub it in to Saul, who is just beginning to realize the inevitable.

Read 1 Samuel 18:1–16; 19:1–18; 20:24–35,41–42.

Saul's hatred

As Samuel prophesied, God is no longer with Saul, and everything he does goes wrong. Twice when Saul tries to kill David, his spear misses. When he sends David to the battlefront, David's prowess wins the love of the people. Even Saul's children give their loyalty to David. Saul realizes that nothing he can do will stop David from becoming king.

World Happenings from 1250 to 900 B.C.

Africa
Poverty and decadence plague the declining Egyptian Empire.

America
By 1000 B.C. the Olmecs in Mexico and the Chavin in Peru establish states with populations in the tens of thousands, along with priesthoods, civil services, and classes of traders and artisans.

China
The first Chinese dictionary is written, including more than forty thousand written characters.

Europe
Classical paganism blooms in Greece. A temple to Hera—worshiped as queen of heaven, goddess of women and marriage, and wife of Zeus (king of the gods)—is built in the tenth century B.C. at Olympia.

India
Basic elements of Hinduism develop, including a belief in a cosmic order and also a class system of priests, nobles, merchants, and workers.

The Near East
The Creation Epic confirms the belief in the Babylonian god Marduk as the maker of the universe. The city of Babylon becomes the spiritual capital of the region.

Jonathan's love

The story of David and Jonathan is one of the world's greatest tales of friendship. Notice how Jonathan's love for David is described, his loyalty and the risks he takes for David. **9**

David: The Loyal Outlaw

David flees to the shrine at Nob, which is near Jerusalem. There he contrives to get food from the priest by lying to him, saying that Saul has sent him on an errand. The priest gives David not only bread from the altar but the sword of Goliath as well. When Saul finds out, he orders the entire city of Nob destroyed, and the only survivor is one of the priest's sons. David, contrite, admits his guilt to the surviving son and offers him protection.

Still loyal to his people, David next rescues an Israelite town from the Philistines. Then he and his troops, a band of several hundred followers, flee to the desert, where David takes refuge in a cave. Pursuing him, Saul stops in the cave to relieve himself and apparently falls asleep. David could kill Saul at that point, but instead he cuts off a piece of his cloak and leaves him sleeping. When Saul emerges, David calls from a distance and tells Saul he means him no harm. As proof David waves the cloth to show Saul that he was close enough to kill him but has instead spared his life. Saul then understands how righteous David is, how deserving he is to be king.

Read 1 Samuel 21:1–10; 22:18–23; 23:1–5; 24:1–22.

No perfect hero

The destruction of the city of Nob at Saul's command is a bad moment in David's

---

9

Have you ever had an experience where being loyal to a friend meant being disloyal to someone else? Write a story featuring young people that illustrates this challenge of loyalty.

I-Witness: Seth

I'm Seth the warrior, and I've fought alongside David for five years, since I was old enough to carry a spear. Why do I fight against Saul? I'll tell you why: Saul's a rotten leader who can't keep the Philistines off our land.

David will. He doesn't have Saul's army, but he's got more brains than Saul has soldiers. He creates big headaches for the Philistines and Saul both!

I don't say this in camp, but once we clear our land of scumbag foreigners and get rid of Saul, I want David to go back to the simple life—like we had in the old days with the judges. Saul's enough to prove that we don't need permanent kings. Kings love wars and taxes. After five years of spilling blood—some of it mine—I'm done with fighting. I'm settling down to a farm and a family.

The harsh landscape of the Judean desert, where David fled for his life from the jealous King Saul

rise to kingship. After all, David has had a part in the terrible deed—having deceived the priest within the hearing of one of Saul's men. Innocent people die because of David's lie. As we will see, David is far from perfect, and the biblical writers let us know about his sins. But despite his human failings, David is still the one chosen to accomplish the divine purposes, and the writers repeatedly hold him up as a model of faithfulness to God.

David's loyalty

As David spares Saul, we see in a touching and beautiful speech that his affection for Saul remains in spite of the king's attempts to kill him. After Saul acknowledges David's goodness and his right to be king, David swears he will never harm Saul's descendants. He keeps this promise even though the unstable Saul continues to hunt him down to destroy him. Loyalty to friends and family proves to be one of David's strongest and most admirable character traits.

Another Outlaw Story

David and his band survive by offering protection to the local inhabitants for a price—food and other provisions. But a rich herdsman whose shepherds have enjoyed David's protection refuses to pay up. When David angrily moves to confront him, the herdsman's wife, **Abigail,** intercepts David with supplies of food and wine, hoping to keep him from annihilating her family and her people. David is appeased, and later, when the herdsman dies, he marries Abigail. Saul has already given David's wife Michal to another man.

Read 1 Samuel 25:18–43.

The politics of marriage

David's marriage to Abigail is prompted by his gratitude and admiration for her character. By contrast, Michal's remarriage was a political move by Saul. By having Michal marry another man, Saul hoped to weaken David's claim to the throne. Later, David will demand Michal back to strengthen his claim. David, as we will see, uses power effectively to further his own purposes. Even as God's chosen one, his trust in God is mixed with some heavy-handed tactics. *10*

The Philistines Versus David and Saul
David decides to seek refuge from Saul, who is still out to get him, by staying with the Philistines. To ingratiate himself with their king, he pretends to attack Israelite towns—something the loyal David would never do to his own people. In reality he is raiding Canaanite villages for their livestock.

Threatened by the Philistines, a desperate, even deranged Saul seeks out a witch to conjure up the spirit of the dead Samuel (earlier he had outlawed such fortune-telling in the land). The ghost of Samuel reveals only that Saul and his sons will perish in battle the next day.

Meanwhile, at the Philistine camp, David is trying to outwit these enemies of Israel. His men, about to march into battle at the rear of the Philistine army, are apparently planning to attack the Philistines from behind during the battle.

But the Philistine chiefs distrust David and instead send him and his troops back to the village where they have been staying.

10

Who is someone you consider powerful? Write a paragraph about what he or she has taught you about the meaning of power and how it should be used.

The Prayer of Israel: "To You, O LORD, I Lift Up My Soul"

To you, O LORD, I lift up my soul.
O my God, in you I trust;
    do not let me be put to shame;
    do not let my enemies exult over me.
Do not let those who wait for you be put to shame;
    let them be ashamed who are wantonly treacherous.

Make me to know your ways, O LORD;
    teach me your paths.
Lead me in your truth, and teach me,
    for you are the God of my salvation;
    for you I wait all day long.

. . . .

Turn to me and be gracious to me,
    for I am lonely and afflicted.
Relieve the troubles of my heart,
    and bring me out of my distress.
Consider my affliction and my trouble,
    and forgive all my sins.

Consider how many are my foes,
    and with what violent hatred they hate me.
O guard my life, and deliver me;
do not let me be put to shame, for I take refuge in you.

(Psalm 25:1–5,16–20)

A waterfall at Ein Gedi oasis in the Judean desert. David sought out such places for refreshment while a fugitive.

Finding it sacked by Canaanite marauders, with all the women and children kidnapped, David rescues the captives and slays their captors. He then distributes the spoils to other towns where he and his troops were best known—a move that was not just generous but politically smart.

Read 1 Samuel 27:1–12; 28:4–20; 29:1–11.

A Tragic End for Saul

Israel's battle goes as prophesied by the ghost of Samuel, and in a tragic end to a career that was once bright with promise, Saul kills himself rather than be captured. The Philistines fasten his body and those of his sons—including Jonathan—to the walls of one of their cities. But the Jabeshites, who were once rescued by Saul, march all night, rescue the corpses, and take them to their own town.

Read 1 Samuel 31:1–13.

Saul's demise, David's rise

The First Book of Samuel completes the first of the major themes in Samuel—namely, the **reign of Saul**. The other theme—the **rise of David to his kingship**—follows in the Second Book of Samuel.

For Review

- ☐ Why does God reject Saul after he becomes king?
- ☐ How does the story of David repeat the theme of God's choosing the weakest and lowest?
- ☐ What two biblical incidents tell of Saul meeting David?
- ☐ Why does Saul want to murder David?
- ☐ With whom does David have a deep friendship?
- ☐ How does David show loyalty to Saul even though Saul wants to destroy him?
- ☐ How does Saul's life end?
- ☐ What is the theme of each of the two Books of Samuel?

At First, King of Judah

Israel is now without a king, but has two rival leaders: Saul's general **Abner** in the north and David in the south. Abner makes Saul's eldest son, **Ishbaal,** king over the northern tribes, although Abner himself really wants to rule. David, with a power base already in the south, is anointed king of the southern

The coffin of a U.S. sailor killed at sea in World War II, being carried ashore. David mourned deeply the deaths of Saul and Jonathan, who both fell in battle.

King David: Nation Builder

David in Mourning

The Second Book of Samuel opens with a different version of Saul's death. A young soldier from the front of Israel's battle reports to David that Saul is dead. The wounded Saul persuaded the soldier to strike him a deathblow, lest Saul be captured by the Philistines. David is furious that the young man would violate "the LORD's anointed" (1:14), even though Saul asked him to finish his life. He has the young soldier killed, and then mourns the death of Saul and Jonathan in beautiful and passionate words. *11*

   Read 2 Samuel 1:17–27.

11

The plot in this story is illustrated in our times by the controversy over assisted suicide. Although physician-assisted suicide is practiced mostly with the terminally ill, the implications go much further. Is it wrong for someone to choose suicide as a means of avoiding suffering? Should one who assists in a suicide be held responsible? Find an article about this topic and write a few paragraphs explaining your point of view. Research what the Catholic Church teaches and include it in your essay.

A monument to David's victory over Goliath, whose giant head is raised in triumph by the young slingshot expert.

tribes of Judah in Hebron. Actually, David is now *publicly* anointed king, because Samuel has already secretly anointed him.

Read 2 Samuel 2:8–11.

Then, King of All Israel

Abner tries to move Ishbaal into the lead over David, but his plan fails. So, aware that David's star is rising, Abner betrays Ishbaal, returns Michal to David, and persuades the northern tribes to choose David for their king. The northerners remember David's loyal service to Saul, assemble together with

12

Is it possible to be intensely loyal to someone who has acted like an enemy to you? Think of someone you care about who has treated you badly. How could you still be loyal to him or her? Write your thoughts in a paragraph.

Judah, and anoint David king over *all* Israel. He is thirty years old.

Murder and Mayhem

Sandwiched between these events is a series of murders and betrayals that sound like they could have come from a contemporary corporate-thriller movie. The plot would go like this:

Abner, the powerful and ruthless vice-president of Israel, Inc., promotes to president the weak son (Ishbaal) of the deceased president (Saul). Abner also takes over the deceased president's mistress and tries to eliminate the lawfully designated president (David) by violence, but fails.

Insulted by Ishbaal, Abner next abandons his candidate for president of the company (Ishbaal) and persuades the stockholders whom he controls (the northern tribes) to vote for the lawfully designated president (David).

Returning from a business trip, Abner is waylaid and murdered by the new vice-president (Joab, one of David's generals), whose brother was slain by Abner. The new president (David) is horrified and mourns Abner's death.

In the meantime two hit men from the north, certain that the president (David) will be pleased if his rival (Ishbaal) is removed, murder Ishbaal. When the appalled president discovers the crime, the hit men are executed.

In short, David's reign begins with a bloodbath.

Read 2 Samuel 2:12–16; 3:6–13; 5:1–5.

More loyalty from David

David could be caught up in trying to destroy his rivals—Saul, Abner, Ishbaal—or at least he could rejoice when they are killed by others. But his response to their deaths is not even relief; it is deep anger at their murderers and profound mourning at the losses. Once David decides he is loyal to Saul, he never turns against him or those close to him. *12*

Jerusalem, the ideal site for David's capital city, has become a holy city for Jews, Christians, and Muslims.

United at Jerusalem

Alarmed at Israel's unity, the Philistines force David into battle, and his victories drive them down to the coastal plain. The Philistines are never again a serious threat.

David's next move is inspired. He captures **Jerusalem,** a Canaanite walled city whose inhabitants have boasted that even the lame and the blind could defend it, and makes it his capital.

Read 2 Samuel 5:17–25; 5:6–16.

Jerusalem as ideal

David's two great feats were ending the Philistine threat and unifying the Israelite tribes. Making Jerusalem his capital was a stroke of genius. Because Jerusalem had never belonged to any one of the twelve tribes, David could not be accused of playing favorites by bringing his court there. Jerusalem was ideally located in territory between the northern and the southern tribes.

History has proven that David's decision was of much greater import than he would ever know. In Jerusalem David established what would become a holy city for Jews, Christians, and Muslims—more than half of all religious believers in the world today.

The Ark Comes to Jerusalem

Aware that the ark of the Covenant is a powerful symbol of God's presence to the people, David brings it to Jerusalem, where it will be housed in a tent. When David joyfully enters the city, dancing before the ark, his wife Michal berates him for acting like a fool. He replies that if to give God praise he must look a fool, he will. The story ends with the note that Michal never bears a child.

Read 2 Samuel 6:1–5, 12–23.

David's devotion to God, Michal's fate

In his devotion David dances exuberantly before God's ark, without concern for how he looks to the people (no one seems to mind his ecstatic dancing except Michal, though). As Michal's contempt toward David shows, she does not see or value his love for God. Apparently no bond of love remains between them; their remarriage was purely political. The text implies that David never makes love to Michal again—a sad ending to a young love for which they had risked so much. *13*

13

Politics, at its worst, can involve using or oppressing people. What does it look like at its best? Write about several examples.

The Davidic Covenant

David reflects that while he is living in a house of cedar, God has only a tent as a dwelling place. That seems unfitting to him, so David plans to build a house for the Lord. But the prophet **Nathan** says no to David's plan. Nathan tells David of God's greater plan for him. God will instead build a different kind of "house" for David. This house of David will not be a building but a royal dynasty, a line of David's descendants that will endure forever. Scripture scholars call this promise by God the **Davidic Covenant.**
Read 2 Samuel 7:1–17.

No temple until later

The prophet Nathan, one of the non-writing prophets, plays an important role in the lives of David and Solomon. In this first prophecy, Nathan reveals God's wish that the temple David is planning be postponed until his future son (Solomon) can build it.

The messianic promise

God promised that David's line would endure forever. In fact David's line endured unbroken for four hundred years; then it dropped into obscurity. Afterward devout Jews remembered this promise and waited for the reappearance of a leader from this royal line to be Israel's **Messiah.** The Hebrew word *messiah* means "the anointed," referring to the anointing of a king. By the time of Jesus, the belief in the coming Messiah was widespread among Jews in Palestine. The early Christians believed the Messiah to be Jesus, who was from the line of David. The Gospel writers referred to Jesus using the Greek word for *messiah—christos,* meaning "the anointed," from which the name Christ comes.
Read Matthew 1:1,12–17; Mark 15:2,26.

David and Bathsheba

As king, David is powerful, wealthy, and undefeated. But after years of war, he is tired, and one spring he stays home from battle. As he strolls on the roof of his house, he sees a beautiful woman bathing nearby. She is **Bathsheba**, whose husband is **Uriah,** a warrior at the battlefront. David sends for her and has sexual relations with her, apparently

A multigenerational family reunion. The "house" that God promised to build for David was not a building but a family—a line of descendants that would endure forever.

with no guilty qualms about breaking the commandment "You shall not commit adultery." *14*

David gets nervous, though, when he finds out from Bathsheba that she is pregnant with his child. He tries to cover up his adultery by bringing her husband, Uriah, back from the battlefront, and telling him he can go home and stay with Bathsheba for a couple of nights. However, the plan fails because Uriah, a man of high principles, refuses to go home and enjoy himself while God's ark is out in the battlefield encamped with the other soldiers.

Desperate to cover up his sin, David has Uriah killed. He does this by directing his general at the front to place Uriah where he will be killed in battle—and this happens. Bathsheba mourns the loss of her husband, but then David sends for her to become his own wife, and she bears him a son.

Read 2 Samuel 11:1–27.

Grievous sins

Despite his devotion to God and his persisting loyalty to family and friends, David has grave flaws. Having given in to his lust for Bathsheba, David then lies and manipulates others to cover up his mistake. But his sins only multiply, resulting in murder. In arranging Uriah's death, David shows his willingness to betray a good and honorable man so as to keep the whole affair secret. David intends to come out of the sordid situation "smelling like a rose."

A Lesson and Repentance for David

David, however, is forced to confront the evil of what he has done, with the help of Nathan the prophet. Nathan presents the king with a parable, asking him to judge this case: A poor man had one ewe lamb that he loved very much, and a rich man had a flock of sheep.

14

Read 1 Corinthians 13:4–7. Write a brief essay explaining the difference between love and lust and between love and infatuation.

British soldiers in the frontline trenches during World War I. David, in a successful attempt to have Uriah killed, placed him in the front line of battle.

The Prayer of Israel: "Have Mercy on Me, O God"

Have mercy on me, O God,
            according to your steadfast love;
according to your abundant mercy
            blot out my transgressions.
Wash me thoroughly from my iniquity,
            and cleanse me from my sin.

For I know my transgressions,
            and my sin is ever before me.
Against you, you alone, have I sinned,
            and done what is evil in your sight,
so that you are justified in your sentence
            and blameless when you pass judgment.

. . . .

Create in me a clean heart, O God,
            and put a new and right spirit within me.
Do not cast me away from your presence,
            and do not take your holy spirit from me.
Restore to me the joy of your salvation,
            and sustain in me a willing spirit.

(Psalm 51:1–4,10–12)

When the rich man had a guest over for dinner, he stole the poor man's ewe instead of slaughtering one of his own for the meal. "What should happen to such a man?" asks Nathan. "The fellow should die!" cries David angrily. And Nathan says, "You are the man!"

Through the parable David recognizes his sin and repents. He has been reminded that though he is a powerful king, he is subject to God and must follow the Law. When David pours out his sorrow, Nathan assures him that God forgives him and will not ask his life—but he will pay for his acts with much trouble and grief in his family.

Sure enough, the son of David and Bathsheba, who was conceived in the adulterous incident, becomes sickly as a child and dies. Later, Bathsheba conceives and bears another son, named Jedidiah but in his adulthood called Solomon.

Read 2 Samuel 12:1–25.

Chosen but sinful

We might be surprised to see such a frank portrayal of David's sins in the Scriptures. After all, he was God's chosen king of Israel, revered through the centuries as a hero and model of faithfulness. Why did such an account of his weakness and sin find its way into the Bible?

The Deuteronomists who put the history together centuries after David were inspired to leave in the account of his acts of adultery and murder. They did not choose to idealize David by ignoring his sinful behavior. They made it clear that David is not above God's Law; he must repent for his sins, and he will suffer greatly for them. The message for us is that God works through limited and sinful persons, with David as a prime example of that. Perhaps that realization can give hope to all of us far-from-perfect human beings—

hope that God somehow brings about the divine purposes even through our flaws and weaknesses. **15**

Rivalry and Treachery in the Family

Nathan's prophecy of evil for David's family is fulfilled in a series of tragedies and treacheries. David has had a number of sons by various wives (polygamy was a common practice, especially among royalty). The obvious heir to the throne is his firstborn, **Amnon.** But the family is wrecked by incest, rivalries, hatreds, murders, and rebellions among the sons. Here is a brief summary of what is told with marvelous detail in the Second Book of Samuel:

- Amnon desires his half sister **Tamar** and rapes her, then turns on her and drives her away. Though angry, David does not punish Amnon because he is his heir to the throne.

- **Absalom,** another of David's sons and the full brother of Tamar, is enraged at Amnon for his horrible deed and has him slain two years later, then escapes to stay away from the angry David for three years.

- David loves Absalom and longs to have him return. After Absalom does come back, he finally reconciles with his father. But his intentions are evil: he begins to subtly undermine the people's respect for David as he plots to take over the kingship.

- Absalom attracts a following among the people, leaves Jerusalem with them, and then declares himself king instead of his father. David weeps for Absalom.

- In the midst of Absalom's rebellion, David is told of the disloyalty of **Mephibosheth** (Meribbaal, in some translations). This man is the surviving son of David's dear friend Jonathan and the grandson of Saul. It is reported that Mephibosheth is trying to take away the throne from David. This is especially hurtful to David because years earlier, after Jonathan's death, he had taken the young man into his court and treated him like a son.

- Absalom proceeds to attack Jerusalem, but David implores his men to protect his enemy Absalom from harm in the battle. But after Absalom is defeated, he is killed in trying to escape. David is heartbroken and mourns him piteously.

Read 2 Samuel 13:1–39; 14:28–33; 15:1–18; 17:7–13; 18:1–17,31–33; 19:1–4.

A grieving woman during a funeral procession in Haiti. David was heartbroken over the death of his son Absalom.

The Empire of David and Solomon

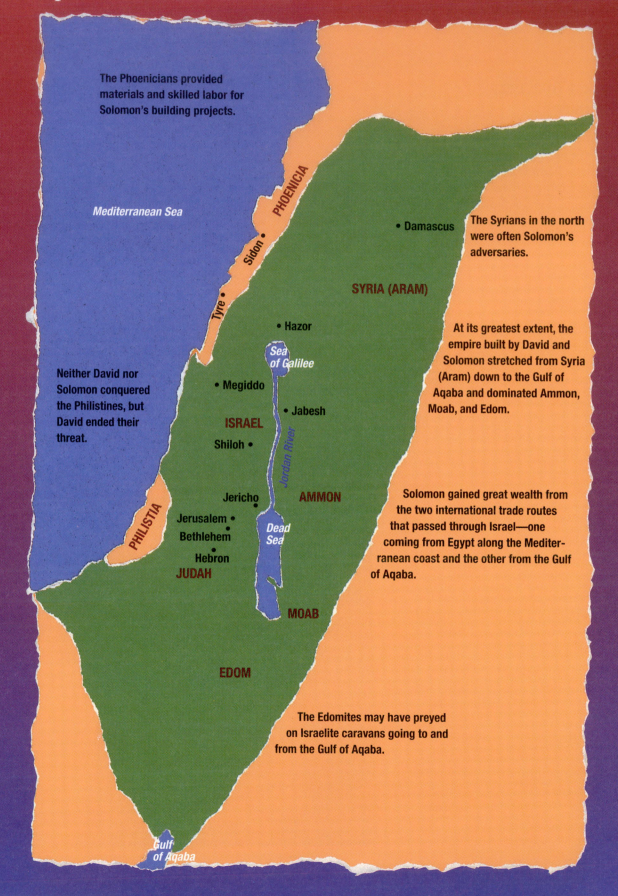

The Phoenicians provided materials and skilled labor for Solomon's building projects.

Mediterranean Sea

PHOENICIA

• Damascus

The Syrians in the north were often Solomon's adversaries.

SYRIA (ARAM)

Sidon •

Tyre •

• Hazor

Sea of Galilee

Neither David nor Solomon conquered the Philistines, but David ended their threat.

• Megiddo

At its greatest extent, the empire built by David and Solomon stretched from Syria (Aram) down to the Gulf of Aqaba and dominated Ammon, Moab, and Edom.

• Jabesh

ISRAEL

Shiloh •

Jordan River

Jericho •

AMMON

PHILISTIA

Jerusalem •

Bethlehem •

Dead Sea

Hebron •

JUDAH

Solomon gained great wealth from the two international trade routes that passed through Israel—one coming from Egypt along the Mediterranean coast and the other from the Gulf of Aqaba.

MOAB

EDOM

The Edomites may have preyed on Israelite caravans going to and from the Gulf of Aqaba.

Gulf of Aqaba

Senseless devotion

Notice that David's loyalty to family is so strong that he refuses to punish Amnon for raping Tamar, he trusts Absalom to come back into his court after killing Amnon, and he fails to recognize Absalom's treacherous intentions. His devotion to his sons seems to make him abandon good sense. *16*

The Ending Years of David's Reign

After the failed revolts, David moves to reconcile the disgruntled tribes in both north and south. He refuses to punish Saul's family—even the treacherous Mephibosheth.

David is enthroned once more in Jerusalem, and the kingdom is restored to a semblance of order. Yet the popularity of the aging king is not what it was. Animosity among the tribes is beginning to surface. And David—worn out, his judgment not always fair—has such bias toward his favorites that it is bound to fuel resentments and rivalries.

David's Legacy: Nation Building, Trust in God, a Promise of Forever

By the end of David's reign, Israel is indeed a nation like other nations, with a king and a capital. David has established his kingship over all the tribes of Israel, built a strong nation that can resist the Philistines, and set up its center in Jerusalem, a city that will embody the hopes and dreams of Israel for centuries to come, even to the present.

The Deuteronomists, who during the exile edited the history of David's times, may have looked back and wondered about the wisdom of Israel's becoming a nation with a king. They knew that the illusions and temptations of power and wealth corrupted most of the kings after David and ultimately led to Israel's downfall at the hands of the Babylonians. Yet they saw in David a model of what the kings, and all Israel, should have been—devoted to God.

Above all else David trusted in God and tried to serve him. When his enemies plotted against him and his own sons became his enemies, David continued to be devoted to God, placing himself in God's care. When he sinned grievously, he threw himself on God's mercy and did not despair. David was not sinless, but he knew that God was the center of his life and his nation's life. He must have been a hopeful example for the exiles, a sign

16

In a paragraph describe a character on television or in a movie who reminds you of Amnon or Absalom.

The artist Michelangelo's statue of the youthful David

Solomon, a son of David and king of Israel

that Israel could be forgiven its many failures and could go on to live faithfully, if only Israel would keep God at the center. [17]

Recall, too, God's promise to David that his royal line would endure forever. This Davidic Covenant became the source of hope among Jews of later times, and even today—hope that a messiah would be born from David's descendants to deliver the people from oppression. The early Christians saw this promise to David as fulfilled in Jesus. [18]

For Review

☐ How does David continue to show loyalty to Saul and those close to Saul?

☐ Why is Jerusalem an ideal choice as capital?

☐ What does David do as he brings the ark of the Covenant into Jerusalem, and what is Michal's reaction?

☐ What is the Davidic Covenant? What is its connection with the later Jewish expectation of a messiah?

☐ How does David sin grievously, and how does Nathan help him to repent?

☐ Why did the Deuteronomists leave the account of David's sins in their history? What message can it give us?

☐ Give three examples of how the sons of David cause him tragedy and grief. In general, what is David's response to their terrible deeds?

☐ What characteristic of David made him a model of what the kings, and all Israel, should have been?

King Solomon: Temple Builder

For the rest of the story of the monarchy, we turn to the two Books of Kings, the last part of the Deuteronomic history edited during the Babylonian exile. They tell of David's son Solomon (the focus of the remainder of this chapter); then the breakup of the nation into the kingdoms of Israel and Judah; the infidelity of their kings; the prophets Elijah and Elisha; and all the events that led finally to the exile.

The Books of Kings show how the nation was mostly unfaithful despite warnings from its prophets. They were written to remind the disheartened exiles in Babylon that it was the people, not God, who broke the Covenant. Yet their restoration in the future would be possible if they would repent and turn to God again.

Passing the Torch to Solomon

As the First Book of Kings opens, David is close to death. His eldest son, **Adonijah,** is trying to take over the throne and even throws himself a party to celebrate. But Nathan the prophet manages to have David promise the throne to Solomon, David's son by Bathsheba. Solomon is then anointed king before his father dies.

On his deathbed David assures Solomon that if Solomon and his line will remain faithful to God, they will always sit on the throne. Then, in what seems a bloody reversal of David's merciful attitudes toward his enemies, David counsels Solomon to settle the old scores. Upon David's death Solomon

<hr />

17

Etched on U.S. currency are the words "In God we trust." Do you think this is true of U.S. citizens, or does our national security depend on trust in weapons, the military, wealth, prisons, and so on? Write an essay on your thoughts and observations.

18

Are you familiar with the story of King Arthur of Britain? Look up the legend of the Round Table. In writing, compare Arthur's story with David's.

does so, killing off several known "trouble-makers" and assuring himself of total control of the kingdom.

Read 1 Kings 1:1–22,28–40,49–53; 2:1–25.

Solomon Asks for Wisdom

To build an alliance with Egypt, Solomon marries the daughter of the Egyptian pharaoh. He also worships at one of the "high places," meaning an outdoor sanctuary.

In a dream Solomon asks God for an understanding heart to distinguish right from wrong. Pleased, God promises Solomon not only the wisdom to judge rightly but riches, glory, and long life as well—if he is faithful. **19**

Read 1 Kings 3:1–14

The high places

The Deuteronomists frowned on outdoor sanctuaries because the Canaanites used them in fertility rites and in the worship of Baal. Although Solomon's worship seems genuine, the story is hinting of evil things to come in its references to the high places—and to Solomon's Egyptian wife.

Solomon's Judgment

Solomon's understanding heart is immediately put to the test. Two prostitutes come before the king—one with a child, one without. The childless woman tells Solomon that each of them bore a child and that the other woman smothered hers in her sleep, then exchanged the dead infant for the live one and now claims him. The woman with the child denies this. The king calls for a sword and suggests that the child be divided and half given to each woman. The true mother, in anguish, cries out that the child should live and gives up her claim to him. Solomon gives the child to that woman, who revealed her motherhood in her desire to save the child's life.

Read 1 Kings 3:16–28.

The hills around Jerusalem. Solomon worshiped at the "high places," or outdoor sanctuaries near Jerusalem.

19

Who or what do you look to for wisdom? Write a paragraph about this source of wisdom in your life.

Solomon's Oppressive System

Solomon, ignoring tribal boundaries, divides the land into twelve new districts and appoints an officer for each region. Then he forms an elite group of administrators and introduces forced labor and taxation to provide supplies for the palace and for government officials.
Read 1 Kings 4:1–7.

20

Find an article about a corrupt or oppressive government of a country in the world today. How do you think world leaders and citizens outside that country can approach this problem? Write an essay about this issue and possible responses or resolutions.

Injustice and exploitation

Peasants in areas of the world like Central and South America have long been exploited by corrupt governments, by wealthy landowners, and by foreign investors. Solomon's glory was built on income raised by oppressing his people in the same way. Farmers and shepherds had to provide palace supplies from their own crops and herds, and take time from their work to hunt wild game for officials. The prophet Samuel had warned about these things long before, when the people first clamored for a king. With the reign of Solomon, the injustice came to pass. **20**

Solomon's Wisdom

Solomon's reputation grows until "all the kings of the earth" know of his wisdom (1 Kings 4:34). He utters three thousand proverbs,

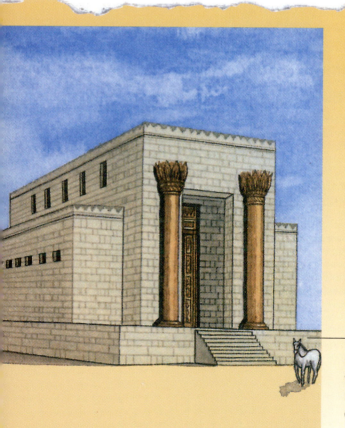

Solomon's Temple

The Bible devotes several pages to the construction, furnishings, and dedication of the Temple at Jerusalem. Indeed, Solomon is probably best known the world over for building his Temple. Financed by taxes, the building was a marvel of cedar beams, bronze pillars, ivory-paneled doors, golden vessels, and carved stonework. Its magnificence rivaled the monuments of Egypt.

The Temple had three chambers, as did the Canaanite temples. The people were relegated to the outer court, the priests and nobles to the inner court. The high priest entered the sanctuary, called the holy of holies (where the ark of the Covenant was housed), only once a year.

Solomon not only designed the Temple on Canaanite models but also adopted temple practices from his neighbors. In some ways Solomon's Temple became a symbol of wealth at the price of justice, and arrogance at the price of faith. Yet the Temple was always regarded as sacred because it was seen as the place where God chose to dwell with the people.

Marvelous though it was, Solomon's Temple marked the beginning of Israel's downfall.

writes one thousand and five songs, and discusses plants, beasts, birds, reptiles, and fishes.

Read 1 Kings 4:29–34 (or 5:9–14 in NAB or NJB).

What kind of wisdom?

The scriptural writers probably exaggerated the number of proverbs and songs that Solomon wrote, but no doubt he was the source of many wise words and a key figure in the intellectual wisdom movement of that time. Entire books of the Bible (in the category of Wisdom books) were later attributed to him, although this does not mean he actually wrote them.

We have to wonder, though, how deep the wisdom of Solomon actually was. True, his reign was a glorious time for Israel in terms of splendor and power and reputation among other nations. But how wise was he in the ways of God? In the end Solomon's reign was a disaster for Israel, a time marked by extravagance in the royal house, harsh oppression of the people, and even, as we will see, idolatry by the king himself.

The Temple as God's House

Rich and powerful, Solomon is now ready to build the Temple in Jerusalem. He asks a Phoenician king to send not only materials but also architects. Because Israel has never built a temple, a Canaanite model must be used. Solomon conscripts thirty thousand workers from his own people in addition to foreign labor. He also builds a fabulous royal palace complex and entire cities for his supplies, chariots, and horses.

The Prayer of Israel: "How Lovely Is Your Dwelling Place"

How lovely is your dwelling place,
    O Lord of hosts!
My soul longs, indeed it faints
    for the courts of the Lord;
my heart and my flesh sing for joy
    to the living God.

Even the sparrow finds a home,
    and the swallow a nest for herself,
    where she may lay her young,
at your altars, O Lord of hosts,
    my King and my God.
Happy are those who live in your house,
    ever singing your praise.

. . . .

For a day in your courts is better
    than a thousand elsewhere.
I would rather be a doorkeeper in the house of my God
    than live in the tents of wickedness.

. . . .

O Lord of hosts,
    happy is everyone who trusts in you.

(Psalm 84:1–4,10–12)

God agrees to be present in the Temple, adding that if Solomon observes the Law and carries it out, Israel will not be forsaken. In a long prayer, Solomon himself wonders if his great accomplishment is futile: Can any building contain God?

When the Temple is dedicated, God repeats the promise made to Solomon and adds a warning: If Solomon and his descendants forsake the Covenant, the Temple will become a heap of ruins. These words must have pierced the hearts of the exiles in Babylon as they listened and remembered their own story of failure.

Read 1 Kings 5:1–6 (or 5:15–20 in NAB or NJB); 6:11–13; 8:27–30; 9:1–11.

A high point on the way down

Israel's Temple, which enthrones the ark of the Covenant and centralizes worship, becomes a source of pride and joy. Yet its building marks the beginning of Israel's downfall. With the growing splendor of Solomon's reign comes oppression such as the people have never known before. *21*

The Queen of Sheba

Solomon is visited by the queen of Sheba, seeking to discover if he is as wise as reputed. The queen asks Solomon some subtle questions—probably traditional riddles, a number of which survive in collections of tales about Solomon. Observing his wisdom and his wealth, the queen is breathless.

Read 1 Kings 10:1–10.

The Sins of Solomon

As Solomon adds to his wealth and his harem, his love for God diminishes. He tolerates shrines where his pagan wives offer sacrifice, and he even joins in worshiping their gods. Finally, unable to distinguish right from wrong, Solomon prefers strange gods to the one God. Then God speaks: Solomon's line will lose the throne and all the tribes but Judah!

Read 1 Kings 11:1–13.

By now Solomon's failure is a foregone conclusion.

Trouble Brewing as Solomon's Reign Ends

After forty years of harsh rule, the discontent of Solomon's people lures his enemies back from exile to harass him. One of these, **Jeroboam,** is chief of the labor force fortifying the Jerusalem walls. Disenchanted, Jeroboam leaves Jerusalem to go north and meets a prophet, who tears his cloak into twelve pieces, one for each tribe. He gives ten of them to Jeroboam and tells him God promises him the throne of Israel in the north if he will follow the ways of God. One tribe, the prophet says, will go to a son of Solomon, so that David's line might continue in Jerusalem.

Solomon orders Jeroboam killed, but he escapes to Egypt to await Solomon's death. When at last Solomon dies, the golden age of Israel comes to an end.

Read 1 Kings 11:26–36,40–43.

21

Being portable, the ark held the Covenant of a people on a journey. The Temple, on the other hand, was set in stone, representing security and stability. Write a reflection on how both the ark and the Temple can remind us of God's presence with us.

An inheritance of idolatry

In forty years Solomon has led Israel from a union of tribes under David, loyal to the Covenant, to subjection and near slavery, not to mention the impending breakup of the kingdom. Although Israel is oppressed by taxes and forced labor, idolatry is the worst of the burdens that the nation has inherited from this golden ruler. Israel, whose identity rests on its fidelity to God, has been led to the worship of false gods. *22*

For Review

☐ Give three examples of Solomon's wisdom.

☐ How does Solomon oppress and exploit the people?

☐ What is God's warning at the time the Temple is dedicated?

☐ What burdens does Israel inherit from Solomon?

Nationhood Revisited

Why did Israel become a nation? There were good reasons, of course. The people wanted unity and strong leadership in the face of threats like the Philistines. Nationhood, too, would make long-term stability and continuity more possible for the Israelites.

Yet with nationhood came many evils—power struggles and betrayals, greed and oppression in the lust for wealth and honor, and the turning away from God, who had made the Israelites a people in the first place.

Imagine the exiles in Babylon wondering, How did we end up in this disaster of exile? With the help of the Deuteronomists, they began to get answers to that troubling question. They saw how they had grown to become a great nation and how that nation had begun to go wrong. It was one thing to sin and repent, as David had done. It was quite another to harden one's heart against God, as Solomon had. So the people recognized that the Covenant had been broken not by God but by kings like Solomon and most of the ones after him, as we will see in the next chapter.

22

In writing, compare and contrast the characters of Saul, David, and Solomon. What did each, in spite of his flaws, contribute to the salvation of Israel?

Ships carrying Solomon's trading goods may have landed at this bay at the northern tip of the Gulf of Aqaba.

7 The Prophets
Crying Out the Word of God

Sebastiya, a modern village that is the site
of Samaria, the capital of the northern
kingdom of Israel

Things went rapidly downhill for Israel after Solomon, as the First and Second Books of Kings tell us. Those scriptures, put in final form by the Deuteronomists during the exile, show how things went wrong for Israel, and why God's people ended up defeated and captive in Babylon some three centuries after Solomon.

The Books of Kings, as we will see shortly, tell the story of the breakup of the kingdom of Israel into **two kingdoms** of north and south, **Israel** and

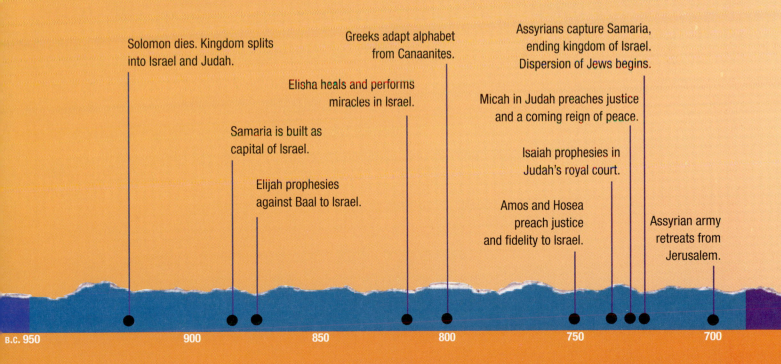

Solomon dies. Kingdom splits into Israel and Judah.

Greeks adapt alphabet from Canaanites.

Assyrians capture Samaria, ending kingdom of Israel. Dispersion of Jews begins.

Elisha heals and performs miracles in Israel.

Micah in Judah preaches justice and a coming reign of peace.

Samaria is built as capital of Israel.

Isaiah prophesies in Judah's royal court.

Elijah prophesies against Baal to Israel.

Amos and Hosea preach justice and fidelity to Israel.

Assyrian army retreats from Jerusalem.

B.C. 950   900   850   800   750   700

A stone carving shows King Jehu of Israel prostrating himself before an Assyrian monarch. Historians prize this artwork from the ninth century B.C. because it is the oldest known portrait of an Israelite.

Judah, and the abandonment of the Covenant by the people, led by their mostly wicked kings. During this time major empires, like the Egyptian, the Assyrian, the Babylonian, and the Persian, were rising and falling as they fought for as much of the known world as they could control, including the regions of Israel and Judah.

The northern and southern kingdoms had to pay tribute to these foreign powers. That is, Israel and Judah were forced to give "gifts" of great value to these empires to keep themselves from being overrun and enslaved. Or at times they agreed to submit to the sovereignty of one empire in exchange for being protected from another. As if that were not enough chaos to handle, at various times Israel and Judah actually were at war with each other.

During the tragic slide toward disaster, first of Israel, then of Judah, prophets came forward. Called by God, they warned the people that they had strayed from true worship and forgotten their role of witness to the Lord before the nations. Because the prophets were faithful to this call, they became the conscience of Israel (both Israel and Judah), risking their lives to condemn the moral laxity of kings and the decadence of their people. Their harsh criticism of greed and idolatry endeared them to only a few followers. But the prophets' ringing accusations and pleas for fidelity and goodness have become a literature ranked among the noblest writings of the ancient world and among the most useful for the modern.

In this chapter, we have already met two of the **former,** or **nonwriting, prophets:** Samuel, who rejected Saul's flawed kingship and anointed David as king; and Nathan, who denounced David's adultery. In the Books of Kings we meet two more of the nonwriting prophets, **Elijah** and **Elisha.** Appealing tales about them were probably collected and passed along by their disciples.

We will also meet for the first time some of the **latter,** or **writing, prophets,** whose messages are passed on to us in separate books of the Bible, which are named for them. Among the writing prophets are **Amos,** a herdsman; **Hosea,** a betrayed husband; the great **Isaiah** of Jerusalem, a confidant and counselor of kings; and **Micah,** a devotee of the poor.

The prophets addressed impassioned pleas to the kings of the north and the south to turn from idol worship and injustice and return to Israel's true God. Most of the kings refused to listen and, together with their people, continued on the path of self-serving. Inevitably this led both kingdoms to exile.

Let's begin the stories of the prophets by laying out what happened after Solomon's death that made the messages of the prophets so necessary.

Prophets to Israel and Judah

ASSYRIAN EMPIRE

The mighty Assyrian Empire threatened the kingdoms of Israel and Judah from the north and destroyed Israel in 721 B.C.

Mediterranean Sea

• Sidon

• Damascus

• Zarephath

PHOENICIA

SYRIA (ARAM)

• Dan

Sea of Galilee

Jezreel •

Jordan River

Samaria •

ISRAEL

Bethel •

Jericho •

Jerusalem •

Dead Sea

JUDAH

PHILISTIA

MOAB

The prophets to the kingdom of Israel included Elijah, Elisha, Amos, and Hosea.

Ezekiel and Second Isaiah spoke words of hope and salvation to the exiles in Babylon.

The prophets to the kingdom of Judah before 700 B.C. included First Isaiah and Micah.

In the years before the Babylonian exile, Jeremiah, Nahum, Habakkuk, and Zephaniah prophesied in Judah. The authors of Lamentations wrote poems of grief after the fall of Jerusalem.

EDOM

After the Babylonian exile, Third Isaiah, Haggai, Zechariah, Malachi, and Joel encouraged the returnees to rebuild the city of Jerusalem and its Temple. The author of Baruch inspired those who lived away from Jerusalem to keep the faith.

The prophet Obadiah condemned Edom, perhaps for helping Babylon to destroy Jerusalem.

Gulf of Aqaba

The Kingdom Breaks Up

Two Kingdoms: Israel and Judah

Following the death of Solomon, the people of the south accept his son **Rehoboam** as their king. But the northern tribes set forth a condition for accepting him as king: Rehoboam must not oppress them as his father did. The elders of the court agree and advise the young king to be a servant to his people, not a slave driver. But Rehoboam instead heeds the counsel of his young comrades, who call for more brutality, and the northern tribes reject him. Thus all Israel is divided into two kingdoms—Israel in the north, Judah in the south—and the unifying work of David is destroyed in the space of two generations. Rehoboam carries on David's royal line, or the house of David, in the south. *1*

When the rebel Jeroboam (whom we met at the end of chapter 6) is declared king in the north, he immediately breaks the Law of God and enshrines two golden calves, one at Dan and the other at Bethel. Then Jeroboam raises up non-Levite priests to offer sacrifices in the north, hoping to keep his people from going south to Jerusalem to worship, where they might rekindle their loyalty to the house of David. His strategy fails, as his dynasty only briefly outlives him.

Read 1 Kings 12:1–20,25–33; 13:33–34.

Why golden calves?

You might be wondering why Jeroboam would be stupid enough to build golden calves at shrines. Wasn't that an obvious act of idolatry that would only make God furious with him?

In hindsight the act looks foolhardy and downright insulting to God. But decisions to do what is evil do not usually appear so black-and-white to those who make them. Let's just speculate on Jeroboam's motives and rationalizing. Imagine this going through his head:

I've got to win the allegiance of a lot of different people up here in the north—not only my own tribes but the native Canaanites, too—so that I can fight off any threats from Rehoboam in the south. If the people can see I've got something to offer them,

---

1

Name a type of leader (such as a bishop, a president, a general, or a principal) and list five ways she or he can be a servant in that role.

The Prophets of Israel After 900 B.C.

The Northern Kingdom of Israel		Before and During the Exile	After the Exile
Elijah	Amos	Jeremiah	Third Isaiah
Elisha	Hosea	Nahum	Haggai
		Habakkuk	Zechariah
The Southern Kingdom of Judah		Authors of Lamentations	Joel
		Zephaniah	Obadiah
First Isaiah	Micah	Ezekiel	Authors of Baruch
		Second Isaiah	

900 – 700 B.C.   700 – 540 B.C.   540 – 400 B.C.

Terraced farmland in the region of Samaria. The prosperous northern kingdom of Israel had rich, fertile land compared with that in the southern kingdom of Judah.

The Wicked Kings of the North

The history of the northern kings of Israel reads like a police blotter:

A string of violent deaths follows the reign of Jeroboam, as the assassination of a king and his whole family becomes a common way for a rival to assume the throne. The sixth king, **Omri,** builds a splendid capital city, **Samaria,** but he, like his predecessors, does "evil in the sight of the LORD" (1 Kings 16:25)—but more so. He is succeeded by his son **Ahab,** the worst of them all. Ahab marries the Phoenician princess **Jezebel,** a fiendishly wicked woman, and they become the villains in the stories about the prophets Elijah and Elisha.

Read 1 Kings 16:23–33.

A strategic marriage

The marriage of King Ahab to the pagan Jezebel is recorded with horror by the Deuteronomists, who knew that Jezebel went on to insist that Baal, not the Lord, be worshiped in Israel. Why did Ahab marry her? Such marriages between royalty of two nations—in this case Israel and Phoenicia—were common ways of building protective alliances against hostile empires. In Ahab's case his marriage gained for Israel the military strength of Phoenicia, but that came at a big price—putting Baal in God's place.

they'll hang in with me. So I'll give them shrines to worship at, and my tribes won't have to go to Jerusalem, where the ark of the Covenant is, to offer sacrifices. In fact I might as well forbid them from going there; it'll only confuse their loyalties.

I can build golden calves for these shrines that are kind of dual purpose. For the Canaanites a golden calf is a symbol of their fertility god, Baal. And for the Israelites, the golden calf can be sort of a throne for our invisible God. That way I take care of everyone's needs, I don't get any flak from the Canaanites, and I keep my tribes away from Jerusalem.

The Israelite tribes, as Jeroboam could have anticipated, soon turned to worshiping the golden calf itself, a terrible betrayal of their relationship with God. Jeroboam's rationalized deed only brought disaster. Many actions of Israel's unfaithful kings that we now view as wicked probably seemed only smart to the kings at the time. *2*

For Review

- ☐ In what ways were the prophets the conscience of Israel and Judah?
- ☐ Why do the northern tribes form their own kingdom?
- ☐ How does Israel's King Jeroboam break the Law of God? Why does he do so?

2

In previous chapters you identified the kinds of false gods people worship today. Write your opinion in response to this question: *Why do people turn to these kinds of false gods?*

Elijah and Elisha in the North

How could the people of Israel become what God had called them to be when each king was worse than the previous one? Who could speak of God to them?

The answer to these questions was the prophets. Among the Israelites, they alone had no interest in power, money, or any approval but God's. They saw, heard, and spoke nothing but God. Moses, Eli, Samuel, and Nathan have been called prophets, and now we meet Elijah and Elisha, nonwriting prophets of the northern kingdom.

Prophesying is often seen as a kind of crystal ball gazing that foresees the future, but the prophets of Israel based their oracles on the will of God. When the kings became obsessed with power and wealth and led their people into idolatry, God called upon certain individuals to warn Israel of the consequences, and those individuals were the prophets.

The purpose of the stories in the Books of Kings about Elijah and Elisha—especially when told to the exiles in Babylon—was to show that when God spoke through the prophets, he expected Israel to listen—or else. Elijah and Elisha were historical figures who, without a doubt, tangled with Ahab and Jezebel. They prophesied from the reigns of the kings of Israel from Ahab to Joash—about 874 to 796 B.C.

Elijah Nourished by a Starving Widow

The stories about Elijah open with God's sending Elijah to tell King Ahab that he will be punished by a terrible drought, because apparently Queen Jezebel has ordered the

World Happenings from 900 to 600 B.C.

Africa
As the Saharan region in North Africa dries up, the inhabitants shift from using horses to camels as mounts and beasts of burden. In this same region, the Phoenicians found the city of Carthage and establish a trading empire in the western part of the Near East.

America
Earlier worship of jaguars as fierce and powerful totems develops into widely successful jaguar cults. Among the Olmecs of Mexico and the Chavin of Peru, these beasts are worshiped at great ceremonial centers.

China
Under the Chou dynasty, an aristocracy rules fiefdoms and presides over the practice of ancestor worship.

Europe
The Iron Age arrives, and with it come the Celts, who use iron tools and weapons to hew and hack their way through central Europe.

India
Hindu priests become the most powerful caste within the social order. Wandering sages, disenchanted with religious rituals, practice yoga and meditation as a means of discovering wisdom.

The Near East
The Assyrian Empire reaches the height of its glory, then disappears when its capital, Nineveh, is destroyed in 612 B.C.

Children at a Catholic school conduct a food drive, practicing the biblical lessons of sharing food with the hungry.

for her last bit of bread. The woman, a pagan like Jezebel, hears the word of God and also obeys. It is a simple tale about saying yes to God and trusting that he will provide whatever is needed.

Jesus told his own people in Nazareth that the pagan widow of Zarephath had more faith and heard the prophets more clearly than they did. They confirmed this by immediately trying to push Jesus off a cliff! *Read Luke 4:20–30.*

God's way is risky—but rewarding. Consider the story of **Dorothy Day.** In 1933, when she was in Washington, D.C., for a hunger march, she prayed with anguish that she might be led to use her gifts for her fellow workers and the poor. Later, she became cofounder of the Catholic Worker Movement, a leading voice of advocacy for justice that today has more than one hundred houses of hospitality for the hungry and homeless in the United States and other countries. [4]

Victory over the Prophets of Baal

Elijah remains with the widow of Zarephath until God sends him back to the court of Ahab. When Ahab blames Elijah for the drought, Elijah challenges the prophets of Baal to a contest to see whose god can produce rain. The prophets (priests in some Bible versions) call to Baal in vain. Elijah taunts them to call louder—perhaps Baal is meditating, napping, or on a journey. The prophets slash themselves in an ecstatic frenzy—but no rain.

Then Elijah builds an altar to the Lord. He digs a trench around it, arranges wood for a fire, kills a bull for sacrifice, and has the people—who have been shilly-shallying between Baal and God—drench it with water.

slaughter of all the prophets of Israel. Elijah is next sent to hide by a stream, where ravens will feed him. When the stream goes dry, he is sent to the village of Zarephath in Sidon (Phoenicia), where a widow will care for him. Upon his arrival Elijah sees the woman and asks her for water and a crust of bread. But she has only enough flour and oil, she says, to make a barley cake for herself and her son before they die of starvation. Elijah promises God's help if she will divide the cake with him. The widow does, and afterward, until the drought is over, her jar of flour and jug of oil are never empty. *Read 1 Kings 17:1–16.* [3]

Saying yes with trust

The obedience of Elijah is contrasted with the disobedience of the king. The prophet goes on a dangerous errand, entrusts his survival to ravens, and asks a starving woman

---

3

Write a modern-day story that tells the lesson of this story about the widow.

4

What are your dreams for the future? Think about ways of helping to heal the world. Then respond in writing to this question: *If anything were possible, what would you do to heal the world?*

He calls for a show of God's power, and fire comes down to consume the bull, the wood, and the stones, even lap up the water. The unfaithful people fall to the ground and worship the God of Israel. Then Elijah has the prophets of Baal killed.

Read 1 Kings 18:17–40.

In this story Elijah accuses the people of halfheartedness in their faith: They must make up their mind. Biblical faith calls for commitment, not standing on the sidelines being careful.

Read Luke 11:23.

God in the Breeze

Angry at Elijah's victory over the prophets of Baal, Jezebel threatens his life. So Elijah flees to the desert, where an angel tells him to journey on to Horeb (Mount Sinai). There he takes shelter in a cave, and when God asks why he has come, Elijah, filled with self-pity, pours out his woe. There is no point in going on, he mourns; all Israel but he, Elijah, has abandoned God.

God bids Elijah to stand outside the cave to experience his presence. First Elijah hears a powerful wind, then he feels an earthquake, then he sees a fire, but God is not in them. At last a gentle breeze ("a sound of sheer silence" [1 Kings 19:12] or "a tiny whispering sound" [NAB]) speaks to Elijah of the presence of God, and Elijah hides his face in shame at his own disbelief and in gratitude for the patience of God. God sends Elijah back to work, reminding him that he

The LORD was not in the wind . . . . not in the earthquake . . . not in the fire . . . . [but in] a sound of sheer silence. **1 Kings 19:11–12**

is not the only one who cares, that seven thousand Israelites have remained faithful.
Read 1 Kings 19:1–18.

God's presence in the small and ordinary

Elijah, feeling he has failed, needs the strength of God's presence. God's strength comes to him not in a big, showy display but in the simplest way. God is like that for us. We may not find God's power in big, obvious successes or triumphs but in his quiet movement in our everyday life. *5*

Condemning Ahab's Greed for a Vineyard

In another Elijah story, King Ahab wants a vineyard belonging to a man named Naboth, but Naboth refuses him because it is his ancestral land, which has always been kept in the family. When Ahab sulks to Jezebel about this refusal, she arranges for Naboth to be killed. She gets false witnesses to testify that Naboth cursed God and the king and thus deserves death by stoning. So Naboth is killed, and because the property of a condemned person reverts to the king, Ahab gets his vineyard in a neat but nasty operation.

God sends Elijah to curse Ahab. Elijah tells the king that as dogs licked the blood of Naboth, they will lick Ahab's blood and devour Jezebel. Elijah also predicts that Ahab's line will disappear. All these things eventually do come to pass.
Read 1 Kings 21:1–29; 22:29–38.

The storytellers may have chosen the image of a fiery chariot and horses to describe the fiery prophet Elijah.

Free to choose

"Where is God?" is our cry when we see villainy like Ahab and Jezebel's—in history or today. But people are free to choose either good or evil. Unfortunately when someone chooses evil, it often destroys the innocent. The answer to "I can't believe in a God who would let this happen!" is "God didn't; *people* did." The alternative to having free will is to be like windup toys with God turning the key.

Ultimately, however, good does prevail. Evil is often self-destructive, while good is usually fruitful and multiplies. Heinous villains like Ahab can be forgotten, while saints who lived as unknowns in their time have later become known all over the world for their quiet, unshowy goodness. **Thérèse of Lisieux,** a young woman who went into obscurity in a Carmelite monastery, lived a loving but quiet life in the late 1800s, and she kept a journal of her reflections. Thérèse never would have expected that after she died at age twenty-four, she would become one of the favorite saints of modern Catholicism and be proclaimed a doctor of the Church. *6*

Off in a Chariot of Fire

Elijah, aware that his life is over, goes to the Jordan River with Elisha, a man who had earlier become his devoted follower. There Elijah parts the water with his cloak, and the two cross over. In their last moments together, Elisha asks for a double portion of Elijah's spirit. Suddenly a flaming chariot with fiery horses comes between the two,

---

5

"We may not find God's power in big, obvious successes or triumphs but in his quiet movement in our everyday life." Read this sentence to three adults you know. Ask them if they believe it is true. If they say yes, ask if they can think of an example of his quiet movement in their life. If they disagree with the statement, ask them to explain their viewpoint. Write the results of your interviews.

6

Write about an experience from your life that shows either the destructive effects of evil or the nature of good, which is fruitful and multiplies.

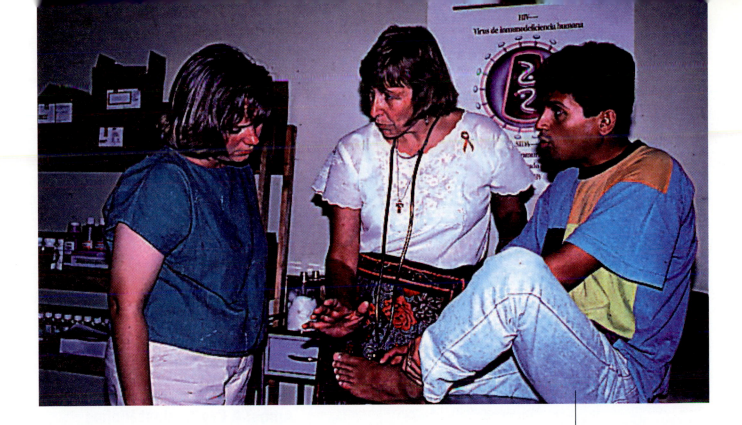

and Elijah disappears in a whirlwind. Elisha watches, crying out. He tears his own cloak in half, strikes the Jordan's water with Elijah's cloak, and returns across the riverbed. For three days a community of prophets of the region search for Elijah but fail to find him.

Read 2 Kings 2:1–17.

Eventually this tale gave rise to the belief that Elijah would return to announce the coming of the Messiah. This tradition was the basis for references to Elijah in the Gospel stories of Jesus and John the Baptist. In Luke the priest Zechariah announces that John the Baptist has "the spirit and power of Elijah" (1:17). In the Gospel of John, John the Baptist is asked if he is Elijah. Later, Elijah appears at the Transfiguration of Jesus Christ.

Read Luke 1:13,17; John 1:19–21; Luke 9:28–33.

Elisha's Miracles

From that time on, Elisha carries on the mission of his mentor, Elijah. His story is an unbroken succession of wonders. Elisha purifies Jericho's water supply, which has been causing deaths and miscarriages. He helps a widow avoid selling her children to pay her debts. He blesses a childless couple, and they beget a son. Later he raises this child from the dead in a manner that strangely suggests artificial respiration. He purifies poisoned stew and multiplies loaves of bread to make enough for a hundred people.

Elisha becomes known, even among foreigners, for his healing powers. In one incident Elisha cures Naaman, a commander in the Syrian army, of leprosy. He does this by having a servant tell Naaman to wash seven times in the Jordan River. Naaman balks at doing this because it seems so simple, but when he gives in and bathes in the river, he is cured. A grateful and humbler Naaman returns to Elisha, believing in Elisha's God. He offers Elisha gifts, but the prophet refuses them. Then Naaman asks for earth from Israel to take home so that every day he can stand and pray to God on Israel's soil.

Maryknoll missioners at a medical clinic in El Salvador with a young man who has AIDS. The healing ministry of the prophet Elisha, and later Jesus, is carried out today in such work.

Even in death Elisha heals. One story tells of how, after Elisha's burial, a dead man's body is thrown into Elisha's grave. When it touches the prophet's bones, it springs to life.

Read 2 Kings 2:19–22; 4:1–44; 5:1–19; 13:20–21. [7]

Multiplying loaves and healing the sick

All four Gospels have accounts of Jesus miraculously multiplying loaves of bread for the hungry crowd, as well as Jesus healing many who came to him in trust. The multiplication of loaves by both Elisha and Jesus were signs of God's loving concern for people, as were the healings they did of the sick and the leprous. To see their miracles as divine tricks intended to impress the crowds is to miss the point. Their concern was for the people, not for raising eyebrows.

We have seen in the Books of Kings the marvelous stories of the nonwriting prophets Elijah and Elisha, of the northern kingdom. Next, we turn to the writing prophets of the north, Amos and Hosea.

For Review

☐ How does the story of Elijah and the starving widow demonstrate trust in God?

☐ In what way does Elijah experience the presence of God at the cave?

☐ How did the biblical storytellers describe Elijah's leaving the earth? What belief arose later about Elijah?

☐ Give four examples of Elisha's miracles.

Amos and Hosea in the North

If, at first glance, the prophets all seem alike, it is for a good reason: They were concerned about the same things. They called Israel and Judah to remember the God who saved them, who made a Covenant with them, who wanted them to return to it and be a blessing to the nations. The prophets' language and symbolic actions said long ago what still needs saying today. However, in other ways the prophets were not alike. Their personalities, backgrounds, ways of speech, and actions were very different—as we will see. [8]

Amos: A Cry Against Riches Gained by Injustice

The time is about 750 B.C., and Jeroboam II is king in prosperous Israel. Amos, a shepherd from Judah, goes north to preach against the sinful kingdom of Israel. Amos is harsh, blunt, and angry—a prophet who is said to roar like a lion.

Amos first appears at Bethel in the north where, after the breakup of David's kingdom, Jeroboam I set up a golden calf. Amos's rustic garments are a sharp contrast to the worshipers' rich attire, but the people recognize the voice of a prophet when he speaks. He condemns their unjust, exploitative actions toward the poor and weak, and tells them God will punish them for this.

7

In a paragraph, respond to the following questions:
- Have you ever used the word *miracle* for an event you witnessed or for a solution to a situation you thought was unsolvable?
- Was the event or the solution a suspending of the natural order? Or did you use the word *miracle* simply to say that it was wonderful beyond expectations? or spooky?
- Did the event have anything to do with faith?

8

Who are the people in your life who keep calling you back to goodness? Name two such persons and describe in writing what message they communicate to you. Do they express this message by their words or by their actions? Explain.

The Prayer of Israel: "Do Not Forget the Oppressed"

Why, O Lord, do you stand far off?
> Why do you hide yourself in times of trouble?
In arrogance the wicked persecute the poor—
> let them be caught in the schemes they have devised.

For the wicked boast of the desires of their heart,
> those greedy for gain curse and renounce the Lord.
In the pride of their countenance the wicked say,
>> "God will not seek it out";
> all their thoughts are, "There is no God."

Their ways prosper at all times;
> your judgments are on high, out of their sight;
> as for their foes, they scoff at them.
They think in their heart, "We shall not be moved;
> throughout all generations we shall not meet adversity."

Their mouths are filled with cursing and deceit and oppression;
> under their tongues are mischief and iniquity.
They sit in ambush in the villages;
> in hiding places they murder the innocent.

Their eyes stealthily watch for the helpless;
> they lurk in secret like a lion in its covert;
they lurk that they may seize the poor;
> they seize the poor and drag them off in their net.

They stoop, they crouch,
> and the helpless fall by their might.
They think in their heart, "God has forgotten,
> he has hidden his face, he will never see it."

Rise up, O Lord; O God, lift up your hand;
> do not forget the oppressed.
Why do the wicked renounce God,
> and say in their hearts, "You will not call us to account"?

But you do see! Indeed you note trouble and grief,
> that you may take it into your hands;
the helpless commit themselves to you;
> you have been the helper of the orphan.

. . . .

O Lord, you will hear the desire of the meek;
> you will strengthen their heart, you will incline your ear
to do justice for the orphan and the oppressed,
> so that those from earth may strike terror no more.

(Psalm 10)

The Prophets   **159**

Let justice roll down like waters, and righteousness like an ever-flowing stream.

Amos 5:24

Amos condemned the rich women of Samaria, describing their extravagant luxury and self-indulgence—all at the expense of the poor.

In Samaria, the capital of the kingdom, Amos condemns the rich women of Samaria, comparing them to fat cattle. He describes a scene like a movie set: Lying on their couches and ivory beds, the Samaritan women loll about and call to their husbands, "Bring us drinks!" They eat lamb and veal from the flocks, drink wine from bowls, and anoint their skin with perfumed oil—all at the expense of the poor! Amos warns that it will not last; the day will come when, like dead animals, they will be dragged away with hooks through their noses and deposited on the refuse heap outside the city.

Read Amos 1:1–2; 2:6–8; 3:1–2,9–11,15; 4:1–3. **9**

Why so angry, Amos?

Amos is not some disgruntled yokel who resents the rich. He is angered by Israel's disregard for God's Law, so lovingly designed to protect the people—both the poor from going hungry and the rich from becoming greedy. The Law was given to Israel when it was called to be God's nation, but now Israel has become like other nations: wealth is in the hands of a few, justice has been corrupted, and poor people are oppressed. **10**

No Empty Ritual: "Let Justice Roll Down"

In an eloquent passage said to have been the favorite of Dr. Martin Luther King Jr., Amos says that the Lord hates and abominates processions, sacrifices, and hymn singing that do not come from sincere hearts. God wants hearts from which justice rolls down "like waters, / and righteousness like an ever-flowing stream" (Amos 5:24).

Read Amos 5:21–24.

Ways of worship

Through Amos's prophesying, God condemns not formal worship but empty worship, in which rituals of praise and sacrifice are not backed up with just actions toward others. False worship continues to be a problem in modern times. Before the civil rights laws and desegregation, widespread discrimination existed in many Christian churches in the United States—with African Americans unwelcome in white churches. Various forms of discrimination still exist in some churches today.

9

Write your thoughts on the following statement: *In our society we sometimes enjoy luxuries at the expense of poor people.*

10

Explain in writing how God's Law can serve to protect poor people in our society from going hungry or rich people from becoming greedy. Name two other ways God's Law can protect people.

160   The Prophets

Amos's Visions of Israel's Final Fate

Amos has visions of Israel's final fate, insights that come to him while he works. Watching locusts eating the crops, Amos sees that Israel is helpless to survive the fate it has brought upon itself. Seeing fire ravage the land during the dry season, he sees Israel being destroyed by the people's sin. Amos sees God measuring a crooked wall, about to collapse, with a plumb line, and he sees that Israel is also about to collapse. Referring to Israel as Jacob, Amos pleads for Israel to God. At first God relents but finally says that Israel has chosen evil; he will leave it to its own destruction.

Amos crosses the line too many times with the powers that be in Israel, and he is ordered by the high priest at Bethel to go back to Judah. He goes, but not without telling off the high priest!

Read Amos 7:1–17; 8:4–12; 9:8–15.

Hosea: God as a Betrayed Husband

A line of corrupt kings makes the last years of Israel (786 to 721 B.C.) a sordid tale. During this period, toward the end of Jeroboam II's reign, the prophet Hosea from the northern kingdom appears. Hosea is involved in a terribly unhappy marriage. **Gomer,** the wife he loves, has deserted Hosea for other lovers —as Israel has deserted God for the Canaanite god Baal. Hosea, out of his own experience of betrayal, finds the words for his oracles to unfaithful Israel.

When Hosea speaks of himself and Gomer, he is telling Israel a parable of its own betrayal of God. If we keep this in mind, we will understand him clearly. The first three chapters of the Book of Hosea deliver his message. The remaining eleven chapters are fragments of oracles condemning Israel's sin.

As the book opens, God commands Hosea to take an unfaithful wife. That is, he is to take a wife who later will be discovered

Seeing fire ravage the land, Amos envisioned Israel being thus destroyed by the people's sin.

to be unfaithful. Looking back, Hosea sees his call to marry Gomer as prophetic. Without his own heartbreak, he could never have understood the magnitude of Israel's betrayal of God. [11]

Hosea and Gomer have three children, to whom Hosea is told to give strange names. In telling his story to the Israelites, Hosea knows these names are symbolic of how God regards the children of the Covenant with Israel. The names stand for or mean, literally, "shameful butchery," "not pitied," and "not my people." By the time the third name is spoken, the people recognize what Hosea is saying—that God will break

11

Many poets and songwriters say their writing is sometimes inspired by heartbreaking experiences. Find a poem or a song that is an example of this and write a paragraph about what the writer seems to have learned from his or her suffering.

I-Witness: Adah

I'm Adah, the younger daughter of Terah, whose family has long been the scribes to the royal court of Israel. No longer: the Assyrians have destroyed cities to the north, and their envoys threaten that we are next.

Our king has all the brains of a fig. He sacrifices with priests of Baal, who prophesy peace and prosperity—to keep their own hides safe! And the king and court go back to partying.

Even commoners know better. In Samaria the other day, I heard a bumpkin preach about our idolatry and ruin. I'm not officially a scribe, but I jotted down his speech. He was honest, and I admire his faith in the Lord's saving power.

Father can get work at the court in Judah, and we are headed south to Jerusalem any day. We will be safer there, but I feel guilty leaving so many to their fate. I pray the Lord's blessings on all those who remain in Samaria!

the Covenant. A more threatening image could not exist. No matter how it sinned, Israel has always presumed that God's Covenant with it would stave off punishment.

Read Hosea 1:1–9. **12**

Be Exiled, but Come Back to Me

Chapter 2 of Hosea takes place in a divorce court, where Hosea testifies to Gomer's unfaithfulness and ingratitude. He is angry, and his plans for her punishment are harsh. She has forgotten that he gave her everything she ever had—grain, wine, oil, silver, and gold. He will take these things away. She has even credited her lovers with the gifts Hosea gave her! He will punish her until at last she is abandoned and forlorn and returns to him.

As Hosea's story proceeds and he speaks of his longing to forgive Gomer and be reunited with her, he fantasizes of days to come.

Strangely, his voice seems to be replaced by the Lord's, as though God is speaking now without the pretext of the parable. God speaks hopefully of the future with Israel:

Therefore, I will now allure her,
and bring her into the wilderness,
and speak tenderly to her.
From there I will give her her vineyards,
and make the Valley of Achor a door of hope.
There she shall respond as in the days of her youth,
as at the time when she came out of the land of Egypt.

(Hosea 2:14–15)

God and Israel will remarry. In a canticle of joy, God promises to make up for every deprivation Israel has suffered. Every good gift will be restored, and their children (the Israelites) will be renamed.

God tells Hosea to seek out Gomer and pay a bride-price for her again—or a ransom should she be a slave or in the hire of Baal's priests as a temple prostitute. Then, after she has been through a period of waiting and faithfulness, he is to take her back.

Read Hosea 2:2–23 (or 2:4–25 in NAB or NJB); 3:1–5.

12

If Hosea were to name his children to symbolize corruption in our time or in our country, what names do you think he might choose? List them and explain their significance.

Gomer and Israel as forever beloved

Hosea is the first book to feature the relationship between God and Israel as a marriage and to use the language and images of marriage in describing it. To God, "infidelity" in Israel's behavior means betrayal of justice, compassion, integrity, or true worship; or as Hosea says, Israel "played the harlot" (2:7, NAB).

According to the custom of the times, Gomer could be sentenced to death for her infidelity. Instead, Hosea wants to punish his wife for a while but then take her back tenderly. Similarly, Hosea is saying that God will not wipe out the Israelites even though they deserve it. God will put Israel through a time of exile and abandonment, and this experience will eventually bring Israel back into its loving relationship with the Lord.

Assyria Defeats and Scatters Israel

Even with the warnings of prophets like Amos and Hosea, chaos and infidelity to God abound in Israel. Palace revolutions, assassinations of kings, and worship of Baal continue to weaken the nation. Israel turns more and more to making deals with foreign powers for security in a hostile world rather than trusting in God. But the overwhelming might of the **Assyrians**—the fiercest, most brutal empire of the ancient Near East—makes it impossible for Israel to be secure. Finally, after a long siege of Israel's capital, Samaria, the Assyrians take the city; the northern kingdom of Israel is finished. (The date, as we estimate it today, is 721 B.C.)

Assyria deports thousands of Israelites, particularly their leaders, forcing them to live in exile in the Assyrian Empire. The Assyrians put their own people in charge of the land that was Israel, and they bring in

Hosea pictured God tenderly welcoming back an unfaithful Israel, like a husband or wife embracing and forgiving an unfaithful partner.

Adolf Hitler and Nazi officers inspect a defeated Paris, France. Like France, which was overrun and occupied by the Germans during World War II, the northern kingdom of Israel was conquered and occupied by forces of the brutal Assyrian Empire.

Scripture scholars tell us that some of the Israelites fled south to Judah, where they knew they would have common religious roots. They hoped that despite past periods of war between Israel and Judah, the southern kingdom would accept them as their fellow Chosen People of God. Some of the fleeing northerners brought their traditional stories and writings with them to Judah. Many of these stories found their way into the Scriptures as they were edited centuries later during the Babylonian exile.

The Samaritans

Later in the history of Judaism and in the Gospels of the New Testament, we will run into people called **Samaritans,** who were intensely disliked by the Jews. Who were they, and why did the Jews have such prejudice against them? They were the descendants of the Israelites who remained in the north after Samaria's collapse (generally the common folk, not the leaders) and intermarried with the foreign colonists brought in by Assyria. So, centuries later, they were like distant lost cousins to the people of Judah. The Samaritans' religion, while it had traces of the old Israelite worship, was seen by Jews of the south as polluted with paganism. So they had no time or regard for anything or anyone Samaritan. *13*

foreign colonists, who will intermarry with the locals. In the Second Book of Kings, the scriptural text describing the dismantling of the northern tribes ends tersely: "The LORD was very angry with Israel and removed them out of his sight; none was left but the tribe of Judah alone" (17:18).

Read 2 Kings 17:5–24.

13

Have you witnessed or experienced cultural, racial, or religious prejudice? What do you think people have learned about this problem since the time of the Samaritans? Write your thoughts in a brief essay.

For Review

☐ What does Amos condemn in Bethel and Samaria?

☐ What kind of worship does Amos criticize?

☐ How is Hosea's relationship with Gomer similar to God's relationship with Israel?

☐ How did the northern kingdom come to an end?

The Assyrians

Sometime after 2000 B.C., history began to hear from the Assyrians, a Semitic group that took its name from its major city, Assur. The story of Assyria tells about alternating periods of domination and decline, and about the struggle for leadership of the region against the rulers of Babylon, a city about two hundred miles southeast of Assur. Assyria was located in the area now belonging to northern Iraq.

The Babylonians are best remembered as culture lovers, and the Assyrians had a reputation as warmongers. The Assyrians often tried to negotiate disputes with their neighbors, but more frequently their kings adopted tactics of terror that made them feared and despised throughout the Near East.

The height of Assyrian domination came in the seventh century B.C. In the reign of Ashurbanipal (668 to 627 B.C.), the Assyrians ruled the largest empire in the world—including all of Iraq, Syria, Lebanon, and Jordan; much of Egypt; and some of Turkey.

Historians compare the Assyrians to the Romans. Like those later empire builders, the Assyrians became efficient administrators and war tacticians. They were one of the first nations to train a professional army and to deploy it in formal lines of battle. And just as the Romans borrowed much of their culture from the Greeks, the Assyrians embraced the Babylonians' literature and their religious, economic, and legal concepts. The Assyrians' lasting achievement was Ashurbanipal's library in his capital city, Nineveh. It contained twenty thousand tablets on such topics as history, astronomy, and mathematics.

At its peak the Assyrian Empire was overextended, undefendable, and doomed to collapse. In 612 B.C., fifteen years after Ashurbanipal's death, Nineveh fell to the Babylonians.

An ancient stone relief depicts the brutality of the Assyrian army, tossing around the heads of their defeated enemies.

A field near Bethlehem in what was the southern kingdom of Judah

Isaiah in the South: The Greatest Writing Prophet

The greatest of the writing prophets was Isaiah. As we will see, the Book of Isaiah was composed by more than one "Isaiah." But before looking at First Isaiah's message, let's back up two centuries to see what events led up to his prophesying in Judah while Israel in the north was heading for its own disaster.

Backing Up: The Southern Kingdom of Judah

Each kingdom—Judah and Israel—had its own kings after Solomon's death in about 922 B.C. But the kings of Judah had one major difference from those of the northern kingdom. Whereas Israel's kings came from a variety of families, Judah's kings all the way down to the Babylonian exile were of the house, or family line, of David. They were direct descendants of King David, with whom

God had made a Covenant pledging that David's royal line would endure forever. So the kings of Judah felt rather proud of that, and secure in the knowledge that their line would continue unbroken.

Recall that Solomon was David's son. After Solomon died, his son Rehoboam (as we have seen earlier in this chapter) ascended to the throne and made a point of being harsh and cruel to the northerners. The breakup of the united nation of Israel into two kingdoms followed shortly after that. Besides being a harsh ruler, unfortunately Rehoboam started things off on a bad foot for Judah by being unfaithful to God.

After Rehoboam the record of the southern kings was mixed but mostly bad. There were a few reformers, like Hezekiah and Josiah. But for the most part Judah's kings were as bad as the kings of the north. Not only did they allow worship of Baal, in some cases they even made room for it in the Temple. Besides that, they were as murderous and treacherous as Israel's kings, with royal assassinations being common— all in the family!

By the 740s B.C., Judah had become idolatrous, prosperous, and greedy. At this time a man named Isaiah had an awesome vision in the Temple at Jerusalem in which he answered God's call to become a prophet to his nation that was in such trouble. The Book of Isaiah is named for this man, the greatest of Judah's prophets. *14*

The Book of Isaiah: A Work of Three Eras

Isaiah of Jerusalem is mentioned in only thirty-nine of the sixty-six chapters of his book, and of these only twelve chapters are from his hand. Why, then, is the entire book called the Book of Isaiah? Is Isaiah the only inspired author of it? Are the other "Isaiahs" inspired prophets also? They are indeed.

The Book of Isaiah is the longest and most influential of the prophetic books, covering from two hundred to two hundred and fifty years and written by a number of authors. It is usually recognized as falling into three parts, the work of three principal authors:

- **First Isaiah,** or **Isaiah of Jerusalem,** who pleaded with Judah's kings and people before the Babylonian exile—chapters 1 to 39

- **Second Isaiah,** who spoke during and at the end of the exile—chapters 40 to 55
- **Third Isaiah,** who was with the people when they returned to Judah from exile—chapters 56 to 66

The entire collection is named after Isaiah of Jerusalem because he was the first and most important contributor. The other "Isaiahs" seem to fall into the category of disciples who shared his vision and passionate desire to bring Israel back to God.

The Book of Isaiah is a story of infidelity, suffering, repentance, and consolation for the people—and of threats, condemnations, promises, and comfort by the prophets. This story is told not so much in events as in oracles and poetry. Isaiah contains some of the most beautiful language in the Bible, spoken by people who were geniuses and saints.

14

List three prophetic messages of our time, that is, messages that challenge us—beyond what is comfortable—to be faithful. In writing, respond to these questions:
- Do people listen to modern prophecies?
- Why or why not? Give examples.

A sing-along concert of Handel's *Messiah,* a well-known symphony that sets magnificent passages from the Book of Isaiah to music.

Writing the Scriptures

Many of the books of the Old Testament were derived from earlier oral versions going back to the time when Israel was a people but not yet a nation. The written versions began later, when a simple system of writing Hebrew became available around 1000 B.C.—the time of David's and Solomon's reigns. The story of writing systems and the Bible is a fascinating one.

Picture writing

In a limited form, writing has been used for over thirty thousand years. In picture writing, realistically drawn figures represent an object, an event, or an idea. For instance, a picture of a hunter, a spear, and a bear can mean "The hunter killed the bear."

Many ancient societies developed writing systems based on picture writing. Over time the written characters became simpler, but each one still represented a word or a phrase. Ancient writers had to learn hundreds, even thousands, of written characters in order to record even brief reports or letters.

Hieroglyphics

We associate the written characters called hieroglyphics with the Egyptians, who carved them on their temples and tombs beginning around 3000 B.C. Actually, the term *hieroglyphic,* meaning "of holy carvings," can refer to any system of highly stylized pictures—such as those once used by the Cretans in the Mediterranean or the Mayans in Central America.

The Egyptians added a special feature to writing by using some of their pictures to represent sounds. We will see in a moment what an important change that was.

Egyptian hieroglyphic writing (pictures)

Persian cuneiform writing (wedge-shaped word symbols)

Greek alphabetical writing (characters that represent sounds)

Alphabetic writing

Egyptian writing influenced the system that the Canaanites invented sometime before 1550 B.C. The Canaanites also used pictures, but eventually they adopted a set of simply written characters— all of which represented consonants.

Think about what that meant: The written characters were linked to sounds, not words. Relatively few characters were needed; a couple of dozen could represent most of the sounds of speech. Now anyone who could learn a simple alphabet could write. Suddenly many more people could become professional writers, or scribes.

Hebrew writings

After the Israelites entered Canaan, they adopted both the language of the Canaanites and their alphabetic writing system. The ease of using an alphabet made it possible to preserve the ideas of common people, not just royalty. In the Scriptures, then, the words of unpopular prophets stand alongside those of powerful kings.

The Greek alphabet

The alphabet moved toward completion when the Greeks borrowed it from the Phoenicians, descendants of the Canaanites, around 800 B.C. Soon after, the Greeks took the final step of using some of the characters to represent vowel sounds. Hundreds of years later, the early Christian writers used the Greek alphabet and language to record the Gospels. A few of the books in the Catholic canon of the Old Testament were written in Greek as well.

This statue of an Egyptian scribe dates from about 2400 B.C. Because the ancient kings were not literate, their scribes could advance to the positions royal administrator and adviser.

The rooftops of Jerusalem

First Isaiah, Isaiah of Jerusalem

Isaiah, son of Amoz, was probably a lad in Judah when the prophet Amos (no relation) preached in Israel. Isaiah lived in Jerusalem during the reigns of four kings of Judah, including the abominable Ahaz and his surprisingly faithful son Hezekiah. Isaiah was married and the father of at least two sons, and he was familiar with the court and a counselor to kings. His Hebrew, the best in the prophetic writings, suggests a high-placed, well-educated—perhaps priestly—family background.

When the young Isaiah has a vision of God in the Temple, at Jerusalem (about 742 B.C.), Judah is in serious peril because of its injustice to the poor and its practice of idolatry. Israel, to the north, has not yet been exiled, but the Assyrian Empire looms ominously over both the northern and southern kingdoms.

The threat of Assyrian invasion sets the scene for the forty years of First Isaiah's career. Israel and Judah, fearful of Assyria, are in danger of invasion, and Israel joins a coalition of neighboring states to stave off

the empire. But Judah refuses to participate in that alliance and instead tries to solve the problem by becoming a vassal of Assyria and paying tribute—all the while dreading the day when its "landlord" might want more.

"Sinful Nation"

The Book of Isaiah does not start in chronological order with the vision and call of Isaiah in the Temple. Rather, the first five chapters get right to the hard message of Isaiah: a savage condemnation of Judah and Jerusalem for infidelity and corruption. These chapters are broken briefly by a hope-filled passage about a day of reconciliation.

The prophet decries the greed and injustice of Jerusalem's leaders and warns that God will punish them if they do not change. He calls Judah to trust in God, not to plot ways to avoid invasion.

The Lord is a forgiving God, no matter how grave the sin. Isaiah assures the people that God promises forgiveness if Judah and

Jerusalem will turn from injustice and idolatry. God can make sin that is as red as scarlet be as white as snow, sin like blood-stained garments to be as white as new wool. A change of heart can show Judah and Jerusalem new ways to solve the dilemma with Assyria. Repentance and prayer can open them to the wisdom of God, who knows how things work.

God will protect the people of Judah—but if they ignore the Lord, no treaty or alliance will be able to save them. Yet Judah and Jerusalem turn a deaf ear to Isaiah's warnings. *Read Isaiah 1:1–4,18–20,24–31.* [15]

God's majesty and goodness

Characteristic of Isaiah's message is his insistence on the majesty and glory of God. He calls God the one to whom all nations and creatures owe existence and, therefore, obedience and honor. Seeing Judah and Jerusalem ignore God's majesty and goodness is the cause of his rage. [16]

To illustrate this point, in Isaiah 1:2–3 the fidelity of the ox and the donkey is contrasted with the infidelity of the people. Even the dumb ox and the stubborn donkey, Isaiah says, recognize their master—but Judah does not. This passage is probably the source of the ox and the donkey in the Christmas manger scene; the Gospels do not mention them.

A Punishment of Judah's Own Making

Isaiah describes the coming fall of Judah and Jerusalem and the people's deportation to foreign lands. Hero, warrior, judge, prophet, elder, captain, nobleman, counselor—all will

Isaiah proclaimed that God can make as white as snow even sin that is as red as scarlet.

15

Find an article that presents an issue in our times that a prophet might address. Write a paragraph explaining what you think the prophet's message would be.

16

Find or create a symbol of God's majesty and goodness and bring it to class.

Seraphim, or angels, symbolized the divinity and mystery of God in the prophet Isaiah's vision in the Temple.

be taken. Only the poor and the weak will be left in the land. Judah and Jerusalem "have brought evil on themselves," says God (Isaiah 3:9). Their leaders have devoured God's "vineyard" (verse 14), wresting loot from the poor, grinding down the helpless. Their punishment is their own doing. They, not God, are responsible for it.

Read Isaiah 3:1–24.

The Vineyard Song: A Brokenhearted Lover

The Vineyard Song is like a country music ballad telling of a brokenhearted lover lamenting betrayal by a faithless sweetheart. It starts with Isaiah telling the story of a friend, but soon the voice of that text changes to the first person and the betrayed lover is revealed to be God, the unfaithful lover to be Judah.

Read Isaiah 5:1–7. 17

Isaiah's Vision and Response: "Here Am I; Send Me!"

Now, after five chapters that give the broad picture of how things were in Judah, Isaiah begins to focus on specific events and the people taking part in them: Isaiah's vision in the Temple, his status as a counselor to kings, and his efforts to make them listen to God.

In the Temple, probably on a feast day, Isaiah has a shattering experience of the All-holy One. He sees God enthroned, surrounded by chanting angels (seraphim), with the divine presence filling the Temple. Overwhelmed by his own sinfulness, Isaiah fears that he will die because he has seen God. But an angel descends and with tongs picks a live coal from the altar and cleanses Isaiah's lips to purify him of his sinfulness. When a voice cries out, "Whom shall I send?" Isaiah answers, "Here am I; send me!" (Isaiah 6:8).

In answer God gives Isaiah a strange errand. He is to make the hearts of the people sluggish—dull their ears and close their eyes to the message of God. In other words, when Isaiah speaks the truth to hearts that are already hard, they will become all the more hardened—not a happy prospect for the young man. Isaiah asks how long this will continue and is told that it will be until exile.

Read Isaiah 6:1–13.

"Holy, holy, holy!"

The angels' hymn in Isaiah 6:3 is sung daily in the contemporary Jewish morning service and is known to Catholic Christians as the Sanctus (meaning "holy") of the Mass. Seraphim with wings covering themselves have become a traditional symbol in religious art.

17

Read Matthew 21:33–41. Jesus frequently quoted from the Book of Isaiah. In writing, compare the symbols and message of the parable of the vineyard with those of the Vineyard Song.

God does not actually sit on a throne, nor do angels use tongs to pick up coals. Isaiah's vision reflects the splendor and language of Temple worship during his time.

A Child Will Be Born: "God Is with Us"

God tells Isaiah to find Judah's young king **Ahaz** outside of Jerusalem, where he is preparing for a siege by Syria (Aram) and Israel (Ephraim), who are in league against him. Isaiah tells Ahaz that faith in God, not elaborate preparations, will overcome these enemies. The prophet bids Ahaz to ask God for a sign. But with a great show of false humility, the young king refuses to ask. (He has already abandoned God, having sacrificed his son by fire and having worshiped false gods on the "high places.")

Isaiah angrily replies that Ahaz will get a sign, like it or not: a virgin ("young woman" in Hebrew) will bear a son named **Immanuel,** meaning "God is with us."

Another of Isaiah's prophecies tells of a blessed child to come with titles that belong only to the greatest of all kings, one who will rule forever.

In another passage Isaiah prophesies that from the "stump of Jesse" (that is, the roots of David's father, Jesse) will come a child who will lead the people to a time of peace never before experienced, symbolized by the contented friendship of traditional enemies from the animal world—like the wolf and the lamb, the calf and the lion (Isaiah 11:1,6).

Read Isaiah 7:1–14; 9:2–7 (or 9:1–6 in NAB or NJB); 11:1–9. **18**

The future king

Isaiah's oracle about the birth of Immanuel has been interpreted in various ways but not, at the time, as a passage about a coming messiah. In the days of Isaiah of Jerusalem, belief in a messiah had not yet developed, so the prophecy seemed to refer to the future birth of a perfect Davidic prince who would rule Judah in an age of peace and justice—thus "God is with us."

Isaiah envisioned a time when old enemies (symbolized by the wolf and the lamb) would come together in peace. Since 1989, members of the Veterans Viet Nam Restoration Project, who were U.S. military personnel in Vietnam during the war of the 1960s and 1970s, have traveled to Vietnam to help with humanitarian projects. Here U.S. veterans and Vietnamese workers begin construction on a house at a social care center for elderly people and orphans.

18

If you could bring together in peace two "enemies"—two groups or persons who are typically hostile to each other—who would they be? Explain in writing how the world would be better if they were at peace.

Mystic Nativity, by fifteenth-century painter Botticelli. Isaiah's words about the coming of the Messiah and the birth of a savior child are a familiar part of the Christmas liturgy.

Christians have always believed that Isaiah's longing for the ideal king, through whom God would be revealed fully, was accomplished in Jesus Christ. The words of Isaiah about the birth of a savior child are familiar to Christians from the liturgy of Christmas:

> For a child has been born for us,
>   a son given to us;
> authority rests upon his shoulders;
>   and he is named
> Wonderful Counselor, Mighty God,
>   Everlasting Father, Prince of Peace.
>
> (Isaiah 9:6)

In Christian belief, the angel Gabriel's announcement to the Virgin Mary fulfills those words: "And now, you will conceive in your womb and bear a son, and you will name him Jesus. He will be great, and will be called the Son of the Most High, and the Lord God will give to him the throne of his ancestor David. He will reign over the house of Jacob forever, and of his kingdom there will be no end. . . . The child to be born will be holy; he will be called Son of God" (Luke 1:31–33, 35). For Christians, Jesus is the **Messiah,** the one to whom Isaiah's prophecies pointed; in him, "God is with us." *Read Matthew 1:22–23.*

Jerusalem Is Saved from Assyria

As the Second Book of Kings (chapter 16) tells it, Assyria comes at Ahaz's invitation and seizes Judah's enemies, Israel and Syria. So Judah is rescued— though not by God's power but by a worldly empire. Ahaz must become a vassal of the Assyrian king in return for protection. To curry favor with his new "master," Ahaz eventually replaces God's altar in the Temple with one to an Assyrian god.

Fortunately Ahaz's son **Hezekiah** is faithful to God. As king of Judah, he destroys the pagan shrines that his father had erected, and he insists that sacrifices be made only in the Jerusalem Temple. Naturally Isaiah is pleased with this turn of events. But meanwhile the northern kingdom of Israel is conquered by Assyria and its leading citizens deported into exile (about 721 B.C.).

When Hezekiah flirts with the idea of revolting against Assyria, Isaiah must warn him away from this. To revolt against such a monstrous empire would be foolish. As a symbol of how Judah will be stripped bare if it revolts, Isaiah walks around Jerusalem in nothing but a loincloth!

A few years later (about 701 B.C.), the Assyrians have captured some of Judah's northern towns. Pressing in on Jerusalem, the Assyrian army is camped outside it, prepared to invade the capital. Even though Hezekiah has previously sent gold from the Temple as tribute to Assyria, this is not enough to keep Jerusalem from being crushed. Hezekiah turns to Isaiah in this dark moment and prays to the Lord for help, and Isaiah assures the king that the city will indeed be saved.

What happens next seems miraculous to the people of Jerusalem. During the night that the Assyrian army is poised to storm the capital, the "angel of the LORD" (2 Kings 19:35) strikes the soldiers down in their camp. Thousands of Assyrians are found dead in the morning. So the survivors, under their king, must retreat to their home capital, Nineveh. *Read 2 Kings 18:1–12; 19:14–20,32–36.*

The Prayer of Israel: "Escaped Like a Bird from the Snare"

If it had not been the LORD who was on our side
   —let Israel now say—
if it had not been the LORD who was on our side,
   when our enemies attacked us,
then they would have swallowed us up alive,
   when their anger was kindled against us;
then the flood would have swept us away,
   the torrent would have gone over us;
then over us would have gone
   the raging waters.

Blessed be the LORD
   who has not given us
   as prey to their teeth.
We have escaped like a bird
   from the snare of the fowlers;
   the snare is broken,
   and we have escaped.

Our help is in the name of the LORD,
   who made heaven and earth.

(Psalm 124)

Judah forever?

The Judahites, grateful to be spared in the nick of time in such an amazing fashion, see their good fortune as a sign of God's favor on Judah. It is one more assurance of God's Covenant with David—that his royal line of Judah's kings will last forever.

As the next chapter shows, this sense of divine protection will backfire on a later generation of Judahites. They will become complacent, refusing to acknowledge that Jerusalem can ever fall to its enemies and turning a deaf ear to prophets who warn them otherwise. "With God on our side," they will reason, "how can we ever be defeated? We can always count on God to work a miracle at the last minute, just like the night the Assyrian army was stricken by an angel of the Lord when they were about to storm Jerusalem."

Sincere trust, according to the Scriptures, goes much deeper than that. *19*

First Isaiah Concludes: Both Disaster *and* Hope Ahead

Isaiah of Jerusalem, as we might expect, is never lulled into complacency. He knows that in the future Judah will not be safe from suffering and even disaster if its kings and people disobey God. His words point to the day when Jerusalem (called Ariel or "altar hearth" in this passage) will be overcome by its enemies because the people's hearts are

19

Respond in writing to the following questions:
- Is the knowledge of God's willingness to forgive an encouragement to laxity and sin? Or does it inspire deeper love and gratitude?
- What about the opinion that a little fear never did anyone any harm—meaning that the fear of hell and damnation is an inducement to avoid sin. Is it? Explain your view.

Catholics in El Paso, Texas, act prophetically by participating in the diocese's March for Life.

far from God. When they worship they are only going through the motions; their "wise" leaders are really foolish.

Isaiah, however, sees beyond the coming disastrous defeat (which will be, more than a century later, the Babylonian exile). On the other side of defeat, says Isaiah, is hope—hope for new life to bloom for Jerusalem out of the desert of exile.

Isaiah of Jerusalem leaves as his heritage a passion for God and an unquenchable hope that Israel will one day reclaim its role as a light to the nations. The Isaiahs who follow him continue his work—begging Israel to be Israel.

Read Isaiah 29:1–4,13–16; 35:1–10.

For Review

☐ What three major parts make up the Book of Isaiah? In what context was each part written?

☐ What is Isaiah's response to the vision in the Temple?

☐ What does the name Immanuel mean? How do Christians understand Isaiah's prophecies about a child to come who will be the ideal king?

☐ How is Jerusalem saved from the Assyrian invasion? How does this event foster a sense of complacency and a refusal to listen to the prophets' warnings in a later generation?

☐ What does Isaiah see ahead for Judah?

Micah in the South: Sympathy from the Bottom of Society

In about the same time period as Isaiah of Jerusalem, there lived Micah, a man of humble origins from the countryside twenty or so miles from Jerusalem. Like Isaiah he was inspired to speak God's truth no matter how unpopular it made him. Unlike Isaiah, who was well educated, Micah's sympathy for the poor came from his own experience near the bottom rung of society's ladder—probably as a farmworker. His language is blunt and uncompromising, and his passionate condemnation of those who oppress the poor reveals an intimate knowledge of the sufferings of poverty.

The Book of Micah is short, only seven chapters, but it contains passages that have become universally known, such as the prophecy of a time of peace when the nations "shall beat their swords into plowshares" (4:3) and the eloquent description of what God requires of us: "to do justice, and to love kindness, / and to walk humbly with [our] God" (6:8). [20]

Exploitation Will Bring Ruin

Micah mourns the crimes of both Israel and Judah. Calling them both Jacob, he describes their sins, the ruin in store for them, and how he goes about lamenting them.

The rich, says Micah, lie in bed at night concocting schemes for depriving the poor. He vividly accuses the nation's rulers of exploiting the people, saying it is like the rulers are tearing the skin off the people and eating it, chopping up their bones like meat for a kettle of stew! But God will punish Jerusalem because of the wicked, unjust deeds of the people.

Read Micah 1:1–9; 2:1–4; 3:1–4,9–12.

Protesters block railroad tracks in Bangor, Maine, that carry nuclear ballistic missiles to their destination on Trident submarines. Micah imagined the day when the nations would "beat their swords into plowshares, / and their spears into pruning hooks" (4:3), and no one would ever train for war again.

Beat Swords into Plowshares

Micah calls for Israel to repent and return to God, and believes that it can happen. He writes hopefully of a time when the nations will walk in the way of the Lord, a time of justice and peace. Creating one of the world's most well-loved images of peacemaking from his own farming background, Micah imagines the day when the nations "shall beat their swords into plowshares, / and their spears into pruning hooks," and no one will train for war (Micah 4:3).

Read Micah 4:1–3.

Isaiah 2:2–4 contains an almost identical passage, and Micah perhaps was Isaiah's source.

Plowshares' actions

Since the 1960s a movement of peace activists in the United States has called itself the **Plowshares.** It has taken Micah's prophecy to heart, living it out in protests against

20

Some Scripture scholars consider Micah 6:8 to be the most powerful passage in his book. Write a one-paragraph response to this question: *Is Micah 6:8 a complete statement of what God requires of Christians?*

God requires us "to do justice, and to love kindness, / and to walk humbly with [our] God" (Micah 6:8).

A Great Shepherd from Bethlehem

Micah foresees a day when a descendant of David's line—from little Bethlehem, hometown of David—will rise up and lead Israel to the Reign of peace and justice. He will shepherd his flock in the strength of the Lord, and "he shall be great / to the ends of the earth; / and he shall be the one of peace" (Micah 5:4–5a).

Read Micah 5:2–5 (or 5:1–4 in NAB or NJB).

"O little town of Bethlehem"

Christians have seen great significance in this passage from Micah, for it points not only to the family of David for the origins of a messiah-king but also to Bethlehem as the place from which the Messiah will come. Two of the Gospels—Matthew and Luke—situate the birth of Jesus in the town of Bethlehem.

war and the instruments of war. Plowshares' actions have been controversial and always thought provoking, if not disturbing, in a society where the existence of nuclear weapons that could destroy the planet is almost taken for granted.

For instance, groups of Plowshares have entered production plants and hammered on the nose cones that carry nuclear warheads to symbolically "beat them into plowshares" —instruments of peace, not war. And they have poured blood on military property to symbolize the transformation of these sites into places of life, not death. For such actions they are tried and usually sentenced to prison. By way of media coverage, thousands of people are made aware of what the Plowshares stand for and against. We might think of them as modern-day Micahs. *21*

What God Requires

In a beautiful, simple statement, Micah puts in perspective what God wants from the people, who are typically so prone to false assumptions. No elaborate sacrificial offerings and rituals are required, Micah says, as he tries point out the emptiness of showy displays. What God requires is sincerity of the human heart, shown in justice, kindness, and humility.

Read Micah 6:6–8.

21

Research one other group or person who works for peace and write an essay about those efforts. Include your reflections on this question: *Do you think it is possible to have world peace—with no threat of war? If so, tell how you imagine this can come about.*

For Review

☐ What experience makes Micah especially sympathetic to the poor?

☐ For what image of peacemaking is Micah well known?

☐ According to Micah, what does God require?

Is Anybody Listening?

Prophets like Elijah and Elisha, Amos and Hosea, and Isaiah and Micah certainly did their job of announcing God's point of view to the rich and powerful of Israel and Judah. They must have wondered, Is anybody listening? For the most part, no matter what the prophets said or did, both kingdoms continued on their downward trek of injustice and idolatry toward the pit of exile.

We who read the prophets today might wonder, too, if they had any impact. (Isaiah of Jerusalem did get a hearing from King Hezekiah, but he seems to have been an exception.) Was their risky, bold truthtelling all in vain?

The Deuteronomists, editing the history of the kingdoms in the Books of Kings, saw the whole thing from the perspective of the exile. For them, the answer to Is anybody listening? was, "Yes! *We* are! We who are in exile see clearly what you prophets were talking about. We have learned from you. Your message has taken root in us, and we will pass it on to future generations."

The words of the prophets continue to be passed on. Some of the great movements of this past century have found their inspiration from the prophets: the civil rights movement, the peace movement, the movements for national and global economic justice. Is anybody listening? Yes, some are. But in every age, humankind is challenged to listen again.

Pope John Paul II addressing the United Nations. This pope has been a prophet in our times, preaching his message of the "Gospel of Life" as a counter to the contemporary "culture of death."

8 The Exile
Prophets of Warning, Consolation, and Hope

Babylon, the city to which the Jews were exiled in 587 B.C., was located on the Euphrates River, shown here in present-day Iraq.

Toward what fate was Judah headed? The Deuteronomists, who composed the biblical history, knew that all the injustice, infidelity, and idolatry of the two kingdoms, Israel and Judah, was to end in crushing defeat for them. First, as we have seen, Israel was defeated by the Assyrians. Then, as this chapter tells, Judah, under its own delusion that Jerusalem could never fall, was overrun by the Babylonians. Its Temple was destroyed, and its citizens captured and exiled to faraway Babylon. From the vantage point of the exile, the Deuteronomists pointed out the path the Chosen People had taken to their own destruction. The ending five chapters of the Second Book of Kings complete the Deuteronomists' history, with accounts of the last of Judah's kings, the defeat of Judah and Jerusalem, and the exile itself.

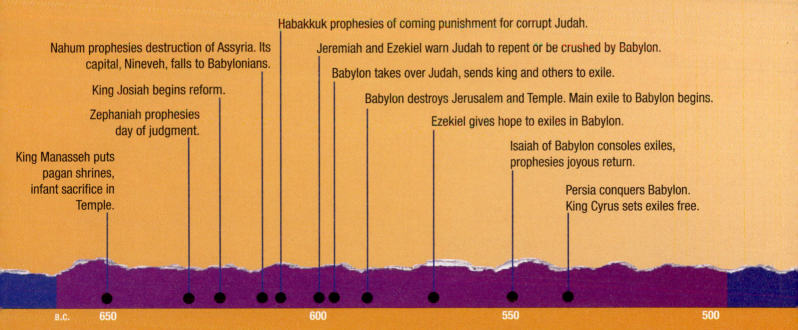

Nahum prophesies destruction of Assyria. Its capital, Nineveh, falls to Babylonians.

King Josiah begins reform.

Zephaniah prophesies day of judgment.

King Manasseh puts pagan shrines, infant sacrifice in Temple.

Habakkuk prophesies of coming punishment for corrupt Judah.

Jeremiah and Ezekiel warn Judah to repent or be crushed by Babylon.

Babylon takes over Judah, sends king and others to exile.

Babylon destroys Jerusalem and Temple. Main exile to Babylon begins.

Ezekiel gives hope to exiles in Babylon.

Isaiah of Babylon consoles exiles, prophesies joyous return.

Persia conquers Babylon. King Cyrus sets exiles free.

B.C.   650   600   550   500

Archbishop Oscar Romero, laywoman Dorothy Day, and Mother Teresa of Calcutta are considered twentieth-century prophets.

The main focus for us, as in chapter 7 of this text, is not so much on the kings, for the most part a disappointing lot, but on the prophets. They confronted and warned the kings before the exile, and then consoled the people and offered them hope once they were defeated and captive in Babylon. The prophets' role, as has been said of modern-day prophets like Dorothy Day (see page 154), was to both "comfort the afflicted and afflict the comfortable."

The story of the exile in this chapter takes us through the Second Book of Kings and covers these prophetic books:

- The Books of **Zephaniah, Nahum,** and **Habakkuk** speak briefly of a coming time when God's justice will finally be done.

- The Book of **Jeremiah** recounts that prophet's call, his futile struggle to make the kings listen to God's message, his persecution, the fall of Judah and Jerusalem, and the exile. It offers the hope of a new Covenant for Israel, written on the people's hearts, after the exile has purified them.

- The Book of **Lamentations** is a group of five poems expressing Judah's grief over the loss of Jerusalem.

- The Book of **Baruch,** although set in Babylon during the exile, was actually written centuries later when many Jews lived dispersed around the Greek Empire far from home and needed encouragement for the hope of return someday.

- The Book of **Ezekiel** tells of that prophet's symbolic actions, his acted-out messages from God before the exile about the impending disaster. During the exile Ezekiel offers a vision of hope and renewal to the people.

- Second Isaiah is filled with hope and expectation of the return to Jerusalem and a coming reign of peace. It also describes a mysterious servant of the Lord who suffers for the sake of the people.

Judah's Slippery Slope: Heading for Disaster

The reforms initiated by Hezekiah, the good king we studied in chapter 7 who heeded Isaiah's advice, do not last long. His wicked son **Manasseh** next rules as king of Judah. Hopelessly dominated by the Assyrian Empire, Manasseh bows to their gods. He abandons God, puts pagan shrines in the Temple, offers his son as a sacrifice, and drenches Jerusalem in blood. The son who succeeds him is assassinated, but his grandson Josiah grows up to be king and one of Judah's great reformers.

A High Point on the Way Downhill

During King Josiah's repair of the Temple in about 622 B.C., a copy of the Book of the Law is found. (This was probably part of what later would be known as the Book of Deuteronomy.) When the king hears it read and then consults the prophetess Huldah to help explain it, he is appalled that Judah has abandoned the Law of God so shamelessly.

So Josiah leads the people in a renewal of the Covenant and a celebration of the Passover, and then commences his reforms. First he destroys pagan altars and executes pagan priests and temple prostitutes. Then, driving north, he reclaims territory lost to Judah for a hundred years—and Israel, it seems, will be its old self again. Assyria, now past its zenith, is fighting for its life far away.

The zealous reform helps slow down Judah's slide to ruin, but unfortunately it does not reverse it. Although external changes occur, most people's hearts are not affected enough to turn things around. Josiah is killed in a battle with Egypt's pharaoh in 609 B.C. The externals of his reform are undone as his son **Jehoiakim,** yet another terrible king, takes the throne of Judah as a puppet of Egypt.

Read 2 Kings 21:1–6,16; 22:1–20; 23:15,19–25.

Josiah Leaves a Legacy

Josiah's zeal for the Covenant, however, has left a deep and lasting impression on some of his followers. Sometime before the exile, a movement that calls the people back to the Covenant springs up. Its leaders—known by us as the Deuteronomists—begin assembling Israel's ancient texts of its history. During and after the exile, they rework and edit these texts to compose the account we have been calling the Deuteronomic history. Without the Deuteronomists we would not have the Bible.

Zephaniah: The Remnant

For almost a century after First Isaiah, there is no prophetic voice in Judah. Then Zephaniah speaks in about 630 B.C., during the early reign of Josiah, a few years before Jeremiah.

Zephaniah's three short chapters tell of "the day of the LORD" (2:3), a time of judgment not only for Judah's enemies but for the unfaithful of Judah and Jerusalem as well. On that day the guilty will be judged for their deeds, not for their religious affiliation.

Zephaniah introduces an idea only briefly touched on by Isaiah and Hosea: The unfortunate and impoverished, the "humble of the land," will become the **remnant,** a new kind of "chosen" from whom God will build the new Israel.

Read Zephaniah 2:3; 3:11–13.

The humble and lowly

Zephaniah's words would have sounded like heresy to the upper-class citizens of the time. The poor were considered sinners. Their poverty made it impossible for them to keep the laws about washing, contributing money, and offering sacrifices—because they could not buy animal offerings. If reduced to begging, people were outcasts; if ill, they were considered unclean. To the respectable Temple-going citizens, the poor were beyond the reach of God.

Words that exalted the lowly were as shocking to the self-satisfied citizens of Jesus' time as they were to the people in the days of Zephaniah—and as they are to some people today.

Read Luke 6:20–26. [1]

A beggar in Jerusalem. Zephaniah spoke of the humble and the lowly as God's chosen ones.

Other individuals during and after Josiah's lifetime call Judah to repentance and hope. Inspired in part by his reform, some of these individuals also inspire the Deuteronomists. These are the prophets of the years before the exile: Zephaniah, Nahum, Habakkuk, and, above all, the great Jeremiah. Of all the prophets, Jeremiah is the one whose spirit is most apparent in the work of the Deuteronomists.

We will consider Zephaniah, Nahum, and Habakkuk, whose books of the Bible are quite short, before moving on to Jeremiah.

1

Write a story or news report about an imaginary society where the poor and lowly people are treated as the most important citizens. Then answer this question in a separate paragraph: *Why is this situation so different from our reality?*

*I will save the lame
and gather the outcast,
and I will change their shame into
praise
and renown in all the earth.*

Zephaniah 3:19

Nahum: Nineveh Will Fall!

Nahum, a little-known prophet, prophesied during Josiah's reign. He spoke several years before the capital of Assyria, Nineveh, fell to the Babylonians in 612 B.C.

As Nahum's book opens, Josiah's reform is in full swing. Nahum is jubilant because it looks like Assyria, Judah's fiercest enemy, will soon be destroyed by Babylon. Assyria has bathed the Near East in blood for three hundred years, devising unspeakable butchery for its captives. Nahum—rejoicing that God will use Babylon as the instrument to punish Assyria—gloats over his vision of its vanquished soldiers, their shields scarlet with blood, and Assyria's queen and her ladies moaning with grief.

Encouraged by Josiah's ongoing reform, Nahum assumes that all will be well in Judah. Nahum does not call Judah to repentance but to hope, because it looks like Judah is getting back on track with the reform and Assyria is soon to be crushed by Babylon. Little does Nahum dream that Judah will become corrupt again and that God will use the same Babylon as an instrument for Judah's purification.

Read Nahum 2:1–9 (or 2:3–10 in NAB or NJB).

Habakkuk: Why, God, Why?

Habakkuk was probably a prophet in the Jerusalem Temple during the reign of Josiah's son, the detestable Jehoiakim—609 to 598 B.C. Habakkuk had a marvelous way with words and wrote his short book at God's bidding after a vision in the Temple. Its third chapter is actually a psalm, probably adapted from Temple worship.

In chapter 1 Habakkuk complains to God that he has prayed endlessly that Judah, corrupted under Jehoiakim, be punished for its injustice and violence. But his prayer has not been heard. Now he wants to know why. When God replies that his prayer *has* been heard and Judah will indeed be punished—by the Chaldeans (Babylonians)—Habakkuk is appalled. An exchange between Habakkuk and God finally leaves the prophet praising him and humbled by his own ignorance of divine ways. **2**

Read Habakkuk 1:1–17; 2:1–20; 3:16–19.

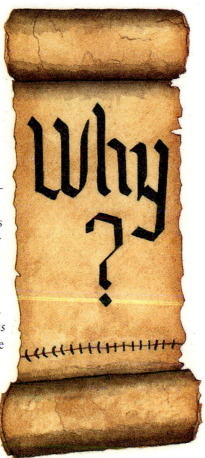

2

Imagine that Habakkuk is a friend of yours who has asked why some misfortune has happened to him. In writing, explain what you would say to him.

The Prayer of Israel:
Wait for the Vision; It Will Surely Come

O LORD, how long shall I cry for help,
and you will not listen?
Or cry to you "Violence!"
and you will not save?
Why do you make me see wrongdoing
and look at trouble?
Destruction and violence are before me;
strife and contention arise.
So the law becomes slack
and justice never prevails.
The wicked surround the righteous—
therefore judgment comes forth perverted.

. . . .

Then the LORD answered me and said:
Write the vision;
make it plain on tablets,
so that a runner may read it.
For there is still a vision for the appointed time;
it speaks of the end, and does not lie.
If it seems to tarry, wait for it;
it will surely come, it will not delay.

(Habakkuk 1:2–4;2:2–3)

Tough questions

Habakkuk's book is the first to introduce the question Why? Why, if God is present, does he seem not to be? Why, when God says that prayer will be answered, does it seem not to be? Why does God not stop human evil? Habakkuk's questioning was a bold step forward in the people's understanding of God: It is all right to challenge and question God.

For Review

☐ What types of reform does King Josiah lead and inspire?

☐ What people does Zephaniah say will become God's remnant, through whom God will build the new Israel?

☐ What kind of questioning did the Book of Habakkuk introduce?

Jeremiah: Persecuted for God's Sake

Jeremiah, one of the great tragic figures of the Bible, preached to the complacent and falsely secure Judahites in the years before the exile, and after Jerusalem was destroyed. More than any other prophet, Jeremiah communicated God's message not only through his words and oracles but also through his own life of suffering and struggle. He "walked the talk," as the saying goes. His message of warning and of the suffering to come was, as you would expect, an unwelcome one.

The role of a prophet is never easy, and that was especially true for Jeremiah. He did not relish the idea of confronting people with truths they did not want to hear. He longed for the security of a normal life, with friends and family who loved him. But instead he did not marry—which was unthinkable for young Jewish men in those days. He was despised and persecuted by the people he was trying to save, and he struggled with God and poured out his anguish over his miserable fate. In spite of repeated failures at reaching the people, he loved and served God all his life—even as he was dragged off to Egypt to an unrecorded death. He lived from about 650 to 570 B.C. ³

The Book of Jeremiah is a combination of poetry, prose, and biographical material combined by the editors (probably the Deuteronomists) in themes rather than in chronological order. This means that writings treating similar themes are found together, even if they describe events that occurred at different times.

Nelson Mandela, former president of South Africa. For decades, Mandela was imprisoned by the country's apartheid regime. He communicated his message, like Jeremiah, not only through words but through the suffering and struggle of his life.

Jeremiah pointed out the inevitable doom to come for Judah and Jerusalem if they did not turn around, but his message did not stop there. From within his own broken heart, he was able to find seeds of hope that would later grow in the hearts of his people—hope that after their period of suffering, God would bring forth something new in them, a new Covenant.

A Reluctant Prophet

Jeremiah was born of a priestly family in a village just north of Jerusalem. We are not told where he is when God calls him at about age twenty, during Josiah's reign. But the calling is an interior experience, profound and frightening. Jeremiah is not eager to respond to the call. When he cries out, "I am too young!" God tells him not to fear: He will put the right words into Jeremiah's mouth. And Jeremiah gives in to God. ⁴

3

Write your opinion on this question: *Why would someone be faithful to God in spite of his or her suffering?*

4

Find an article about a child or a teenager who has said or done something that inspired and taught an important lesson to adults. Write your reflections on this article in a paragraph or two.

A young student, calling on the Chinese people to resist their communist leaders in a 1989 uprising. Jeremiah also was called to a prophetic role at a young age.

Who, me?

Notice that to tell the bad news to Judah, God chooses a young man who feels terribly inadequate for the task. Being hated by others is not Jeremiah's idea of a good time. He is not nervy, like some people who really enjoy telling others off. But God thinks Jeremiah *is* up to the task. Perhaps God even prefers that the message come through a tenderhearted young man, rather than someone who relishes a fight.

Jerusalem, Your Time Is Coming!

After King Josiah is killed in a battle with Egypt, the Egyptians choose his son Jehoiakim to be king of Judah. Jehoiakim, a contemptible monarch, then sides with Egypt in its struggle against the king of Babylon, **Nebuchadrezzar II,** for control of the region around the eastern Mediterranean. Jeremiah despises Jehoiakim's politicking, and is convinced that God will use Babylon to punish Israel for its unrepentant heart.

Through Jeremiah, God warns that Judah and Jerusalem will get the punishment their crimes deserve. When God bids Jeremiah to search the city for an honest person, he can find none. The people have filled their houses with loot taken from the poor and have grown rich and fat—all the while winking at evil. Their time is coming!
Read Jeremiah 4:18; 5:1–5,26–29.

Jeremiah has two visions: He sees a branch of an almond tree—also called a watching tree—symbolizing that God is watching to see if Judah and Jerusalem will change. The prophet also sees a boiling cauldron tipped on a hearth in the north, meaning that God will summon kingdoms from the north to be poured out over Judah if it does not change. These warnings, says God, will outrage people and create enemies, so Jeremiah must stand fast.
Read Jeremiah 1:1–19.

Asking for the consequences

To ignore God's instructions for how things work is to ask for the consequences. Similarly, every car manual tells us that driving a car without oil in it will ruin the engine. Yet every day, car engines burn out from lack of oil, and the carmaker who wrote the manual cannot be held at fault.

Jeremiah's prophecies were not predictions of what was bound to happen but of what *could* happen if people and nations continued to be hard-hearted. Alas, they were not willing to change.

Why so smug, Judah?

Why did the Judahites feel so confident in ignoring Jeremiah's message? They had convinced themselves that God would never allow Jerusalem to be overcome. After all, the holy Temple was there, the place of God's dwelling. They remembered the incident (see 2 Kings 19:32–36) a century earlier, during Hezekiah's reign, when Jerusalem was under siege by the Assyrian army, but a mysterious "angel of the LORD" (2 Kings 19:35) had killed the Assyrians just as they were about to break through the walls of the city. They saw this apparent miracle, and the pledge that God would be with David's royal line forever, as proof that they were safe. God would never permit Jerusalem or the house of David to be destroyed.

The Temple: No Guarantee of Safety

God tells Jeremiah to preach in the Temple, and Jeremiah warns his listeners that even the Temple does not assure God's presence. Unless they stop oppressing aliens, shedding innocent blood, and worshiping idols, unless they treat their neighbors with justice and show mercy to widows and orphans, they will be lost. How can they steal, murder, commit adultery and perjury, worship strange gods—and still believe they are safe? **5**

Outraged, the priests and court prophets start a riot and call for Jeremiah's death. Fortunately Jeremiah is whisked away while the ruckus is being quelled, and he escapes alive.
Read Jeremiah 7:1–15.

In the Gospels the Temple is again called "a den of robbers" (Matthew 21:13) (or thieves). Who says that?
Read Matthew 21:12–13.

The hillside slums of Rio de Janeiro, Brazil, contrast with luxury hotels and high-rises just blocks away. Jeremiah warned those who grow rich at the expense of poor people that their time of punishment was coming.

5

Write your responses to these questions:
- What behaviors do you regularly see or hear about that are unsafe?
- Are people generally aware of the risks and consequences of such behavior?
- If so, why would they choose to engage in dangerous behavior? If not, what would it take to raise their awareness?

At one point in his prophesying, Jeremiah wore a wooden yoke that ordinarily harnessed a work animal to the plow—to symbolize Jerusalem's coming oppression by Babylon.

Although the king and his prophets would like to believe that Jeremiah does not speak for God, they are deeply threatened by him. His words have the ring of truth.

Read Jeremiah 29:1–14; 27:12–15. **8**

Prophet and traitor?

Jeremiah will be accused of treason—of deserting to the Babylonians and demoralizing the army with his call for surrender. He will be beaten and imprisoned, and court nobles will throw him into a muddy, deep cistern to die (fortunately he will be saved by the secret intervention of an Ethiopian courtier). Such harsh treatment is not surprising for a man who says that surrender to the enemy is better than fighting for king and country. But God wants Judah to repent, and the purification of exile is the only means left, as Isaiah said long before and Jeremiah understands.

A New Covenant

The times are indeed bleak for Jeremiah. Yet in such a dark moment, God speaks to him of a great hope—the future return of the people from exile. Moreover, God says that the people will not simply return home to their same old ways, their same broken relationship with him. No, they will be made anew as God's beloved! At that time he will make a **new Covenant** with the people, writing the Law on their hearts instead of on stone tablets. He will forgive their evil and remember their sin no more.

Read Jeremiah 31:31–34.

The Law written on their hearts

The new Covenant prophesied by Jeremiah will be a turning point for Israel. The Law, the basis of the Sinai Covenant, would no longer be merely a matter of external practices and norms imposed from outside the person. In this new Covenant, the Law would be written on each person's heart. Each individual would know God and what he wants from deep within. This would be the fruit of the people's long period of suffering in exile. **9**

Jeremiah's own sorrow and suffering—we can think of it as an exile from his own people—has brought him to a deep and intimate relationship with God. He has struggled mightily within his soul to come to an acceptance of his own suffering, and to find security in God alone. Now he is telling Israel that it must do the same. Out of Israel's acceptance of its exile will come hope—hope for an entirely new, living relationship with God.

8

Answer these questions in writing:
- How do you know the truth when you hear it?
- What can stand in the way of your hearing the truth?
- If possible, give examples of your experience with hearing or not hearing the truth.

9

We follow some laws or rules simply because that is what is expected of us *and* we know we might be punished for disobeying them. Think of a law or rule that is instead "written on your heart"—one you follow because, in your heart, you know it is right and good.

Create a sign or poster that states the law or rule and illustrates it, if possible, with symbols, photos, or other artwork.

A stone relief of Near Eastern people being led into exile, from the ancient palace at Nineveh

A prophesy fulfilled by Christ

The early Christians brought a special perspective to Jeremiah's prophesy of a new Covenant. They believed—as Christians do today—that his prophesy was ultimately fulfilled in Jesus Christ, whose teaching established the terms of the New Covenant and whose death and Resurrection sealed it. In the Gospel of Luke, Jesus refers to the New Covenant during the institution of the Eucharist at the Last Supper. For Christians, this new law of love is written on their hearts by the grace of the Holy Spirit.

Read Luke 22:14-20.

The Second Exile: Jerusalem Destroyed

In 587 B.C. time finally runs out for Jerusalem. The Babylonians return, breach the city's walls, and torch its buildings. The Temple is destroyed, and many of the people are deported to Babylon. King Zedekiah is captured, forced to see his sons slain, and then blinded and hauled off in chains to Babylon.

Jeremiah stays behind with the Judahites still in Jerusalem, and tells them they will be safe if they remain in the ruined city and give in to Babylonian rule. Once again the people refuse to listen to Jeremiah.

They flee to Egypt, seeking comfort and security, taking Jeremiah and his scribe, Baruch, with them. Few of them will ever return to Jerusalem.

With that, Jeremiah disappears. No one knows what happens to him. One tradition holds that he is murdered in Egypt by his fellow Judahites, which is possible but not recorded anywhere. Baruch, however, returns to Jerusalem.

Read Jeremiah 39:1–14; 42:1–12; 43:1–7.

The power of failure

Contemporaries of Jeremiah saw him as a complete failure. His people never paid attention to his warnings. He was despised by almost everyone, and he was dragged off to die in a land he never wanted to be in. *10*

Later, though, Jeremiah's failure was remembered by the exiles and succeeding generations of Jews—including Jesus and his followers. They saw the "failure" of Jeremiah's

10

A piece of spiritual wisdom heard in our times is "We are not called to be successful. We are called to be faithful." Write about how this relates to the experience of Jeremiah, and about how it relates to your life.

Catholic musician Tony Melendez, born without arms, plays guitar and sings at a youth gathering. As Jeremiah reminds us, new life and hope can emerge from suffering and apparent tragedy.

life, like the sorrow and humiliation of the exile, as a seed of hope and transformation. Israel's heart was broken so that God could at last enter it. Indeed the exile turned out to be the time when Judaism as a religion came to birth. Its Scriptures, its monotheism, its Law-centeredness, its prayer and worship, and many of the practices we know today were fruits of that period.

The experience of Jeremiah and the exile was that failure and suffering do not have to crush us. Our own heart can be made anew through sorrow, and we can find new life once again. *11*

The next two books of the Old Testament, Lamentations and Baruch, are connected with Jeremiah in tradition.

Lamentations: Judah Grieves

The Book of Lamentations is a collection of five hymns of grief composed shortly after the fall of Jerusalem. Although not written by Jeremiah, these dirges have been attributed to him because the writer sounds like Jeremiah. Each chapter is a separate poem, perhaps each by a separate author.

The first, second, and fourth chapters are funeral laments for the lost Jerusalem. The third chapter tells of the author's suffering and of the hope that one day God will bring it to an end. The fifth chapter is the voice of a people admitting their guilt, expressing their hope, and praying for restoration. The Book of Lamentations seems to have helped Judah by giving it a way to grieve—recalling its agony, lamenting, and asking for healing.

Read Lamentations 1:1–7,10,18–19; 2:11–13.

11

Write a character sketch of Jeremiah, responding to these questions:
- Is he like a person you know or know about?
- What is his most outstanding trait?
- Whom would you cast as Jeremiah in a movie?
- What will you remember about him?

The Prayer of Israel: Grieving for Jerusalem

My eyes are spent with weeping;
    my stomach churns;
my bile is poured out on the ground
    because of the destruction of my people,
because infants and babes faint
    in the streets of the city.

They cry to their mothers,
    "Where is bread and wine?"
as they faint like the wounded
    in the streets of the city,
as their life is poured out
    on their mothers' bosom.

What can I say for you, to what compare you,
    O daughter Jerusalem?
To what can I liken you, that I may comfort you,
    O virgin daughter Zion?
For vast as the sea is your ruin;
    who can heal you?

(Lamentations 2:11–13)

Baruch: Keep the Faith!

The Book of Baruch, though attributed to Jeremiah's faithful scribe, Baruch, was written by several authors centuries after the exile. Its setting is the exile, but it was actually meant to nurture the faith of the later Jews of the Dispersion (those living away from Jerusalem) and to encourage them to return home someday. The scribe Baruch probably did inspire the Jews during the exile, reminding them of Jeremiah's witness, and the authors of the Book of Baruch hoped they too would touch the hearts of their fellow Jews far from home. *12*

Chapter 6 of Baruch is a letter attributed to Jeremiah but was actually written much later, like the rest of the book. The letter is a powerful and amusing ridicule of the idols that surround the Jews in these far-off lands. These idols have tongues smoothed by woodworkers and covered with gold and silver, but they cannot speak. They are decked out in garments like men, wrapped in purple, but are not safe from moths or corruption. Lamps are lighted for them, but they cannot see. If they fall to the ground, they must be picked up. They need dusting; their faces are black from the smoke

12

Do you know of someone who is far from home and needs support and encouragement? If so, write a letter to that person.

of candles, and when the bats and the swallows light on them . . . !

The point is this: Do not be fooled, you faraway sons and daughters of the one God; there is no other God but the Lord.

Read Baruch 6:1–22 (Baruch, chapter 6, is called the Letter of Jeremiah in some versions of the Bible).

For Review

- [ ] What is Jeremiah's reaction to God's calling him to be a prophet?
- [ ] Why are the Judahites so confident in ignoring Jeremiah's message that the time of disaster is coming?
- [ ] What aspects of Jesus' life and ministry reminded the early Christians of Jeremiah?
- [ ] What is Jeremiah's message to the people after the first exile?
- [ ] How will the new Covenant differ from the old, according to God's message to Jeremiah?
- [ ] What happens to Jerusalem and its people in 587 B.C.?
- [ ] What understanding did later Jews come to have about the "failure" of Jeremiah's life?
- [ ] How did the Book of Lamentations help Judah?

Ezekiel: From Hearts of Stone to Hearts of Flesh

Like Jeremiah, Ezekiel prophesied in Jerusalem in the years before the exile. And as Jeremiah did, he confronted the hard hearts of the people, shaking them out of their complacency and letting them know that the time of God's patience with them was just about up.

After Jerusalem fell, Ezekiel was one of those deported to Babylon. He is best known for his prophesying there, where he inspired hope in the discouraged exiles that all was not over for Israel: God had forgiven Israel and would create it anew, giving it a new heart and a new spirit. *13*

Unlike the other prophets, Ezekiel's gifts were not writing and poetry but drama, symbol making, and storytelling. This fiery prophet certainly had dramatic flair, so much so that he often seemed out of his mind to people, or possessed by a demon. But Ezekiel was possessed by God, driven to communicate his messages in vivid, unsettling ways.

The Prophets of Israel After 900 B.C.

The Northern Kingdom of Israel

Elijah   Amos
Elisha   Hosea

The Southern Kingdom of Judah

First Isaiah   Micah

Before and During the Exile

Jeremiah
Nahum
Habakkuk
Authors of Lamentations
Zephaniah
Ezekiel
Second Isaiah

After the Exile

Third Isaiah
Haggai
Zechariah
Joel
Obadiah
Authors of Baruch

900 – 700 B.C.

700 – 540 B.C.

540 – 400 B.C.

An Awesome Call

Ezekiel's life of prophecy begins with being called through a strange vision. He sees a bright light in a chariot drawn by four winged creatures, each with four faces—those of a lion, an ox, an eagle, and a man. On a throne above the creatures is a being of light resembling a man, which appears to be a likeness of the glory of the Lord.

A voice instructs Ezekiel to tell the people of the Lord's displeasure with them, and it bids him to eat a scroll on which God has written words of lamentation and mourning and woe. When he does eat the scroll, the taste is as sweet as honey. God tells Ezekiel that he must speak the message of woe to the people.

Ezekiel is warned that the people will be stubborn and hard-hearted, but he must not be afraid of them; he must stand his ground. And he must communicate to them through actions, not simply words. God tells him to be silent until bidden to speak. Ezekiel is no longer his own man; he is God's.

Read Ezekiel 1:4–14,26–28; 2:2–10; 3:1–11.

Sweet as honey?

What could be sweet about a scroll containing words of woe? Perhaps the sweetness is a symbol of how good it is to know the truth, even when the truth seems bitter, because ultimately the truth frees us. "Sweet as honey" also seems to convey how good it is to know what God is calling us to do— even when the thing we are called to do is very hard—because God will be with us through it all. *14*

On an unbaked clay brick, Ezekiel built a model of Jerusalem under siege.

Prophetic Actions and Storytelling

With one bizarre wordless performance after another, Ezekiel tries to convince the people of Jerusalem that their rescue is *not* at hand, Jerusalem will *not* be saved, and exile will last a long time. But up until Jerusalem is captured, they continue to believe that because Jerusalem has the holy Temple, God will come charging in to save them.

Here are some examples that show the amazing lengths this prophet goes to in his efforts to get through to the people:

- Ezekiel makes a model of Jerusalem on an unbaked clay brick, using sticks and stones around it to signify a siege with battering rams, towers, and ramps. He wedges a large iron griddle into the ground behind the "city," and he lies down and gazes at it for over a year. This symbolizes God watching Nebuchadrezzar's siege of Jerusalem but doing nothing about it. *Read Ezekiel 4:1–8.*

13

Where do you find comfort and hope when you are in trouble? Think of one such source and write a poem, prayer, or reflection about it.

14

Ezekiel says that the scroll describing God's mission for him tastes as sweet as honey. Write a half page about your own discovery that doing what is right, even if it is difficult, could be said to taste sweet.

- Ezekiel cuts off his hair and beard, burns one-third of it within his model city, strews a third around the city and strikes it with a sword, and tosses the final third in the wind. A few hairs he keeps in the hem of his garment, but even some of these will be burned. This striking dramatization signifies that Jerusalem will be cut down, with some people dying of pestilence, some being slain, and some being exiled. Only a few will return. *Read Ezekiel 5:1–3,11–12.*

- Ezekiel packs his baggage, leaves his house, and goes through an elaborate acting out of escaping from the city. Later he explains that his actions represented King Zedekiah in disguise escaping the city. But the king will be caught, blinded, and taken to Babylon, where he will die. Ezekiel stands in front of the people and trembles as he eats bread and water—as they will do when they are captives. *Read Ezekiel 12:1–16.*

- Ezekiel tells the whole history of Israel through an allegory—a symbolic story. It is a love story reminiscent of the prophet Hosea's, in which Jerusalem proves to be God's vain and faithless spouse. Only when Jerusalem has shamed herself entirely—taking countless lovers, paying for their services, destroying her beauty, and behaving worse than her sisters Sodom and Samaria—only then will God forgive her and renew their marriage. *Read Ezekiel 16:1–63.*

- Ezekiel's wife, the delight of his eyes, dies and he is told by God not to show his grief. His silence embodies a message to the people. Ezekiel tells them that the delight of *their* eyes—the Temple, Jerusalem, and all its people—will also be taken from them. Ezekiel's failure to mourn outwardly for the loss of his dear wife symbolizes the people's not mourning their lost relationship with God. *Read Ezekiel 24:15–27.*

Even through the tragedy of his wife's death that he is not allowed to mourn, Ezekiel tries to communicate the truth to the people of Jerusalem. But they continue in their hard-heartedness, brushing him off with the attitude, "Okay, okay, we heard you the first time. Now don't bother us!" [15]

Denial does not serve the people well. Jerusalem does fall and is utterly destroyed. All that Ezekiel, like Jeremiah, has prophesied comes about. Unlike Jeremiah, however, when the city is captured, Ezekiel does not stay behind with those who remain there. He accompanies the exiles on their long journey through the desert to Babylon.

15

List symbolic actions—like Ezekiel's—that people might take to get across a message about one of the following issues:
- nuclear waste disposal
- air pollution
- endangered life-forms
- destruction of water supplies

Ezekiel's prophetic actions, often wordless, were much like the performances of a mime, who communicates silently.

"A New Heart . . . and a New Spirit" Within

Once the disaster he prophesied has become reality, Ezekiel's role with the people changes. He now becomes a counselor, a teacher, an inspirer to the disheartened exiles. No longer do they need to hear of God's anger but of his tender mercy. By living through their sorrowful time of exile, their hearts will be softened and made anew.

In a passage that echoes the new Covenant prophesied by Jeremiah, Ezekiel hears God speak through him these great words of hope to the people: "A new heart I will give you, and a new spirit I will put within you; and I will remove from your body the heart of stone and give you a heart of flesh" (Ezekiel 36:26). God will bring the exiles back to their land, where what has become desolate will flourish again, and where the ruined towns will be full of people once more.

Read Ezekiel 36:22–36.

The Vision of the Dry Bones

Despite Ezekiel's hopeful words, the exiles still feel not only discouraged but lifeless. Their life as a people seems over; they are dead. "Our bones are dried up," they moan (Ezekiel 37:11). Ezekiel has a vision of a valley filled with dry bones. And when God asks him, "Can these bones live?" (37:3), Ezekiel replies that only God knows. With this, he is told to say, "O dry bones, hear the word of the LORD" (37:4). As he speaks there is a rattling sound, the bones come together,

sinew and flesh covering them, but the bodies have no life. Ezekiel is told to call forth breath, or spirit, for the bones; he does, and suddenly standing before him is a vast array of living people. This is the whole house of Israel, whose grave of exile God

I will put my law within them, and I will write it on their hearts; and I will be their God, and they shall be my people. **Jeremiah 31:33**

The Babylonians and the Exile

The city of Babylon dates from before 2000 B.C. but did not achieve fame in the ancient world until the reign of King Hammurabi (1792 to 1750 B.C.). Hammurabi is famous for his code of laws. For the next twelve hundred years or so, the rulers of Babylon withstood the sieges and sackings of, and were sometimes governed by, many other nations, like Assyria.

Babylon had inherited from its predecessors a rich cultural and religious tradition going back to 4000 B.C. The Babylonians themselves produced extensive literature, including the famous *Gilgamesh Epic,* the story of a Babylonian king's failed search for immortality. Cities under Babylonian rule were governed by law, with courts and police, contractual business arrangements, and the guarantee of private property. Among their other accomplishments, the Babylonians designed the Hanging Gardens, famous as one of the Seven Wonders of the Ancient World. Because Babylon heard and often acted upon the will of its people, some scholars refer to it as a primitive democracy.

In 612 B.C. the Chaldeans (who had taken over Babylon from the Assyrians) demolished the Assyrian capital, Nineveh. Twenty-five years later the Chaldean king Nebuchadrezzar II destroyed Jerusalem and carried the citizens of Judah into exile in Babylon—a tactic often used to destroy a people's will to resist foreign rule.

Although the Jews came to Babylon as captives, they were not slaves. In fact during the exile there, they played an important part in the empire's economy and became farmers, bankers, merchants, artisans, contractors, and landowners. Some Jews felt enough at home to take Babylonian names. However, they were not permitted to worship their God publicly, and this led them to focus on the written and shared word of God instead of the sacrifices of the Temple.

In the centuries that followed the exile, many Jews remained in Babylon and were true to Judaism. They trained exceptional scholars in the Mosaic Law, and in the sixth century B.C. produced the Babylonian Talmud—the most influential Jewish writing other than the Jewish Bible.

An artist's reconstruction of ancient Babylon, with the blue Ishtar Gate in the foreground and the fabled Hanging Gardens to the right

will open, to lead them back to their land and to give them a new spirit, and there they will turn to God once more.

Read Ezekiel 37:1–14. [16]

16

Ezekiel uses the image of dry bones to describe the Israelites, who have become lifeless and faithless. Think of something in your life that appears lifeless. What kind of image would you use to describe it? Draw or describe the image and write a paragraph explaining it.

A resurrection

Probably the most familiar of the Ezekiel stories, his vision of the dry bones is about a kind of spiritual resurrection—the raising up of a nation that has lost hope. Israel has tried to manipulate its own fate and has failed lamentably; now it is God, whom they have ignored, betrayed, and rejected, who alone can save them—and will.

Christians have seen in Ezekiel's vision of the dry bones coming to life an image of Jesus' Resurrection and the new life his rising brings to those united with Christ. The passage is one of those read at the Catholic Easter Vigil service on Holy Saturday.

The Vision of a New Jerusalem

The last chapters of Ezekiel are a vision of the return to Jerusalem, the rebuilding of the Temple, and the return of the glory of God. The Lord orders Ezekiel to tell the priests and the people how to worship; celebrate feast days; and observe the laws of ritual, the rules for nobles, and the laws for division of land. Then Ezekiel announces that the name of the city shall henceforth be "The LORD is There" (48:35). But Ezekiel does not live to see Jerusalem again—except in his vision. He dies in exile.

Read Ezekiel 43:1–9; 48:35.

After years of his message of repentance being ignored, Ezekiel became the herald of Israel's hope, at long last its teacher and counselor. One can imagine that when the exiles, filled with remorse, finally asked him, "Why did it happen?" he reminded them of their infidelities. But far more eagerly, he recalled for them the mercy of their God, a saving God.

For Review

☐ What were Ezekiel's gifts that he used in prophesying?

☐ Give three examples of Ezekiel's dramatic actions and the message he tries to convey through each of them. What is the people's attitude in response?

☐ What passage in Ezekiel echoes the new Covenant prophesied by Jeremiah?

☐ How does Ezekiel's vision of the dry bones relate to Israel? to Jesus?

Second Isaiah: Toward a Joyous Return

Isaiah of Jerusalem, as we have seen, prophesied more than a century before the exile. Scholars call him First Isaiah because he was the inspiration for the later "Isaiahs," whose writings follow his in the Book of Isaiah. First Isaiah is comprised of chapters 1 to 39.

In Babylon toward the end of the exile, around 550 B.C., lived a prophet (or prophets) whom scholars call Second Isaiah, author of chapters 40 to 55 of the Book of Isaiah. Before we consider his message, let's picture the setting in which the message was given.

Life in Babylon

Imagine what the exiles' life was like after several decades in Babylon. Although they were captives in the sense that they could not leave, the exiles were not treated as slaves, forced to labor for the empire or held in prison camps. They had a certain freedom in Babylon. So as Jeremiah had advised them, the people did settle down, build homes, plant gardens, and develop businesses. Babylon was a sophisticated, wealthy city compared to Jerusalem, and many exiles became prosperous and comfortable there as the years went on.

Religious renewal

Although the Babylonians permitted some freedom in economic life, Jews were not allowed to build a temple or practice their religious rituals in any public way. The Babylonians' temples were the only ones in town. Jews who could not stomach worship of the strange Babylonian gods, like Marduk, tried to preserve their religious identity and heritage as best they could.

So the Jews carefully preserved the words of the prophets and the sacred writings of the Torah. Much of the Jewish Bible, as we

I-Witness: Saul

I'm Saul. My family lives within the walls of Babylon but runs a trading company that reaches all over the empire and even beyond it to Jewish communities far away. My grandfathers were merchants in Jerusalem before its destruction, and we were able to rebuild our business quickly here—even build it up.

I work long days and look forward to a day of study at school. The locals don't get it: Why take a day off from business? But the Sabbath is commanded by the Lord in the Scriptures—which we read and listen to and the scholars argue over at school on our day off. At home the Sabbath is a time for resting and enjoying great food.

Babylon is okay, but we will never be Babylonians. They sacrifice at temples, but their religious life ends at the gates. Our Lord does not live in any one place. We pray every day to the Lord, who is the master of time, creator of history, and promiser of our destiny as a holy people.

Jews learn the sacredness of the Sabbath at a young age. Here children practice for the lighting of Sabbath candles.

have noted, came into its final form in this period. The people gathered together as families or in community to read the Scriptures, pray, and chant their hymns and psalms.

The exile proved to be a time of great creativity for Israel, as the religion focused more on the word of God and the communi-ty, and less on the place of worship, the Temple. It was then, too, that male circumcision, kosher dietary practices, and the Sabbath as a day of rest became so significant. These customs reminded the Jews of *who they were* as God's Chosen People. *17*

17

When we are separated from someone or something that means a great deal to us, we may try to keep alive memories of that person or thing through familiar rituals, symbols, and so on. Write a brief reflection about a time you experienced this.

Tensions and compromises

The religious renewal drew many in the Jewish community closer together. But Babylon with its sophisticated ways no doubt was alluring to many Jews, especially the younger ones. As the decades in Babylon went on, and Jerusalem seemed farther and farther away, people must have wondered whether the Lord had forgotten them or was simply a weak God. There must have been arguments between parents and children, sisters and brothers, grandparents and grandchildren, even neighbors, over following the old ways and being faithful to the one and only God. Some may have been tempted to throw their allegiance to the chief Babylonian god, Marduk, who, they thought, must be more powerful than the God of the Israelites. Why not go with a winner? A little compromise could lead to a lot of success. (This, of course, had always been Israel's temptation.)

So Jews in Babylon in 550 B.C. varied in their faithfulness to God. Some compromised to the extent that they blended in with the Babylonians. Even among faithful Jews, many were content to stay in Babylon with their established homes and businesses. They could express their religious identity through their customs, their Law, and their worship centered on the Scriptures and prayer; they did not require the Temple in order to be faithful to God.

Consolation and hope

Second Isaiah had a challenge—to raise the hopes of the people for the day when they would make a joyous return to Jerusalem. That day would come soon—in 538 B.C., when Cyrus, king of Persia, overcame the Babylonians and set the exiles free. By that time almost all the original exiles had died. Their offspring would need to be passionately inspired to make the difficult journey across the desert back to Judah and the ruins of Jerusalem, beginning life over again. In fact only a fraction of the Jews in Babylon did return. *18*

The chapters of Second Isaiah are full of joyous expectation of the return to Jerusalem; of the Promised One, the Messiah; and of the day when all nations will gather to worship God in justice and peace. Appropriately, these writings are called the Book of Consolation. Included also are four songs of a mysterious servant of God, one whose mission is to bring salvation to all peoples through his own suffering.

Cyrus the Anointed: Liberator

Second Isaiah foresees the day when God will summon **Cyrus the Persian** to overthrow Babylon and to allow Israel to return home. The exile will end with a new Exodus!

Cyrus is called God's anointed, and God calls him by name. Cyrus does not know the one God, being ruler of a foreign empire with its own gods. But that does not stop God from choosing him to be the instrument of his blessings. God is ruler and creator of *all* the earth—that means foreign nations and kings. "I am the LORD, and

there is no other" (Isaiah 45:5). God joyously bids nature to let justice descend from the heavens like rain, and salvation bud forth from the earth.

Read Isaiah 45:1–8.

A good ruler, God's chosen

Unlike other conquerors, Cyrus does not resort to rape, genocide, or the deportation of populations. He allows conquered peoples to return home, asking only that when they worship their gods, they pray for him as well. God calls Cyrus the anointed out of respect for his kingship.

In Isaiah 45:1–8 we see not only a picture of a liberating Cyrus but, even more important, the image of a "universal" God. This is the God of *all* the nations, who can accomplish the divine purposes through anyone, of any nation, of any religion.

At the ancient Persian palace at Persepolis is a sculpture of a griffin, a winged supernatural animal. Although Cyrus the Persian had different beliefs than those of Judaism, the Jews saw him as God's anointed, sent to liberate them.

18

Is there something in your religious or ethnic heritage that your family values deeply—that is, passionately? If so, bring in a symbol or story about it. If not, ask your parents or grandparents if they have had such a feeling or experience in their family.

Comfort My People

In Second Isaiah, God offers comfort and shows the exiles that the way home will be made ready for them: "Comfort, O comfort my people" (40:1).

A voice cries out:
"In the wilderness prepare the way of
          the LORD. . . .
Every valley shall be lifted up,
     and every mountain and hill be
          made low."

(40:3–4)

God will come to lead Israel home—like a shepherd who leads his flock and carries his lambs in his arms. For anyone who is afraid or discouraged, God offers strength:

Those who wait for the LORD shall renew
          their strength,
     they shall mount up with wings like
          eagles,
they shall run and not be weary,
     they shall walk and not faint.

(40:31)

Read Isaiah 40:1–11,27–31.

Preparing the way of the Lord
In the Gospels, John the Baptist uses the passage from Second Isaiah about one who prepares the way of the Lord. This Gospel reading and many other hope-filled passages from Second Isaiah are part of the Christian liturgies for Advent, the season of anticipating the coming of Jesus Christ.
Read Luke 3:2–6.

19

Among your acquaintances, family members, and neighbors, identify someone who is a bruised reed. Write a note to that person, expressing your concern.

The Songs of the Suffering Servant

In Second Isaiah appears the mysterious **suffering servant,** an innocent man who suffers greatly—not as punishment for his own sins but in order to save the people from theirs. In the songs of the suffering servant, his identity is not clear. Often he seems to be the people Israel, sometimes the prophet, sometimes a composite portrait of Israel's great men, an ideal of what Israel is called to be. Christians have always seen a prophetic image of Christ in the suffering servant.

In the first song, God speaks of a chosen one, one set above others. He has been given God's spirit, and his mission is to bring justice to the nations. He will not raise his voice in noisy authority but will speak with gentleness and act tenderly toward the "bruised reed"—hopeless Israel. *19*

He was wounded for our transgressions, crushed for our iniquities;

by his bruises we are healed.

Isaiah 53:5

In the next song, the speaker is the prophet. He likens himself to a sharp-edged sword, a polished arrow that God had hidden in a quiver. He was called from his mother's womb to restore Israel as a light to the nations—so that the salvation of the Lord can reach to the ends of the earth.

In the third song, the servant is subject to insults and derision, he is beaten, his beard is plucked, his face is spat upon. Patiently he endures this abuse, certain that God will uphold him. His tormentors will wear out, he says, like moth-eaten clothing.

In the fourth song, the suffering servant seems to be an embodiment of Israel, who, before finally being exalted, is first spurned and avoided and so disfigured as to seem inhuman. The people think that he is being punished for his sins, but in reality he is suffering for the nation's wrongdoing. Like a lamb led to slaughter, he is taken away, "cut off from the land of the living" (Isaiah 53:8), and buried in a criminal's grave, although he has done no wrong. But because he has "poured out himself to death" (53:12) and was counted among the wicked, he will win pardon for the sins of many.

Read Isaiah 42:1–4; 49:1–6; 50:4–9; 52:13–15; 53:1–12.

The way of salvation through suffering

In the songs of the suffering servant, Second Isaiah introduces a new concept, a different way for Israel to be a light to the nations. Israel's light will shine not through being a glorious nation, as many Israelites in former times believed. No, Israel will bring salvation to the whole world through its willingness to suffer for the sake of others.

Jesus as the suffering servant

Today the songs of the suffering servant (Isaiah 52:13–15; 53:1–12) are used in the Good Friday liturgy, the memorial of Christ's death on the cross. Christians interpret the suffering, death, and triumph of the servant as a prophetic image of Jesus.

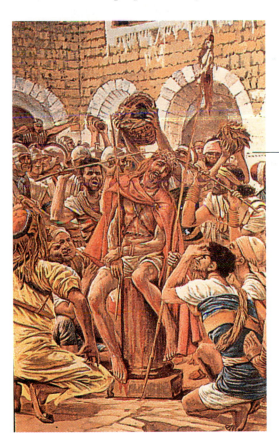

A nineteenth-century depiction of the crowning of Jesus with thorns. Christians interpret the suffering servant of the Book of Isaiah as a prophetic image of Jesus.

The Jews of the Dispersion

Beginning with the eighth century B.C., many Jews were forced to leave Israel, victims of the power games played by the Assyrians, the Babylonians, and the Persians. Jewish refugees and deportees settled in cities around the Near East and became artisans and merchants.

Some Jewish communities were large, prosperous, and long-lived, like the group remaining in Babylon after the exile, which survived into the Middle Ages. The largest of all the Jewish communities was in the Egyptian city of Alexandria, a cultural and literary hub of the Near Eastern world. In the last centuries before Christ, its Jewish population grew to nearly one million.

In Alexandria, in the third century B.C., Jewish scholars began work on the *Septuagint,* the Greek translation of the Old Testament and today the oldest complete version in existence.

Within the Alexandrian community, as elsewhere, many Jews chose to abandon the Law and adopt the local lifestyle. Others kept the Sabbath and the dietary laws, continued to regard Jerusalem as their spiritual capital, contributed to the upkeep of the Temple, and made pilgrimage there.

At the same time, Jewish communities built synagogues, where worship, education, and traditional celebrations could take place. The synagogue, a prominent part of life for Jews, also played a vital role in the origins of Christianity. In the Gospels we find Jesus attending synagogue services and teaching there.

But the Jews of the Dispersion often paid a heavy price for their clannish ways and unusual customs. Mob attacks on Jews—called pogroms in modern times—were reported in the records of Alexandria and Rome.

As the gods of the ancient world lost their attraction, people hungered for a more spiritual and moral religion, and many were attracted to Judaism. In the time of Jesus, millions of Jews lived throughout the whole Roman Empire. The growth of a large Jewish population in Roman times suggests that Jews earnestly pursued their mission to reveal the one God to the world, and that they actively sought—and received—converts.

Jews from around the world come to Jerusalem and visit the holy Western Wall, what remains of the old wall around the city.

Potential believers could not always make a full commitment to Judaism, however—perhaps because of the stigma of circumcision or the fear of persecution. Such seekers became an eager audience for the early Christian missionaries, who did not demand compliance with the Jewish regulations. Saint Paul gained many converts with his teaching that salvation depended on faith in Jesus Christ, not on obedience to the Law.

The Dispersion continued to be the determining element in Jewish history for many centuries. Then, in the twentieth century, six million Jews were killed in Europe under the Nazis during World War II (known as the *Shoah,* or the Holocaust). At last many in the world community came to recognize that the Jews ought to have a homeland. The modern state of Israel was formed in 1948, which gave the Jews back their ancestral homeland in Palestine. The formation of the modern Israel, however, has left the Arabs of Palestine, both Muslim and Christian, without *their* homeland, and the region has suffered from conflict and war as a result.

As the ancient prophets saw it, the infidelity of the Jews caused the Dispersion, but in time the Dispersion proved the durability of their faith. Judaism survived the destruction of both nation and Temple in A.D. 70 and, lived out in settings far from home, became one of the most creative and moral forces in history.

The Dispersion of the Jews by A.D. 400

RUSSIA

CENTRAL ASIA

Caspian Sea

Atlantic Ocean

GERMANY

Danube River

Black Sea

Tigris River

Euphrates

GAUL (FRANCE)

BALKANS

Babylon

Persian Gulf

Ephesus

Antioch

Rome

Corinth

Damascus

SPAIN

•Jerusalem
PALESTINE

Mediterranean Sea

Alexandria

Nile River

ARABIA

AFRICA

EGYPT

Red Sea

★ Large Jewish community

■ The Jewish Dispersion by A.D. 100

■ The Jewish Dispersion by A.D. 400

Beginning with the Assyrian deportations of Israelites in 721 B.C. and the Babylonian exile in 587 B.C., Jews were gradually dispersed across the Mediterranean world and the Near East.

In A.D. 70 Jerusalem and the Temple were destroyed. By A.D. 135 Jews were not even allowed to enter Jerusalem.

By about A.D. 400 Jews had settled throughout the Roman Empire.

The Tenderness of God

To the complaint that he has forgotten Jerusalem, God responds, through Second Isaiah, with one of the most beautiful passages in the Scriptures. Even a mother might forget her infant or be without tenderness for the child of her womb, but God will never forget Israel. **20**

In another passage God becomes a woman in labor, gasping and panting as she struggles to bring forth Israel as a reborn nation.

Read Isaiah 49:14–15; 42:13–14.

Come to the Feast!

A joyful poem in Second Isaiah invites the people to a great feast: All those who thirst, come to the water! Come and enjoy the rich food of God's life. It's free, and it's the kind of food and drink that satisfies—not the kind that leaves you empty and parched.

Second Isaiah closes in a hymn of joy, with God promising peace, mountains that break into song, trees that clap their hands, cypresses instead of thornbushes, myrtle instead of nettles. No wonder the returning exiles leave Babylon with high and hope-filled hearts!

Read Isaiah 55:1–13.

20

Write about three examples from the Old Testament in which God shows the Israelites that he will never forget them.

As pictured in Isaiah's hymn of joy, when God's reign of peace comes, there will be beautiful myrtle, *above,* instead of nettles and thornbushes, *right,* trees will clap their hands, and mountains will break into song.

Feminine Images of God

Christians have traditionally referred to God as Father; Jesus, after all, teaches us to pray to "our Father." So we might be surprised to find God described as a woman or mother in Isaiah and other places in the Old Testament (see, for example, Isaiah 66:13, Psalm 131, Proverbs 9:1–6, and Wisdom of Solomon 6:12–20).

God is pure spirit, neither male nor female. But both male and female images of God help us to more fully appreciate how good and wonderful God is, because at their best, both women and men—as creatures made equal in God's image—reflect something of God (see *Catechism of the Catholic Church,* numbers 239 and 370). Isaiah's image of God as mother must have been a powerful reminder of God's intimate care for his people, just as it can remind us today of God's motherly care for each of us.

For Review

- [ ] Where and when did the prophet (or prophets) known as Second Isaiah live?

- [ ] In what ways was the exile a time of religious renewal for the Jews? What tensions and compromises did they face?

- [ ] What was Second Isaiah's challenge?

- [ ] Why does the suffering servant suffer? How have Christians understood the image of the suffering servant?

- [ ] What images does Isaiah, chapter 55, use to convey hope?

The Fruits of Exile

The prophets Jeremiah, Ezekiel, and Second Isaiah guided Israel through its time of purification in exile, calling the people to a deeper relationship with God. Judaism as a religion, with its unswerving belief in the one and only God, its Law and distinctive practices, and its rootedness in the written word of God, was born in exile. Jeremiah and Ezekiel saw the new Covenant that was coming for Israel. And Isaiah and Jeremiah pointed to the transforming and saving power of suffering, rather than its being simply a punishment for sin. That insight into suffering would be crucial to the Jews throughout their history of oppression and persecution up to the present, and to Christians in their belief in the saving power of Christ's suffering and death, leading to resurrected life.

At the end of the exile, relatively few Jews returned to Jerusalem to begin again. Those who did saw themselves as the "faithful remnant" prophesied by Zephaniah and others. However, that did not make the Jews of the Dispersion *unfaithful*. For them as well as for the returning exiles, the fruit of the exile was new life. With the center of the Jews' faith in their Scriptures and their distinctive practices, Judaism was no longer tied to one particular land, Israel, and one place of worship, the Temple. It became a portable religion, which later spread throughout the Greek and Roman Empires. Its portability enabled Jews to be faithful wherever they were, truly a "light to the nations."

The Prayer of Israel: "Come to the Waters"

Ho, everyone who thirsts,
    come to the waters;
and you that have no money,
    come, buy and eat!
Come, buy wine and milk
    without money and without price.
Why do you spend your money for that which is not bread,
    and your labor for that which does not satisfy?
Listen carefully to me, and eat what is good,
    and delight yourselves in rich food.
Incline your ear, and come to me;
    listen, so that you may live.
I will make with you an everlasting covenant,
    my steadfast, sure love for David.
                 (Isaiah 55:1–3)

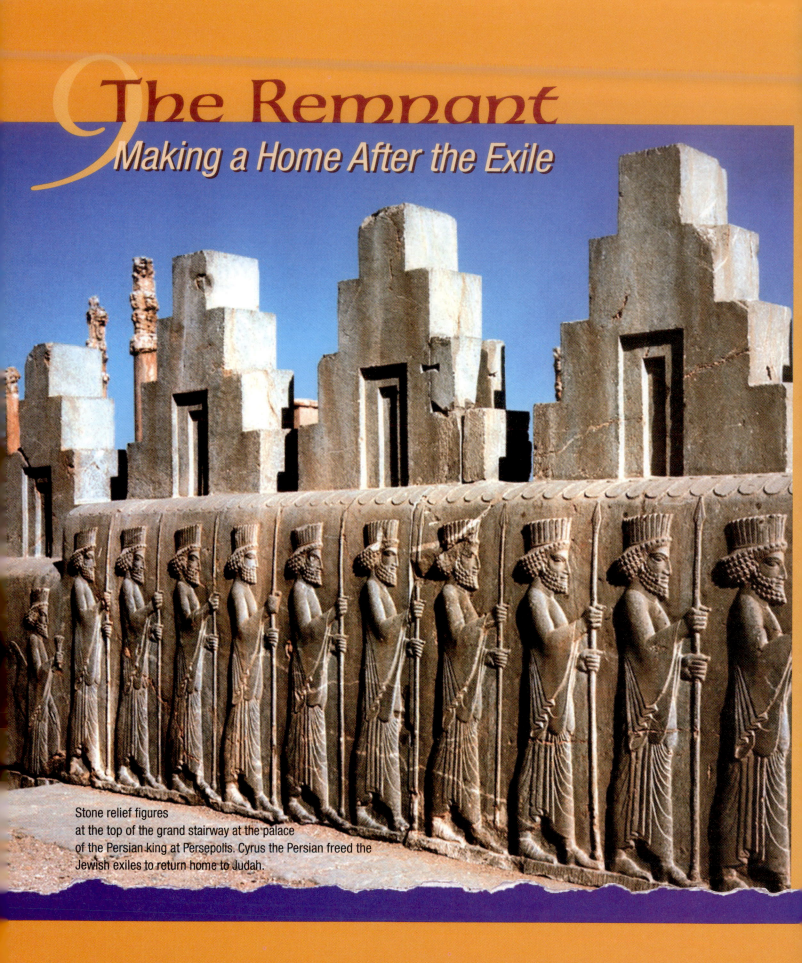

9 The Remnant
Making a Home After the Exile

Stone relief figures
at the top of the grand stairway at the palace
of the Persian king at Persepolis. Cyrus the Persian freed the
Jewish exiles to return home to Judah.

L iberation finally came for the exiles in Babylon. As Second Isaiah had foreseen, Cyrus, the king of Persia, was the liberator, taking over Babylon in 539 B.C. and issuing an edict the next year that freed the exiles to return home to Judah.

This chapter tells what happened after the exiles returned to Jerusalem—the period known as the **restoration.** We will see how the exiles struggled with discouragement, as they sought not only to rebuild the city and the Temple but also to establish a clear sense of their own identity as Jews. (After the exile the term *Jew*—from *Judah*—came into common use, along with *Jewish* and *Judaism*.)

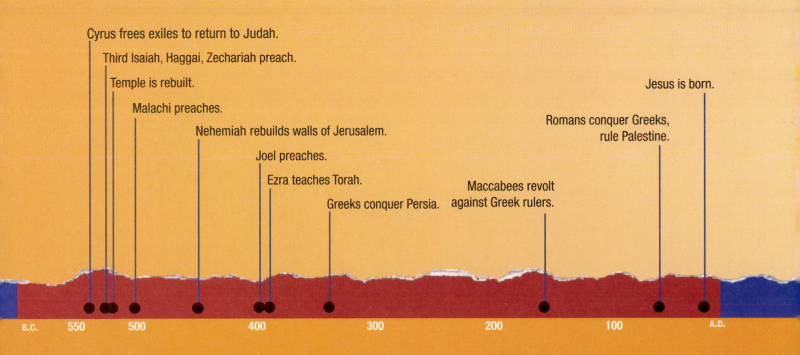

Cyrus frees exiles to return to Judah.

Third Isaiah, Haggai, Zechariah preach.

Temple is rebuilt.

Malachi preaches.

Jesus is born.

Nehemiah rebuilds walls of Jerusalem.

Romans conquer Greeks, rule Palestine.

Joel preaches.

Ezra teaches Torah.

Maccabees revolt against Greek rulers.

Greeks conquer Persia.

B.C. 550   500   400   300   200   100   A.D.

A road through the countryside in Israel

In 538 B.C. a group of exiles made the long trip back to Judah, followed by later groups over the decades. Most of the exiles, however, remained in and around Babylon, where life was more certain. The ones who returned to Judah thought of themselves as "the remnant"—those few in number but strong in faith that Zephaniah and other prophets had foretold would be the basis of a new Israel.

This group of exiles came home quite literally. But even more important, they needed to come home in a spiritual sense by reinforcing and defending the major beliefs and practices of Judaism. The period after the exile was a time to build a strong spiritual center, a vital faith that Jews could carry with them into foreign lands—like Egypt, Greece, and other places around the Mediterranean Sea where Jews eventually did form communities. With a vital spiritual center, wherever they lived, the Jews would be "at home."

This meant setting boundaries—not the geographical kind like the borders of a country or city but the spiritual kind that define the limits of a person or group: "This is *who we are.* There are certain things we do, and certain things we don't and won't do. These are the lines we must not cross if we are to be faithful to who we are." For the Jews such boundaries were essential if they were to survive as a people in strange lands where they were treated as aliens if not as enemies. Their boundaries gave them a spiritual home that would endure despite the many attempts through the centuries to wipe out the Jewish people. [1]

Because so much of Jewish practice developed during the period after the exile, scholars say that Judaism as the religion we know came to birth in those years.

Boundaries or limits help us to know who we are. The boundary, or rule, of participating in Sunday Mass helps Catholics to identify themselves as children of God who are responsible to one another.

At the beginning of this chapter, we will see how, in the two **Books of Chronicles,** the history of Israel was told again, up through the exile. Then the Books of **Ezra** and **Nehemiah** continue with the story of the return from exile, the rebuilding of Jerusalem and the Temple, the people's recommitment to the Law, and the centering of their religion in the Jewish Bible. Woven throughout this chapter are the messages of prophets, who urge the people to faithfulness and hope: **Third Isaiah, Haggai, Zechariah, Malachi, Joel,** and **Obadiah.**

Finally, we will consider the Jewish people's struggle to maintain their identity and boundaries in the face of the power and allure of the Greek Empire, which conquered the region in 330 B.C. The two **Books of Maccabees** tell of a period of terrible persecution of the Jews by the Greeks that began about 175 B.C. They also tell of the Jews' brave resistance to oppression that led to a time of limited independence for Judah. The **Book of Daniel,** written amid cruelty and torture at the hands of the Greeks, offers inspiration and hope by drawing on stories of a courageous figure named Daniel, who faced oppression during the exile in Babylon. Both the Second Book of Maccabees and Daniel express belief in an afterlife and the hope of resurrection, concepts that emerged in Judaism in the two centuries before the birth of Jesus.

1

Think of a group to which you belong—such as a church, a family, a club, a team, a school—that has a strong sense of identity. Then write a paragraph that describes *who you and the other members are* as a group.

Chronicles: History as It Should Have Been

The two Books of Chronicles were written sometime after the rebuilding of the Temple, possibly about 400 B.C. The books retell Israel's history in terms of its meaning in God's unfolding plan, rather than in factual, chronological events. They are a valuable prologue to the Books of Ezra and Nehemiah, named for two men whose leadership in Jerusalem was key to the development of modern Judaism.

Why are we told still another version of Israel's history, one that skips over large chunks of it, puts the emphasis on David and Solomon—omitting all their sins—and still claims to be inspired Scripture?

The Books of Chronicles were the writer's effort to put things in focus. They reminded the Jews that they were called to be a priestly people and a holy nation, not an empire. The Chronicler was not concerned with Israel's scandals, wars, or wealth. Israel's political greatness was over, but that did not matter because by holding to the ideal set forth by David, Israel would keep on course to the spiritual greatness that was its destiny.

So the Chronicler made David and Solomon the key figures in his saga and retold their story the way it *should* have happened, with the warts removed. He recalled how David took Jerusalem, rebuilt it, made it the capital of the twelve tribes, and brought the ark of the Covenant there. David dreamed of a house for God, purchased land for it, drew plans, provided materials, wrote regulations for the Temple, trained choristers and musicians, and even wrote music for Israel's worship. Much of this information appears for the first time in Chronicles.

The story of Solomon is told with emphasis on his wealth, his building and dedication of the Temple, and his wisdom—no mention of his idolatry. Only when the Chronicler got to the stories of the later kings who led Israel into infidelity, idolatry, and exile did he criticize and condemn. He ended with the decree of Cyrus, which at last freed Israel to return from exile to Jerusalem to start again.

The Deuteronomists, in the Books of Samuel, portrayed David as a great warrior-king and a repentant sinner. The Chronicler, however, presented David as a liturgist and leader in worship, in order to inspire the Jerusalem community to return to a vibrant religious life. **2**

Read 1 Chronicles 22:1–6,17–19; 28:9–21; 2 Chronicles 6:1–11.

For Review

☐ What kind of boundaries did the returning exiles need to set?

☐ What did the Chronicler's history emphasize about David and Solomon? Why was the history written this way?

A depiction of King Solomon dedicating the original Temple. The Books of Chronicles tell about Solomon as an ideal leader.

2

The Chronicler rewrote Israel's history the way it *should* have happened. Try doing the same: rewrite an incident in your life to make it come out as you wish it had.

The Return: Discouragement and Struggle

When Home Is Not What You Imagined

The first six chapters of the Book of Ezra are about the return home from exile in 538 B.C. (The book was named for a priest and scribe, Ezra, who came from Babylon to lead a religious renewal in Jerusalem about a hundred years after the exiles returned to Judah. So Ezra himself does not appear in the book named for him until chapter 7.)

The book opens with the decree of Cyrus giving freedom to all the Jewish exiles in the Persian Empire who wish to return to Jerusalem. Cyrus suggests that the exiles remaining behind in Babylon contribute supplies to those who are returning and that all artifacts taken from Solomon's Temple be restored.

The exiles start out from Babylon full of hope and excitement, buoyed by Second Isaiah's prophecy of a new Jerusalem. But when they arrive in Jerusalem, they find nothing but a miserable little village perched on a pile of rubble—its wall and Temple in ruins—and ahead of them a future promising nothing but hardship. Judah is an impoverished land spanning a mere twenty-five miles from north to south. The poor residents of the land, descendants of the Jews that were left behind at the time of the exile to Babylon, resent the newcomers. To the north the Jews of Samaria observe the returnees with suspicion. It hardly seems to the exiles like a great homecoming! What about the glorious vision of a new Jerusalem?

The exiles resettle in their ancestral towns and several months later gather in the city to offer sacrifice. Led by **Zerubbabel** (a grandson of King Jehoiachin and thus a descendant of David) and the high priest

The returning exiles found their beloved Temple in ruins, requiring a major rebuilding project.

Joshua, they lay a foundation for a new Temple and commence work.

News of this enterprise travels to the north, and the Samaritans come down to help, saying that they too worship Israel's God. But to the exiles, who consider themselves the remnant (the *true* Israel), these hybrid Jews are not Jews at all, and their offer is rebuffed. The angry Samaritans return to the north and report the project to their Persian rulers as rebellion. Because

Samaritans still exist today as a small sect of Judaism. Here a Samaritan priest displays an ancient scroll of the Torah.

Cyrus is dead and the present king is unfamiliar with the decree permitting the Jews to rebuild their Temple, the work is halted—for eighteen years.

Read Ezra 1:1–4; 4:1–24.

A legacy of prejudice toward the Samaritans

The Samaritans were Jews whose ancestry went back to the time of the northern kingdom of Israel, with its capital in Samaria. Recall that when the northern kingdom's elite were deported to Assyria in 722 B.C., foreign settlers were brought in to colonize the former Israel. The foreigners were ordered by the Assyrians to marry with the local Israelites and worship Israel's God as well as their own gods. The result was a weakening of tribal identity and religious fidelity. The Samaritans—the descendants of the Jews and foreign settlers of the north—were regarded as inferior by the Jews of the south, not "real" Jews, and this prejudice carried over into Jesus' time and beyond. **3**

Third Isaiah: Get Back on Track, Keep the Vision Alive!

The last eleven chapters of Isaiah (chapters 56 to 66) focus on the state of affairs in Jerusalem after the return of the exiles. The writings speak of the far-from-glorious state of affairs in the Jersualem community, painting a sad picture of the returnees' behavior as they struggle to get back on track again but fail at it. The vision of a new Jerusalem painted by Second Isaiah during the exile obviously has not yet "come true" for the returning exiles. The prophet or prophets known as Third Isaiah, probably disciples of Second Isaiah writing around 540 to 510 B.C., respond to the grim reality of what the returnees face. Third Isaiah challenges the people to look deeper into the vision that inspired them, to see it as a promise for a day when they have grown into God's plan for the whole world. They are not there yet.

Third Isaiah sees things going downhill rapidly after the arrivals' shock at the ruin in Jerusalem, followed by the obstruction of their Temple project. Laxness and religious apathy settle over the community like a blight. The poor are reduced to hopelessness, the rich care only for themselves, the leaders are faithless, and infidelity and idol worship are rife.

When the rich ask why God ignores their fasting and prayer, the answer is that he desires *true* fasting. True fasting is working for the release of the unjustly imprisoned, freeing the oppressed, sharing bread with the hungry, sheltering the homeless, and clothing the naked. For people who fast in this compassionate sense, God promises them great renewal: "Then your light shall break forth like the dawn, / and your healing shall spring up quickly" (Isaiah 58:8).

Read Isaiah 58:1–11.

3

Are you surprised to find so much prejudice in the Bible? Write a one-paragraph answer to this question: *Is prejudice more prevalent in society today than it was in biblical times?*

Third Isaiah tries to stir the people to believe in their own possibilities. If they will learn the ways of justice, God's glory will be with them, they will shine forth a great light, and the nations of the world will gather around them. No more will Jerusalem be called forsaken; instead it will be the hope of the world. One will appear who is anointed to bring good news to the oppressed, release the captives, and heal the brokenhearted. The new heavens and the new earth will come to pass, and all the world will worship the Lord.

Read Isaiah 60:1–7; 61:1–2; 66:18–23.

Jesus in the synagogue

As Luke's Gospel account tells it, centuries after Isaiah, Jesus reads aloud in his hometown synagogue the passage about the anointed one, proclaiming that it is now fulfilled.

Read Luke 4:16–21.

The Book of Isaiah is a masterpiece of the Old Testament. First, Second, and Third Isaiah have different authors, moods, and historical settings, but together they weave a theme: God's love for Israel and tender care

Isaiah says that God's people will shine as a light for the nations, giving hope to the poor and the oppressed. In Philadelphia, former welfare recipients have moved from joblessness to hopefulness. They started their own company, a home health aide agency, with a grant from the Catholic Campaign for Human Development.

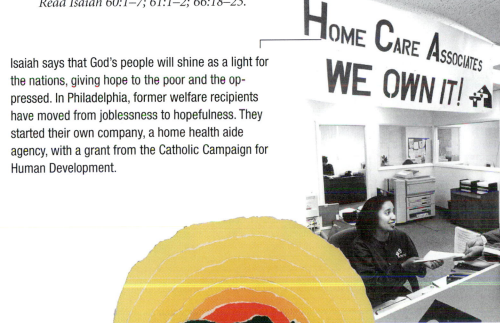

The spirit of the Lord God is upon me,
   because the Lord has anointed me;
he has sent me to bring good news to
      the oppressed,
   to bind up the brokenhearted,
to proclaim liberty to the captives,
   and release to the prisoners.

Isaiah 61:1

World Happenings from 600 B.C. to 1 B.C.

Major religious and philosophical movements arise in the period preceding Jesus' life—movements that shape our ideas about God and goodness today.

China

The teacher K'ung Fu-tzu, better known as Confucius (551 to 479 B.C.), promotes social ethics, stressing traditional values, courtesy, and good government. His contemporary Lao-tzu writes the Tao Te Ching, which prescribes living in joy and harmony with nature. Their complementary systems—Confucianism and Taoism—guide Chinese culture and politics into modern times.

Greece

In Athens during the fifth and fourth centuries B.C., democracy blooms, and thinkers such as Socrates, Plato, and Aristotle lay the foundations for Western philosophy, emphasizing a systematic search for wisdom.

India

The monk Vardhamâna (599 to 527 B.C.) establishes Jainism, a religion based on equality and non-violence. (India's present-day dominant religion, Hinduism, eventually adopts nonviolence as part of its own teachings.) About the same time, the prince Siddhartha Gautama (563 to 483 B.C.) has a spiritual awakening and, as the Buddha, teaches the principles of meditation and moderation. Although it does not take firm root in India, Buddhism spreads throughout the rest of the Eastern world.

The Near East

The prophets of Israel and Judah preach monotheism and justice—religious and social ideas that become core beliefs in the great Western religions.

The reformer priest Ezra revives the Jewish community in Jerusalem, teaching the obligations and restrictions set down in the Torah. Later tradition acclaims Ezra to be a second Moses.

In the sixth century B.C., the reformer priest Zoroaster revolutionizes Persian religion with his teachings on free will and the afterlife.

for Zion, or Jerusalem. Particularly in Second and Third Isaiah, we find the notion of **universalism,** the dream that God's love for Israel will make it a "light to the nations," ultimately bringing together all nations and peoples of the earth under his Reign. *4*

4

What do you think it means to bring together all nations and peoples of the earth under God's Reign? Is it possible to unite all people? Find an article that illustrates a step toward this vision and write a one-paragraph reflection about it.

For Review

☐ What do the exiles find when they return to Jerusalem?

☐ Why were the exiles prejudiced toward the Samaritans?

☐ According to Third Isaiah, what is the true fasting that God desires?

☐ What is meant by the notion of universalism in Second and Third Isaiah?

Right: The humble sanctuary at Chimayo, New Mexico, where faith-filled pilgrims come to pray for God's healing. *Far right:* A grand church in Munich, Germany. Haggai would wonder, which serves God better?

The Second Temple: A Focus for Faith

Despite Third Isaiah's attempts to keep the vision of Israel's destiny alive, many of the returning exiles are still disheartened and cannot seem to get back on track. After Jerusalem has languished in apathy for eighteen years, the prophets Haggai, Zechariah, and Malachi appear. They are appalled that God's people have forgotten their calling and realize that the Temple is crucial if the Jews are to keep their religious identity. They waken the people with powerful oracles.

Haggai: No House for God?

Haggai, a speaker with a concise, humorous style, would probably be a political organizer today. He sees the delay in rebuilding the Temple as not entirely the fault of the Samaritans. Poverty, and the powerlessness that goes with poverty, is widespread in Jerusalem, and the rich care only for getting richer—so who is surprised that the leaders are halfhearted and the people religiously lax? They seem to agree on one thing only: there are more important things to do than re-build a temple that has been in ruins for almost seventy years.

Without the Temple, however, Haggai believes that the Jerusalem community will lose its faith. Haggai rails at the people for ceasing work on God's house when they have found time to build their own. His eloquence moves Zerubbabel (named governor of Judah by the Persians) and Joshua, the high priest, to action. The people join them, hasten to the site, and begin work.

Read Haggai 1:2–15.

Later in the same year (520 B.C.), God asks the people if they are discouraged with their efforts. In truth the new building they are constructing does not remotely compare with Solomon's great Temple. God tells them to take courage, "for I am with you" (Haggai 2:4). But their fervor is centered on the building project, not on the state of their lives or their worship, and they fail to understand.

Read Haggai 2:3–5. **5**

5

Imagine an ideal building for worship. Explain in writing what it looks like and why.

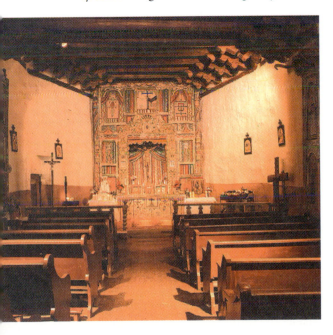

Zechariah tells of a messiah of the poor, who will ride a humble, peaceful donkey and be the people's true shepherd.

Creating a sacred space

God makes a strong point about the appearance of the Temple being built: The people of Jerusalem need the Temple in order to focus their faith on God's presence among them, worship together as a community, and renew their commitment to his call. But the Temple's size and furnishings should be a minor concern.

Yet, right down to the present, people often tend to focus on the beauty and splendor of their worship spaces more than on the sacredness of what happens within them. **6**

Zechariah: The Messiah Will Come

Zechariah was a visionary concerned with the coming of the Messiah, a Davidic king who would rule in peace and justice, uniting all the nations in the worship of God. (Isaiah's universalist theme is also evident in Zechariah). The New Testament contains over seventy references to Zechariah, mainly

6

Why was there no reason for the Jews to feel ashamed of the second Temple? Write your answer as if you were a Jew who helped rebuild the Temple.

in the Book of Revelation. The two halves of the Book of Zechariah are written by two different authors. One is Zechariah, who spoke shortly after Haggai; the other is an anonymous prophet about two hundred years later. Scholars have named them First and Second Zechariah.

First Zechariah sees Zerubbabel, the heir to David's throne, as a messianic figure. He thinks that all God's promises to Israel will be fulfilled in Zerubbabel and all the nations will come together in the worship of God under him. (In actuality, however, Zerubbabel never is made king but only governor; the high priest Joshua has more authority than he. After the exile it is the high priests, not kings, who are the highest leaders of the Judah community. Zerubbabel and the royal line of David disappear from view.)

A beautiful description of messianic times ahead is given: Jerusalem will be a city where the elderly enjoy their leisure and where children play in safety. People will speak the truth, and days of fasting will be occasions for joy.

Read Zechariah 8:1–8.

Like the earlier chapters, Second Zechariah (chapters 9 to 14) has a messianic focus. Now, though, the expected messiah is not a rich and powerful king but a peaceful messiah of the poor. We know this from the images the prophet uses. Warrior-kings always ride horses; the messianic king of peace will ride a white donkey—a symbol of peace. The horse, the chariot, and the bow—all symbols of war—will be banned by the messianic king.

Chapter 11 provides an allegory of a shepherd: the people wander like sheep without a shepherd until the prophet becomes the true shepherd. In chapter 12 the prophet shows Jerusalem, stricken with guilt, grieving for someone they have apparently murdered and seeking forgiveness. It is easy to understand why the early Christians saw these images as referring to Christ.

Read Zechariah 9:9–10; 11:4–5,7; 12:10.

Jesus and Zechariah

As a good Jew, Jesus was aware of Zechariah's prophecies about the Messiah and saw them as related to his own life and mission. On the Sunday before his death, he chose to enter Jerusalem as the peaceful king, riding on the back of a donkey, as Zechariah described. And the shepherd passages in Zechariah, together with those in Ezekiel, may have been the source of Jesus' perception of himself as the Good Shepherd.

Read Matthew 21:1–9; John 12:12–16; John 10:7–15.

Malachi:
Sacrilege, Despite the Temple

The prophet Malachi spoke sometime after the Temple rebuilding project was completed (515 B.C.), but before the coming of Nehemiah as governor of Judah (445 B.C.). Malachi's book reveals the dismal conditions in Jerusalem, even though the people now have a Temple in which to worship. Malachi is a pen name meaning "my messenger."

The Book of Malachi depicts faith at its lowest in Jerusalem. The sacrifices offered in the Temple can only be called sacrilegious— with blemished, lame, and blind animals offered instead of the perfect ones required by the Law. God, through the prophet Malachi, suggests that the priests try giving such gifts

to the governor and see what he says! All over the world, says God, the Gentiles worship with pure offerings, but his own people profane the altar and call worship a burden.

The people are as guilty as the priests. Returning from exile, the men have divorced their Jewish wives and married rich pagan women in order to live more prosperously. They have not only broken vows to God and to their wives but also deprived the community of its rightful children. Indeed, they now believe that "all who do evil are good in the sight of the Lord" (Malachi 2:17), and claim that it is unjust of God not to agree.

Read Malachi 1:6–8,10–14; 2:7–8,13–17.

Malachi announces that God will send a messenger to prepare the people for the coming of judgment. He will be like a refiner's fire that burns the impurities out of gold or like the fuller's lye with which the new wool is cleansed. The people ask, "How shall we return to the Lord?" and Malachi tells them to *tithe*—that is, donate a tenth of their income. Evidently the storehouses in the Temple are empty because the offerings have been stolen. Shallow faith has led the people to admire the successful as the blessed, to approve even prosperous evildoers who hold God in contempt. But, says Malachi, God is keeping a record. Only repentance will save the people.

Read Malachi 3:1–10. [7]

7

The spirit behind tithing is that we give the first 10 percent of our income to charity and to our church, trusting that God will take care of our needs, no matter what financial struggles we might meet. The giving should happen *before* we buy anything or pay our bills, not from leftover money. Tithing is an act of justice and an act of faith. Answer the following questions in writing:

- If you were to tithe each month, to whom would you want to give your money?
- What things might you have to give up in order to tithe?
- What is your opinion about tithing? Do you think you could do it?

The people of Judah after the exile have put their hopes once again in a building, the Temple, to ensure they have God's favor. Yet the Temple is far from a guarantee of righteousness, as prophets like Jeremiah knew before the exile. If worship in the Temple is not sincere, it is as good as worthless.

Something more profound than building a second Temple is needed to bring about the community's renewal.

For Review

☐ According to the Book of Haggai, when the people finally get around to building the new Temple, what do they focus on? What should they focus on?

☐ How does the image of the Messiah differ between the first half of Zechariah and the second half?

☐ What behaviors does the prophet Malachi object to among the priests? among the people?

A homeless woman huddles with her child as shoppers pass by in Russia. Malachai warned against a shallow faith that leads people to hold fast to their money and possessions, that leads them to admire success and prosperity above all else.

The Prophets of Israel After 900 B.C.

The Northern Kingdom of Israel

Elijah   Amos
Elisha   Hosea

The Southern Kingdom of Judah

First Isaiah   Micah

Before and During the Exile

Jeremiah
Nahum
Habakkuk
Authors of Lamentations
Zephaniah
Ezekiel
Second Isaiah

After the Exile

Third Isaiah
Haggai
Zechariah
Joel
Obadiah
Authors of Baruch

900 – 700 B.C.   **700 – 540 B.C.**   **540 – 400 B.C.**

Renewal: Drawing the Community's Boundaries

Renewal of the Judah community came through the two greatest leaders of Judah after the exile. Nehemiah was a governor, and Ezra was a priest. Together, they gave the people something they desperately needed at that time—a sense of the boundaries of Judaism and therefore of the people's own identity, who they were as Jews.

Nehemiah and Ezra labored in Jerusalem while Judah was under the reign of the tolerant Persian Empire. Little did they know that after them, terrible times would be ahead for Judah. The territory would one day fall under the harsh rule of the Greek Empire, then the Roman Empire. Without the firm boundaries set by Ezra and Nehemiah, Judaism as a religion would have been washed away in the coming centuries of oppression.

Nehemiah: Rebuilding the Walls

Much of the Book of Nehemiah, written beginning in 445 B.C., was taken from Nehemiah's private journal and was meant for God alone. It reveals to us one of the most admirable people in Israel's history—a model public servant.

Nehemiah, a Jew, has a privileged position in the court of the Persian king in the empire's capital. His brother comes from Jerusalem and tells of the city's walls still in ruins, gates gutted, and people demoralized, and Nehemiah grieves and fasts for several days. With the sympathetic king's consent, Nehemiah travels to Jerusalem. There, on a moonlit night shortly after his arrival, with only a handful of companions, Nehemiah rides around the city's walls to inspect the ruins. The walls are so devastated that at times he has to dismount and walk his horse through the rubble.

In the following days, Nehemiah calls everyone in the city to rebuild the walls of Jerusalem. This will protect the city and also recover its former status in the eyes of neighboring peoples. Impressed with his words, the people of Jerusalem want to start work immediately. Neighboring governors accuse the Jews of rebellion and try to frustrate the work. But Nehemiah promises that God will help the people, and the task gets under way.

Read Nehemiah 1:1–4; 2:1–20. **8**

Start with something concrete

The walls of Jerusalem are, quite literally, its boundaries. Nehemiah is less interested in these physical boundaries than in the clear spiritual boundary lines that say, "This is Jewish; that is not." But the walls of the city symbolize the outlines of Judaism's identity. And they are a good place for Nehemiah to start. After all, secure walls will make the inhabitants of Jerusalem safe from foreign attack. In order to attract people to live in the city, Nehemiah has to provide them with a sense of security.

Involving the Whole Community

True to Nehemiah's leadership as a model public servant, he involves the whole community in the construction project. A long list of workers rebuild the walls and gates of the city. The high priest and his staff build the sheep gate, the gate closest to the Temple. The guilds of goldsmiths and

---

8

Find or write a story about a person or a group that possesses perseverance and inner strength in the face of great difficulty. What or who do you think inspires the person or members of the group to keep struggling for what is important to them?

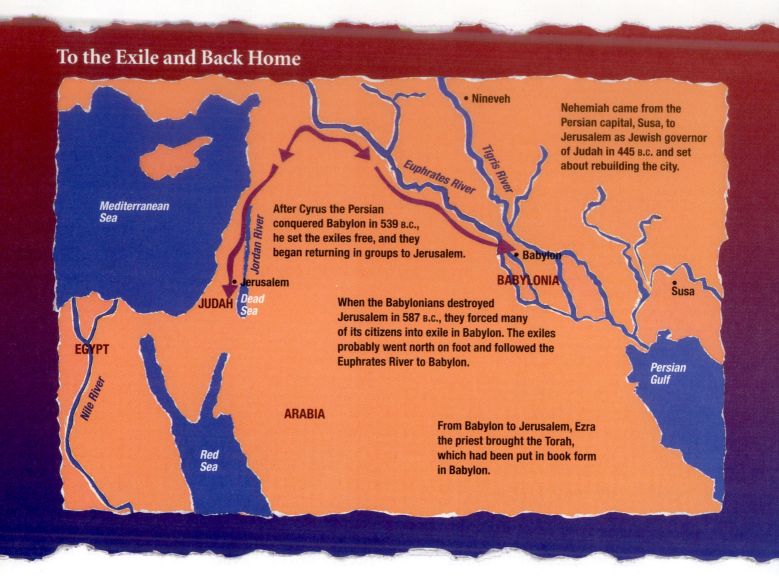

Nineveh •

Nehemiah came from the Persian capital, Susa, to Jerusalem as Jewish governor of Judah in 445 B.C. and set about rebuilding the city.

Euphrates River

Tigris River

Mediterranean Sea

Jordan River

After Cyrus the Persian conquered Babylon in 539 B.C., he set the exiles free, and they began returning in groups to Jerusalem.

• Babylon

BABYLONIA

• Jerusalem

JUDAH

Dead Sea

• Susa

When the Babylonians destroyed Jerusalem in 587 B.C., they forced many of its citizens into exile in Babylon. The exiles probably went north on foot and followed the Euphrates River to Babylon.

EGYPT

Nile River

Persian Gulf

ARABIA

From Babylon to Jerusalem, Ezra the priest brought the Torah, which had been put in book form in Babylon.

Red Sea

perfumers build; fathers and sons build; and one man who has no sons builds with his daughters. The list recorded in the book is a tribute to Nehemiah's record keeping. It also shows how an inspired leader could get the people to roll up their sleeves and begin work lifting rock out of decades of debris to rebuild Jerusalem.

The enemies of the rebuilders try to attack them, but Nehemiah posts guards, arms whole families, and stations a trumpeter to blow an alarm. He writes in his journal that in readiness for an attack, neither he nor his attendants take off their clothes, even at night.

Read Nehemiah 3:1–2,12.

Insisting on Justice

Before the walls are completed, Nehemiah hears the common people cry out against the affluent people of Jerusalem. The common folk have had to pawn their fields, vineyards, homes, and even sons and daughters in order to buy grain to eat. Now some of their daughters are even being molested by wealthy kinsmen.

Nehemiah is outraged. He orders the wealthy to return everything to the people they have cheated and to repay any interest they have charged. Modeling the justice he wants to see in the community, he and his friends and family loan money and grain to the poor without charge. The wealthy

A display of Middle Eastern food. During the rebuilding of Jerusalem's walls, Nehemiah spread a table of food and wine for the workers at his own expense.

people agree to do as he says, and Nehemiah makes them swear to it in the presence of the priests.

Read Nehemiah 5:1–13.

Leading by Serving

As governor of Judah, Nehemiah refuses to use an expense account, to benefit from taxes, or to take land for himself. During the rebuilding of the walls, he sets a table with food and wine for the workers, at his own expense.

But even a model public servant can have enemies. Two men, Sanballat and Tobiah, resent Nehemiah's power. They try to ambush him, they start a smear campaign, and they even try to lure him into the Temple and arrest him. Nehemiah avoids their schemes, and at last the walls are finished. He orders that the gates never be opened before the sun is hot and always be closed before sundown, and he has a guard stationed at all times.

The Jewish leaders take up residence in Jerusalem, and lots are cast among the people to decide who will live there; the rest of the Jews must reside in the other cities. The wall is finally dedicated with great ceremony, and after the religious rituals are celebrated, a gigantic feast is held for all. **9**

Read Nehemiah 5:14–19; 6:1–15; 11:1–2; 12:27–31.

Key Boundaries: Honoring the Sabbath, Not Marrying Foreigners

Nehemiah journeys back and forth between the Persian court and Jerusalem several times. Returning to Jerusalem for the last time, he finds that his archenemy Tobiah is living in the Temple and that the tithes of grain, wine, and oil for the Temple attendants have been stolen or given away. He has Tobiah thrown out, the chambers purified, and the supplies restored. He calls back the Levites, who have gone home to grow food

9

Think of someone who is a leader, but leads in a servantlike way. That is, she or he does not act superior but tries to serve the people rather than dictate to them. Describe the person in writing.

An opulent shopping gallery. Nehemiah scolded the people for their greed; instead of keeping the Sabbath holy by worshiping and resting, they were conducting trade and shopping.

(they were responsible for caring for the Temple). He appoints trustworthy administrators.

But another, even worse situation is brewing. The Jerusalem farmers and merchants are not keeping the Sabbath—they are conducting trade in the city—and the people are shopping on the Sabbath! Nehemiah reminds them that it was such contempt for the Law that led to Israel's downfall in the past and orders the city gates sealed before the Sabbath and opened only when it is over.

Next, Nehemiah condemns the Jews who have married foreign women and whose children cannot even speak Hebrew. He curses those Jews and has them beaten—so dangerous does he believe this mixing of blood to be for the future of Israel. He warns the other Jews not to give their children in marriage to these half-breeds—as they appear to him. He reminds the people of how Solomon married foreign wives and dissipat-

ed the blood of the Davidic line, causing the nation to be divided. He conducts a rite of cleansing to free them of all foreign contamination, and with a brief summary of the provisions he has made for the Temple, his book abruptly comes to a close.

Read Nehemiah 13:4–31.

Why so strict, Nehemiah?

Nehemiah's two final reforms pose tricky questions and may seem quite extreme to us. To understand his motives, we must put ourselves in his time.

Buying and selling on the Sabbath was forbidden by the third commandment. According to the Book of Exodus, the penalty for doing so in Moses' time was death (Exodus 35:1–2). In Nehemiah's time people were not, as many are today, required by their employers to work three shifts or rotate schedules—sometimes on the Sabbath. If they worked or traded on the Sabbath, it was for greed. The prophets loudly condemned the attitude that put money and profit before religious commitment, and Nehemiah was in their tradition, as was Jesus (see Matthew 6:24). *10*

10

Write a paragraph that expresses what the prophets might say to our society about our attitude toward money and profit.

The second reform was insisting that Jews not marry foreigners. In Nehemiah's time intermarriage was the quickest way to weaken a people's religious commitment. That was why the Assyrians had demanded that the settlers in the old northern kingdom marry the local Israelites. Those conquerors wanted to weaken the Israelites' sense of who they were as a community and make them easier to control. And as Nehemiah knew, all the years in Babylon had led many Jews to wonder if the Babylonian god Marduk was not the equal of, or even superior to, Israel's God. The threat of divided loyalties was real and had hurt the people in the past. So the requirement that Jews marry only Jews made sense; they needed a clear identity with undivided hearts if they were to go forward as a united people.

Ezra: Recommitting to the Law

Ezra was a priest and scribe who lived in Babylon about a hundred years after the exile. He came to Jerusalem sometime in the period of Nehemiah, probably on a visit. The sequence of events is a bit confusing, but it seems Ezra then went back to Babylon, returning to Jerusalem after several decades.

Ezra loved the Torah—the collection of Scriptures that comprises the first five books of the Bible (Christians call those books the Pentateuch). We can imagine that in Babylon, Ezra was an ardent student of the Torah, perhaps even helping to edit it into book form. Ezra understood that faithfulness to the Law of Moses, God's commandments at the heart of the Torah, was essential for Jews.

We first hear about Ezra in the Book of Nehemiah. But we know about his later work in Jerusalem from the Book of Ezra, where his personal journal is quoted in chapters 7 to 10.

A Jewish bride and groom are together under a ritual scarf, symbolizing their unity, as they stand before the rabbi on their wedding day.

The Prayer of Israel: How to Be Happy

Happy are those
    who do not follow the advice of the wicked,
or take the path that sinners tread,
    or sit in the seat of scoffers;
but their delight is in the law of the LORD,
    and on his law they meditate day and night.
They are like trees
    planted by streams of water,
which yield their fruit in its season,
    and their leaves do not wither.
In all that they do, they prosper.

The wicked are not so,
    but are like chaff that the wind drives away.
Therefore the wicked will not stand in the judgment,
    nor sinners in the congregation of the righteous;
for the LORD watches over the way of the righteous,
    but the way of the wicked will perish.

(Psalm 1)

Helping the People Remember Who They Are

Nehemiah, chapter 8, opens with the people gathered at the water gate. Ezra is reading aloud the Book of the Law, probably the Torah, to the men, the women, and all the children who can understand. When he concludes, they fall to their knees weeping. Both Ezra and Nehemiah bid them to rejoice, not weep, and they celebrate the event as a time of renewal.

The following week the people celebrate the feast of Booths—another name for Sukkoth. For seven days they live outdoors in booths made from tree branches. This is to recall their ancestors' years in the wilder-ness, when God provided for them whatever they needed before they entered Canaan. A number of days after the festival, dressed in sackcloth and covered with ashes, the people confess their sins. Ezra retells the history of Israel to the people and calls them to make a new pact with God. Once again they commit themselves to the Law and reject the sins of their past.

Read Nehemiah 8:1–18. **11**

Firming Up the Boundaries

Ezra evidently goes back to Babylon, but years later (about 398 B.C.) he returns to Jerusalem to do what his heart is set on do-ing—teaching the Torah to the people of Judah. The Persian king gives him permis-sion to go and to take along any Jews who want to go. Ezra is given gold and silver to be used in Temple worship, and the king decides that no taxes will be imposed on anyone who works in the Temple. Obvious-

11

Answer these questions in writing: *When you recall your past, what are you grateful for? What do you regret about your own actions?*

ly, the king wants Ezra to succeed in his mission to Jerusalem.

Once settled in Jerusalem, Ezra turns his attention to reports that in spite of Nehemiah's warnings, the Jews have continued to marry foreign women. Nehemiah set the boundary that Jews may marry only within Judaism in an effort to unify the people and keep them from abandoning their faith. But now that boundary has broken down.

Ezra tears his cloak, pulls out his hair and beard, and in a retelling of Israel's past infidelities, begs God to pardon its wickedness now. Weeping, the people offer to put aside their foreign wives and children. Then after Ezra has prayed, he announces that they must do so at once! But it is the rainy season, and the people, shivering in the cold rain, beg for more time. They are given two months to complete the arrangements. The Book of Ezra ends with this forlorn statement: "All these had married foreign women, and they sent them away with their children" (10:44).

Read Ezra 7:1–27; 8:21–23, 31–33; 9:1–15; 10:1–17, 44.

Hard but necessary boundaries

Again, as with Nehemiah we may wonder at the extreme nature of Ezra's rules about marriage. Were Ezra and Nehemiah rigid men who promoted intolerance and downright bigotry against outsiders? Or were they actually wise leaders who knew that if Judaism was to be cohesive and unified in their time, it had to be exclusive?

Whatever we may think of Ezra and Nehemiah as persons, history has shown that their policies were effective. At a time when the Jewish community was disintegrating, they set the hard but necessary boundaries that would ensure the survival of Judaism.

Ezra's greatest gift to Judaism was his preaching of the Law, or Torah, the core of the Jewish Bible, which had been put into book form in Babylon. He thus provided a

At the festival of Simchas Torah, Jews celebrate the completion of the annual reading of the Torah. They carry the Scriptures in procession while singing and dancing.

kind of constitution for the Jews—rooting their lives in a common faith and a common code of behavior. Judaism has survived because it is centered in the Bible. As people of the Book, they could continue faithfully even after the Temple was destroyed by the Romans in A.D. 70 *12*

Critiques of narrow-mindedness

Some good, faithful Jews in the time of Ezra and Nehemiah no doubt took issue with a certain narrow-mindedness, legalism, and self-righteousness that resulted from their exclusivist policies. Scripture scholars speculate that two books of the Bible were attempts to critique those attitudes.

Recall that the Book of Ruth, probably written after the exile, is a story about a Canaanite woman in the time of the Judges who marries an Israelite and becomes the great-grandmother of King David. So, the author of Ruth seems to be saying, we would not have had our hero David without his ancestor, a foreign woman. God works in mysterious ways, so don't close off your heart.

12

Have you ever had a teacher who was passionate about the subject he or she taught? Write about that teacher and tell how you were affected as a student.

The Book of Joel focuses on a plague of locusts, symbolizing a coming catastrophe if the people refuse to repent.

Then, as we will see in the next chapter of this course, the Book of Jonah is a satirical story of a prophet who bitterly resents it when Judah's old enemies, the Assyrians, repent of their sins and receive God's mercy. The author of the book intended to get across God's universal love for all peoples. But he also must have enjoyed poking fun at the mean-spiritedness of the fictitious prophet Jonah. He held up Jonah's image like a mirror to those Judahites who got carried away with their prejudices.

Joel: Locusts!

The Book of Joel is thought to have been written around 400 B.C.—close to the time that Ezra urged the people to recommit themselves to the Law. The book focuses on a plague of locusts that ravages the land. The plague symbolizes the coming catastrophe of God's judgment on the people for their continuing infidelity.

Joel paints the picture of the plague vividly. Everyone is weeping and wailing. Wheat, barley, fig trees, pomegranates, date palms, and apple trees have dried up. Barns have collapsed; cattle and sheep have perished. Joel bids the people to don sackcloth, proclaim a fast, and beg God to spare them. After the people have fasted and prayed, God promises plenty and peace again.

Read Joel 1:1–12; 2:12–18,28 (or 3:1 in NAB or NJB).

Joel contains some passages that may be familiar to you. One passage (2:12–18) is often heard in Catholic churches on Ash Wednesday, when the forty-day fast of Lent begins. Another passage (2:28, or 3:1 in NAB or NJB) is also well known:

> I will pour out my spirit on all flesh;
> your sons and your daughters shall prophesy,
> your old men shall dream dreams,
> and your young men shall see visions.

Saint Peter would quote these words from Joel in his sermon on the first Pentecost. *Read Acts 2:14–17.* **13**

Obadiah: Woe to Edom!

Obadiah, the shortest book in the Bible, is a one-chapter attack on Edom (a small state in what is now Jordan), possibly for its part in the Babylonians' sack of Jerusalem. Because Esau, the founder of Edom, and Jacob were brothers (recall their rivalry for Abraham's blessing in the Book of Genesis), Obadiah accuses Edom of fratricide—killing one's brother. Edom has been gloating over its brother's ruin, looting his goods, and selling his survivors.

Obadiah is sure that Edom will pay for its crimes, and that Israel deserves better times ahead—and will see them.
Read Obadiah 1:10–15,17,21.

For Review

☐ When Nehemiah arrives in Jerusalem, what is the first project he calls the people to work on?

☐ Give three examples of characteristics that made Nehemiah a model public servant.

☐ What two reforms does Nehemiah enforce? Why were these important boundaries?

☐ What was Ezra's greatest gift to Judaism? How has this gift helped Judaism to survive?

☐ What does the plague of locusts in the Book of Joel symbolize?

13

Write a paragraph about what you think this passage from Joel could mean for our day.

Keeping the Faith Alive Under Fire

The last part of this chapter takes the story of Israel up to about one hundred years before the time of Jesus. We will focus on the two Books of Maccabees and the Book of Daniel, which have as their context the period of Jewish resistance to Greek domination. Before we look at those books, let's get a picture of the historical situation they responded to.

Greek Rule: Being Jewish in a Greek World

The identity of Judaism became firmly established with Ezra and Nehemiah's reforms, which the Persians not only tolerated but supported. However, the era of tolerant Persian oversight ended when the young Greek ruler **Alexander the Great** conquered the Persian Empire in 330 B.C. Then for about two centuries, the **Greek Empire** dominated Judea (the Greco-Roman name for Judah), with periods of terrible persecution that severely tested the faith of the Jews.

The problem of Greek domination was not just that the Greek rulers were harsh and powerful, at times punishing the Jews with torture and death for practicing their religion. Perhaps the subtler but greater problem was the *allure* of the sophisticated Greek lifestyle and bold new way of thinking. The Greek style included the belief that human reason is more important than religious faith, the emphasis on the individual over the community, and an appealing culture of philosophy, drama, literature, science, architecture, and athletic games.

During peaceful periods, when there was not open persecution, the Greek way of life must have seemed quite exciting and "the latest thing" to young Jews, who were accustomed to being considered strange in

The Greek Empire, established by the young ruler Alexander the Great, was oppressive to the Jews at times but also alluring in its sophisticated culture. *Above:* An ancient outdoor theater where classic Greek drama was performed.

The Arch of Titus in Rome contains a scene celebrating the fall of Jerusalem in 70 C.E., in which Romans take the precious menorah from the Temple as loot.

Athens and Rome—and Jerusalem

The golden age of Greece, before the rise of Alexander the Great, was dominated by the city-state Athens, whose highly developed culture spread rapidly throughout the region of the Aegean Sea. Twice in the fifth century B.C., Athens led a military alliance of smaller Greek cities against invasions by the Persians. After peace was re-established, Athens acquired wealth, produced magnificent architecture—such as the buildings of the Acropolis—and nurtured the concept of a democracy, which allowed its male citizens to vote and to judge cases in courts of law.

Athens' politicians, philosophers, poets, dramatists, and artists produced works held in the highest esteem all over the world, works that have given "the classical period" and "the classics" their name.

Even after the death of Alexander in the second century B.C. and the conquest of Greece by Rome, Greek culture continued to dominate the eastern Mediterranean. Its language became an international tongue that even found its way into the Gospels and the Epistles. Greek culture continued to inspire the art and literature of the Romans, although the Greek democratic form of government, and Rome's republican model, began to disappear. By the time of Jesus, emperors and not the senate ruled the Romans—among whose captive peoples was a rebellious province called Judea.

The first Jewish revolt, which was crushed by Titus—son of a Roman emperor—cost a reputed one million Jewish lives. In A.D. 70 Titus destroyed Jerusalem and the Temple, which was never rebuilt. And in the year A.D. 135 following a second rebellion, Jews were forbidden to enter Jerusalem.

the Greek world because of their religion. With the Greek language becoming popular, many young people did not even learn Hebrew anymore. And within a few generations, Greek became the language of everyday life for most Jews. In fact some of the later books of the Bible were originally written in Greek because so many Jews did not understand Hebrew. *14*

14

Think of an example of persons or groups who are in conflict because one side wants to take on the new and the other wants to hold on to the old. Then share your opinion on this question: *Is it possible to accept and adapt to the new and yet remain faithful to the old?*

Imagine what a struggle the Greek influence must have caused within the Jewish community. How could Jews live with the rapid introduction of Greek language, philosophy, and customs, yet remain faithful to the God of Israel? The boundaries set so firmly by Ezra and Nehemiah were under attack as the dominant Greek culture eroded traditional Jewish life.

Some Jews insisted on the old ways, allowing no concession to Greek thinking or customs. Another group believed that compromise was possible, that adaptation to things Greek—even abandonment of Jewish religious practices—was the realistic method of survival. These two groups grew further and further apart. Soon their conflict mushroomed into full-scale civil war between the pro-Greek Jews and the anti-Greek Jews.

Like the Amish people today, whose traditions and appearance make them stand out as different from the rest of society, Jews of the second century B.C.E. seemed peculiar to the Greek culture that surrounded them.

The anti-Greek Jews' resistance to Greek domination grew until the Greek Seleucid dynasty that controlled Judea decided to squash the opposition. This situation is the historical context for the Books of Maccabees and the Book of Daniel. *15*

The Books of Maccabees: Taking On the Greek Empire

The two Books of Maccabees were written by two unknown authors around 100 B.C.— but they are set in the period of harsh Greek persecution that began in 175 B.C. First Maccabees is a history of the revolt of the Jews under the domination of Greek rulers. It tells of the struggle of Judas Maccabeus and his brothers to free the Jews from Greek control, confirms that God is with the people, exalts the Jews who remain faithful, and condemns the apostates (those who have renounced their faith).

Second Maccabees tells in detail of a cruel persecution of the Jews. It confirms belief in the resurrection of the dead, the intercession of the saints, and the offering of prayers for the dead.

Greek Oppression Heats Up

The First Book of Maccabees opens when the Seleucid king **Antiochus IV** comes to the throne in 175 B.C., calling himself Epiphanes, meaning "God made visible." His subjects soon change this name to Epimanes, meaning "madman."

15

If you were told by the government that you no longer are allowed to express your faith or practice your religion—under threat of death—what effect would that have on your life? Describe in writing what you would do and how you might feel about the situation.

An ancient Greek sculpture of a discus thrower. Discus is still one of the sports in the Olympic Games, world athletic competitions that originated with the Greeks.

burn houses, kill people, and build a citadel, or fortress. The citadel is to house more military troops who will occupy Jerusalem; it is also to be a haven for protecting the apostate Jews, those who have abandoned Judaism.

When these measures fail to counter Jewish resistance, Antiochus orders that everyone in his realm must embrace his religion. Under penalty of death, the Jews must abandon their Law, destroy their scrolls, offer sacrifices to Greek gods, cease circumcision, and ignore their dietary rules. The Temple is defiled by the occupiers, the altar profaned with sacrifices of swine, and, most horrible of all to the Jews, an altar to the god Zeus is erected on the altar of holocausts! But many Jews stand firm in their resolve to be faithful.

Read 1 Maccabees 1:1–63.

Heroic Martyrdom for the Sake of the Young

At this time a Jewish elder named **Eleazar** has been arrested by the Greeks for his refusal to eat pork, a meat forbidden by Jewish Law as being unclean. In charge of his execution are young Jews who work for the Greek authorities. They have known Eleazar all their lives and are deeply disturbed at the thought of his death. They propose to bring him meat that is not pork but looks like pork. He can eat it without breaking the Law yet dupe the king by seeming to eat pork. Eleazar replies to their scheme in effect, "If you think that to save my life for a few short years, I would scandalize all the young who are watching me, you are quite mistaken." And he dies, "leaving in his death an example of nobility and a memorial of courage, not only to the young but to the great body of his nation" (2 Maccabees 6:31).

Read 2 Maccabees 6:18–31.

In Jerusalem the pro-Greek Jews, led by a corrupt high priest, build a gymnasium where young men participate in athletic events naked—a practice that the traditional Jews condemn; those in the games hide their marks of circumcision so as not to be obviously Jewish. Then when Antiochus takes the treasures from the Temple to pay for his military adventures, animosity among the faithful Jews mounts. Two years later Antiochus sends a military force to Jerusalem to control the anti-Greek Jews. The soldiers

I-Witness: Esdras

I'm Esdras and running was my game. I practiced hours each day—javelin throwing, wrestling—but mainly distance running. I'm light and long-legged, so I could run the sandals off almost anybody.

I have trained since childhood, but now, when I am old enough to participate in the big events in Jerusalem, they won't let me in. "They" meaning the Jews who love Greek ways.

I love Greek ways too. I speak in Greek, and the whole idea of athletic games came here from the Greek world. But I'm a Jew and a Jew first. I can't go onto the athletic field naked, and even if I could, I wouldn't hide that I'm circumcised—the mark of my faith.

My family applauds my decision to leave athletics, but I don't think they realize how much it hurts. I wonder about my future too. My family hasn't any wealth or influence, so I counted on being a champion. Champions are treated well by the Greeks. Now what do I do with my life?

Norwegian "Eleazars" stand up to the Nazis

During the Second World War, the country of Norway, conquered by Nazi Germany, witnessed its own "Eleazar-like" example of integrity. When the fascist puppet government ordered all teachers to promote fascism in their classrooms and join a fascist union, the teachers refused—knowing they risked death. Instead, they each read this statement to their students:

"The teacher's vocation is not only to give children knowledge; teachers must also teach their pupils to believe in and uphold truth and justice. Therefore, teachers cannot, without betraying their calling, teach anything that violates their conscience. . . . That, I promise you, I shall not do." (Quoted in Sider and Taylor, *Nuclear Holocaust and Christian Hope,* page 239)

Five hundred teachers were arrested and hauled off to a concentration camp in the frigid north of Norway. As trainloads of teachers went through the mountains, Norwegian children lined the railroad tracks to sing patriotic songs and encourage their teachers. Two teachers died in the camp.

Like Eleazar's loving, courageous witness to young Jews under Greek oppression, the teachers' message of integrity to their students and the world will last forever.

A Mother and Her Seven Sons: We Shall Live Again

The Second Book of Maccabees tells about the same period of persecution under Antiochus IV as in the First Book of Maccabees. A remarkable incident testifies to the courage and magnificent faith of the Jerusalem Jews.

A mother and her seven sons are arrested for refusing to eat pork. When torture fails to persuade them, the mother is forced to watch all her sons, from the eldest to the youngest, endure unspeakable torments and be put to death, after which the mother is also slain.

As several of the sons go to their horrible deaths, they and their mother proclaim their belief that they will live again with God and one another. "'One cannot but choose to die at the hands of mortals and to cherish the hope God gives of being raised again by him. But for you there will be no resurrection to life!'" (2 Maccabees 7:14) one

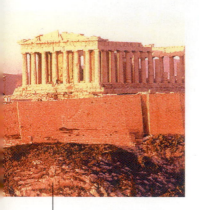

The Parthenon, the temple to the Greek goddess Athena, is built on the Acropolis, the fortified height of ancient Athens, Greece.

brother, near death, declares to his torturers. And the last brother to be killed says, "For our brothers after enduring a brief suffering have drunk of ever-flowing life, under God's covenant" (7:36). The account remarks, simply and eloquently, "So he died in his integrity, putting his whole trust in the Lord" (7:40).

Read 2 Maccabees 7:1–42. **16**

The belief in resurrection

The story of the martyrdom of the mother and her seven sons is a powerful testimony to the belief in **resurrection**— that God will raise the just to new life after death. This belief was just emerging within Judaism in the late centuries before Christ. Belief in resurrection also appears in the Book of Daniel.

The Maccabees: A Revolt That Succeeds

The remainder of the First Book of Maccabees tells of an exciting military adventure—how a Jewish family led by one brother named **Judas,** also called **Maccabeus** (the hammerer), takes on the mighty Greek Empire (a revolt that began in 166 B.C.) and

manages to achieve a measure of independence for little Judea. Along the way the rebels also kill pro-Greek Jews. In the Maccabees' mind, violent resistance is the only way left to keep the Jewish faith alive under such an oppressive empire.

We will not go into the ins and outs, plots and betrayals involved in the Maccabees' winning this degree of independence for Judea, which can be read in the First Book of Maccabees. It is enough to say that by 164 B.C. the Jews take back control of the Jerusalem Temple, which has been defiled by the Greeks. The region continues to be under Seleucid rule. But for certain periods, interspersed with wars and persecutions, Judea is allowed to govern itself—until the Roman Empire takes over Judea in 63 B.C. **17**

The Origins of Hanukkah

The Jewish **feast of Hanukkah** has its origins in the celebration that followed the rededication of the Temple after the Greeks had defiled it. Here is how it came about:

The Maccabees find the Temple forlorn and abandoned—its altar desecrated, the gates burned, and weeds growing in the courts.

16

Eleazar, the teachers from Norway, and the mother and her seven sons all showed incredible faithfulness and integrity. The choices they made were not just for themselves, but more important, for the people who were watching them. Through our choices we may teach or influence others toward good or away from it. Write about a situation when you might have influenced another person by the choices you made.

17

Write your thoughts on these questions:
- Is violent resistance the only way to overcome oppression?
- If so, why do you think that way?
- If not, what are other solutions?

First they mourn; then they get to work. They purify the sanctuary and the courts, remove the profaned altar and build a new one, make new sacred vessels, light a new lamp, hang curtains, and place fresh loaves on the altar of holocausts. A year from the day of its defilement, the Temple is consecrated again. The people celebrate for eight days, and Judas decrees that these days be celebrated on the anniversary every year. This is the event celebrated by our Jewish brothers and sisters on their feast of Hanukkah.

Read 1 Maccabees 4:36–59.

The Festival of Lights

On the celebration of Hanukkah, Jews tell a much-loved legend not found in the Bible:

When the priests, led by Judas Maccabeus, were about to light the menorah, the seven-branched candelabra, they were alarmed to find that the specially prepared oil was gone. Jugs of this oil were always kept sealed by the high priests, but only one small jar was left—barely enough oil for one night. But to their delight, the oil miraculously lasted for eight full days while the people celebrated and prepared more oil.

Hanukkah, which takes place in early December, is also called the Festival of Lights and is celebrated for eight days with prayer and praise. In Jewish homes tiny candles or oil lamps are lighted on a candelabra, one each day, and gifts are given to the children.

In the Temple, the menorah had seven branches for candles. Today during Hanukkah, Jews have a nine-branched menorah. One candle is used to light the other eight, representing the eight days that the oil miraculously lasted during the Maccabees' celebration of rededicating the Temple.

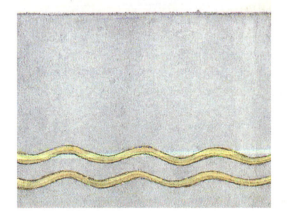

Daniel: Stories and Visions for the Faint of Heart

"Resist Greek oppression with all your heart! Do not give in to the Greeks and do not compromise the faith!" This was the message the Jewish people needed to hear during the era when the Greek Empire threatened to wipe out their religion. The spiritual boundaries of Judaism, drawn so firmly by Ezra and Nehemiah three centuries earlier, had to be defended, or Judaism would cease to exist and Israel would never become a light to the nations. *18*

The Maccabees offered a strategy of resistance—a military campaign for Jewish independence. But the anonymous author of the Book of Daniel offered a different response—a spiritual and theological approach that contrasted sharply with the

18

The biblical Jews wanted to preserve their heritage—a desire we can all share. Write a paragraph detailing your ethnic background and describing any family customs and stories associated with it.

The Book of Daniel tells of steadfast trust in God, not violence, as the response to religious persecution. *Left:* Pakistani soldiers in 1998 attack Christians who nonviolently protest the country's laws that discriminate against Christian beliefs. *Right:* The United Farm Workers, a union founded on Christian nonviolent principles, marches to honor its founder, Cesar Chavez.

violent strategy of the Maccabees. Writing during the time of the Greek persecution, the author of Daniel tried to inspire the Jews to *nonviolent* resistance, with a radical trust in God's power to make everything come out right in the end. Both approaches aimed at preserving the boundaries of Judaism and remaining faithful to God. But the Maccabees focused on human power and might to set things right, while the author of Daniel held out God's love and justice as the ultimate power that saves.

Although the stories and visions in the Book of Daniel are set in Babylon in the time of the exile, they really address the situation of the Jews under Greek rule. But to keep from being killed himself by the Greeks, the author had to avoid any direct references to the Greek oppressors in his writing. So the book is filled with code names and plenty of analogies to the plight of the Jews living under Greek rule, which they, but not the Greeks, would have readily understood. It was a clever way to resist—inspiring frightened people with hope-filled

stories and visions from another time and place. It was not unlike what the black slaves of the U.S. South did, as they fired up their dreams of freedom by telling the old stories of Moses and the escape of the Israelites from slavery in Egypt, all through God's power.

In the Fiery Furnace and the Lion's Den

Chapters 1 to 6 of Daniel tell stories about a young man named **Daniel** and his friends who, in the time of the exile in Babylon, refuse to give in to their rulers' demands that they worship idols. Most familiar are the stories of the three young men in the fiery furnace and the story of Daniel in the lion's den. In these wonderfully told stories, we see that the refusal to give up the faith leads to fierce persecution. But in the end, God's power saves the resisters from harm.

Read Daniel, chapters 3 and 6. (The NAB and NJB versions include the entire text of chapter 3; the NRSV puts the verses of a prayer and a song of praise into the apocryphal or deuterocanonical Scriptures.) **19**

19

Martyrs are people who are persecuted and killed because they refuse to abandon their faith and religion. Find out about a martyr and write an essay about her or him.

No harm done?

What was the author of the Book of Daniel trying to say to young Jews under Greek persecution? On face value we might

think the stories mean: "Go ahead. Refuse to give in to the Greeks. You'll never be killed anyway because God will not let them harm you." But the author and the Jews of his time knew that Jews who resisted the Greeks were being killed on a regular basis. They would have been aware of persons like Eleazar and the mother and her seven sons, martyrs for Judaism who suffered brutal torture before dying.

The storyteller of Daniel was trying to say something deeper to the Jews under Greek persecution: *Ultimately, you will not be harmed. You may die in the physical sense, but your spirit will not be crushed. God will be with you and save you for the kind of life that lasts forever.*

In the twentieth century, such a hope has inspired nonviolent resistance leaders. For instance, **Martin Luther King Jr.,** of the U.S. civil rights movement, and **Mohandas Gandhi,** of the movement for India's independence from Britain, were eventually assassinated for their causes. Likewise people like the teachers of fascist Norway risked death because they believed in something more precious than physical life—their own lasting integrity and that of their nation. **20**

The Book of Daniel, like the Second Book of Maccabees, points to life after

Mohandas Gandhi, *left,* believed in the power of "soul force" or "truth force" over evil and oppression. Similarly, the story of Daniel in the lions' den affirms that integrity, faith, and trust in God ultimately will save us from harm.

20

Write a letter—you can send it if you wish—to someone who is going through a time that seems overwhelming and defeating. What words of hope can you offer?

The Prayer of Israel: "We Will Not Fear"

God is our refuge and strength,
    a very present help in trouble.
Therefore we will not fear, though the earth should change,
    though the mountains shake in the heart of the sea;
though its waters roar and foam,
    though the mountains tremble with its tumult.

There is a river whose streams make glad the city of God,
    the holy habitation of the Most High.
God is in the midst of the city; it shall not be moved;
    God will help it when the morning dawns.
The nations are in an uproar, the kingdoms totter;
    he utters his voice, the earth melts.
The LORD of hosts is with us;
    the God of Jacob is our refuge.

Come, behold the works of the LORD;
    see what desolations he has brought on the earth.
He makes wars cease to the end of the earth;
    he breaks the bow, and shatters the spear;
    he burns the shields with fire.
"Be still, and know that I am God!
    I am exalted among the nations,
    I am exalted in the earth."
The LORD of hosts is with us;
    the God of Jacob is our refuge.

(Psalm 46)

death, to resurrection, and to an unquench-able hope in God despite circumstances that seem overwhelming and defeating.

Visions of How It Will All Turn Out

With chapter 7 of Daniel, the book turns to Daniel's bizarre and disturbing visions. In one dream, four powerful beasts—repre-senting four nations that are Israel's ene-mies—rise out of a boiling sea. But God condemns them and gives dominion to "one like a son of man" (7:13, NAB)—meaning one like a human being—whom all peoples and nations will one day serve as king in an everlasting reign.

Read Daniel 7:12–14.

In a later vision, an angel tells Daniel that great anguish will one day come to his people but that the just will be delivered from harm. Many "who sleep in the dust of the earth shall awake, some to everlasting life, and some to shame and everlasting contempt" (Daniel 12:2). Those who lead others to justice will shine like the stars for all eternity. These words affirm a belief in the afterlife and in resurrection similar to the belief we saw in the Second Book of Maccabees.

The Son of Man

Jesus used the term *Son of Man* eighty-two times in the Gospels, sometimes clearly referring to himself. Christians have always seen Jesus Christ as the fulfillment of the promise in the Book of Daniel of the coming reign of "one like a son of man."

Read Matthew 26:59–64.

Apocalyptic literature

Daniel's visions in chapters 7 to 12 are prime examples of **apocalyptic literature,** a form of writing widely used in Judaism from about 200 B.C. to A.D. 200. The Book of Revelation in the New Testament is also of this type. This kind of writing is characterized by strange symbolic images that represent events, places, and even particular people of the time in which it is written. Usually that is a period of crisis or persecution, such as the persecution of the Jews by the Greeks or of the early Christians by the

The strange symbolism of apocalyptic literature is depicted in this fourteenth-century French tapestry.

"Many of those who sleep in the dust of the earth shall awake, some to everlasting life, and some to shame and everlasting contempt." **Daniel 12:2**

Romans. Thus the author uses a pseudonym to disguise the writer's identity. The literature's bizarre symbols are code language for those "in the know," which keeps the true subject of the writing secret from the oppressors.

Apocalyptic writing was intended to give hope and inspiration to those oppressed by powerful forces. It affirms that in the great cosmic struggle between good and evil in the world, the power of good—that is, the power of God—will prevail in the end. For those who are in distress, apocalyptic literature offers a bold, rallying vision of God's ultimate triumph over injustice and suffering. It proclaims with deep conviction that in the end God is in charge, and he will win. The message for the audience, in so many words, is this: "Bear suffering patiently now and keep your faith, because one day God's victory will be ours!"

Apocalyptic literature has often been misunderstood to predict certain real events in the future. For example, some have claimed the Book of Revelation predicts a global catastrophe like nuclear war or the fall of particular world powers like the Soviet Union. We are living in a new millenium, and as expected, we have heard a great flurry of claims that symbols from apocalyptic literature, particularly the Book of Revelation, are being played out in contemporary world events. However, such claims show an inadequate understanding of apocalyptic literature and are distractions from the powerful message that the writer intended.

For Review

- Besides the Greeks' persecution of the Jews, what aspects of Greek domination threatened traditional Jewish life?
- In what ways does King Antiochus Epiphanes persecute Jews in Jerusalem?
- Why does Eleazar not eat meat that looks like pork, even though doing so would save his life?
- What story in the Second Book of Maccabees gives testimony to the belief in a resurrection and afterlife?
- What event in Jewish history is celebrated each year on the feast of Hanukkah?
- Contrast the Maccabees' strategy of resisting the Greeks with that of the author of the Book of Daniel.
- In whom do Christians see fulfilled Daniel's prophecy of the coming reign of "one like a son of man" (Daniel 7:13, NAB)?
- Why does apocalyptic literature, like that in the Book of Daniel, use strange symbolic images and code language? What is the intent of the authors of this type of literature?

Up to the Time of Jesus

The scriptural history of Israel comes to an end with the Maccabees accounts and the apocalyptic visions of Daniel, which emerged from the period of Greek persecution. As noted earlier in this chapter, in 63 B.C. the Romans conquered the Greeks and took over the region of Palestine, in which Judea was located. At the time of Jesus' birth (about 5 B.C.), the little territory was tightly under the huge thumb of the **Roman Empire,** the most powerful and efficient of the ancient empires. Many Jews put their hopes in a messiah sent from God, "one like a son of man" (Daniel 7:13, NAB). They believed this messiah would save them, transforming them from a humiliated, subjugated people to a people whose destiny as a beacon of God's love and light to the world would finally be fulfilled.

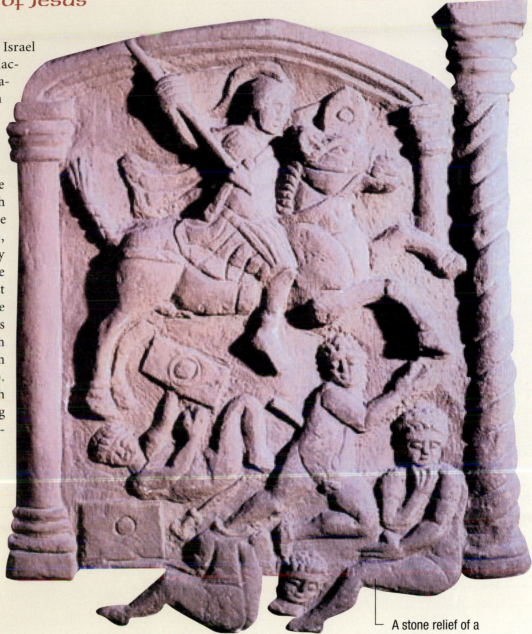

A stone relief of a brutal Roman conquest

10 Wisdom and Wit

Seeking the Ways of God

The wisdom books explore the meaning and purpose of human existence: Why are we here? Where are we going?

During the centuries before the birth of Jesus, as noted in chapter 9, the people of Israel were under foreign domination. Judah (later called Judea) fell under Babylonian control, followed by Persian, Greek, and finally Roman rule. In the Dispersion that resulted, Jews were scattered beyond Palestine to places far from home, where they settled as strangers in strange lands. Whether in Judea or far away, Jews were controlled by the major empires. So they had to respond to the challenges that foreign cultures and powers brought to every aspect of their life.

The Old Testament books considered in this chapter were composed at various times after the Babylonian exile, some quite late, when foreign influences were swirling around Judaism. First the chapter focuses on six **wisdom books: Proverbs, Job, Ecclesiastes, Sirach, Wisdom,** and the **Song of Songs.** Then it turns to the wonderful stories told in the Books of **Tobit, Judith, Esther,** and **Jonah.** The **Psalms,** also counted among the wisdom books, will be treated in chapter 11.

In different ways the authors of the books covered in this chapter tried to address questions such as these:

- What does it mean to be a wise person?
- What is the meaning and purpose of life? Where are we going?
- Why do good people suffer and bad people prosper? Why should we be good in a world that is unfair?
- How can we live good and faithful lives when surrounded by those who are hostile to our beliefs?

Life According to Proverbs, Job, and Ecclesiastes: What's It All About?

Before exploring the first three of the wisdom books, let's look at biblical wisdom literature in general. It grew out of a kind of writing that flourished in non-Jewish cultures of the ancient Near East, especially in Egypt. These earlier writings instructed administrators in royal courts on how to act. They contained maxims on the acquiring of virtues and, often, on the problem of good versus evil—although they were not religious texts.

Influenced by such literature, Jewish sages (wise teachers) adapted these kinds of wisdom writing to Israel's own faith, which saw God as the source of all wisdom. Israel's wisdom books speak to the individual about the wholeness and integrity of a good life, and about the personal disintegration caused by sin. The goal of the biblical teachers of wisdom was to inspire moral integrity.

Proverbs: What Is a Good Life?

The Book of Proverbs appeared sometime after the Babylonian exile, during the period of the second Temple. It consists of several collections of wisdom teachings, intended to instruct the young especially. Some sections of the book are probably from as early as Solomon's monarchy, when scribes in the royal court collected and wrote down wise sayings.

Proverbs, like other wisdom writings, is concerned with how to live a good life; it is full of down-to-earth, practical advice. Here is a sampling:

- *Parenting.* "Discipline your children while there is hope; / do not set your heart on their destruction" (19:18).
- *Communication.* "A soft answer turns away wrath, / but a harsh word stirs up anger" (15:1).

Laborers harvesting the fields on a farm in Israel. Many of the proverbs affirm the value of hard work and condemn idleness.

A Jewish Orthodox school in Jerusalem

- *Attitudes.* "Pride goes before destruction, / and a haughty spirit before a fall" (16:18).

- *Manners at court.* "A gift opens doors; / it gives access to the great" (18:16).

- *Work.* "In all toil there is profit, / but mere talk leads only to poverty" (14:23).

- *Conducting business.* "The integrity of the upright guides them, / but the crookedness of the treacherous destroys them" (11:3).

- *Reputation.* "A good name is to be chosen rather than great riches, / and favor is better than silver or gold" (22:1).

- *Leadership.* "If a ruler listens to falsehood, / all his officials will be wicked" (29:12).

- *Gossip.* "A perverse person spreads strife, / and a whisperer separates close friends" (16:28).

- *Learning.* "A fool takes no pleasure in understanding, / but only in expressing personal opinion" (18:2).

- *Relationships with neighbors.* "A generous person will be enriched, / and one who gives water will get water" (11:25). *1*

You may have noticed in these examples a literary device that is typical of wisdom sayings. The same wise truth is stated in two ways. For instance: "Misfortune pursues sinners, / but prosperity rewards the righteous" (13:21). We might imagine young Jews of biblical times memorizing these sayings in school, with the teacher calling out the first half of the proverb, and the students responding with the second. It could have been an enjoyable way to learn, especially with the clever word plays and sounds that can be appreciated only in the sayings' original Hebrew language.

1

Choose one of these proverbs and write about an experience from your life that illustrates its meaning.

Rash words are like sword thrusts, but the tongue of the wise brings healing.

Proverbs 12:18

According to Proverbs, success and prosperity, rightly gained, are the reward for a virtuous life. Honor, dignity, and a good name are a person's memorial—there is no hint of an afterlife. The importance of living prudently, honestly, generously, and diligently can be seen in a famous passage about the "ideal wife," which ends the Book of Proverbs. *Read Proverbs 31:10–31.* **2**

You might wonder, Where is God in all this wisdom? Most of the sayings do not mention God. However, the perspective of the Jewish sages was that true wisdom is from God, no matter where we find it—in the advice of family and friends, in common sense, in nature, even in other cultures with their appealing wisdom sayings. The sages saw the world as full of God's wisdom. Strikingly, in chapters 8 and 9 of Proverbs, wisdom is portrayed poetically as a woman who came forth from God in the beginning before the world was created. She was with God as the "master worker" while the heavens and the earth were made; thus wisdom fills the whole world. So it is not surprising that the sages looked to everyday experience of the world to find wisdom. *Read Proverbs 8:1–11,22–31.* **3**

In Proverbs, wisdom is portrayed as a woman who was with God at Creation as the master worker.

Wisdom's feminine voice

Proverbs' image of God's wisdom as a woman adds a feminine voice and quality to the traditional Jewish image of God as masculine. This feminine image of wisdom has been called Lady Sophia, after the Greek word for wisdom.

Of course we know that God is neither man nor woman. God is personal but transcends the human categories of gender. The biblical writers used male and female images to describe God because that was what they knew of persons from their human experience.

Catholic Tradition has often read the beautiful passages on wisdom in the Old

---

2

Write three proverbs that would be good advice for our age.

3

Write about someone you know who is wise. Give an example of a circumstance when he or she demonstrated wisdom.

Testament as related to Mary, the mother of God. Mary is called the Seat of Wisdom in some prayers of the liturgy.

Job: Why Do the Good Suffer?

While the wisdom writers of the Book of Proverbs taught that a virtuous life brings success and prosperity, an unknown Jewish sage after the Babylonian exile was questioning that mentality. "Wait a minute," he must have reasoned, "it's not necessarily the case that good people have wealth, health, and the admiration of their family and community. What about the good people who have a miserable life of poverty, sickness, and rejection? And what about the wicked people who have tons of money and a grand, comfortable life? How do you explain that?" Most Jews of the time, including this sage, did not believe in an afterlife where good could be rewarded and evil punished. They thought that rewards and punishments had to be given out in this life, or never at all.

Many people today, even those who believe in the afterlife, struggle with the same kind of questions: Why does a mother of three young children die? Why do people starve in a famine while others have so much food they don't know what to do with it? Why were six million innocent Jews killed by the Nazis during World War II? The dilemma of why the good suffer and the wicked prosper in this life is known as the **problem of evil.** We first saw this issue raised in Israel's consciousness by the prophet Habakkuk, who asked, "Why?" (See page 186 of this text.) *4*

The author of the Book of Job struggled with that dilemma and wrote a poetic story considered one of the world's great literary treasures. In it a virtuous and prosperous man named Job loses everything—wealth, family, health. He bears his suffering patiently, trusting in, not questioning God.

Read Job 1:1–22; 2:1–13. (The figure of Satan in the story is not meant to be the devil but a heavenly prosecutor whose job is

to test the genuineness of human virtue. The author used this angel merely as a device to get the story moving, not to imply that God ever initiates human suffering.)

In his suffering Job finally calls out, "Why?" and curses the day he was born. His friends insist that Job's sin must be the reason for his misfortune, that if he prays to God and repents, all will be well again. But Job disagrees, arguing with them in a series of disputes.

Read the following passages from Job:

- *3:1–3,11–26 (Job's cries)*
- *4:7–9 (the words of Job's friend Eliphaz)*
- *6:8–10,24–25 (Job's reply to Eliphaz)*

Jews in the Warsaw ghetto in Poland being taken off to a concentration camp during World War II. The Book of Job and people throughout history have asked, Why do the innocent suffer?

4

Have you ever asked *why* in the face of something terrible and undeserved? If so, write a brief reflection about it.

- *8:3–7 (the words of Job's friend Bildad)*
- *11:1–6 (the words of Job's friend Zophar)*
- *13:1–5,15–16 (Job's reply to Zophar)*
- *27:3–6 (Job's words to Bildad)*
- *33:1–6,8–13 (the words of a young man named Elihu)*

At last, after all the arguing has brought no satisfying answers, God, who has been silent all along, speaks out of a whirlwind to Job:

"Where were you when I laid the foundation of the earth?
    Tell me, if you have understanding.
Who determined its measurements—surely you know!" (Job 38:4–5)

In a long discourse, God reminds Job that he, not Job, is the Creator of the universe who sustains everything in existence. Job, awed and humbled, admits that the mystery of life is too great for him to understand. God's wisdom is far beyond his own. At last Job believes this truth and accepts what has happened.
    Read Job 38:1–30; 39:19–30; 42:1–6. [5]

The "answer"
Christians believe that all suffering—even suffering caused by natural events—is the consequence of Original Sin (see page 33). But this doctrine was not fully understood by the author of the Book of Job, so the author does not give a definite answer to the question of why good people suffer. But the author clearly dismisses the easy answers of Job's smug friends—that suffering is a punishment from God and prosperity is a sign of God's approval. Rather than answers, the story leaves Job with a sense of humility in the face of mystery: some things are simply beyond the grasp of the human mind, and all we can do is bow before the mystery of God.

The message of the Book of Job is that even in the darkest moments, God is in charge, loving and caring for us through it all.

Ecclesiastes: Is Life Lived in Vain?

Another sage reflected on the meaning of life during the time the Jews were under Greek rule, about 250 B.C. Like the author of Job, he questioned the common notion that virtue leads to good fortune, and wickedness to misfortune. "It's not so simple! Life is a lot messier than that," he seemed to say. His res-

[5]
What do you think of God's "answer" to Job? Write your own response to God.

ponse was the Book of Ecclesiastes, a Greek word for the name Qoheleth, which is Hebrew for "teacher." (His pupils thought of him as *the* teacher.)

The book is known for what appears to be a pessimistic outlook on life. Where Habakkuk and Job asked God, "Why?" Qoheleth's response to life's inconsistencies was, "Who's surprised?" On the other hand, he may have been the kind of man who liked to startle his students with unexpected questions and provocative comments—just to make them think. For example:

- In his book Qoheleth says that nothing makes a difference—people are born, die, and are forgotten, and there is nothing new under the sun: "Vanity of vanities! All is vanity!" (1:2). (Here *vanity* means "futility" or "meaninglessness.")

- Then he reverses this dour comment with his famous poem (3:1–8): "For everything there is a season, and a time for every matter under heaven. . . ."

- At the poem's conclusion he seems to say that all things, including reward for the righteous and punishment for the wicked, will be accomplished in God's time (3:17), though we cannot expect to understand God's ways.

Qoheleth worried about injustice and wickedness and about their victims, who were doomed, he believed, to a dead end in earthly life. As for eternity, he knew nothing of a heaven hereafter. But in the end he came to the conclusion that life was a mystery he could not solve. The sensible thing, he says in his book, is to accept it from the hand of God and enjoy it as well as one can.

Read Ecclesiastes 1:1–11; 2:18–26; 3:1–22. [6]

For Review

- [ ] What was the main goal of the biblical teachers of wisdom?
- [ ] Give three examples of quotations from the Book of Proverbs that give practical advice.
- [ ] According to Proverbs, what is the reward for a virtuous life?
- [ ] What is meant by the problem of evil?
- [ ] What is the message of the Book of Job?
- [ ] What conclusion does Qoheleth come to in Ecclesiastes?

A businessman surveys what is left of his office after a tornado. The author of the Book of Ecclesiastes questioned the common notion that virtue leads to good fortune, and wickedness to misfortune.

6

Write a reaction to Qoheleth's attitude toward life. Do you agree or disagree with him? Why?

Wisdom and Wit **251**

I-Witness: Sheba

My name is Sheba, and I live in Alexandria, Egypt—the land where our ancestors lived in slavery under the ancient pharaohs. Pharaohs still reign, but since the time that Alexander was buried here, they are Greeks. We have had queens as well as kings among these Greek pharaohs.

Women count for something in Greek philosophy as well as politics. In Greek tradition wisdom is a goddess, Athena. I like that thought, although I am devoutly Jewish, and I love that the Torah was first translated intro Greek here.

While I don't read or write myself, I have good ears and a good mind. I hear my father and brothers and their friends discussing the latest thinking on many topics. Once in a while, they let me join their conversations. And in the forums, I sometimes stop to listen to the public debates. Alexandria's great teachers, Greek and Jewish, make it the most exciting city in the world.

Sirach:
Wisdom in the Teachings of Israel

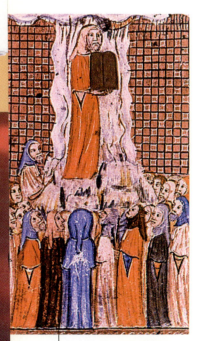

A depiction of Moses at Mount Sinai giving the Ten Commandments to the Israelites

A man named Jesus ben Sirach ran a school for scriptural study and Jewish wisdom in Alexandria, Egypt (then under the Greek Empire), and wrote between 200 and 175 B.C. He wanted to instruct his fellow Jews who were confused by the philosophical questions of the Greeks. He wrote that all wisdom comes from God—not from Greek thought!

The Book of Sirach depicts wisdom as a woman who was with God at Creation—like the image described in the Book of Proverbs. Unlike most Jewish wisdom literature, though, Sirach is deeply concerned with the history of Israel, its heroes, and its institutions. According to Sirach, wisdom's home is in Israel. Wisdom is found specifically in the teachings of Israel as given by God, and keeping the Commandments is the way to wisdom. (The book's alternate name is Ecclesiasticus, which means "church book," but that title should not be confused with Ecclesiastes.)

The advice given in the Book of Sirach is as full of wisdom for us as it was for the ancients.

Read Sirach 1:19–23; 2:1–6; 3:1–4; 4:1–5,8–10; 5:9–14 (or 5:11–17 in NAB); 6:8–12,14–17; 11:1–3,7–9; 24:1–8. [7]

In praise of wisdom

Chapter 24 of Sirach is one of the greatest writings about wisdom in the Bible. Sirach says that wisdom came forth from the mouth of God to make her dwelling with Jacob's people. He is reminding the Jews, and us, that God's wisdom is far above the wisdom of the world.

7

If you were to personify wisdom, would it be young or old? male or female? human or another animal? Create a written portrait of wisdom. Once you have thoroughly described wisdom, let it speak: what is its wisest saying?

Wisdom's testing

Wisdom tests us with difficulties. Times of difficulty can be seed times, times for growing strong.

A story is told of a man who saw a monarch butterfly struggling to get out of its cocoon. Wanting to help it, he took his penknife and carefully slit the cocoon to free the butterfly. To his astonishment, the butterfly gave a few flutters and died. Cutting it free was the worst thing the man could have done. The butterfly needed to struggle in order to strengthen its wings.

The Song of Songs: Human and Divine Love

The Song of Songs is one of the wisdom books, but it differs from the others in theme and concern. Rather than a book of teachings about wisdom, it is a collection of love poems written by unknown authors sometime after the Babylonian exile, about 450 B.C. It is a dialogue between a bridegroom and a bride, who speak of their love and longing for each other, with now-and-again asides from their friends. Some of the most beautiful, passionate poetry in the world can be found in this book. (At one time the book was attributed to King Solomon, so in some Bible versions it is called the Song of Solomon.)

Why is the Song of Songs a book of the Bible, when it does not even mention God? Some people think even its language of love and sexuality are inappropriate for a holy book. But the ancient Jews and Christians who decided to include it in their respective Bibles recognized that God designed human love as a powerful and holy bond. In itself, human love is good and a gift from God.

Early interpreters of the book saw the work as a religious allegory. For both Jews and Christians, the bride and groom's mutual love was an image of God's love for and passionate devotion to Israel. For Christians, it was also a figure of Christ's love for his "bride," the Church, and also for the soul of an individual believer.

In the Song of Songs, the bride describes herself as dark, like the tents of Kedar that are woven from black goat's hair. She wistfully asks where her lover pastures his sheep. It is the kind of yearning all lovers know.

Read Song of Songs 1:5–7.

The bride compares herself to a flower of the field, unlike the exotic blooms that grow in the gardens of the rich. But the groom says that compared to the other women, she is a lily among thistles!

Read Song of Songs 2:1–6.

A walled garden has long been a symbol of virginity. The groom sings with joy of the maiden who has kept herself for their bridal union.

Read Song of Songs 4:12–16. (In chapter 4, verse 12, the term *sister* is one of endearment, not kinship.) [8]

The bride longs to be as close to the groom as the name seal that he wears on a cord about his neck, resting on his heart. She would be one with him—as he and his name are one. In this passage we hear the well-known tribute to the power of love:

8

Do young people today see virginity as positive for someone who is not married? Give your opinion in a paragraph.

Set me as a seal upon your heart,
    as a seal upon your arm;
for love is strong as death,
    passion fierce as the grave.
(Song of Songs 8:6)

Read Song of Songs 8:6–7.

Love can overcome death. This is the wisdom offered us by the Song of Songs.

For Review

☐ According to the Book of Wisdom, what is our destiny as humans?

☐ How does the Book of Sirach differ in its concerns from other wisdom literature?

☐ What is the Song of Songs? According to early Jewish and Christian interpreters, what is it meant to symbolize?

**Love is strong as death
passion fierce as the grave.**

Song of Songs 8:6

Stories of Encouragement: Faith and Goodness Triumph

As we saw in earlier chapters of this course, the stories of Jacob, Rebekah, David, Saul, Jonathan, and the rest, take us through the history of Israel's calling to be God's people. The later stories that are covered in the remainder of this chapter were tales told during the centuries after the Babylonian exile; they were meant to inspire courage and faith in times of trial. The stories reminded the people over and over that goodness and faithfulness will triumph in the end. The Books of Tobit, Judith, and Esther are listed among the historical books of the Bible; Jonah is listed as a prophetic book. However, all these books are treated here as story books because modern Scripture scholars have determined that they are not accounts of historical events. As story books, however, they are inspired by God, conveying God's truth just as the historical accounts of the Bible do.

The Book of Tobit is a wisdom tale about a noble and faithful elder who remains steadfast in the face of personal disaster.

The Book of Judith tells of a courageous woman who defies all the stereotypical notions of "how women are supposed to be." Saving her people from the Assyrian army with wit and wisdom has made Judith a favorite hero for many.

The Book of Esther, on the other hand, is about a naturally timid woman—a queen—who risks her life to save her people from a wicked schemer who plans to slay them. Esther is a model for those who are not brave.

The Book of Jonah, a humorous portrayal of a fictitious prophet, gets across an important lesson: God's love and mercy reach far and wide across cultural and religious boundaries.

As you read the stories from the Bible, try to imagine yourself as a young person in Judea listening to them at a family or community gathering. The young boy Jesus, of the family of Joseph and Mary, would have been raised on these wonderfully entertaining, inspiring—and inspired—stories.

Tobit: The Faithful Jew

The Book of Tobit was written by an unknown author about 200 B.C., to encourage faithful Jews to be righteous and patient during the difficult period of Greek oppression. The story is set around five hundred years earlier, in the Assyrian capital of Nineveh after the fall of the northern kingdom of Israel.

The story is of a good, faithful Jew, Tobit, and his family. Tobit's love for his fellow Israelites extends to burying their corpses in a time of Assyrian persecution—even at great risk to his own life.

Teenagers at a Jewish prayer vigil in Seattle, Washington

During the feast of Purim, Jewish children have fun dressing up as the characters in the story of Esther.

the king that the Jews are treasonous people, and the king goes along with Haman's plan.

At Mordecai's urging, Esther agrees to plead for the Jewish people before the king. But she is terrified to go to court without the king's summons; such an improper act could risk her death. She decides to risk it for the sake of her people.

Esther, shaking with fear, appears before the king, and when he welcomes her, she faints. Finally, she invites the king and Haman to be her guests at dinner. After the meal Esther is too timid to tell the king what is on her mind. Instead, she asks that the two men return the next evening, when she will explain her purpose.

That night the king learns that Mordecai once uncovered a plot in the court to kill him, but has never been rewarded for this good deed. The king determines to honor Mordecai—unaware that Haman hates the man.

When Haman appears, having built a gallows on which to hang Mordecai, the king asks him what he should do to honor a certain man. Thinking that he himself is the man, Haman dreams up an elaborate procession. The king, pleased, says in effect, "Splendid—now go do it for Mordecai." Needless to say, it ruins Haman's day.

The next evening, when Esther is once again with the king and Haman, she tells the king that one of his nobles wants to murder the queen (herself) and all her people. Outraged, the king asks who, and Esther points to Haman. Wicked Haman now grovels before Esther, the king is wild with anger at him, and in the end it is Haman, not Mordecai, who hangs on the gallows.

Read Esther, chapters 1 to 7. [11]

versions—around 485 to 464 B.C. The place is Susa, a Persian city where many Jews of the Dispersion settled.

King Artaxerxes orders his queen to step down from the throne after an incident when he feels humiliated by her. To replace her he searches the kingdom for the most beautiful, pleasing woman in the land. Esther, a Jew, is encouraged by her cousin Mordecai to come forward and "try out" for the role of queen—without revealing that she is Jewish. Her loveliness and simplicity immediately win the king's heart.

As queen, Esther gains knowledge of a plot by the prime minister, Haman, to slaughter all the Jews in the land. Haman has a grudge against Mordecai, who refuses to bow to him, and he wants to punish not only Mordecai but all his people. Haman convinces

Purim

The Jewish feast of Purim, dear to Jews everywhere, honors the courage of the gentle and beautiful Esther, who overcame her fears to save her people. It gets its name from the lot—the *pur*—that Haman drew to determine the date of the slaughter of the Jews. Purim is

---

11

In the last century, a "Haman" killed six million Jews in Europe and millions of other Europeans. Who was he? Explain in writing how such crimes can evolve within a community or a country.

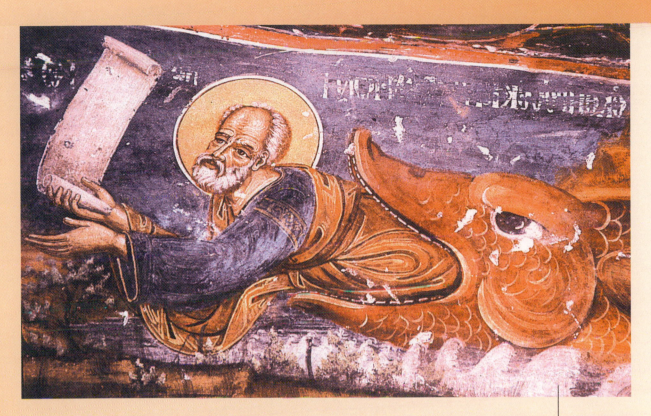

An ancient painting on a monastery wall of Jonah and the whale

one of the feasts that Jesus must have celebrated in the synagogue as a child, booing Haman and cheering Esther as the story was read and the listeners reacted with high spirits.

Jonah: A Parable of Mercy

The Book of Jonah, only four chapters long, uses some humorous satire to make its serious point—that God's mercy extends to all, not just to the "insiders." The book is fiction, including its main character. Its author is unknown, and its setting is the Assyrian Empire around 750 B.C.—although Jonah was written in the fifth century B.C. Jonah the prophet is depicted satirically; he is obviously not in the great tradition of the prophets Isaiah, Jeremiah, and Ezekiel. Rather, he is portrayed as a somewhat scatterbrained, self-serving fellow who sulks when God turns out to be more merciful to sinners than he expected or wanted.

God tells Jonah to go to Nineveh, the capital of Assyria, and warn its people that their wickedness is known and is about to be punished. To Jonah the Ninevites are filthy pagans, and he wants nothing to do with them. So instead of doing as God instructs, he flees on a ship bound for a distant land. Out on the sea, a terrible storm comes up, and the ship's crew blames Jonah for their disaster and casts him overboard. *12*

Jonah is swallowed by a fish, in whose belly he remains for three days and three nights until the fish belches him up on shore. Having gotten Jonah's attention by the ordeal in the sea, God sends Jonah to Nineveh a second time. This time he goes and delivers the message of the coming doom. After only one day of Jonah's preaching, the people

12

Have you ever "run away" from a difficult situation like Jonah did? Did running away work? Write down your story and include the consequences of your running away.

Modern Branches of Judaism

Judaism today has three main branches—**Orthodox, Reform,** and **Conservative.** They all share belief in the one God and in the moral truths revealed in the Torah. However, they differ in the extent to which they observe the traditional ritual and dietary laws. Even within each branch, there is quite a variety in terms of practice. In the United States, with more Jews than any other country, Conservative Jews are the largest branch, followed by Reform Jews, and then Orthodox Jews.

Orthodox Judaism, the oldest group, calls itself Torah-true Judaism because of its strict observance of the Law of Moses, including rules for worship, the Sabbath, diet, family rituals, and festivals. It was Orthodox Jews who first came to the Americas from eastern Europe.

Reform Judaism arose in the nineteenth century from the desire to adapt to modern society. It held to the high moral ethic of the Law, but it dispensed its members from most of the ritual and dietary laws. This liberal branch found many adherents in the United States, where Jewish people enjoyed greater freedom and acceptance than elsewhere, and wanted to fit into society rather than stand out as peculiar because of their customs. In the last several decades, however, Reform Judaism has returned to some of the ritual and dietary traditions. Reform Jews call their houses of worship "temples" rather than "synagogues," and they now ordain women rabbis. They are known as firm supporters of many justice causes.

Conservative Judaism formed later in the nineteenth century as a reaction against Reform Judaism, which, it was thought, had abandoned too much of the Law. It lies between the strict Orthodox and the liberal Reform branches. Its members keep the ritual traditions of Judaism but adapt them or allow departures from them in keeping with modern needs. Women are beginning to become rabbis in the Conservative branch.

Within and beyond the three main branches of Judaism are other smaller groups and movements. **Reconstructionism,** a twentieth-century cultural and spiritual movement that branched off from Conservatism, aimed to revitalize Judaism and ensure the creative survival of the Jewish people. The movement, which has its own synagogues, fosters the art, music, language, literature, and customs of Jewish civilization.

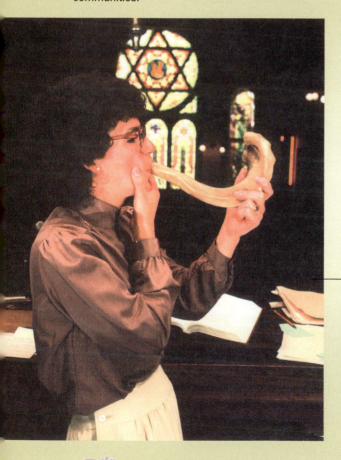

Hasidic Jews in Brooklyn, New York. Strict rules govern the relations of men and women in Hasidic communities.

A woman rabbi of a Reform Jewish temple in Greenburg, Mississippi, blows a ritual shofar—a ram's horn trumpet.

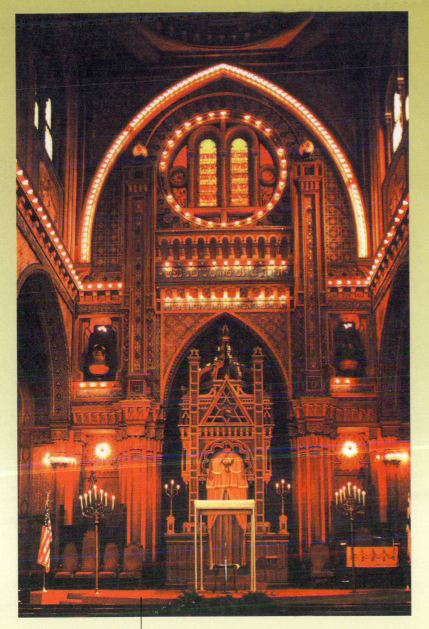

A Conservative Jewish synagogue in Cincinnati, Ohio

A group that arose within Orthodox Judaism is known as the **Hasidim** (which means "pietism"). It was part of a mystical movement that developed in reaction to scholarly approaches to Judaism. Rather than intense study of the Scriptures, Hasidic Jews concentrate on simple, heartfelt faith, prayer, and personal devotion. A large concentration of Hasidic Jews is located in Brooklyn, New York, where they are recognized by their very traditional appearance and practices.

A movement called **Zionism** came about in the late 1800s, and today has members within all major branches of Judaism. Named for *Zion,* the Jewish poetic term for Jerusalem and the Holy Land, the movement sought to return dispersed Jews to their ancient homeland in Palestine and to once again build their own nation there. Since the state of Israel was established in 1948, Zionism has focused on support for that nation amid conflicts with its Arab neighbors and with the Palestinians of the land.

During the devastating ***Shoah*** (Holocaust) of World War II, six million Jews were executed by Nazi Germany—about one-third of all the Jews in the world. This reality has made a deep impact on the survivors of the horror, on the Jewish people as a whole, and on the entire world.

The population of Jews worldwide has climbed steadily since the end of World War II, when it was about 11 million. Today about 13.5 million Jews live around the world, with most living in three major centers—the United States, Israel, and Russia, in that order.

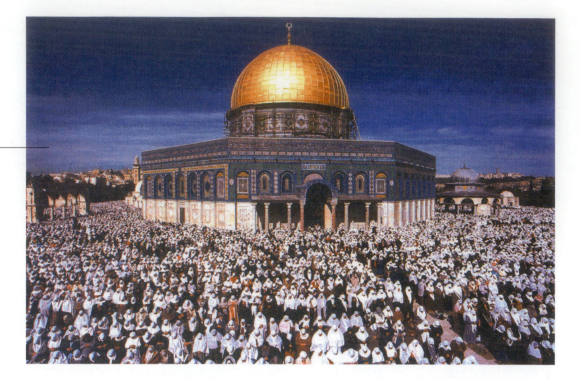

Muslim worshipers at Islam's holy Dome of the Rock, Jerusalem. The Book of Jonah suggests that everyone, including those of religions different from our own, is an insider when it comes to God's love and mercy.

repent, fast, and call loudly to God for mercy for their past wickedness. Upon hearing Nineveh repent, God decides not to destroy the city after all.

But even though God is pleased, Jonah is not. He throws God's mercy back in his face. This was the reason he refused to go to Nineveh in the first place: he knew that God would be too kindhearted to the people. Jonah would rather die than lose his credibility as a prophet when his message of doom and destruction does not come true.

God makes it clear to Jonah that this grumpy prophet has no good reason to be angry. If Jonah is so concerned about himself, shouldn't God be concerned about and show mercy to the city of Nineveh and its

120,000 people, "who do not know their right hand from their left" (Jonah 4:11)? And the book ends; we never hear Jonah's answer.

Read Jonah, chapters 1 to 4. **13**

We are all "insiders"

Recall that in the period when Jonah was written, Ezra and Nehemiah had worked to purify Judaism of foreign elements and build the boundaries of Jewish identity. Some Jews then took this to mean that Israel *alone* could be worthy of God's mercy. The Book of Jonah was probably written to argue against that narrow-minded spirit.

Through his brief satire on a fictitious prophet, the author wanted to remind his audience that God called Israel to be a light to the rest of the world, not to assume that others were beyond the reach of God's love and the hope of salvation. The book has a message for us today as well: We may be tempted at times to think we are better than others; we may forget that the "worst people" are still loved tenderly by God and deserve our respect. The Book of Jonah reminds us that no

13

Answer the following question in writing: *What do you think could have been Jonah's answer to God's question at the end of the Book of Jonah?*

one—no religion, culture, nation, or subgroup—is beyond God's reach. We are all "insiders" when it comes to God's love and mercy.

For Review

- [ ] What does the Book of Tobit remind us about?
- [ ] What did the author of Judith try to emphasize?
- [ ] What story is remembered and celebrated in the Jewish feast of Purim?
- [ ] What was the author of the Book of Jonah trying to tell his audience?

Wisдom anд Virtue foR Then anд Now

Judaism before Jesus was engaged in a kind of ongoing conversation—with itself, with God, and with the cultures in which it was immersed. Consider the variety of outlooks in the wisdom books, each helping to build up a rich tradition of insights on the meaning and purpose of life. That these outlooks vary and differ gives us a sense of the depth of God's wisdom, which cannot be penetrated by any single point of view.

Even the Books of Tobit, Judith, Esther, and Jonah are like responses, in story form, to the issues facing Judaism in those late centuries. But they speak just as powerfully to Christians today who are trying to live faithful lives while immersed in a society that is often in tension with Christian values. The virtues these stories encourage—generosity, faithfulness, trust, steadfastness, piety, heroic courage, humility, simplicity, and mercy—are all desperately needed in our day. The God who is worshiped by Christians and Jews today inspired those stories, and the ancient conversations that produced them, as gifts for all eras and times.

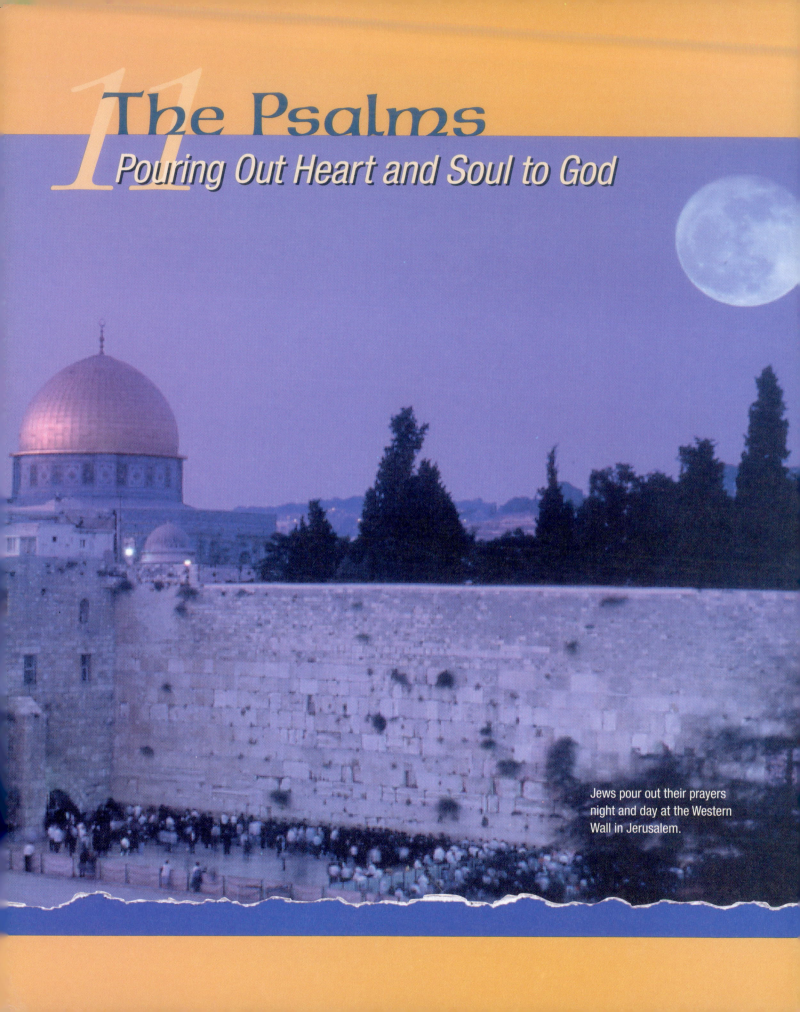

11 The Psalms
Pouring Out Heart and Soul to God

Jews pour out their prayers night and day at the Western Wall in Jerusalem.

In This Chapter . . .

- **The Psalms as Songs of the Heart**
- **Psalms of Lament: Crying Out in Suffering**
- **Psalms of Thanks and Praise: Celebrating Who God Is**
- **"Everything I Ever Needed to Know . . ."**

Throughout this course passages from the Book of Psalms have come up often in the featured sections called "The Prayer of Israel." Those sections have shown how the Psalms and other prayers can be connected with the life and history of the people of Israel. Many psalms, as you have probably noticed, refer to specific events and persons from biblical history. So you are already somewhat familiar with the Psalms.

This chapter focuses on what the Psalms can teach us about how to pray—whether we are praying with the beautiful poetry of the Psalms or with our own words, using our own experiences.

The Psalms as Songs of the Heart

To begin, let's consider one particular prayer, Psalm 116. Try to imagine an experience or event that could have prompted this prayer in the heart of the person who originally wrote it.

I love the LORD, because he has heard
　　my voice and my supplications.
Because he inclined his ear to me,
　　　therefore I will call on him as long as I
　　　live.

The snares of death encompassed me;
　　the pangs of Sheol laid hold on me;
　　I suffered distress and anguish.
Then I called on the name of the LORD:
　　"O LORD, I pray, save my life!"

Gracious is the LORD, and righteous;
　　our God is merciful.
The LORD protects the simple;
　　when I was brought low, he saved me.
Return, O my soul, to your rest,
　　for the LORD has dealt bountifully with
　　　you.

For you have delivered my soul from death,
　　my eyes from tears,
　　my feet from stumbling.
I walk before the LORD
　　in the land of the living.
I kept my faith, even when I said,
　　"I am greatly afflicted";
I said in my consternation,
　　"Everyone is a liar."

What shall I return to the LORD
　　for all his bounty to me?
I will lift up the cup of salvation
　　and call on the name of the LORD,
I will pay my vows to the LORD
　　in the presence of all his people.
Precious in the sight of the LORD
　　is the death of his faithful ones.
O LORD, I am your servant;
　　I am your servant, the child of your
　　　serving girl.
　　You have loosed my bonds.
I will offer to you a thanksgiving sacrifice
　　and call on the name of the LORD.
I will pay my vows to the LORD
　　in the presence of all his people,
in the courts of the house of the LORD,
　　in your midst, O Jerusalem.
Praise the LORD!

Arising from Experience

We do not know what experience originally prompted the heartfelt words of Psalm 116, but we can imagine. Perhaps the psalmist was deathly ill, and then got better. Maybe she or he was the victim of vicious gossip or false accusations. Perhaps the accusers were so cruel to the person that it felt like being near death—and then her or his reputation was restored when the truth came out. Or the psalmist might have been attacked and beaten on the road, or nearly killed in a fierce battle, and survived to tell the story.

Whatever the experience behind the prayer, the psalmist wanted to give thanks to God for the marvelous rescue. In this case that meant going to the Temple in Jerusalem, where the Lord was believed to dwell, and offering a sacrificial animal in thanksgiving.

Although we do not know exactly what situations prompted the authors of the Psalms to write them, the strong feelings these prayers express could apply to situations in any place or time. In every era since biblical times, people have found that the Psalms say what is in their heart, and so they have been central to Jewish and Christian prayer and worship. Today, thousands of years after they were composed, we can identify our own life circumstances with the Psalms. *1*

Lament, thanks, and praise

Many scholars categorize the Psalms by the sentiments they express. The Book of Psalms has three major types of prayers:

- **psalms of lament,** which express grief and complaint to God for suffering and beg for help

A patient who was resuscitated from a cardiac arrest—"brought back from the dead"—is discharged from the hospital.

- **psalms of thanks,** which express gratitude for God's good deeds
- **psalms of praise,** which celebrate the wonder and majesty of God

We have already seen prayers like the psalms of lament in the Book of Lamentations, considered in chapter 8 of this text. Recall that those were laments over the destruction of Jerusalem by the Babylonians at the time of the exile.

It is not always clearcut which category a psalm is in, because many psalms express more than one sentiment. A psalm, for instance, might have features of both lament and praise, or praise and thanks. But most psalms focus predominantly on one sentiment or another—like Psalm 116 above, which is one of thanks.

Read Psalms 86 (lament), 30 (thanks), 104 (praise).

Later in this chapter, we will consider the psalm types of lament, praise, and thanks in more detail. *2*

1

Imagine how Psalm 116 could apply to your own situation or that of someone you know, and describe that situation in writing. Remember that being rescued from death does not have to be taken literally: "death" can mean the painful loss of someone you love, the heartbreak of enduring parents' separation, or the anguish of being rejected by others.

2

Compare Psalm 104 to chapter 1 of Genesis and make a collage that tells the glorious story of God's Creation.

Parched land in Israel

The Jordan River at its source

Developed over Centuries

Scholars believe that the Psalms were composed throughout several centuries, from about 1000 to 300 B.C. Half of them are attributed to King David, but it is likely that he wrote only a few psalms, if any at all. They were written in his spirit, though, and a number of them have a "tag line" at the beginning that identifies a certain situation in David's life. For example, Psalm 63, attributed to David, is preceded by the tag line, "A Psalm of David, when he was in the Wilderness of Judah" (that is, hiding out from the jealous King Saul). But the psalm is not about David's experience alone; it is the prayer of anyone who longs for God. In its first verse, for example, Psalm 63 uses the image of the desert wilderness to point to the inner thirst for God:

O God, you are my God, I seek you,
    my soul thirsts for you;
my flesh faints for you,
    as in a dry and weary land where there
        is no water.

O God, you are my God, I seek you, my soul thirsts for you.

Psalm 63:1

Another example of a tag line related to David is the one for Psalm 51, a plea for God's mercy and forgiveness: "A psalm of David, when Nathan the prophet came to him after his affair with Bathsheba" (NAB). Recall that David had an affair with Bathsheba, and ordered that her husband be put at the front line in battle so he would be killed. David had sinned grievously and needed forgiveness. Psalm 51 expresses what anyone who regrets an awful deed can pour out to God. Here are its first two verses:

Have mercy on me, O God,
    according to your steadfast love;
according to your abundant mercy
    blot out my transgressions.
Wash me thoroughly from my iniquity,
    and cleanse me from my sin.

These tag lines remind us of the kinds of events in biblical history that could have prompted such prayers. But the Psalms most likely were composed decades or centuries later, not at the time of those particular events. The full collection of 150 psalms was put together from many shorter collections. The Book of Psalms as we now have it is divided into five smaller books. *3*

Used in Worship

The Psalms can be used for personal, private prayer, but most were probably written with community worship in mind.

Sung, not said

Today it is common to *read* or *say* the psalms in prayer. But the psalms are beautiful works of poetry originally set to music; they were composed to be *sung* in public worship. Some of the tag lines for the psalms even include musical instructions: "with stringed instruments" (Psalm 54); also "according to Lilies" (Psalm 69) and "according to The Deer of the Dawn" (Psalm 22)—both melodies that would have been known by the ancient worshipers.

Some of the psalms are intended to be sung along with certain liturgical actions or services, for example, "for the memorial offering" (Psalm 38) and "A song for the Sabbath Day" (Psalm 92). A whole group of psalms (120 to 134) are given the tag line "A Song of Ascents." These would have been sung as pilgrims to the holy city of Jerusalem ascended the hill in procession to worship in their revered Temple. For instance, here are the first two verses of Psalm 122:

I was glad when they said to me,
    "Let us go to the house of the Lord!"
Our feet are standing
    within your gates, O Jerusalem.

Shared experiences, shared sentiments

A psalm can express a whole community's sentiments about some experience they have shared—a victory, a defeat, or perhaps the renewal of spring as the land comes alive again. When it expresses a shared experience, singing the psalm together in worship bonds the people to one another and to God.

Some psalms point to specific events in the history of the people, for instance, Psalm 137, which recalls the exile in Babylon. Imagine how powerful it must have been for

3

Psalms were often written as reflections on biblical events that happened many years earlier. Choose a story from the Old Testament and find a psalm that captures the spirit of the event or persons featured in the story.

Israeli men weep over the death of a friend killed in a bombing.

those who understood the choking grief of exile to sing this psalm together:

By the rivers of Babylon—
    there we sat down and there we wept
    when we remembered Zion.
On the willows there
    we hung up our harps.
For there our captors
    asked us for songs,
and our tormentors asked for mirth, saying,
    "Sing us one of the songs of Zion!"

How could we sing the LORD's song
    in a foreign land?
If I forget you, O Jerusalem,
    let my right hand wither!
Let my tongue cling to the roof of my
    mouth,
    if I do not remember you,
if I do not set Jerusalem
    above my highest joy.

(Verses 1–6) **4**

4

Can you recall a time when your whole school went through something very significant together? Perhaps it was the death of a student or a faculty member, the closing of your school, or a major victory in a contest or sports event. The community liturgy at such times may seem more heartfelt than usual, because everyone has shared in the major event and brings strong feelings about it to the worship. People seem more open to God.

Consider such a significant event in your school's life, either real or imaginary, and write a description of it. Suppose you have been asked to choose a psalm, or an excerpt from a psalm, for the schoolwide liturgy centered on that event. You hope it will express people's strong feelings and help them be open to God. What psalm, or psalm verses, would you choose, and why? Explain in writing.

The Responsorial Psalm: Sung from the Heart!

In Catholic congregations during Sunday Mass, people are encouraged whenever possible to *sing* the responsorial psalm, the psalm response to the first Bible reading. Typically a cantor sings the verses and then leads the congregation in singing a refrain (also called an antiphon) after each verse.

The beautiful melody and words can go with people throughout their week, like background music reminding them of God's loving presence and at times expressing just what is in their heart. Here, for example, are a few refrains that are sung with the psalm verses in many Catholic congregations around the country. You may even be familiar with their melodies:

- "The Lord is my light and my salvation, of whom should I be afraid, of whom should I be afraid?" (*Gather,* number 39).
- "All the ends of the earth have seen the power of God; all the ends of the earth have seen the power of God" (number 95).
- "Shepherd me, O God, beyond my wants, beyond my fears, from death into life" (number 31).
- "The Lord hears the cry of the poor. Blessed be the Lord" (number 48).
- "Be with me, Lord, when I am in trouble, be with me, Lord, I pray" (number 85).
- "To you, O Lord, I lift my soul, to you, I lift my soul" (number 36).

Maria Kujawa, a senior, is one of several high school students who serve as cantor at Masses in their parish, Saint Mary's in Winona, Minnesota. She explains what it means to her to lead the congregation in the responsorial psalm:

> In the years since I began being a cantor, the prayer aspect of it has grown for me. I realize that I'm not up there to perform for people; I'm there to help them worship by singing.
>
> I love the responsorial psalm. It is usually slow and reflective, and it stays with you. When I sing the verses, I realize it's important for people to understand the words. Then when they join in on the refrain, they are really participating in the whole psalm. They remember that refrain, and they grow from it. It is really such a privilege to be able to help people pray in that way.

Maria Kujawa

In the Christian liturgy

From early Christian times, followers of Jesus prayed the Psalms. Jesus himself had prayed them as a good Jew. In the local synagogues, where the earliest Christians worshiped (considering themselves still Jews), the Psalms were a part of the Jewish service of the word—as they are today. The service of the word consisted of readings from the Torah and the Prophets, with psalms sung in response to the readings.

In the liturgy of the word. Toward the end of the first century A.D., Christianity and Judaism split, and Christians were no longer allowed in the synagogues. But they continued to have their own service of the word modeled on the Jewish service, with readings and psalms. That service evolved into what today Catholics call the liturgy of the word, the first part of the Mass (another term for the Eucharist).

The liturgy of the word includes Bible readings, which are the word of God. The first reading is followed by the "responsorial psalm"—the people's response to the gift of God's word. So the Psalms play an important role in the Mass, as well as in most Christian worship services.

"You make the clouds your chariot, you ride on the wings of the wind."

Similar to the sayings in the Book of Proverbs (studied in the previous chapter), the Psalms include much repetition—expressing the same idea in more than one way. Psalm 51, also quoted earlier in this chapter, gives numerous examples of this:

Create in me a clean heart, O God,
    and put a new and right spirit within me.
Do not cast me away from your presence,
    and do not take your holy spirit from me.
        (Verses 10–11)

The first part of each verse above is echoed by the second part of the verse. And sometimes, as in Psalm 20:8, the two parts of a verse express the same idea (in this case, "our victory") in two contrasting ways:

They [the enemy] will collapse and fall,
    but we shall rise and stand upright.

Structuring the Psalms with such repetition and contrast made them easier to remember. It also helped the person praying to dwell on the ideas and let them sink in, as one line added another layer of understanding to the previous one. This device also lent itself to chanting the verses of the Psalms back and forth between two groups during worship.

Concrete language

Another literary feature of the Psalms that makes them beautiful poetry is their use of concrete, not abstract, language. To see the difference, compare these two styles of prayer:

1. O God, you are the all-powerful supreme being of the whole universe.

2. Bless the LORD, O my soul.
    O LORD my God, you are very great.
  You are clothed with honor and majesty,
    wrapped in light as with a garment.
  You stretch out the heavens like a tent,
    you set the beams of your chambers on
      the waters,
  you make the clouds your chariot,
    you ride on the wings of the wind,
  you make the winds your messengers,
    fire and flame your ministers.
        (Psalm 104:1–4)

In the liturgy of the hours. The Psalms are also a major part of the liturgy of the hours, the official daily prayer of the Catholic Church. Also called the Divine Office, the liturgy of the hours is designed to be prayed at specified times of the day, ideally by a community. In it, the Psalms are interspersed with biblical and other readings, hymns, and seasonal prayers. Over four weeks' time, almost the entire Psalter (Book of Psalms) is prayed during the liturgy of the hours. The Psalms, beloved to ancient and modern Jews, are the same prayers that have nourished and expressed the Catholic Church's daily worship for centuries.

The Psalms as Poetry

Certain literary qualities of the Psalms make them ideally suited to prayer, whether they are used in a group or in solitude.

Easily remembered and chanted

The Psalms were written to be prayed from memory, not read. The beautiful sounds in the original Hebrew poetry helped people to remember them, but these sounds are lost in the translation to English. But even in English we can see other devices that would make the Psalms easy to remember.

The first uses abstract language to describe God's power, whereas the second, the psalm, uses concrete language—lengthier than the first but more appealing. The psalm verses are full of similes and metaphors, vivid images that help us to *sense* the power of God, not simply to acknowledge the concept. They are full of action as well: God does not "stand still" but moves in the world; he is active and at work making things happen! These metaphors are not meant to be scientific understandings, but poetic figures of speech that bring to life the abstract notion of an all-powerful supreme being. **5**

If a psalmist wished to tell of being saved by God, he or she would not say simply, "Salvation came from God," an accurate but unpoetic statement. Instead, the psalmist might pour out the seeable, hearable, touchable, feelable, even smellable words of Psalm 40, letting us know just what being saved felt like:

I waited patiently for the LORD;
    he inclined to me and heard my cry.
He drew me up from the desolate pit,
    out of the miry bog,
and set my feet upon a rock,
    making my steps secure.
He put a new song in my mouth,
    a song of praise to our God.
Many will see and fear,
    and put their trust in the LORD.
                (Verses 1–3) **6**

The Psalms contain some of the most moving poetry the world has ever known. But they are much more than that. They are God's inspired gift to us, coming through the earthy humanity of the psalmists who wrote them. Through the Psalms God helps us pour out the deep longings, great sufferings, and ecstatic joys of the human heart and release them into his loving care.

We will next turn to the major types of psalms—lament, thanks, and praise—to discover how they can heal and transform us.

For Review

- ☐ Name and define the three major types of psalms.
- ☐ When were the Psalms composed?
- ☐ How were the Psalms originally intended to be used?
- ☐ How are the Psalms used in the Christian liturgy?
- ☐ Describe two poetic features of the Psalms.

"[God] drew me up from the desolate pit." A counselor and an outreach worker lead a support group for survivors of domestic violence.

---

5 Find three metaphors about God in the Psalms that you find comforting or disturbing. Write each down and explain how it makes you feel and why.

6 Write your thoughts on what the "desolate pit" and "miry bog" could mean in a young person's life.

Psalms of Lament: Crying Out in Suffering

Have you ever been so low that you felt completely overwhelmed, unable to keep going, desperate for relief from the burdensomeness of life? Or have you ever known someone who felt this way? Maybe it was a real, external event that brought this on—like the death of someone close, the breakup of a family, or a false accusation of some terrible deed. Perhaps the cause was more internal—like an awful sense of worthlessness or failure. Or a combination of external and internal causes could have brought on this person's overwhelmed, devastated condition.

A Prayer of Anguish

Such a state of mind and heart is a moment for a psalm of lament. Hear, for example, these verses from Psalm 69:

Save me, O God, for the waters have come up
    to my neck.
I sink in deep mire,
    where there is no foothold;
I have come into deep waters,
    and the flood sweeps over me.
I am weary with my crying;
    my throat is parched.

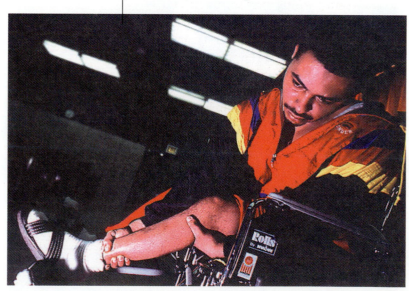

A young man paralyzed by a gunshot wound in Brooklyn, New York. "But I am lowly and in pain; let your salvation, O God, protect me."

My eyes grow dim
    with waiting for my God.

More in number than the hairs of my head
    are those who hate me without cause;
many are those who would destroy me,
    my enemies who accuse me falsely. . . .
. . . .

But as for me, my prayer is to you, O Lord.
    At an acceptable time, O God,
      in the abundance of your steadfast love,
        answer me.
With your faithful help rescue me
    from sinking in the mire;
let me be delivered from my enemies
    and from the deep waters.
Do not let the flood sweep over me,
    or the deep swallow me up,
    or the Pit close its mouth over me.

. . . .

You know the insults I receive,
    and my shame and dishonor;
    my foes are all known to you.
Insults have broken my heart,
    so that I am in despair.
I looked for pity, but there was none;
    and for comforters, but I found none.
They gave me poison for food,
    and for my thirst they gave me vinegar
      to drink.

Let them be blotted out of the book of the
      living;
    let them not be enrolled among the
      righteous.
But I am lowly and in pain;
    let your salvation, O God, protect me.

I will praise the name of God with a song;
    I will magnify him with thanksgiving.
. . . .

Let the oppressed see it and be glad;
    you who seek God, let your hearts revive.
For the Lord hears the needy,
    and does not despise his own that are in
      bonds.

(Verses 1–33)

I-Witness: Sarah

Lord, I'm Sarah, your servant, daughter of Benjamin and Miriam. Touching the wall of your Temple, under its torchlights, I seek comfort in your nearness.

My sister's baby died many days ago. Today we learned of it from friends who arrived here in Jerusalem.

We couldn't help. We didn't even know her baby was ill. My mother's wailing filled the street, and my father's face is pinched with pain.

I am here at the Temple because even you seem far away. Or are we just so small that you couldn't see what was happening to our family? I'm confused. Why do you make life so hard at times?

You have been with me throughout my life, and I know you are with me now. I'm not asking for an answer. There is nothing to say. But here, standing at your Temple, I know you are with me.

These excerpts show the elements found in most psalms of lament, though not necessarily in this order. See if you can identify where the following five elements are in the verses above:

1. an address to God
2. a complaint or account of the misery suffered
3. a plea for help
4. an affirmation of trust in God
5. a statement praising God [7]

From Voicing the Pain to Being Transformed

A psalm of lament gives loud and emotional voice to a complaint or a series of them. The details of the suffering endured may take up most of the verses. (Descriptions of the vicious behavior of enemies can be especially lengthy!) But the psalm eventually moves beyond pouring out all the woes of the heart to turning those woes over in trust to God, whose wisdom and enduring love are beyond all imagining. It ends with praise of God.

It's about trust

The ancient Jews prayed fervently for an end to suffering and injustice, just as modern-day people do. The psalms of lament voice the deep pain people are suffering, but in the process they recall God's goodness and justice, mercy and kindness, power and awe. This is the God who has rescued the people over and over, who has worked wonders for them. This is the God who can turn the impossible into the possible and real. This is the God who has never abandoned them, and never will. Through pouring out their pain and entrusting themselves into God's care, those who pray these psalms are consoled and gradually transformed. They become centered in God. No matter what the circumstances of their life, they know their hope is in God.

Read Psalm 42.

A theme song of tears and trust

In ancient times a Jew might have gone to the Temple with a great sorrow or suffering, asking for a prayer that would help present the concern to God. The Temple priest, then, would give the person a particular psalm that fit her or his needs, encouraging the person to recite and memorize it, and to make it like a heartfelt theme song that could be prayed back home any time of day or night.

7

Find a newspaper or magazine article that tells of a situation of great suffering. Using the five elements listed above, tell about the story in the style of a psalm of lament.

A young girl places a candle outside the United States Embassy in the wake of the September 11, 2001, terrorist attacks on the United States.

Suppose, for instance, that a man living in Judah in about 350 B.C. becomes widowed when his wife dies giving birth. He is grief stricken for months and cannot seem to go ahead with life. His small piece of land lies neglected; he cannot care for his children. At the Temple the priest encourages the man to pray every day what we now know as Psalm 77 and to let it become a part of him. The man does so faithfully. Slowly, over weeks and months, his deadened heart comes alive again. But he is changed from before his grief began. His eyes radiate a quiet hope now, even when he is having a hard day. He has gradually put his trust in God, and allowed God to become the center of his life.

Read Psalm 77. **8**

Why So Brutally Honest?

Although psalms of lament are among the most numerous and favorite of the Psalms, they contain some features that people find troubling. For one thing many of the lament psalms convey some shocking emotions—things that might seem out of place in a

book of prayer, let alone the inspired word of God. Why are these messages there?

The lament psalms let it all hang out—anger at God, blaming and questioning him, rage at enemies, despair, desire for revenge. You may be horrified at some of the sentiments. For instance, recall Psalm 137, the sad song of the exiles in Babylon about longing for Jerusalem. If you check out verses 7 to 9, which are usually not recited or sung in worship, you will see that the psalmist wishes the Babylonians' babies would be smashed against the rocks.

Why are the Psalms so blunt? Why do they seem to hold nothing back when it comes to negative emotions? Are they even disrespectful to God at times?

Consider the opening words of Psalm 22, which may be familiar to you as the words Jesus says (in Matthew's and Mark's Gospels) while dying on the cross: "My God, my God, why have you forsaken me?" (Psalm 22:1). One might wonder: Is the psalmist accusing God of abandoning him? Is that okay? Isn't God offended by that kind of talk?

**Bringing the whole,
uncensored self to God**

The language of the Psalms is not business-as-usual, nice, cover-up talk. It includes the most raw emotions. It is honest. The greatest gift one can bring to God is the gift

8

Choose a verse from Psalm 77 that is meaningful or interesting to you and write a reflection about it.

I will call to mind the deeds of the LORD;
I will remember your wonders of old.

Psalm 77:11

Mourners at the burial for victims of an earthquake in Mexico City.

of one's whole self—honest, true, uncensored, even flawed with sin. But to feel negative emotions and bring them to God is not the same as *acting* on those emotions. Just because the psalmist says to God, "I wish that such-and-such person was dead!" does not mean the psalmist may go out and kill such-and-such person, or cause anyone else to do so. The desire for revenge shows that the psalmist is only human, not perfect. *9*

Letting go

Expressing the awful feelings to God is only part of the movement of a psalm of lament, as noted. Pouring out the complaint is meant to help the person *let go* of the feelings and entrust them to God's care, not hold onto them. The complaint of a psalm always alternates with sentiments of trust, praise, and gratitude, as the burden is given over to God. Check out the rest of the verses of Psalm 22 (the psalm Jesus cried from the cross). You will see that the psalm moves back and forth from fright and desperation to soaring gratitude, trust, and praise of God. Above all else, praise has the last word.

Read Psalm 22.

9

Write your thoughts on these questions:
• How do you feel about being completely honest with God?
• If a person is not able to be honest in relationships with other people, is it possible to have an honest relationship with God?

The Psalms   **281**

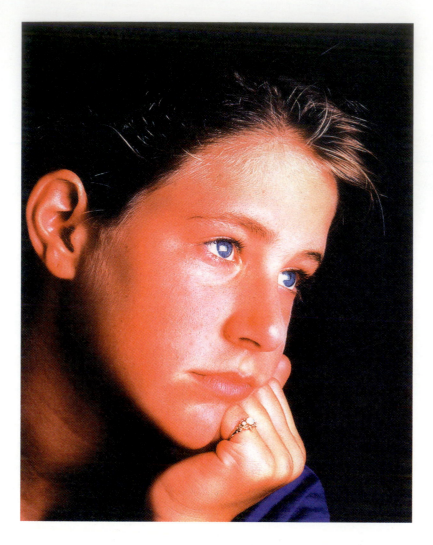

cruel people tried to exploit others, sometimes right within their own community. And even a few mean, gossipy neighbors, just as today, were prone to destroying the reputations of others.

Enemies within ourselves

Today, too, evil is in the world. We can recognize it as "the enemies"—injustice, war, oppression, greed, addiction, abuse, violence, disregard of human life, and cruelty. But unlike the ancients, who saw enemies as completely "out there" in other persons, groups, and empires, we know now that so much of "the enemy" is within ourselves as well. Modern psychology has pointed out the human tendency to project onto other people whatever we do not like in ourselves. Thus we may notice and call attention to faults in others that are actually our own worst tendencies. One way to discover our own faults is to pay attention to what traits in others really irritate us. These are probably things we cannot stand in ourselves.

We need to look at the language about enemies in the Psalms with that kind of insight. "The enemy" is rarely just the "bad guys" out there. The enemy is within us, too. It is all those negative parts of ourselves that we have not yet turned over to God's transforming love.

So when in the Psalms we pray about the enemies who are out to take our life, to ensnare us, to torment us, we may certainly have some particular people in mind. We may also be thinking of some oppressive, cruel systems that cause injustice and misery for poor people in the world; we would be right to consider them enemies. But we also need to be aware that the enemy is not all "out there"—that some of what we find evil in the world really resides within us as well. We may be greedy or selfish; we may want to control others; we may want to make ourselves look good or be successful at the expense of others.

What About Those Enemies?

We see a lot of enemies in the psalms of lament. At times it seems as if the psalmists have a sort of persecution complex. They see plots and snares everywhere. The "bad guys" are always out to get them.

Enemies "out there"

Certainly a great many real, unimagined enemies had to be contended with in the ancient times when the Psalms were composed. Enemies of Israel attacked its towns and raided them for spoils. Empires tried to dominate the Israelites and subject them to slavery and persecution. Greedy,

A Psalm of Lament from Three Viewpoints

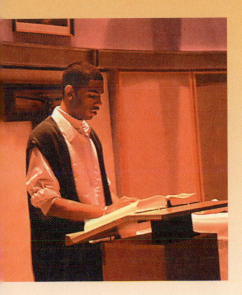

Consider the different ways in which Dan, Moira, and Jesse relate to a psalm of lament during a class prayer service:

Dan has heard from his girlfriend that she wants to break off their relationship. This is devastating to him; he simply cannot imagine life without her. At the class prayer service, Dan recognizes his own plight and suffering in the words of a psalm of lament. Like the psalmist, he feels overwhelmed and hopeless, as if his life is at an end. If only God would help him get through this. Praying that psalm seems like just what he needs to do right now.

Moira, on the other hand, is on top of the world. She just got good news about winning an art contest, and she is looking forward to homecoming. At the service Moira notices how different her own outlook is from the psalm's. She feels great today! But then she remembers someone who does not feel great today. Grandma had a stroke a year ago, and she has not been able to regain her strength. When Moira was at her grandma's apartment last week, Grandma was so discouraged she had tears in her eyes. Moira realizes she can join in the psalm by praying it for Grandma. It's a way to be united with Grandma in her suffering and to ask God's help for her.

Jesse is having an average day—no big highs or lows. During the service the psalm does not seem to speak of his own experience today. He may not feel fabulous, but he sure doesn't feel like the guy in the psalm! Then he remembers hearing once that Jesus, being Jewish, probably prayed all the psalms at some point in his life on earth. If Jesus prayed this one, maybe it was on the night before he died, when he was in agony in the garden. Jesus would have felt like the person in this psalm. As Jesse prays the psalm with the class, he realizes that he is a little closer to understanding what Jesus went through.

Dan, Moira, and Jesse represent three viewpoints from which we can pray the psalms:

- from our own viewpoint as experiencing what is described in the psalm
- from the viewpoint of others with whom we can be in solidarity
- from the viewpoint of Jesus

Transforming, not smashing, enemies

God does not want to smash the enemies "out there." He wants to transform them by love. Likewise, God does not want to smash the sinful tendencies within us but to transform them by love. First, however, we must be aware of what those tendencies are and give them over with trust to him. That is part of praying the psalms of lament with a sincere heart.

Read Psalm 64. **10**

For Review

☐ What are the five elements found in most psalms of lament?

☐ Is it acceptable to have in our own heart the kind of brutally honest language and sentiments that are in the psalms of lament? Why or why not?

☐ How should "the enemies" in the Psalms be understood?

10

Describe three insights or lessons you have learned in your life about how to treat "enemies." From whom did you learn these lessons?

Psalms of Thanks and Praise: Celebrating Who God Is

With the psalms of thanks and of praise, the spotlight moves off the needs of the person praying to shine on God, the source of all goodness. These psalms come from an attitude of humility, one that acknowledges, "*I am not the center of the universe. You are,* God."

Psalms of thanks and of praise are similar to each other and often do overlap, because God can be thanked and praised almost in the same breath. However, psalms of thanks most often express gratitude to God for answering some specific prayer (perhaps a psalm of lament) and for rescuing the person or the community from a terrible situation. Psalms of praise, on the other hand, tend to be more general, focusing on the goodness, power, and majesty of God, not on a particular request that he answered.

Both kinds of psalms have similar elements:

1. an introductory word or statement of praise
2. the reason for the praise, or what the person praying is grateful for
3. another statement of praise

A Spirit of Gratitude

Let's try to enter into the spirit of gratitude expressed in Psalm 30:

I will extol you, O Lord, for you have drawn me up,
    and did not let my foes rejoice over me.
O Lord my God, I cried to you for help,
    and you have healed me.
O Lord, you brought up my soul from Sheol,
    restored me to life from among those gone down to the Pit.

Sing praises to the Lord, O you his faithful ones,
    and give thanks to his holy name.
For his anger is but for a moment;
    his favor is for a lifetime.
Weeping may linger for the night,
    but joy comes with the morning.

. . . .

"You have turned my mourning into dancing." Children dancing at a refugee camp in Malawi, Africa

You have turned my mourning into dancing;
 you have taken off my sackcloth
 and clothed me with joy,
so that my soul may praise you and not be
 silent.
 O Lord my God, I will give thanks to
 you forever.

(Verses 11–12)

Even when we do not feel grateful, we can pray a psalm of thanks, trying to be open to its spirit. Little by little we may find ourselves growing in gratitude.
Read Psalms 23, 34, 136. **11**

Up from the pit

Psalm 30, like a number of others, refers to "Sheol" and the "Pit," as a place from which the psalmist was rescued. The ancient Jews for the most part did not believe in an afterlife of heaven or hell. Rather, they thought that all who died, whether good or bad, entered a shadowy underworld, Sheol, which, in their belief, was a void (the Pit). Formless, lifeless, completely removed from God's presence, the inhabitants of Sheol were basically in a state of nonexistence. It was a terrible condition, much to be dreaded.

When the psalmist says the Lord brought him or her up from Sheol, we do not know just what that means. The psalmist could have been near death from illness. To make the psalm our own, though, we do not need to have been dying. We can substitute for Sheol and the Pit our own experiences with the small deaths of everyday life—rejection, humiliation, failure, loss. Then we can pray the psalm in gratitude for God's bringing us

through those deaths into new life and hope again: "You have turned my mourning into dancing" (verse 11).

Letting Loose with Praise

With wonder and jubilation, God is praised in Psalm 47, and everyone is invited to join in the celebration:

Clap your hands, all you peoples;
 shout to God with loud songs of joy.
For the Lord, the Most High, is awesome,
 a great king over all the earth.
He subdued peoples under us,
 and nations under our feet.
He chose our heritage for us,
 the pride of Jacob whom he loves.

God has gone up with a shout,
 the Lord with the sound of a trumpet.
Sing praises to God, sing praises;
 sing praises to our King, sing praises.
For God is the king of all the earth;
 sing praises with a psalm.

(Verses 1–7)

If you can imagine that your school's basketball team just won the state championship in overtime, and is being welcomed back home that night at a rally in the gym,

11

Rewrite Psalm 136 to include the people, things, events, and so on, for which you are most grateful to God. For example: "*Who provides me with a safe home,* for his steadfast love endures forever."

you might have an idea of the atmosphere surrounding the above psalm. You can almost hear the band playing, the people clapping, the shouts and cheers of joy, the chanting and wholehearted singing. That is the spirit of the psalms of praise. They bring people out of themselves to focus ecstatically on the One who is worthy of all praise.

Why is God praised? Two themes come up over and over in the Psalms:

- God's wonderful deeds and goodness to the people, again and again

- the beauty and intricacy of all creation, which God has brought into existence and sustains with love

Read Psalms 96, 100, 139.

Becoming a Song of Praise

The sense of wonder and awe so apparent in the psalms of praise may not come easily to us. For small children, wonder seems to come naturally. But in our contemporary society, at a certain point in growing up, a more matter-of-fact way of looking at the world tends to take over. The phrase "What you see is what you get" expresses this attitude, a kind of flat numbness to the wonder of the world. There is nothing else beyond the obvious—no mystery, no unseen loving power at work in our life and in the universe, no glory shining within each leaf, each person. That attitude is so contrary to the sense of wonder that fills the Psalms.

Perhaps the psalms of praise can be a "school" for us modern-day people, helping us to see things we have never seen before. As we pray these songs of praise over a long time, maybe *we ourselves* will become a song of praise, joining with all creation in a hymn to our Creator.

Make a joyful noise to the LORD, all the earth;
    break forth into joyous song and sing praises.

. . . .

Let the sea roar, and all that fills it;
    the world and those who live in it.
Let the floods clap their hands;
    let the hills sing together for joy
at the presence of the LORD, for he is coming
    to judge the earth.
He will judge the world with righteousness,
    and the peoples with equity.
                    (Psalm 98:4–9) *12*

For Review

- ☐ What are the elements of psalms of thanks and of praise?

- ☐ What did "Sheol" and the "Pit" mean to the ancient Jews?

- ☐ What themes come up in the Psalms as reasons for praising God?

12

Find a picture that expresses a feeling of praise and write a brief reflection, poem, or prayer about it.

"Everything I Ever Needed to Know . . ."

As inspired writings the Psalms are a loving gift from God to us, for they show us the way to a genuine relationship with him. To paraphrase a well-known essay about learning everything needed for life in kindergarten, we can say, "Everything I ever needed to know about prayer, I learned in the Book of Psalms."

With the Psalms as our teacher, what lessons can we learn about relating to God? Here are a few:

• Let your prayer grow out of your own everyday experiences. The stuff of your life is what God wants to hear.

• Don't be afraid to share what is in your heart with God, no matter how negative you feel. Pouring yourself out in all honesty to him is the beginning of a *real* relationship—and he can handle it.

• Give your burdens over to God in trust that he will know what to do with them. In trusting him you will be transformed because you will become centered in him.

• See God's hand at work in your life, now and in your past. Talk about how grateful you are for the ways God has been loving you.

• Cultivate a sense of wonder and awe. Be amazed by things. Resist becoming jaded. Let the mystery of God tickle your imagination.

• Celebrate from the bottom of your toes, with all your heart.

Praise the LORD!
Praise God in his sanctuary;
    praise him in his mighty firmament!
Praise him for his mighty deeds;
    praise him according to his surpassing
        greatness!

Praise him with trumpet sound;
    praise him with lute and harp!
Praise him with tambourine and dance;
    praise him with strings and pipe!
Praise him with clanging cymbals;
    praise him with loud clashing cymbals!
Let everything that breathes praise the LORD!
Praise the LORD!

(Psalm 150) [13]

13

Take an experience from your life and tell about it in the style of a psalm of lament, thanks, or praise.

The New Testament

God's Love Story Fulfilled in Jesus

Ruins of a synagogue at Capernaum, Israel. Jesus probably preached in synagogues like this one.

Our study of the Old Testament has come to an end. We have reflected on the marvelous stories and characters of the Old Testament, the ups and downs of the biblical people's journey with God, the passionate teachings of the prophets on justice and faithfulness, and the beautiful, moving prayer that expressed Israel's struggle to walk in his ways. *1*

In the beginning of this course, the Bible was described as God's love letter to us. In the Bible we meet the living God, who reaches out to us in love through the great Story of our salvation. At the close of the Old Testament, there is a sense of expectant longing for God's love to be fully realized in the world. There is an urgency to have his Reign of justice and peace over all the earth become a reality.

This "love letter" continues with the New Testament, in which the story of God's love for humankind is fulfilled. The Reign of God is inaugurated on earth with the Incarnation, the event in which the divine Son of God "became flesh and lived among us" (John 1:14) in order to save all humanity from sin and death. (The literal meaning of the word *Incarnation* is "in the flesh.") As Catholics recite in the Nicene Creed, "for our salvation he came down from heaven: by the power of the Holy Spirit he was born of the Virgin Mary, and became man."

1

Leaf through the chapters of this book to recall the course contents. Also read over some of your responses to the reflection activities presented in the margins of this book. Then answer the following questions in a one-page essay:

- What is one significant idea about the Old Testament that you learned in this course?
- What is one significant personal insight—a lesson about yourself—that you gained through this course?

A view of Nazareth, Jesus' hometown, today

An incident told in one of the Gospels in the New Testament provides a link between the Old Testament and the New. Picture the scene:

It is about ninety years since the Roman Empire has taken over the region of Palestine. The Jews live as an oppressed people, subjugated by a mighty dictatorship in the very land God promised to Abraham and his descendants so long ago.

Many Jews have put their hopes and dreams in the coming of a messiah, one anointed by God to save them from oppression and misery. Prophets have spoken and written of such a messiah for hundreds of years, and now the people's expectation of a savior has reached a fever pitch.

One day in a town called Nazareth in Galilee (the northern district of Palestine), a young man who was raised in the town enters the local synagogue for Sabbath worship.

He stood up to read, and the scroll of the prophet Isaiah was given to him. He unrolled the scroll and found the place where it was written:
"The Spirit of the Lord is upon me, because he has anointed me
to bring good news to the poor.
He has sent me to proclaim release to the captives
and recovery of sight to the blind,
to let the oppressed go free,
to proclaim the year of the Lord's favor."
And he rolled up the scroll, gave it back to the attendant, and sat down. The eyes of all in the synagogue were fixed on him. Then he began to say to them, "Today this scripture has been fulfilled in your hearing." (Luke 4:16–21)

In this dramatic moment, the young man, Jesus of Nazareth, identifies himself as the one fulfilling the prophetic message of Isaiah 61:1–2.

The four Gospels go on to tell of Jesus' ministry among the people. As a preacher, teacher, and healer, Jesus proclaims God's mercy and all-embracing love and calls them to love as his Father does. Although his message is not a rallying call for rebellion, the authorities are threatened by him. Eventually Jesus is arrested, tortured, and crucified, dying a criminal's death on a cross.

Could this poor victim of the Roman Empire possibly be the Messiah?

Three days after Jesus' death and burial, his followers encounter him risen from the dead! They begin to grasp that all God's promises to Israel have been fulfilled in Jesus (whom they call the Christ, meaning "the

The love of God in Christ Jesus is remembered and shared at the sign of peace in the liturgy of the Eucharist.

anointed," "the messiah"). They come to recognize that Jesus was more than any messiah they could have dreamed of. They believe that the man who walked the earth with them and suffered and died for them was also the Son of God, now risen from the dead in glory. They see that God was revealed to them fully through Jesus, and that the Holy Spirit will be with them forever to help them be faithful witnesses to the love of God in Christ Jesus. The New Testament records the inspired faith testimonies of those early followers of Jesus.

One of the New Testament writings, the Letter to the Hebrews, proclaims this sacred belief: "Long ago God spoke to our ancestors in many and various ways by the prophets, but in these last days he has spoken to us by a Son" (1:1–2).

The Story of God's boundless love for us began with Creation and culminates in Jesus Christ, the fulfillment of all God's loving promises. So the Old Testament and the New Testament form one continuous story, and we cannot appreciate one without the other.

May the study of the Old Testament you have undertaken in this course enrich your mind and make ready your heart for all that God pours out to you in love as you walk your journey of life.

Long ago God spoke to our ancestors in many and various ways by the prophets, but in these last days he has spoken to us by a Son. **Hebrews 1:1–2**

Index

Italic numbers are references to photos, illustrations, maps, or timelines. Pronunciations of many biblical names and terms are given in parentheses.

Pronunciation Key

Symbol	Sound	Symbol	Sound	Symbol	Sound	Symbol	Sound
a	**c**at	g	**g**ood	ng	si**ng**	s	**s**o
ah	f**a**ther	h	**h**ot	o	h**o**t	sh	**s**ure
ahr	l**ar**d	hw	**wh**ether	oh	g**o**	t	**t**oe
air	c**are**	i	**i**t	oi	b**oy**	th	**th**in
ay	p**ay**	*i*	sk**y**	oo	f**oo**t	uh	**a**go
b	**b**ug	ihr	**ear**	*oo*	b**oo**t	uhr	h**er**
ch	**ch**ew	j	**j**oke	oor	p**oor**	v	**v**ow
d	**d**o	k	**k**ing	or	f**or**	w	**w**eather
e, eh	p**e**t	l	**l**ove	ou	h**ow**	y	**y**oung
ee	s**ee**m	m	**m**at	p	**p**at	z	**z**one
f	**f**un	n	**n**ot	r	**r**un	zh	vi**s**ion

A

Aaron: God's punishment of, 82–83; golden calf of, 69; and Pharaoh, 56, 57; priesthood status of, 71, 80

Abigail, 128

Abner, 131, 132

Abraham [Abram]: age at death of, 45; arrival in Canaan, 14, 27, 37, *42;* God's Promise to, 16, 37–38, 39; God's test of, 43–44; God's visitation to, 39–40; hospitality of, 40, *41;* map of journeys of, *42;* name change of, 39; pleading for Lot, 40–41

Abraham's test, 43–44

Abram (ay' bruhm) [Abraham], 37–38, 39. *See also* Abraham

Absalom (ab' suh-luhm), 137, 139

Achan (ay' kan), 101

Adam and Eve, 32–33

Adonijah (ad-uh-n*i*' juh), 140

adultery: commandment against, 66; committed by David, 135

Africa: 2000–1700 B.C., 44; 1700–1250 B.C., 79; 1250–900 B.C., 126; 900–600 B.C., 153

afterlife. *See* resurrection

Ahab (ay' hab), 152, 153, 154, 156

Ahasuerus (uh-has-y*oo*-air' uhs) [Artaxerxes], 261–262

Ahaz (ay' haz), 170, 174; Isaiah's prophecies to, 173

Ai (*i*), 101

Alexander the Great, 18, *20,* 231, 232

Alexandria: Jewish community in, 206, *207*

alphabetic writing, 15, 53, 147, *168,* 169

America: 2000–1700 B.C., 44; 1700–1250 B.C., 79; 1250–900 B.C., 126; 900–600 B.C., 153

Amish, *233*

Ammonites (am' uh-n*i*ts), 125

Amnon (am' non), 137, 139

Amos (ay' muhs), 147, 149, 151, 196; Book of, 23, 24; on Israel's collapse, 161; as pre-exilic prophet, 24; riches condemned by, 158, 160

ancestor worship, 153

Antiochus IV (an-t*i*' uh-kuhs), 233–234

apocalyptic literature, 241–242

Aqaba (ah' kuh-buh), **Gulf of,** *145*

Arabs: Ishmael as father of, 43; of Palestine, 206

Arch of Titus (t*i*' tuhs) [Rome], *232*

Aristotle, 218

ark of the Covenant, *124;* brought to Jerusalem, 133; housed in the Temple, 144; at siege of Jericho, 99; tabernacle of, 71

Artaxerxes (ahr-tuh-zuhrk' seez) [Ahasuerus], 261–262

Ashurbanipal (ash-uhr-ban' uh-pahl), **library of,** 165

Assur (as' uhr), 165

Assyrians (uh-sihr' ee-uhns): ascendancy of, 79, 165; Babylonian cultural influence on, 165; conquest of Israel by, 15, 17, *20*, 147, *150*, 163–164; destroyed capital of, 153, 165, 181, 185; intermarriage requirement of, 164, 227; Jerusalem saved from, 174–175, 189; Judah as vassal of, 170, 174; and story of Jonah, 263, 266; and story of Judith, 260–261; and story of Tobit, 257–259

Athens, *18, 218,* 232

B

Baal (bay' uhl) [Canaanite god], 100, 141, 152, 166; and Elijah, 154–155; and Gideon, 107, 109

Babel (bay' buhl), 36

Babylon (bab' uh-luhn): as capital of Near East, 126; conquest of Judah by, 17, 27, 181, 191–193, *224;* cultural and religious tradition of, 165, 200; fall of Assyria to, 185; polytheistic myths of, 29

Babylonian (bab-uh-loh' nee-uhn) **exile:** beginning of, 15, 181, 191; Deuteronomic self-examination in, 95–96, 100, 145; Ezekiel's vision of, 199–200; Jeremiah's response to, 191, 192, 193; Jews' lifestyle during, 200, 201; Josiah's reform before, 87–88; liberation from, 18, 181, 203–204, 211–212, 215–216, *224;* monotheism proclaimed during, 17; religious renewal in, 193–194, 201–203, 209; route to and from, *224;* Sabbath custom in, 31, 202; and writing of Exodus, 53–54, 62; and writing of Genesis, 27–28, 31, 51

Babylonian Talmud, 200

Balaam's (bay' luhm) **oracle,** 83

ban, the: broken by Achan, 101; broken by Saul, 125; at Jericho, 100

Barak (bair' ak), 106

Baruch (bair' uhk), 193; Book of, 23, 24, 182, 195–196

Bathsheba (bath-shee' buh), 134–136, 273

bedouin: defined, 43

Benjamin, 47, 49–50

Berlin Wall, *99*

Bethel (beth' uhl): Amos at, 158; golden calf shrine at, 151; meaning of, 46

Bethlehem, *83;* David's hometown of, 125, 126; in Micah's prophecy, 178

Bible: human aspect of, 21; inspired by word of God, 8, 9; magisterium's interpretation of, 11; outlined story of, 8; reason to study, 10–12; three parts of Jewish, 19; writing systems and, 168–169. *See also* Old Testament

biblical period: events of, 16–19; timeline of, 14–15

Birmingham jail, *60*

blood rituals: to atone for sin, 76–77; to seal covenants, 68

Book of the Covenant, 67

Booths, feast of. *See* Sukkoth

Botticelli (bah-tuh-cheh' lee): *Mystic Nativity, 174*

Brueghel (br*oo*' gehl), **Jan, the Elder,** *32*

Buber (b*oo*' buhr), **Martin,** 25

Buddhism, 218

Burmese refugees, *55*

burning bush, 56

C

Cain and Abel, 34–35

Caleb (kay' luhb), 81

Canaan (kay' nuhn): Abraham's arrival in, 14, 27, 37, *42;* Covenant's promise of, 16; Israelites' settlement in, 17, 97–99, 105–106; Jacob's journey to, *42,* 46–47; Joshua's promised entrance into, 81, 85, 96–97; Philistines' conquest of, 93; Rahab's betrayal of, 97; route from Egypt to, *84;* tribes of Israel in, *108*

Canaanites (kay' nuh-n*its*): alphabetic writings of, 15, 53, 169; Deborah's victory over, 106–107; god Baal of, 100, 107, 109, 154–155; golden calf of, 152; outdoor sanctuaries of, 141; temple model of, 142, 143

Canticle of Deborah, 106, 107

Canticle of Moses and Miriam, 60, 61

Capernaum (kuh-puhr' nay-uhm), **Israel,** *124, 288*

Carthage, 153

Catholic canon: Old Testament books of, 22–24

Catholic Tradition: on adultery, 66; on Creation, 32; defined, 11; on good confession, 77; on Judaism-Christianity linkage, 19; and liturgy of the hours, 276; and liturgy of the word, 275; magisterium's interpretation of, 11; on source of suffering, 34; on wisdom's feminine voice, 248–249

Catholic Worker Movement, 154

Chaldeans (kal-dee' uhns), 200

Chavez, Cesar, *238*

China: 2000–1700 B.C., 44; 1700–1250 B.C., 79; 1250–900 B.C., 126; 900–600 B.C., 153; 600–1 B.C., 218

Christians: Balaam's oracle for, 83; Covenant of Sinai for, 69; Jerusalem for, 133; Judaism's links to, 19, 21–22, 25; Psalms in liturgies of, 275–276; Sabbath celebration of, 32

christos (kris' tohs) [the anointed], 134

Chronicles, Books of, 22, 23, 213, 214

circumcision, 39, 202, 234

confession: in sacrament of reconciliation, 77

Confucius [K'ung Fu-tzu], 218

Conservative Judaism, 264, *265*

Epistle to the Hebrews, 77, 291

Esau (ee' saw), 230; birthright stolen from, 45–46; Jacob's peace with, 47

Eskimo culture, 44

Esther, Book of, 22, 23, 245, 257, 261–263

Ethiopia, Africa, *110*

Euphrates (y*oo*-fray' teez) **River,** *180*

Europe: 2000–1700 B.C., 44; 1700–1250 B.C., 79; 1250–900 B.C., 126; 900–600 B.C., 153

evil. *See* problem of evil

evolutionists: Creation account by, 32

Exodus, Book of, 22, 23, 91; burning bush of, 56; Covenant of Sinai in, 16, 63, 68–69; enslaved Israelites of, *52*, 55–57; escape from Egypt in, 16, 53, 59–62, 93; God's thirteen attributes from, 71–72; and Passover celebration, 58–59; plagues of, 57–58; Ten Commandments of, 64–68; written during exile, 53–54, 62

Ezekiel (i-zee' kee-uhl), 151; Book of, 23, 24, 182; death of wife of, 198; exiled to Babylon, 196; hopeful visions of, 181, 199–200, 201; pre-exilic prophecies of, 181, 197–198

Ezra (ez' ruh): Book of, 22, 23, 213, 215; committed to Torah, 211, 227, 228, 229; on intermarriage, 229; resettled in Jerusalem, 15, 18, 215, *224;* as second Moses, 218

F

Fall, the: and human suffering, 33

false witness: commandment against, 67

famine in Near East, 49

father of the Arab peoples [Ishmael], 39, 43

feminine images of God, 208

Fertile Crescent, *42*

firstborn of Egypt: death for, 57, 58

First Isaiah, 147, 149, 151, 196; on fall of Judah, 170–172, 175–176; Hezekiah counseled by, 174; hopefulness of, 176; Immanuel prophecy of, 173–174, 290; pre-exilic writings of, 167; Temple vision of, 170, 172–173; Vineyard Song of, 172

Flood, the, 35

forgiveness: of God, 170–171, 192; of Joseph, 50–51

former prophets [nonwriting prophets], 149

free choice: and human suffering, 34, 156

G

Galilee, Israel, *104*

Gandhi, Mohandas, 239

Garden of Eden, The [Brueghel], *32*

Genesis, Book of, 22, 23, 91; Abraham's test in, 43–44; Babylonian myths versus, 29; God's promise to Abraham in, 16, 37–38, 39; Hagar story of, 41–42; hospitality in, 40–41; Isaac and Rebekah romance of, 44–45; Jacob stories of, 45–47, 49–50; Joseph's forgiveness in, 50–51; polygamy in, 39; prehistory stories of, 29–36; return to Canaan in, 46–47; written during exile, 27–28, 31, 51

Gentile: as ancestor of David, 113, 116

German church, *218*

Gibeonites (gib' ee-uh-n*i*ts), 101

Gideon (gid' ee-uhn), 105, 107, 109

Gilgamesh Epic, 200

gleaning the field, 114, 115

God: and Abraham's test, 43–44; betrayal of, in Hosea's parable, 161–162; as forgiving, 170–171, 192; goodness of, 29–31, 171; Habakkuk's questioning of, 185–186; Israel's marriage to, 162–163; as loving, 8, 70, 89; of Moses and Miriam's canticle, 61; as the one God, 38, 56, 64, 190; providence of, 79; speaking to, in psalms, 279, 280–281, 287; Thirteen Attributes of, 71–73; Yahweh name of, 56, 64–65. *See also* word of God

golden calf: of Aaron and Israelites, 69; of Jeroboam, 151–152

Goliath (guh-li' uhth), **David and,** 125–126, *132*

Gomer (goh' muhr), 161–162, 163

Gospels: Elijah in, 157; Jacob's star in, 83; Old Testament beliefs in, 290–291; Second Isaiah in, 204; synagogue's role in, 206; writing system for, 169

"Grateful Dead, The" [folktale], 259

Greek Empire: 600–1 B.C., 218; Book of Daniel's approach to, 237–239; conquered by Romans, 211, 243; golden age of, 232; Jews oppressed by, 18, 213, 233–234; Maccabees' revolt against, 15, 211, 236–237; Persia conquered by, 211, 231

Greeks: alphabetic writings of, 147, *168*, 169; body and soul concepts of, 253; culture of, 231–232; language of, 232

griffin sculpture, *203*

Gutenberg, Johannes, 15

H

Habakkuk (huh-bak' uhk), 151, 181, 185–186, 196; Book of, 23, 24, 182

Hagar (hay' gahr), 38–39, 41, 42

Haggai (hag' i), 151, 196, 211, 213, 219; Book of, 23, 24

Haiti, *87, 137*

Haman (hay' muhn) [Book of Esther], 261, 262–263

Hammurabi (ha-muh-rah' bee), 14, 200

Handel: *Messiah, 167*

Hanging Gardens of Babylon, 200

Hannah, 122

Assyria, 174–175, 189; in Second Isaiah's prophecies, 203–204. *See also* Temple of Jerusalem

Jesse, 115, 125

Jesus: Bethlehem birthplace of, 126, 178; birth of, 15, 211; Deuteronomy quoted by, 89, 90; of house of David, 121, 134, 140; and Isaiah's prophecy, 173–174, 290; Jeremiah's parallels with, 191; as Messiah, 8, 18; Passover rituals of, 58–59; and stories of Joseph, 51; as suffering servant, 205; and widow of Zarephath, 154; and Zechariah's prophecy, 221

Jews: in Babylonian exile, 17–18, 27–28, 200, 201–203; Creation story of, 29–31; current population of, 265; Dispersion of, 206, *207*; Greek cultural influence on, 231–233; Greek oppression of, 18, 213, 233–234; intermarriage by, 164, 221, 226, 227; liberated from Babylonian exile, 18, 181, 203–204, 211–212, 215–216, *224*; in revolt against Greeks, 15, 211, 236–237; Sabbath celebration of, 32; sacrilegious sacrifices of, 221; the Shema prayer of, 88, 89; Temple rebuilt by, 18, 211, 219–220; use of term, 211. *See also* Israelites

Jezebel (jez' uh-bel), 152, 153–154, 155, 156

Joab (joh' ab), 132

Joash (joh' ash), 107

Job (johb), **Book of,** 22, 23, 245, 249–250

Joel, 151, 196, 213; Book of, 23, 24, 230

John, Gospel of, 157

John Paul II, *19, 179*

John the Baptist, 157, 204

Jonah, Book of, 23, 24, 245; fictitious prophet of, 230; inclusive message of, 257, 266–267; whale story of, 263

Jonathan: David's friendship with, 126, 127; death of, 130, 131

Jordan River, *272*; Elijah and Elisha crossing, 156–157; Joshua and Israelites crossing, 97–98; valley of, *116*

Joseph [husband of Mary], 126

Joseph [son of Jacob], 48–49, 50–51

Joshua [high priest], 215, 219, 220

Joshua [leader of Israelites], 14, 17; crossing the Jordan, 97–98; death of, 103; defeated at Ai, 101; God's promise to, 81, 85; leadership qualities of, 103, 104; and Rahab's bargain, 97; at siege of Jericho, 99–100; victorious at Gibeon, 101–102

Joshua, **Book of,** 22, 23; brutal warfare imagery of, 100–101; Canaan as gift in, 98; instructions for ritual in, 99; sun standing still in, 101–102

Josiah's (joh-si' uh) **reform,** 87–88, 181, 183, 185

jubilee: Holiness Code on, 78

Judah (joo' duh) [brother of Joseph], 48

Judah [southern kingdom]: Assyrian threat to, 170, 174–175; Babylonian conquest of, 17, 27, 181, 191–193, *224*; David as king of, 131–132; Isaiah's condemnation of, 170–172, 175–176; Israel separated from, 15, 147–149, 151; Jeremiah's message to, 187, 188–189, 191; Josiah's reforms in, 87–88, 183, 185; Micah's condemnation of, 177; northern tribes' flight to, 164; pictures of, *28, 118, 128, 130, 166*; prejudiced against Samaritans, 164, 216; prophets to, *150,* 151; return of exiles to, 15, 215–217; ruled by David's house, 166

Judaism: after time of Jesus, 18–19; Christianity's links to, 19, 21–22, 25, 69, 83, 133; postexilic birth of, 212; renewal of, during exile,

193–194, 201–202, 209; Roman converts to, 206; the Shema prayer of, 88, 89; spiritual boundary lines for, 223, 227–228, 238, 266; three modern branches of, 264; use of term, 211

Judas Maccabeus (ma-kuh-bee' es), 233, 236, 237. *See also* Maccabees, Books of

Judea (joo-dee' uh). *See* Judah

Judean desert, *118, 128, 130*

judges: in cycle of deliverance, 105; inclusion of Samson with, 111–112; names of, 105; as temporary leaders, 120

Judges, Book of, 22, 23, 105–107, 120

Judith, Book of, 22, 23, 245, 257, 260–261

K

Kadesh-barnea (kay' desh-bahr-nee' ah), 82, *84*

King, Martin Luther, Jr., 60, *85,* 160, 239

Kings, First Book of, 22, 23, 119, 121, 140, 147–148

Kings, Second Book of, 22, 23, 140, 147–148, 164

kosher dietary rules. *See* dietary rules

L

Laban (lay' buhn), 46

Lamentations, Book of, 23, 24, 182, 194, 271

Lao-tzu, 218

Last Supper, 58–59

latter prophets [writing prophets], 149

Law, the [Mosaic Law]: biblical books addressing, 22, 75; broken tablets of, 69–70; Deuteronomy's refinement of, 86–87; of the new Covenant, 192; observance of, by branches of Judaism, 264; the Shema as essence of, 89. *See also* Torah, the

T

tabernacle, 71

Tabernacles, feast of [Sukkoth], 71, 228

Tamar (tay' mahr) 137, 139

Tanzania, Africa, *82*

Tao Te Ching, 218

Temple of Jerusalem: Babylonian destruction of, 181, 193; built by Solomon, 15, 17, 119, 142, 143–144, *214*; Isaiah's vision in, 170, 172–173; Jeremiah preaching in, 189; Josiah's repair of, 183; rebuilding of, 18, 211, 219–220; reclaimed by Maccabees, 236–237; Roman destruction of, 15, 19, 232; as sacred space, 220; sacrifices of atonement in, 76–77; sacrilegious sacrifices in, 221; tabernacle within, 71

Ten Commandments [Decalogue], 64–68; destroyed tablets of, 69; Deuteronomy account of, 86; as rules that free, 68

tent of the meeting: ark of the Covenant in, 71; God's presence before, 70

Teresa of Calcutta, Mother, *182*

Thérèse of Lisieux, 156

Third Isaiah, 24, *150*, 151, 196, 211, 213; return of exiles in, *167*, 216–218; universalism theme of, 217–218

Thirteen Attributes of God, 71–73

threshing floor, 114

tithing, 221

Titus (ti' tuhs), 232

Toaff, Elio, *19*

Tobiah (toh-bi' uh), 225

Tobias (toh-bi' uhs), 258–259

Tobit (toh' bit), **Book of,** 22, 23, 245, 257–258

Torah (toh' ruh), **the,** 19; at bar mitzvah, *9*; biblical books of, 22; Ezra's commitment to, 211, 227, 228, 229; scriptural authority of, 22. *See also* Law, the

Tradition. *See* Catholic Tradition

Trojan War, 79

twelve, symbolic significance of, 102

twelve tribes of Israel, 102; David's unification of, 120–121, 133; judges of, 105; map locations of, *108*

two kingdoms of Israel and Judah, 147–148. *See also* Israel; Judah [southern kingdom]

U

United Farm Workers, *238*

United States Embassy, *280*

universalism: in Books of Isaiah, 203, 217–218; defined, 218; of Zechariah, 220

unleavened bread: in Communion, 59; for Passover, 58, 59

Ur (oor), 44

Uriah (yoo-ri' uh), 134, 135

V

Vardhamâna, 218

Veterans Viet Nam Restoration Project, *173*

Vietnam, *41, 173*

Vineyard Song [Isaiah], *172*

virginity, 255

W

Warsaw ghetto, *249*

Washington, D.C., *121*

Western Wall [Jerusalem], *6, 39, 206, 268*

widow of Zarephath (zair' uh-fath), 154

winnowing the grain, 114

wisdom: feminine voice of, 248–249; Sirach's depiction of, 254–255; of Solomon, 141, 143

Wisdom, Book of, 23, 24, 245, 252–253

wisdom books, 245; body and soul concepts of, 253; feminine wisdom in, 248–249; list and description of, 22–24; origins of, 246; passionate poetry of, 255–256; practical advice of, 246–247; problem of evil in, 249–251

Wisdom of Solomon. *See* Wisdom, Book of

word of God: Bible inspired by, 8, 9; salvation through, 35–36

World War I, *135*

worship. *See* ritual

writing prophets, 149

writing systems: Greek adaptation of Canaanite, 147; history of, 168–169; invention of alphabetic, 15, 53; invention of hieroglyphic, 14, 15; with pictures, in China, 79

Y

Yahweh (yah' weh): commandment against speaking, 64–65; interpretation of, 56; titles substituted for, 56–57

yoke, *192*

Yom Kippur (yom-kip' uhr) [Day of Atonement], 77

Z

Zarephath (zair-uh-fath), **widow of,** 154

Zechariah (zek-uh-ri' uh) [priest in Gospel of Luke], 157, 221

Zechariah [prophet], *150*, 151, 211; Book of, 23, 24, 213; messianic prophecies of, 220–221

Zedekiah (zed-uh-ki' uh), 191, 193, 198

Zephaniah (zef-uh-ni' uh), *150*, 151, 181; Book of, 23, 24, *182*; on God's remnant, 184, 212

Zerubbabel (zuh-ruhb' uh-buhl), 215, 219, 220

Zionism (zi' uh-nizm), 265

Zoroaster, 218

Acknowledgments *(continued from page 2)*

The scriptural quotes on pages 163 and 240 are from the New American Bible with revised New Testament. Copyright © 1986, 1991 by the Confraternity of Christian Doctrine, 3211 Fourth Street NE, Washington, DC 20017. All rights reserved.

All other scriptural quotations in this book are from the New Revised Standard Version of the Bible. Copyright © 1989 by the Division of Christian Education of the National Council of the Churches of Christ in the United States of America. All rights reserved.

The abbreviation NJB in this book refers to the New Jerusalem Bible.

The quotation on page 25 is from *The Writings of Martin Buber,* edited by Will Herberg (Cleveland: World Publishing Company, 1956), page 275.

The quotation on page 235 is quoted from *Nuclear Holocaust and Christian Hope: A Book for Christian Peacemakers,* by Ronald J. Sider and Richard K. Taylor (Downers Grove, IL: InterVarsity Press, 1982), page 239. Copyright © 1982 by Ronald J. Sider and Richard K. Taylor.

The quotation on page 252 is from *Meditations and Devotions of the Late Cardinal Newman* (New York: Longmans, Green, and Company, 1911), pages 301–302. Copyright © 1893 by Longmans, Green, and Company.

The quotations on page 275 are from *Gather: Comprehensive* (Chicago: GIA Publications, 1994), numbers 39, 95, 31, 48, 85, and 36. Copyright © 1994 by GIA Publications, Chicago. All rights reserved. Used by permission.

Photo Credits

Tsafrir Abayov: page 206
AKG Berlin/SuperStock: page 249
© Paul Almasy/CORBIS: pages 203, 210
AP/Wide World Photos: pages 19, 103, 135, 222, 251, 253, 280
Bill Aron/Getty Images: page 9
Rob Atkins/Getty Images: pages 4–5 (top), 14–15 (top)
Bruce Ayres/Getty Images: page 199
Scott Barrow, International Stock Photo: page 45
© Dave Bartruff/CORBIS: pages 38, 44

© Morton Beebe, S.F./CORBIS: page 167
© Annie Griffiths Belt/CORBIS: pages 270, 274
© Bettmann/CORBIS: pages 60, 65, 113, 160, 239 (left)
Daniel Blatt: pages 4–5 (bottom), 14–15 (bottom), 26, 46, 130, 133, 141, 191, 209 (right), 248, 262
By courtesy of the Board of Trustees of the Victoria and Albert Museum, London, Bridgeman Art Library, London/SuperStock: page 32
© Bojan Brecelj/CORBIS: pages 1, 16, 24–25, 247
Catholic Campaign for Human Development: page 217
K. M. Chaudhry, AP/Wide World Photos: page 238 (left)
© Jacques M. Chenet/CORBIS: page 179
Paul Chesley/Getty Images: page 6
© John H. Clark/CORBIS: page 123
K. Condyles: page 278
© Richard A. Cooke/CORBIS: page 155
Digital image © 1996 CORBIS; original image courtesy NASA/CORBIS: pages 90, 90–91
Francisco Cruz/SuperStock: back cover inset, pages 2–3
Ron Dahlquist/SuperStock: page 256
© Donna DeCesare: page 264 (top)
© Francoise de Mulder/CORBIS: pages 33, 110
Laurence Dutton/Getty Images: page 68
© Ecoscene/CORBIS: page 189
Editorial Development Associates: pages 170, 272 (right), 285
Mary Farrell: page 275
© Kevin Fleming/CORBIS: page 233
© Owen Franken/CORBIS: pages 87, 94, 121, 134, 227
© Michelle Garrett/CORBIS: page 225
© Raymond Gehman/CORBIS: page 161
Getty Images: page 236
© Philip Gould/CORBIS: pages 163, 265
George Grigoriou/Getty Images: page 18
© Darrell Gulin/CORBIS: pages 67, 286 (right)
Sonia Halliday Photographs: pages 205, 263, 267
Ansell Horn: page 271
© Jeremy Horner/CORBIS: page 261

© Hulton-Deutsch Collection/CORBIS: pages 131, 164

International Stock Photo: pages 244, 250

Jewish Museum, New York/SuperStock: pages 125, 140, 214

© Wolfgang Kaehler/CORBIS: pages 168 (right), 231 (top)

© Steve Kaufman/CORBIS: page 62

© Earl Kowall/CORBIS: page 41

Jack Kurtz: page 176

© David Lees/CORBIS: page 231 (bottom)

© Charles & Josette Lenars/CORBIS: page 166

© George Lepp/CORBIS: page 255

Erich Lessing, Art Resource, New York: pages 51, 57, 64, 193

© Barry Lewis/CORBIS: page 198

Michael Lichter, International Stock Photo: page 99

Mark Ludak: page 238 (right)

Marquette University Archives: page 182 (center)

Maryknoll: pages 82, 157

© Stephanie Maze/CORBIS: page 226

© Joe McDonald/CORBIS: page 101

Laurence Monneret/Getty Images: page 208

© Kevin R. Morris/CORBIS: page 259

© David Muench/CORBIS: page 183

© Marc Muench/CORBIS: page 276

Musee du Louvre, Paris/Lauros-Giraudon, Paris/SuperStock: page 169

Museum of Tapestries, Angers, France/Lauros-Giraudon, Paris/SuperStock: page 241

© NASA/CORBIS: page 35

© The National Gallery Collection; by kind permission of the Trustees of the National Gallery, London/CORBIS: pages 111, 174

National Museum of Antiquities, Scotland/Bridgeman Art Library, London/SuperStock: page 243

Tom Nebbia: page 83

© Richard T. Nowitz/CORBIS: pages 28, 58, 92, 104, 118, 146, 152, 220, 272 (left), 287, 288, 290 (left)

© Diego Lezama Orezzoli/CORBIS: page 168 (center)

Courtesy of the Oriental Institute of the University of Chicago: page 200

© Gianni Dagli Orti/CORBIS: pages 190, 234

Gene Plaisted, The Crosiers: pages 11, 77, 97, 124, 184

L. Prosor/SuperStock: page 12 (right)

Z. Radovan, Jerusalem: cover wrap, pages 10 (bottom), 29, 39, 54, 59, 74, 88 (right), 100, 114 (left and right), 116, 120, 132, 145, 148, 165, 209 (left), 212, 216, 229, 232, 254

© Carmen Redondo/CORBIS: page 168 (left)

Cindy Reiman: page 277

© Roger Ressmeyer/CORBIS: page 80

Rimkus, Catholic News Service: page 194

© Jeffrey L. Rotman/CORBIS: page 63

Andy Sacks/Getty Images: page 72

Saint Peter's Basilica, Vatican, Rome/SuperStock: page 48

© Flip Schulke/CORBIS: page 85

Michele Setboun/Getty Images: page 128

James L. Shaffer: pages 8, 12 (left), 76, 95, 154

Ian Shaw/Getty Images: page 66

Kay Shaw: page 286 (left)

Hugh Sitton/Getty Images: page 52

© Leif Skoogfers/CORBIS: page 182 (left)

© Richard Hamilton Smith/CORBIS: pages 171, 252

© Paul A. Souders/CORBIS: pages 81, 137, 246

© Ted Spiegel/CORBIS: pages 115, 257

Johnny Stockshooter, International Stock Photo: page 268

SuperStock: pages 17, 180, 219 (left and right)

Tom Till/Getty Images: page 43

Arthur Tilley/Getty Images: page 282

John Turner/Getty Images: page 73

© David Turnley/CORBIS: page 187

© Peter Turnley/CORBIS: pages 34, 102, 188

Penny Tweedie/Getty Images: page 284

Veterans Viet Nam Restoration Project: page 173

Steven Weinberg/Getty Images: page 36

© David H. Wells/CORBIS: pages 202, 264 (bottom)

© Nik Wheeler/CORBIS: page 281

© Gavin Wickham, Eye Ubiquitous/CORBIS: page 182 (right)

W. P. Wittman Limited: pages 10 (top), 21, 23, 88 (left), 213, 283, 291

David Young Wolff/Getty Images: page 178

© Alison Wright/CORBIS: page 55

© Michael S. Yamashita/CORBIS: page 139

© Yogi, Inc./CORBIS: page 177

Zoom 77/AP Wide World Photos: page 266